# 「彼(かれ)」 KARE First Love ⑩

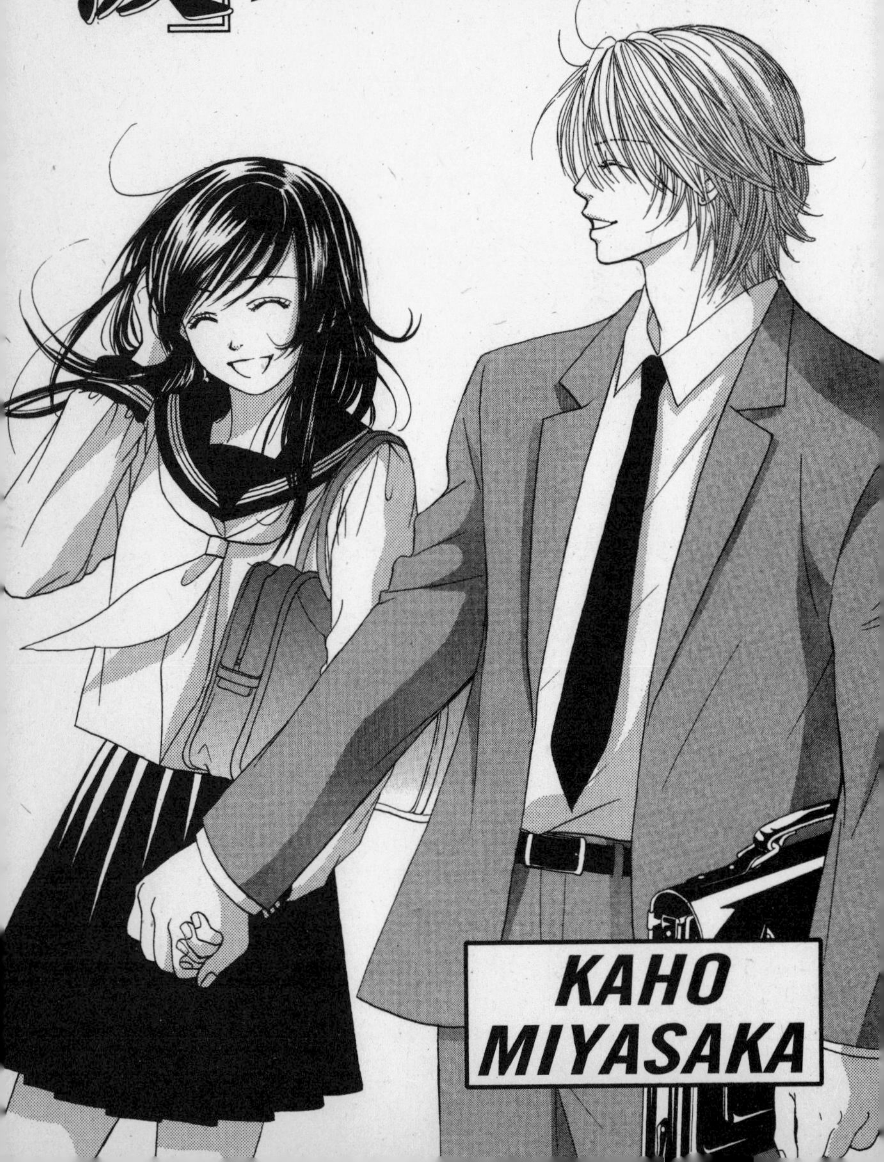

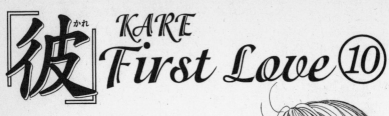

KAHO MIYASAKA

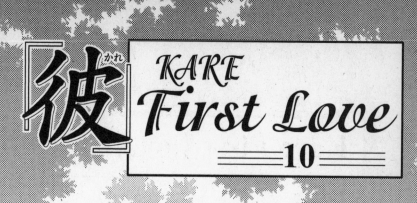

「彼」かれ

# KARE First Love

10

CONTENTS

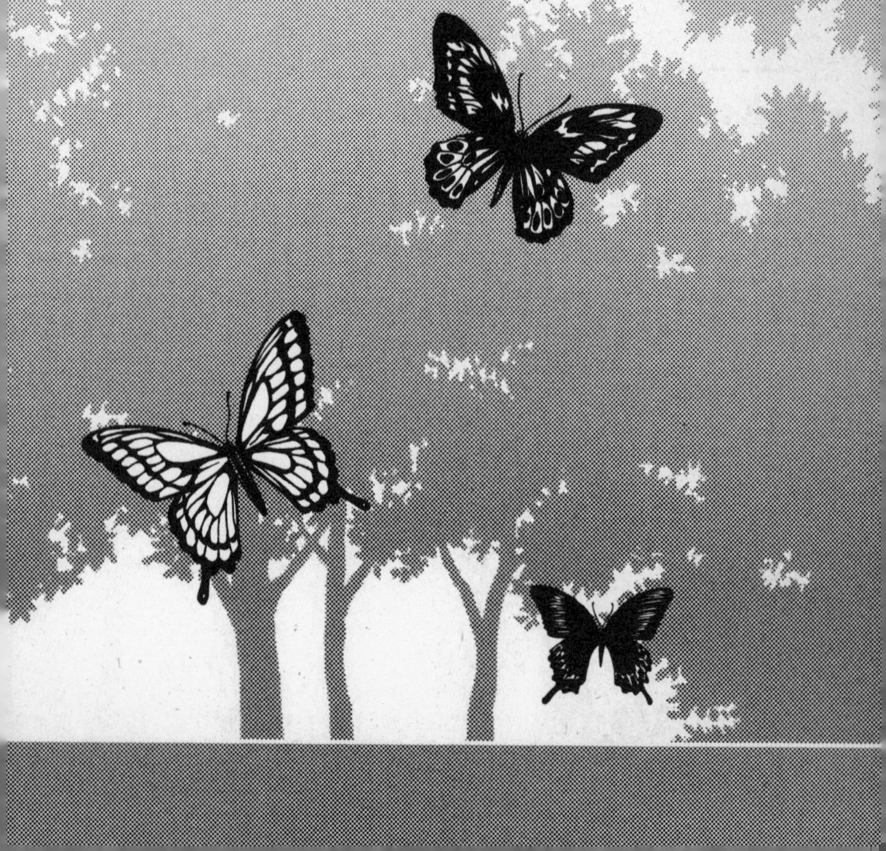

# Kare First Love...6

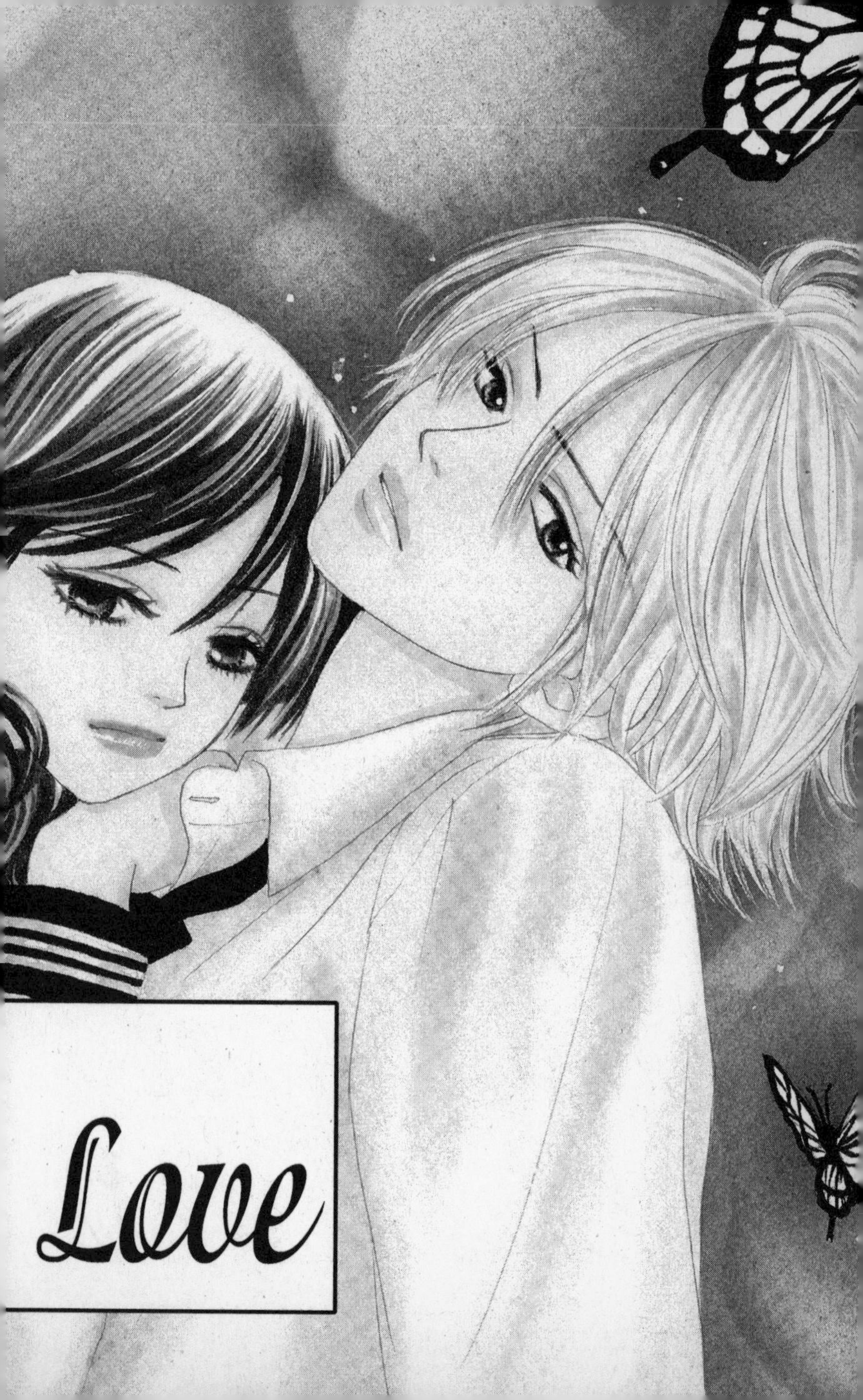
Love

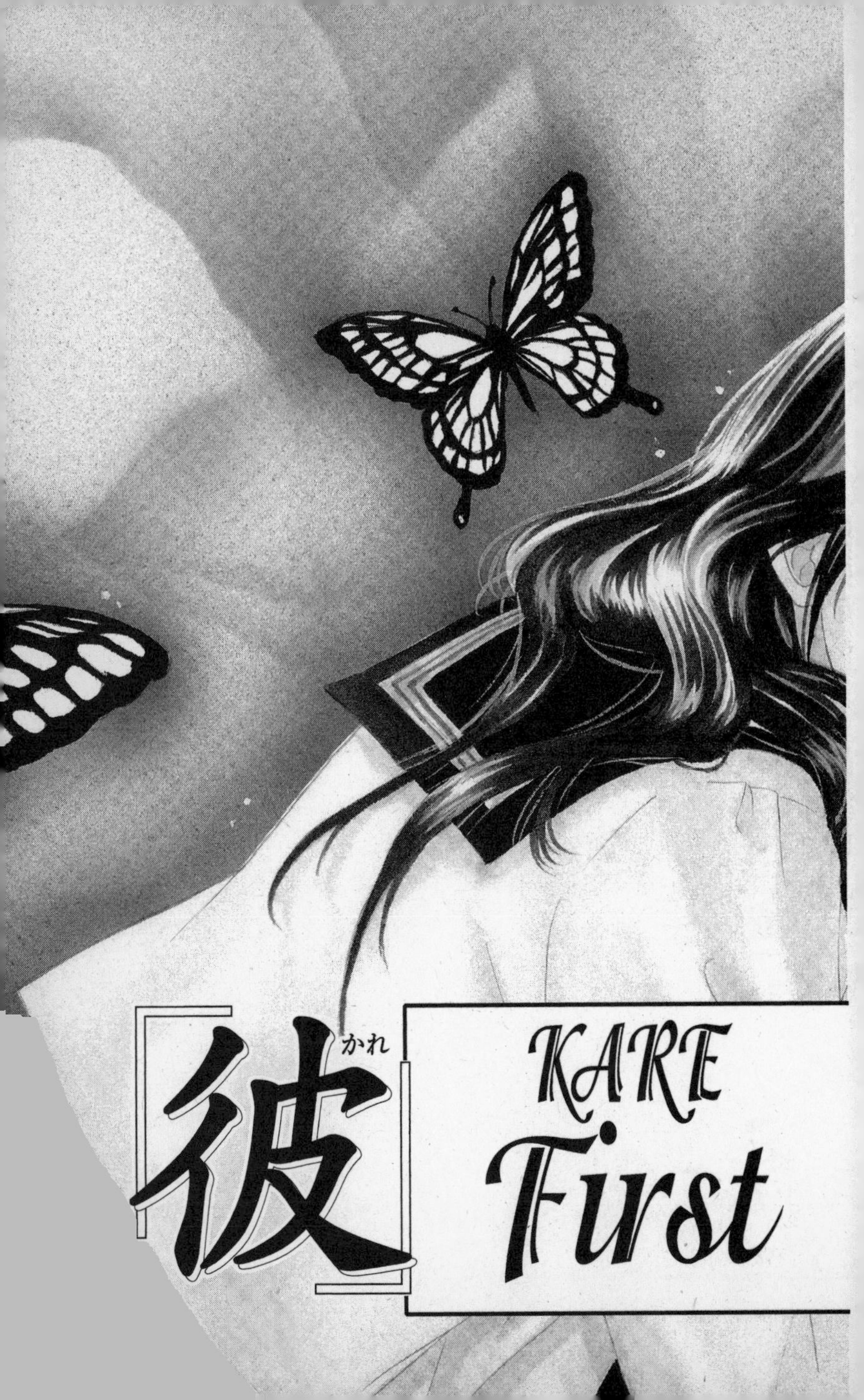
「彼かれ」
KARE
First

# Characters and Story Digest

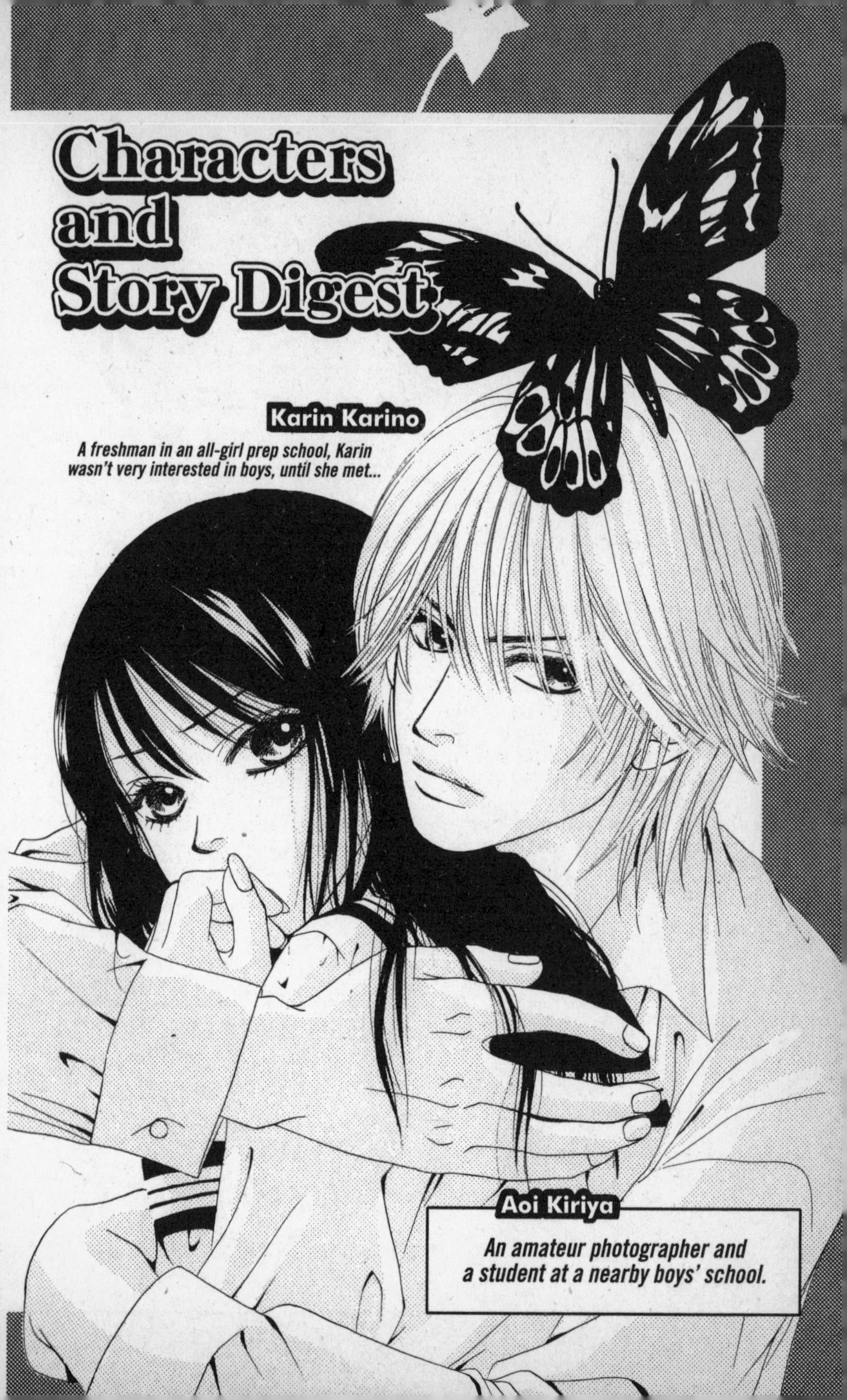

**Karin Karino**

*A freshman in an all-girl prep school, Karin wasn't very interested in boys, until she met...*

**Aoi Kiriya**

*An amateur photographer and a student at a nearby boys' school.*

# KARE First Love

## 彼

**10**

Karin chose an all-girls' school because
she was never really comfortable around
boys. It might not have been bliss, but she
managed. Everything changed when she
met Kiriya on the morning bus and the two
fell in love.

For their first summer vacation together,
the two went to Okinawa with their friends
and stayed on the same beach where Kiriya's
older brother died. They spent the night
together, but Karin drank too much... and the
vacation ended with her virginity intact.

When Karin accompanied Kiriya to visit the
set of his idol, a photographer and director
named Shinji Takagi, some video footage
of Karin ended up being used in a TV
commercial without her consent. At first
this caused a fight between the lovers, but
in the end it brought them closer together
and they quietly consummated their
relationship...

Just as Kiriya decided to enter a photo
contest in which Shinji would judge, Kiriya's
father ordered him to return home and
prepare himself to take over the family
business. Kiriya made a deal with his dad:
if he could get first place in the contest,
he would be able to pursue a future in
photography. In the end, he only took
third. Kiriya resolved to give up photography, but Karin convinced him to
confront his father with his wishes.
Will the two come to terms...?

Karin's best friend. She's interested
in Kiriya's friend Hiromu...

**Shoko Akiba**

Kiriya's older brother's widow,
Karin's confidante and advisor.

**Shinji Takagi**

A photographer, who was friend
and rival to Kiriya's older brother.

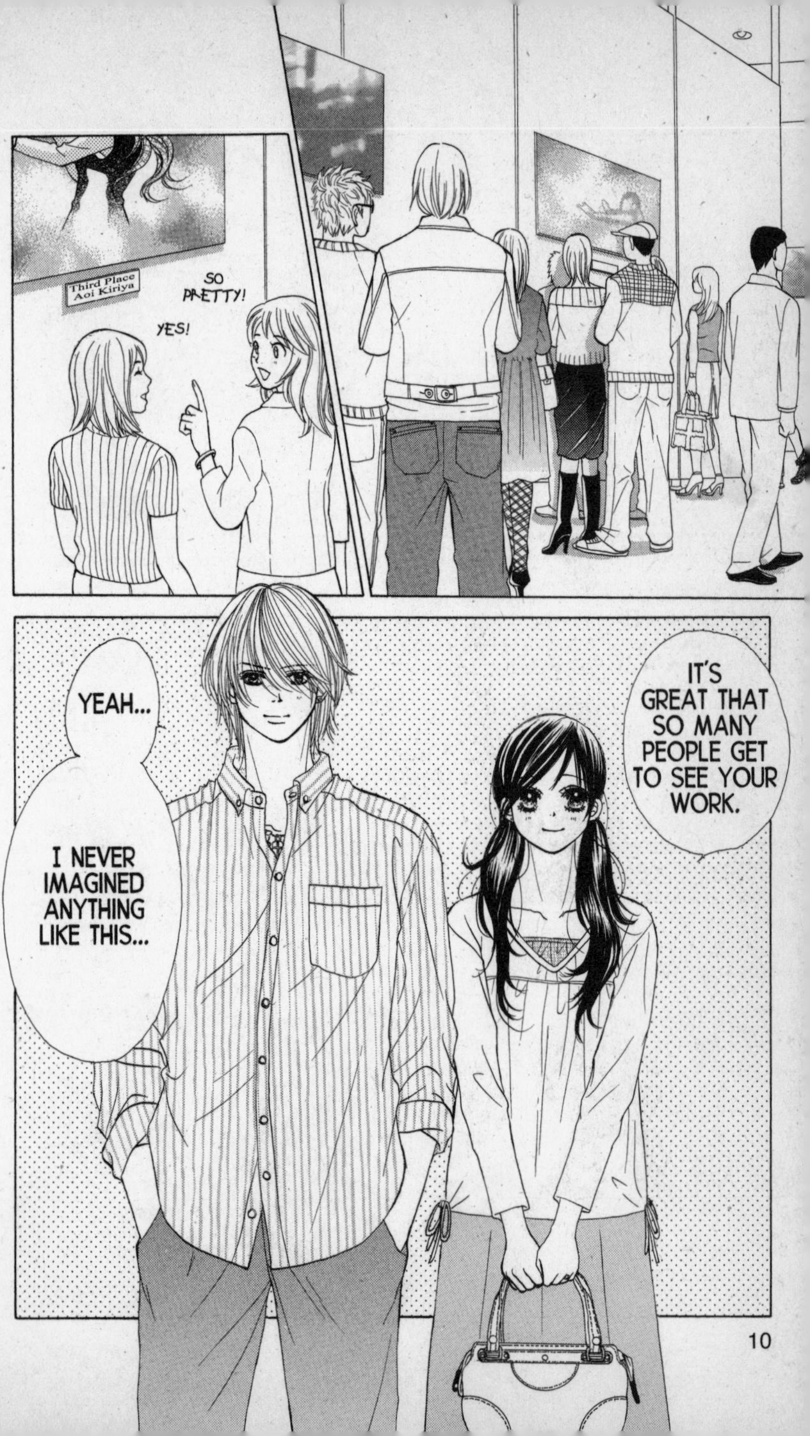
Third Place
Aoi Kiriya
SO PRETTY!
YES!
IT'S GREAT THAT SO MANY PEOPLE GET TO SEE YOUR WORK.
YEAH...
I NEVER IMAGINED ANYTHING LIKE THIS...

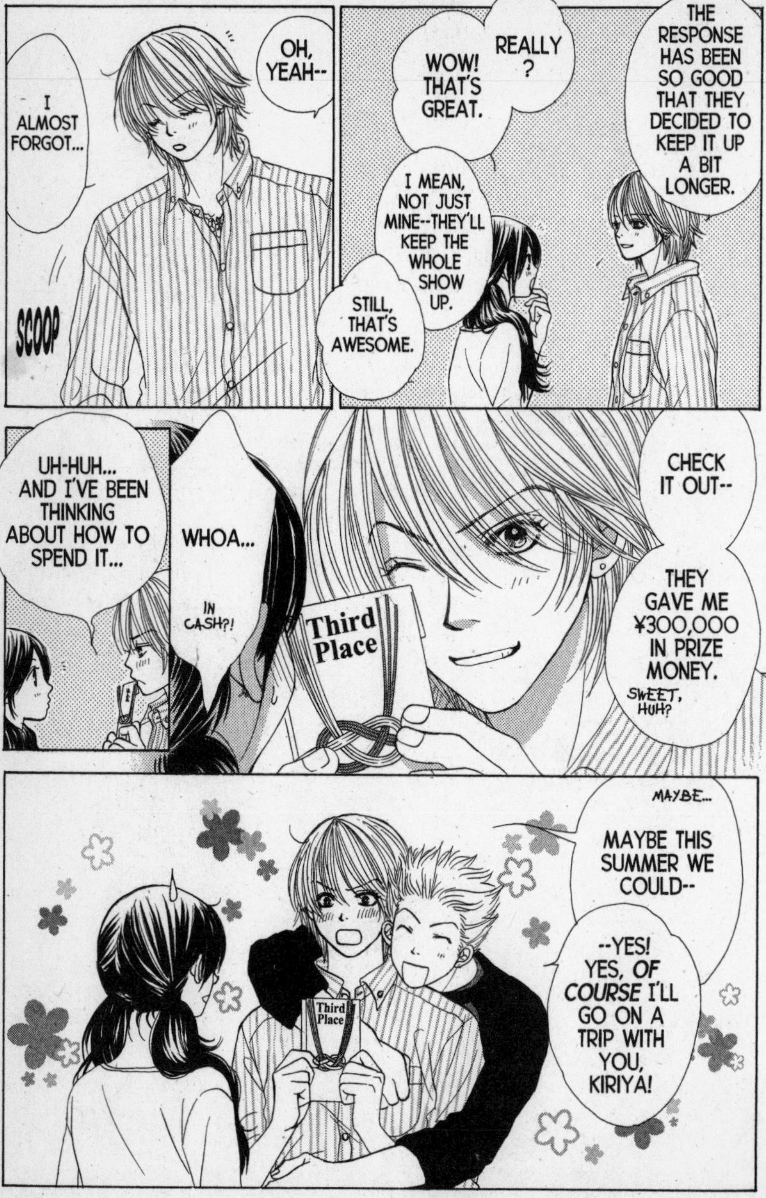
THE RESPONSE HAS BEEN SO GOOD THAT THEY DECIDED TO KEEP IT UP A BIT LONGER.
REALLY?
WOW! THAT'S GREAT.
I MEAN, NOT JUST MINE--THEY'LL KEEP THE WHOLE SHOW UP.
STILL, THAT'S AWESOME.
OH, YEAH--
I ALMOST FORGOT...
SCOOP
CHECK IT OUT--
THEY GAVE ME ¥300,000 IN PRIZE MONEY.
SWEET, HUH?
Third Place
WHOA...
IN CASH?!
UH-HUH... AND I'VE BEEN THINKING ABOUT HOW TO SPEND IT...
MAYBE...
MAYBE THIS SUMMER WE COULD--
--YES! YES, *OF COURSE* I'LL GO ON A TRIP WITH YOU, KIRIYA!
Third Place

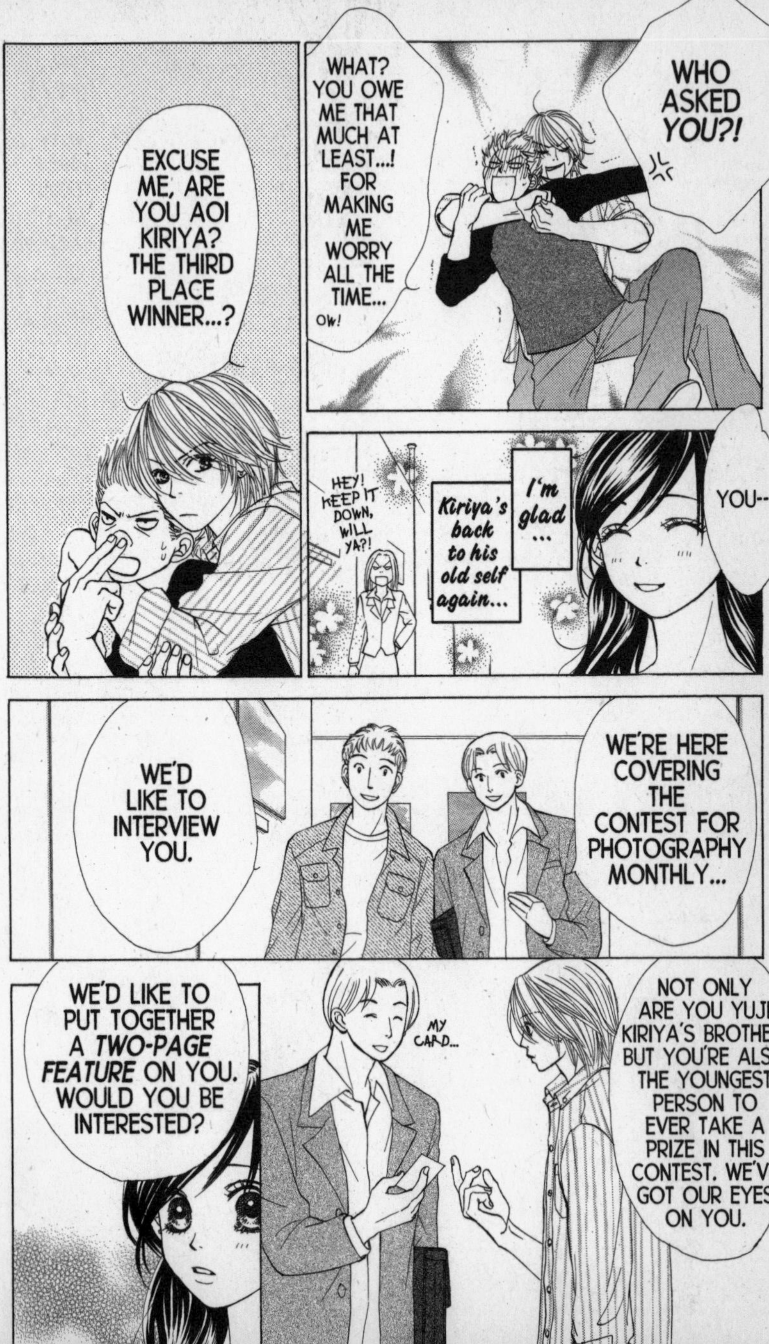
WHO ASKED YOU?!
WHAT? YOU OWE ME THAT MUCH AT LEAST...! FOR MAKING ME WORRY ALL THE TIME...
OW!
YOU--
I'm glad...
Kiriya's back to his old self again...
HEY! KEEP IT DOWN, WILL YA?!
EXCUSE ME, ARE YOU AOI KIRIYA? THE THIRD PLACE WINNER...?
WE'RE HERE COVERING THE CONTEST FOR PHOTOGRAPHY MONTHLY...
WE'D LIKE TO INTERVIEW YOU.
NOT ONLY ARE YOU YUJI KIRIYA'S BROTHER, BUT YOU'RE ALSO THE YOUNGEST PERSON TO EVER TAKE A PRIZE IN THIS CONTEST. WE'VE GOT OUR EYES ON YOU.
MY CARD...
WE'D LIKE TO PUT TOGETHER A TWO-PAGE FEATURE ON YOU. WOULD YOU BE INTERESTED?

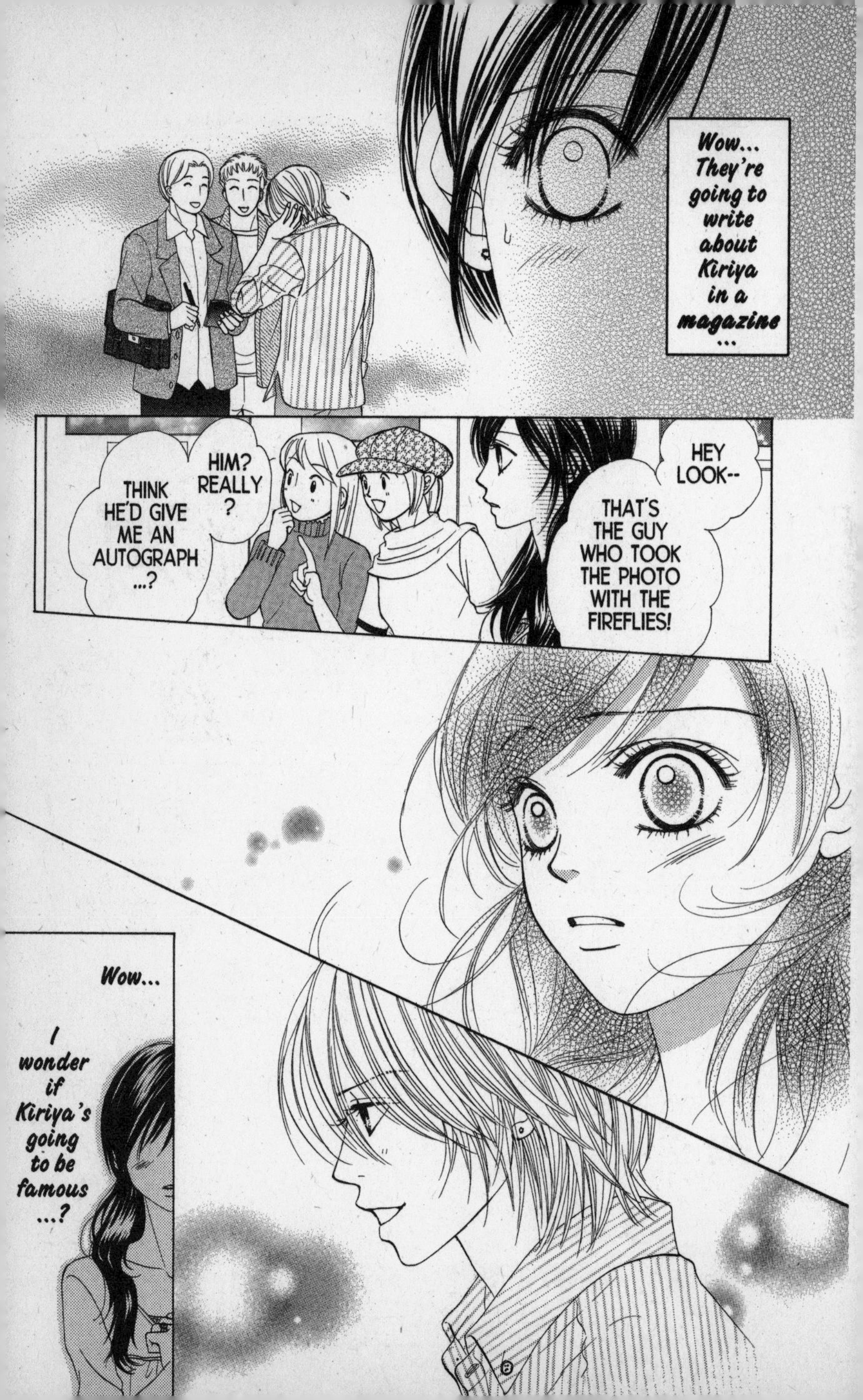
Wow... They're going to write about Kiriya in a magazine...
HEY LOOK--
THAT'S THE GUY WHO TOOK THE PHOTO WITH THE FIREFLIES!
HIM? REALLY?
THINK HE'D GIVE ME AN AUTOGRAPH ...?
Wow...
I wonder if Kiriya's going to be famous ...?

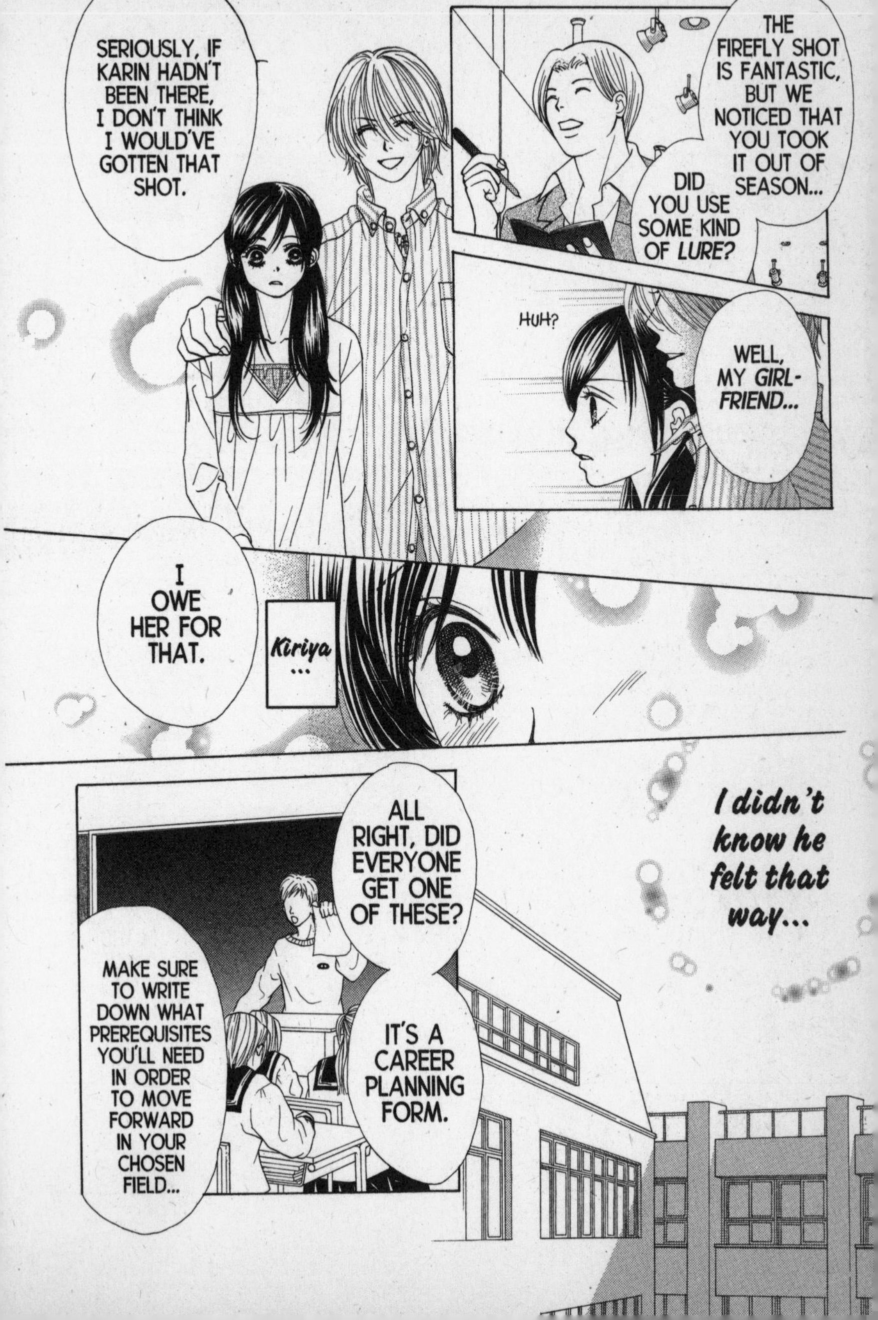
THE FIREFLY SHOT IS FANTASTIC, BUT WE NOTICED THAT YOU TOOK IT OUT OF SEASON...
DID YOU USE SOME KIND OF *LURE*?
WELL, MY *GIRL-FRIEND*...
HUH?
SERIOUSLY, IF KARIN HADN'T BEEN THERE, I DON'T THINK I WOULD'VE GOTTEN THAT SHOT.
I OWE HER FOR THAT.
Kiriya...
I didn't know he felt that way...
ALL RIGHT, DID EVERYONE GET ONE OF THESE?
IT'S A CAREER PLANNING FORM.
MAKE SURE TO WRITE DOWN WHAT PREREQUISITES YOU'LL NEED IN ORDER TO MOVE FORWARD IN YOUR CHOSEN FIELD...

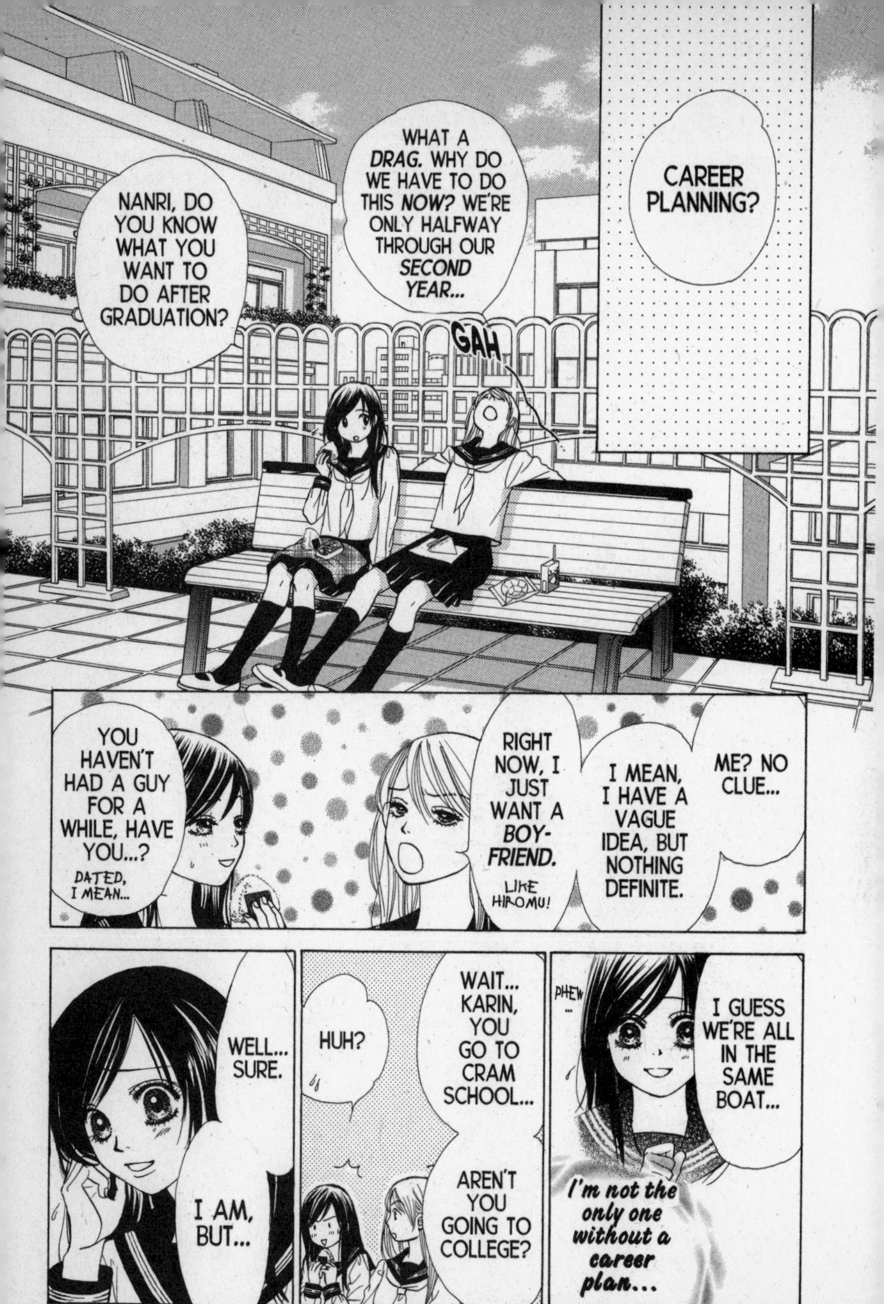
CAREER PLANNING?
WHAT A *DRAG.* WHY DO WE HAVE TO DO THIS *NOW?* WE'RE ONLY HALFWAY THROUGH OUR *SECOND YEAR...*
GAH
NANRI, DO YOU KNOW WHAT YOU WANT TO DO AFTER GRADUATION?
ME? NO CLUE...
I MEAN, I HAVE A VAGUE IDEA, BUT NOTHING DEFINITE.
RIGHT NOW, I JUST WANT A *BOY-FRIEND.*
LIKE HIROMU!
YOU HAVEN'T HAD A GUY FOR A WHILE, HAVE YOU...?
DATED, I MEAN...
PHEW...
I GUESS WE'RE ALL IN THE SAME BOAT...
*I'm not the only one without a career plan...*
WAIT... KARIN, YOU GO TO CRAM SCHOOL...
AREN'T YOU GOING TO COLLEGE?
HUH?
WELL... SURE.
I AM, BUT...

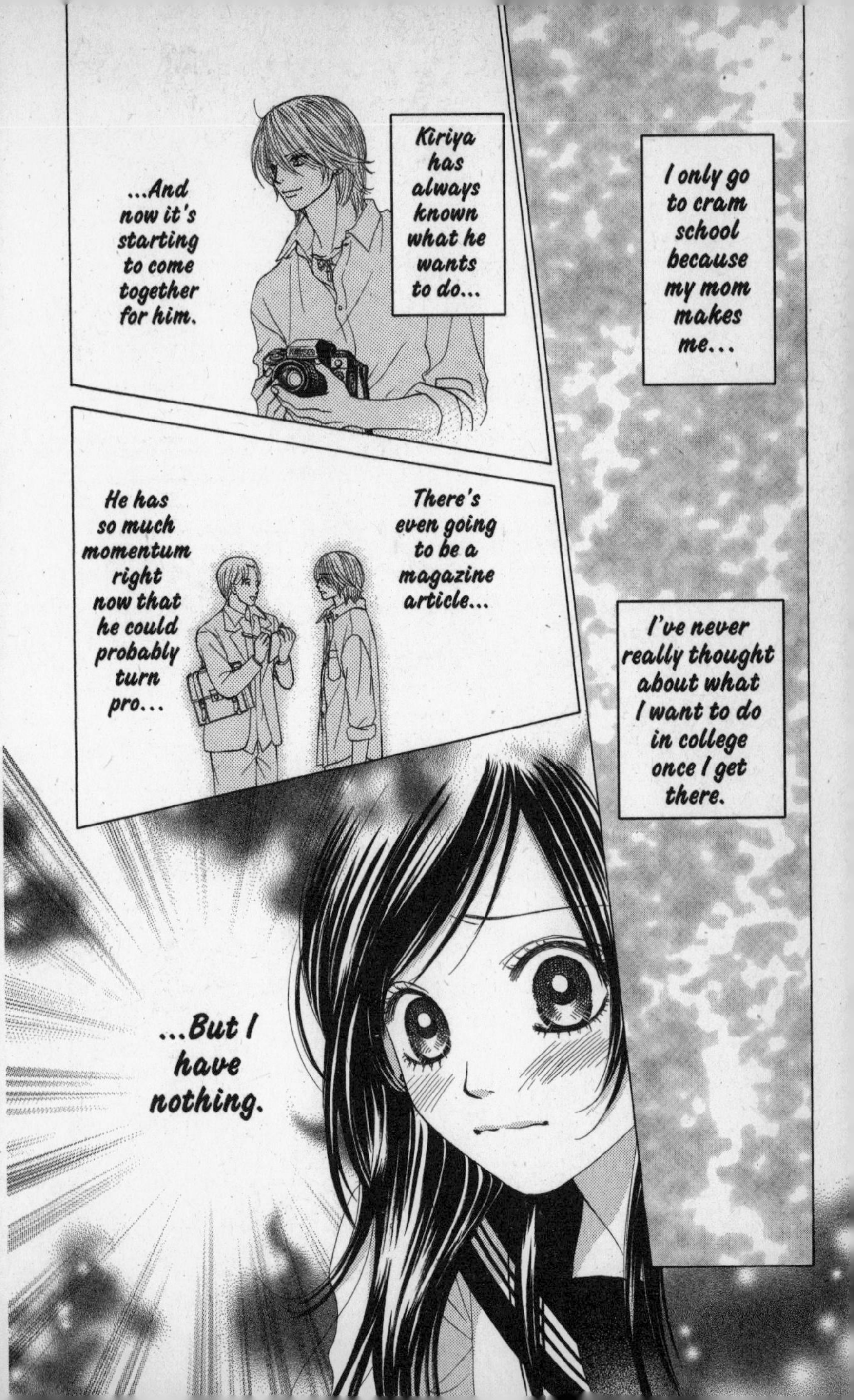
Kiriya has always known what he wants to do...
...And now it's starting to come together for him.
There's even going to be a magazine article...
He has so much momentum right now that he could probably turn pro...
I only go to cram school because my mom makes me...
I've never really thought about what I want to do in college once I get there.
...But I have nothing.

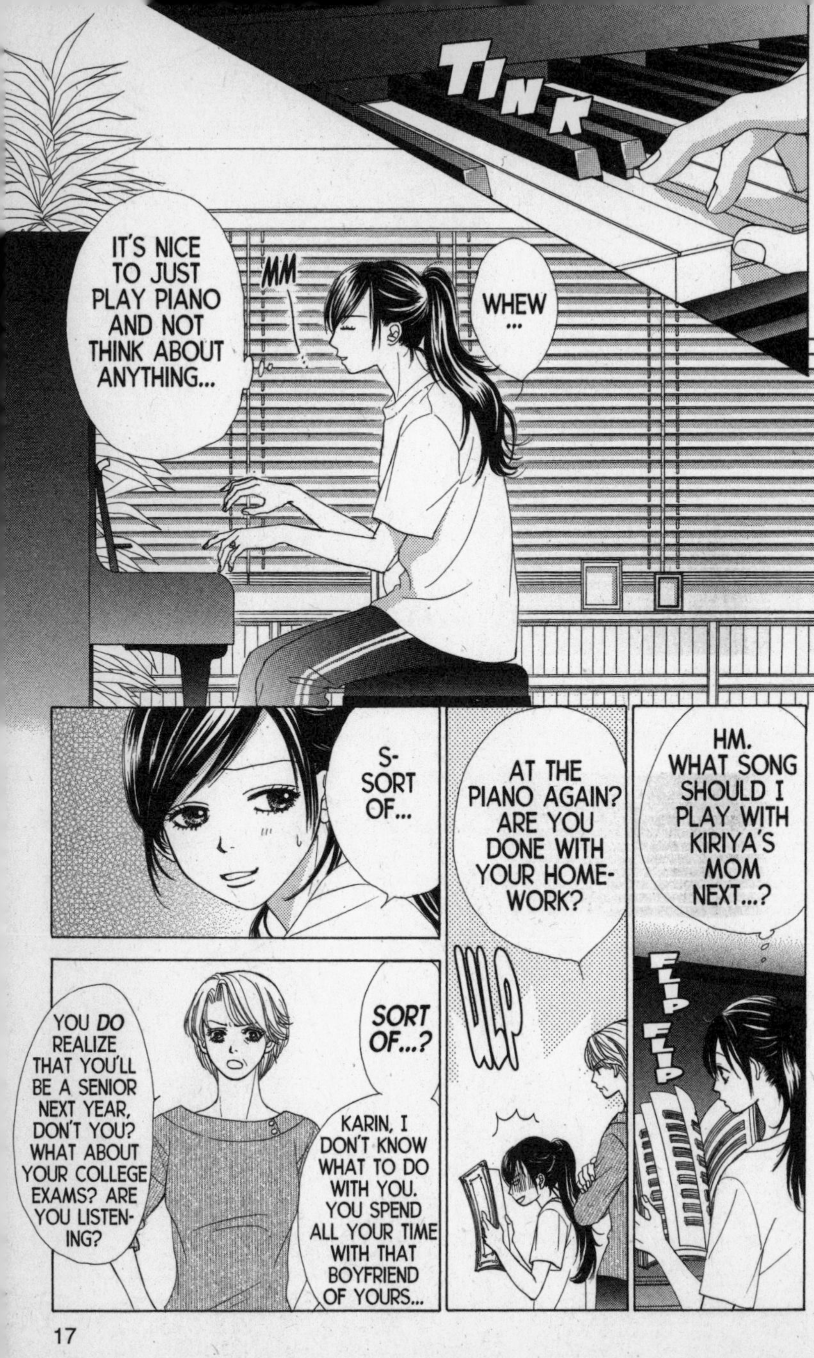
TINK
WHEW...
MM
IT'S NICE TO JUST PLAY PIANO AND NOT THINK ABOUT ANYTHING...
HM. WHAT SONG SHOULD I PLAY WITH KIRIYA'S MOM NEXT...?
FLIP FLIP
AT THE PIANO AGAIN? ARE YOU DONE WITH YOUR HOME-WORK?
GULP
S-SORT OF...
SORT OF...?
KARIN, I DON'T KNOW WHAT TO DO WITH YOU. YOU SPEND ALL YOUR TIME WITH THAT BOYFRIEND OF YOURS...
YOU DO REALIZE THAT YOU'LL BE A SENIOR NEXT YEAR, DON'T YOU? WHAT ABOUT YOUR COLLEGE EXAMS? ARE YOU LISTEN-ING?

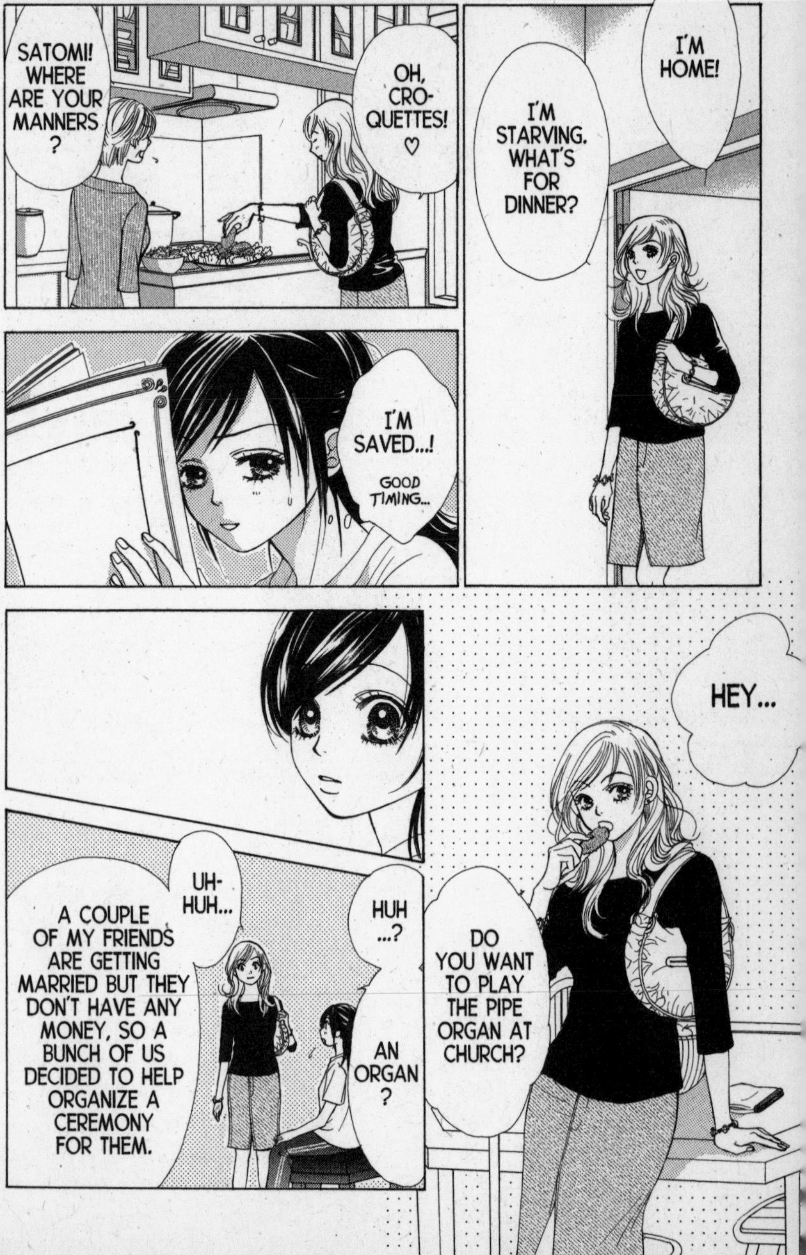
I'M HOME!
I'M STARVING. WHAT'S FOR DINNER?
OH, CRO-QUETTES! ♡
SATOMI! WHERE ARE YOUR MANNERS?
I'M SAVED...!
GOOD TIMING...
HEY...
DO YOU WANT TO PLAY THE PIPE ORGAN AT CHURCH?
HUH...?
AN ORGAN?
UH-HUH...
A COUPLE OF MY FRIENDS ARE GETTING MARRIED BUT THEY DON'T HAVE ANY MONEY, SO A BUNCH OF US DECIDED TO HELP ORGANIZE A CEREMONY FOR THEM.

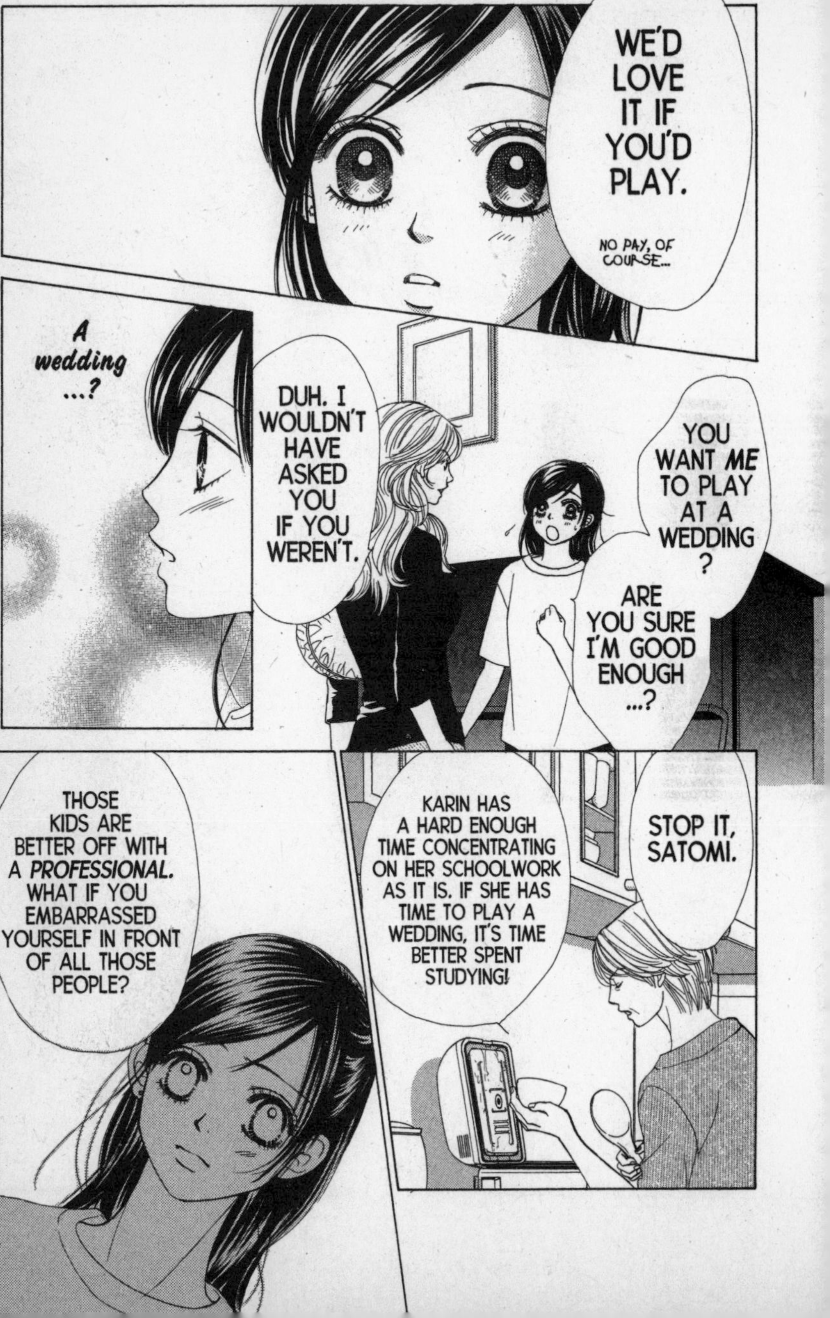
WE'D LOVE IT IF YOU'D PLAY.
NO PAY, OF COURSE...
YOU WANT *ME* TO PLAY AT A WEDDING?
ARE YOU SURE I'M GOOD ENOUGH...?
DUH. I WOULDN'T HAVE ASKED YOU IF YOU WEREN'T.
A wedding...?
STOP IT, SATOMI.
KARIN HAS A HARD ENOUGH TIME CONCENTRATING ON HER SCHOOLWORK AS IT IS. IF SHE HAS TIME TO PLAY A WEDDING, IT'S TIME BETTER SPENT STUDYING!
THOSE KIDS ARE BETTER OFF WITH A *PROFESSIONAL.* WHAT IF YOU EMBARRASSED YOURSELF IN FRONT OF ALL THOSE PEOPLE?

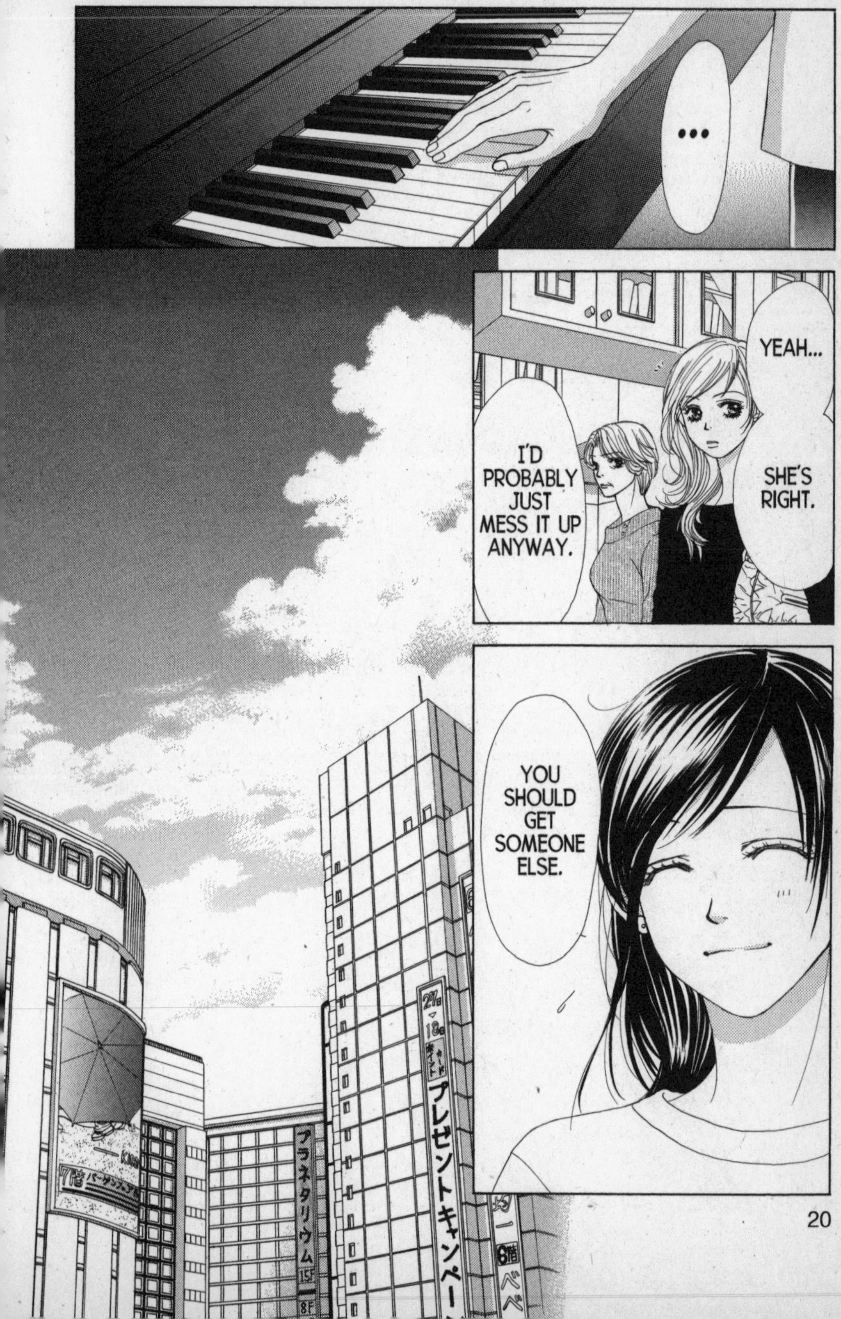
...
YEAH...
SHE'S RIGHT.
I'D PROBABLY JUST MESS IT UP ANYWAY.
YOU SHOULD GET SOMEONE ELSE.
プレゼントキャンペー
プラネタリウム

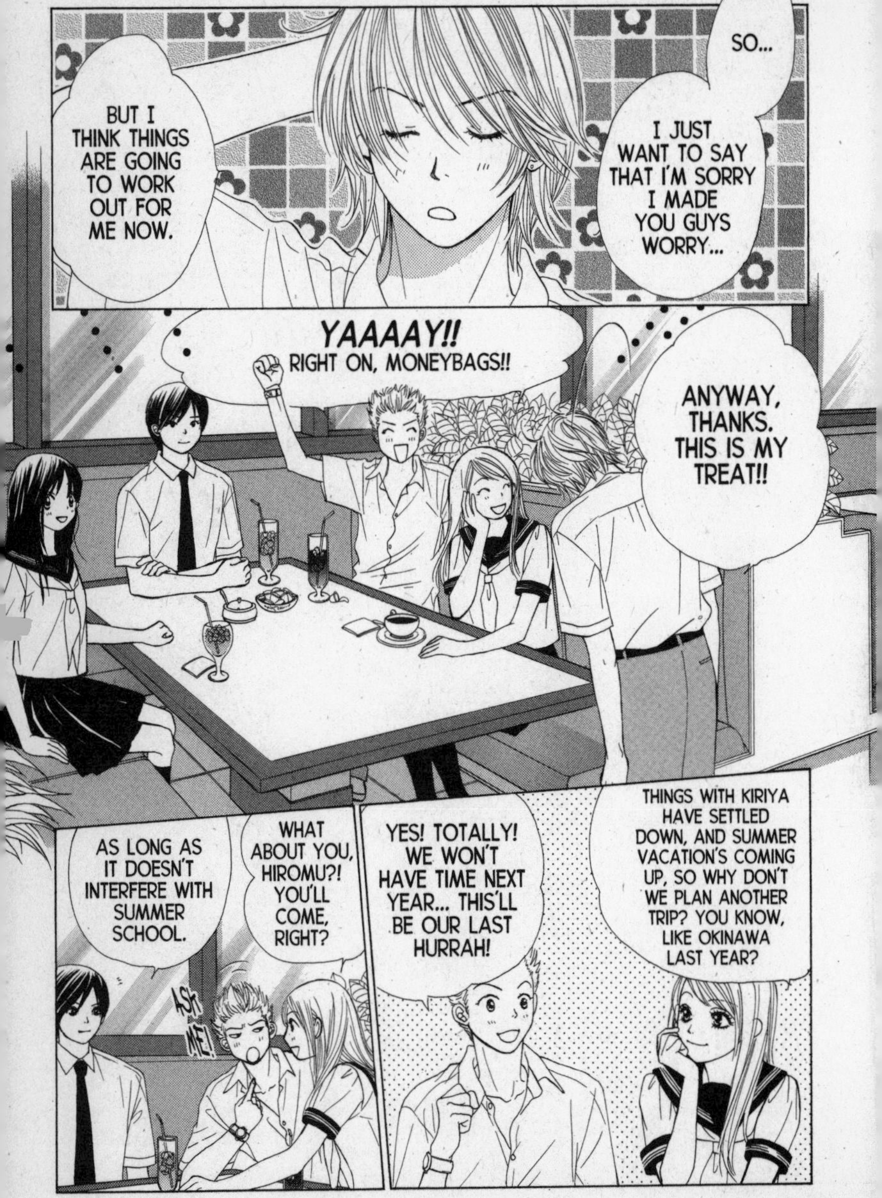
SO...
I JUST WANT TO SAY THAT I'M SORRY I MADE YOU GUYS WORRY...
BUT I THINK THINGS ARE GOING TO WORK OUT FOR ME NOW.
ANYWAY, THANKS. THIS IS MY TREAT!!
YAAAAY!! RIGHT ON, MONEYBAGS!!
THINGS WITH KIRIYA HAVE SETTLED DOWN, AND SUMMER VACATION'S COMING UP, SO WHY DON'T WE PLAN ANOTHER TRIP? YOU KNOW, LIKE OKINAWA LAST YEAR?
YES! TOTALLY! WE WON'T HAVE TIME NEXT YEAR... THIS'LL BE OUR LAST HURRAH!
WHAT ABOUT YOU, HIROMU?! YOU'LL COME, RIGHT?
AS LONG AS IT DOESN'T INTERFERE WITH SUMMER SCHOOL.
ASK ME!

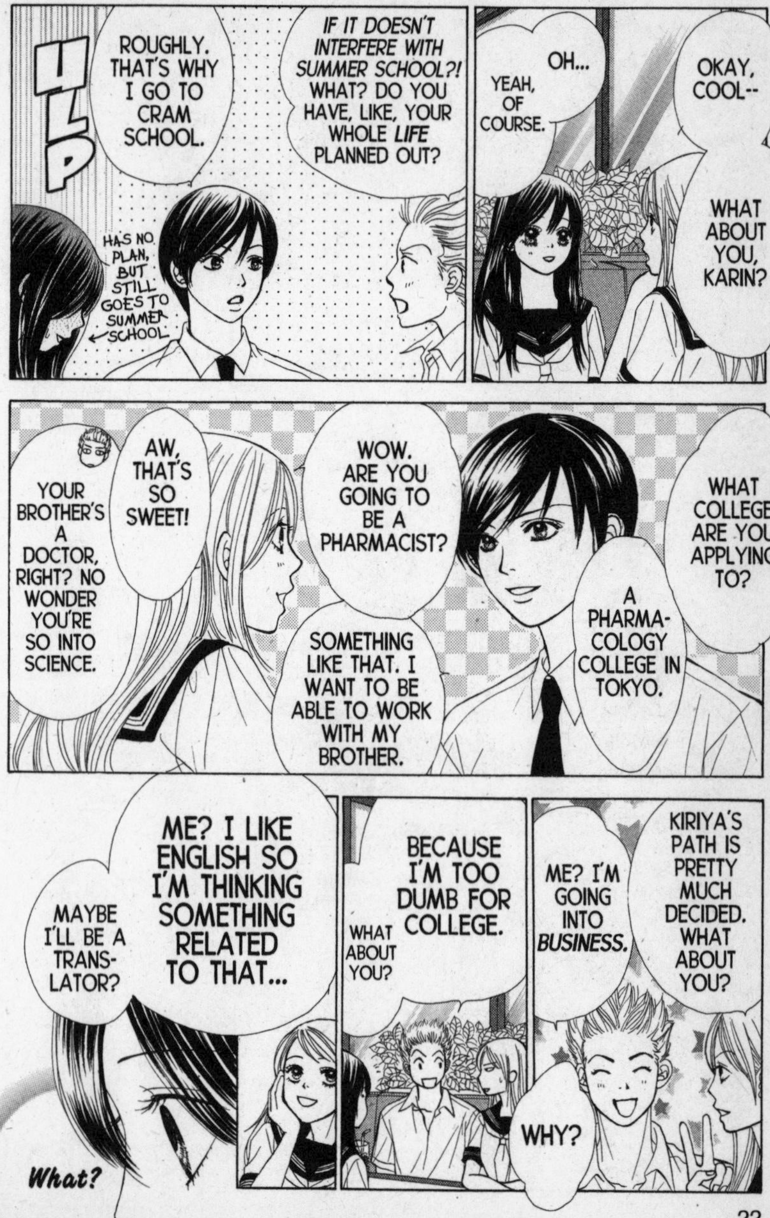
OKAY, COOL--
WHAT ABOUT YOU, KARIN?
OH...
YEAH, OF COURSE.
*IF IT DOESN'T INTERFERE WITH SUMMER SCHOOL?!* WHAT? DO YOU HAVE, LIKE, YOUR WHOLE *LIFE* PLANNED OUT?
ROUGHLY. THAT'S WHY I GO TO CRAM SCHOOL.
ULP
HAS NO PLAN, BUT STILL GOES TO SUMMER SCHOOL
WHAT COLLEGE ARE YOU APPLYING TO?
A PHARMACOLOGY COLLEGE IN TOKYO.
WOW. ARE YOU GOING TO BE A PHARMACIST?
SOMETHING LIKE THAT. I WANT TO BE ABLE TO WORK WITH MY BROTHER.
AW, THAT'S SO SWEET!
YOUR BROTHER'S A DOCTOR, RIGHT? NO WONDER YOU'RE SO INTO SCIENCE.
KIRIYA'S PATH IS PRETTY MUCH DECIDED. WHAT ABOUT YOU?
ME? I'M GOING INTO *BUSINESS.*
WHY?
BECAUSE I'M TOO DUMB FOR COLLEGE.
WHAT ABOUT YOU?
ME? I LIKE ENGLISH SO I'M THINKING SOMETHING RELATED TO THAT...
MAYBE I'LL BE A TRANSLATOR?
What?

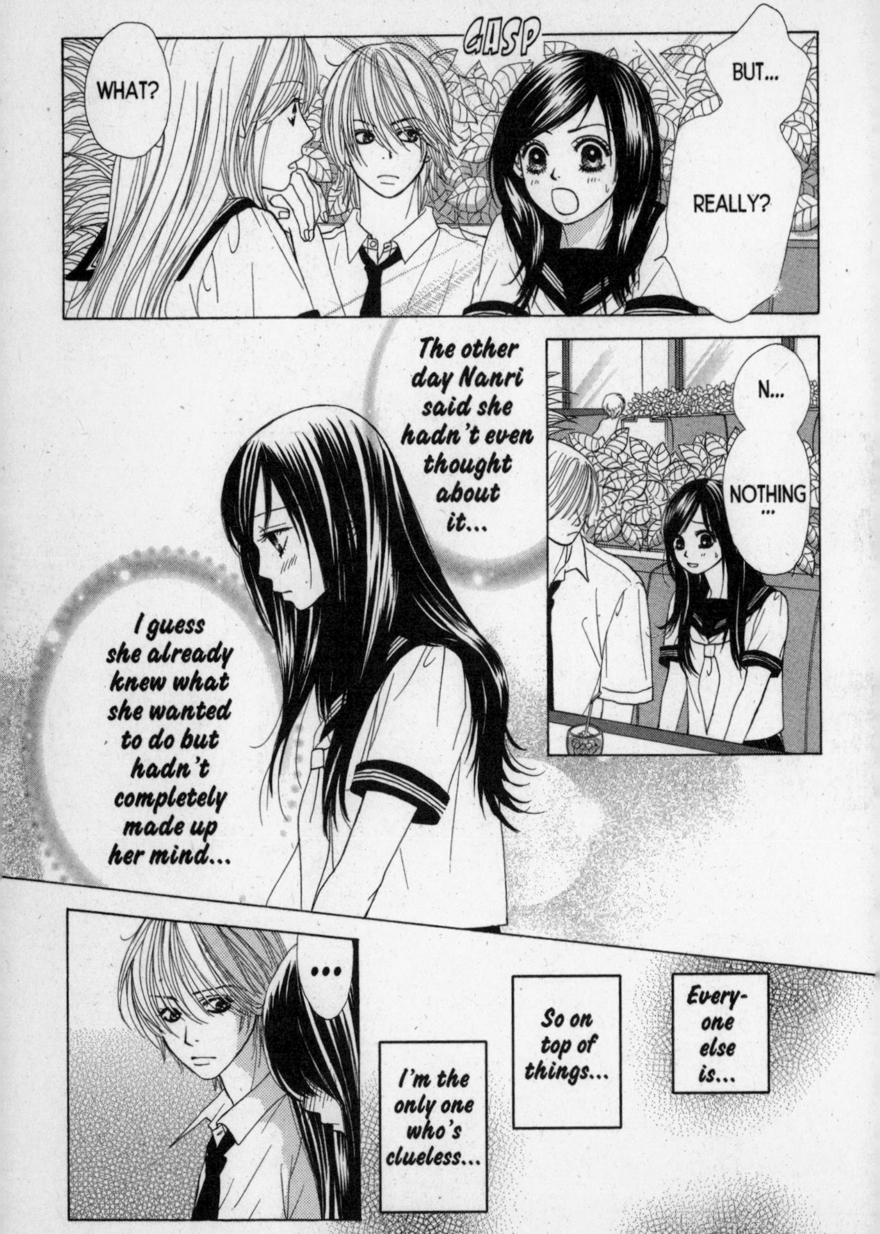
BUT... REALLY?
GASP
WHAT?
N... NOTHING...
The other day Nanri said she hadn't even thought about it...
I guess she already knew what she wanted to do but hadn't completely made up her mind...
Every-one else is...
So on top of things...
I'm the only one who's clueless...
...

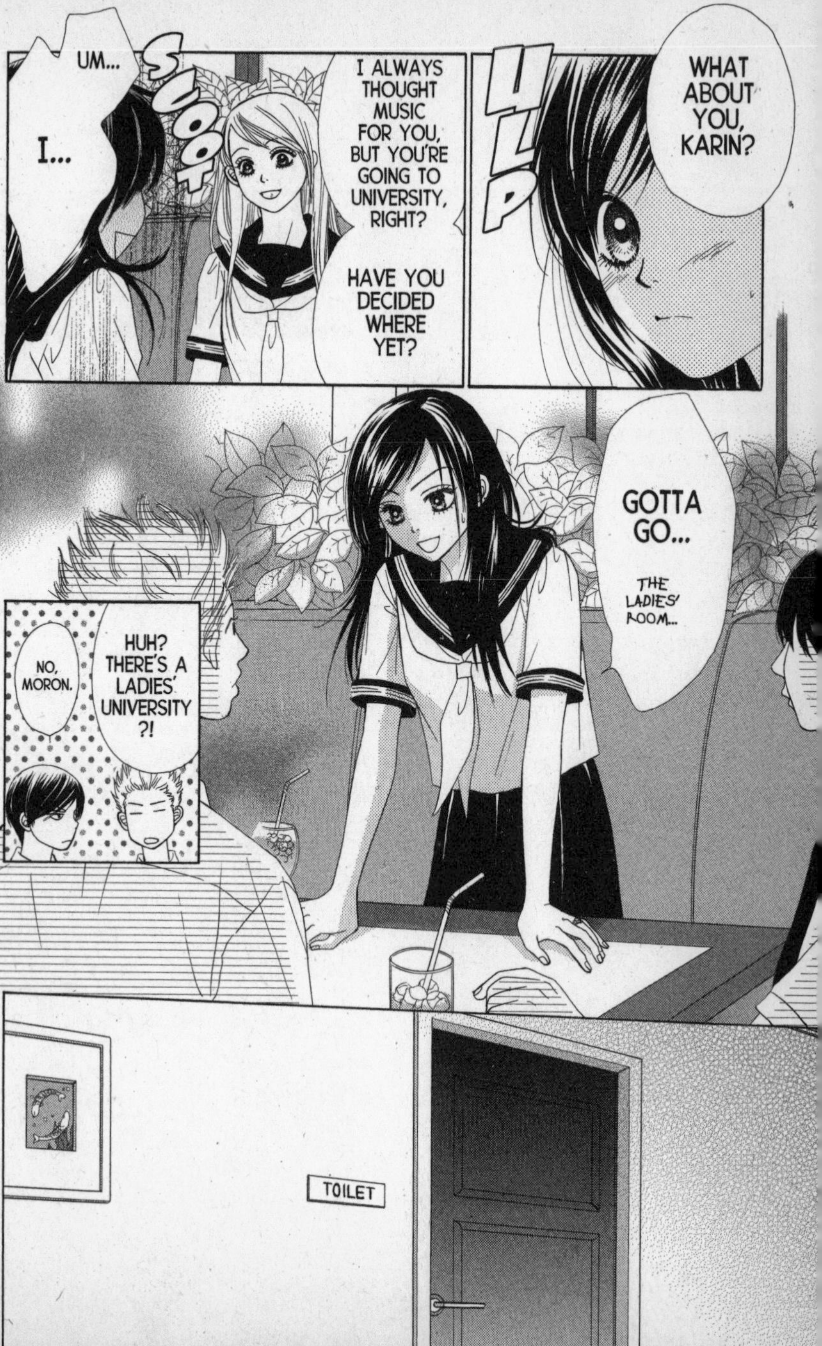
WHAT ABOUT YOU, KARIN?
ULP
I ALWAYS THOUGHT MUSIC FOR YOU, BUT YOU'RE GOING TO UNIVERSITY, RIGHT?
HAVE YOU DECIDED WHERE YET?
SWOOT
UM...
I...
GOTTA GO...
THE LADIES' ROOM...
HUH? THERE'S A LADIES' UNIVERSITY ?!
NO, MORON.
TOILET

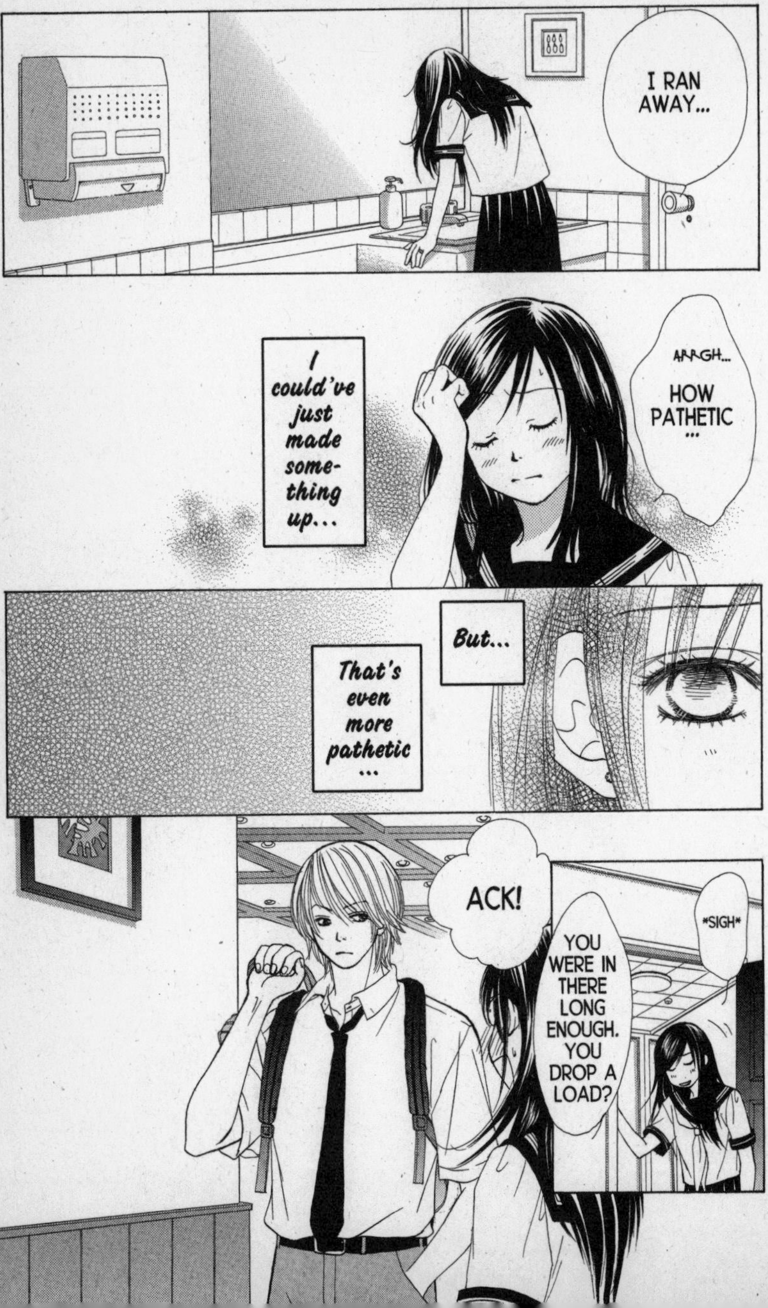
I RAN AWAY...
ARRGH... HOW PATHETIC...
I could've just made some-thing up...
But...
That's even more pathetic...
*SIGH*
YOU WERE IN THERE LONG ENOUGH. YOU DROP A LOAD?
ACK!

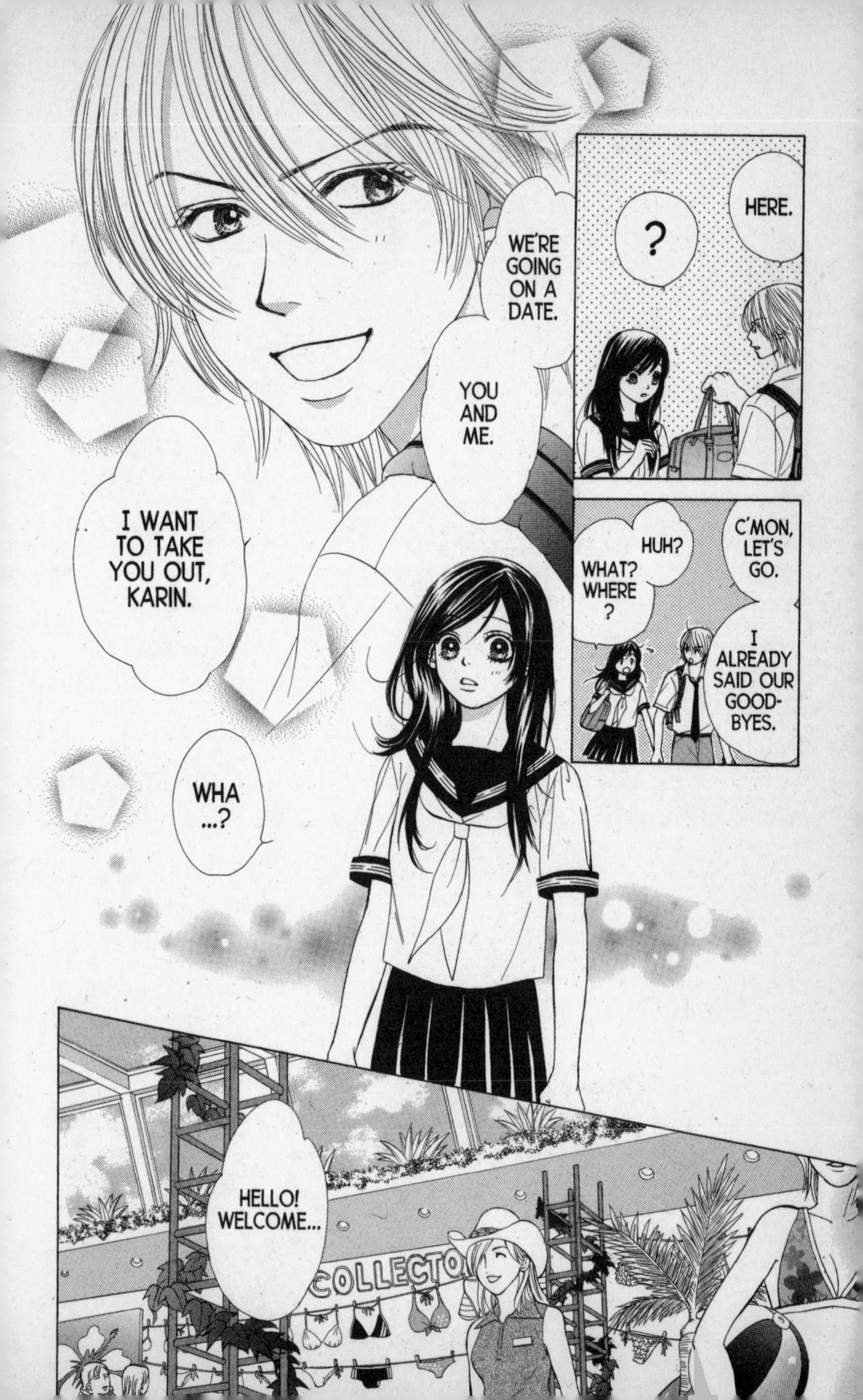
HERE.
?
C'MON, LET'S GO.
I ALREADY SAID OUR GOOD-BYES.
HUH? WHAT? WHERE?
WE'RE GOING ON A DATE.
YOU AND ME.
I WANT TO TAKE YOU OUT, KARIN.
WHA ...?
HELLO! WELCOME...

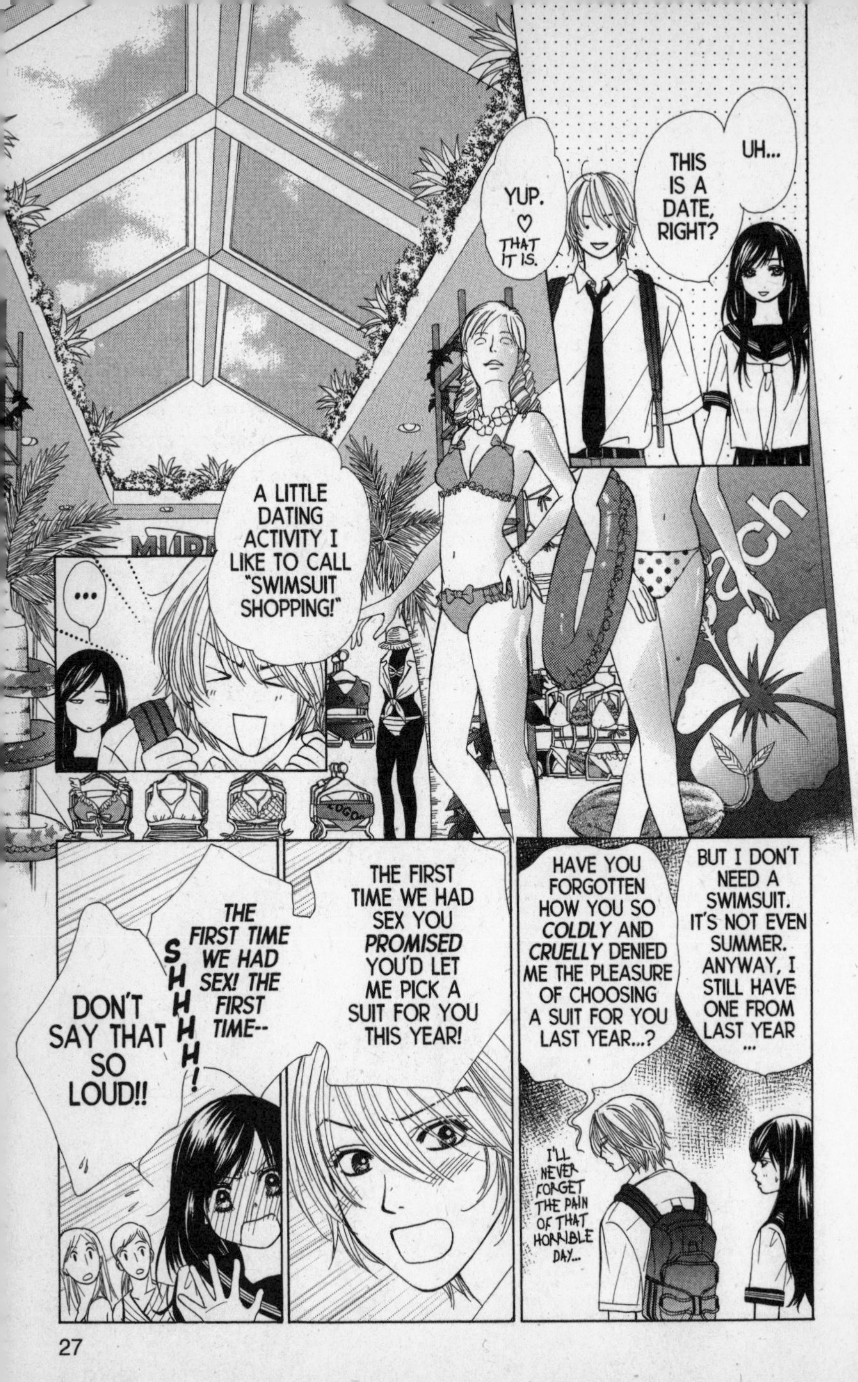
UH... THIS IS A DATE, RIGHT?
YUP. ♡ THAT IT IS.
A LITTLE DATING ACTIVITY I LIKE TO CALL "SWIMSUIT SHOPPING!"
...
BUT I DON'T NEED A SWIMSUIT. IT'S NOT EVEN SUMMER. ANYWAY, I STILL HAVE ONE FROM LAST YEAR ...
HAVE YOU FORGOTTEN HOW YOU SO COLDLY AND CRUELLY DENIED ME THE PLEASURE OF CHOOSING A SUIT FOR YOU LAST YEAR...?
I'LL NEVER FORGET THE PAIN OF THAT HORRIBLE DAY...
THE FIRST TIME WE HAD SEX YOU PROMISED YOU'D LET ME PICK A SUIT FOR YOU THIS YEAR!
THE FIRST TIME WE HAD SEX! THE FIRST TIME--
SHHHH!
DON'T SAY THAT SO LOUD!!

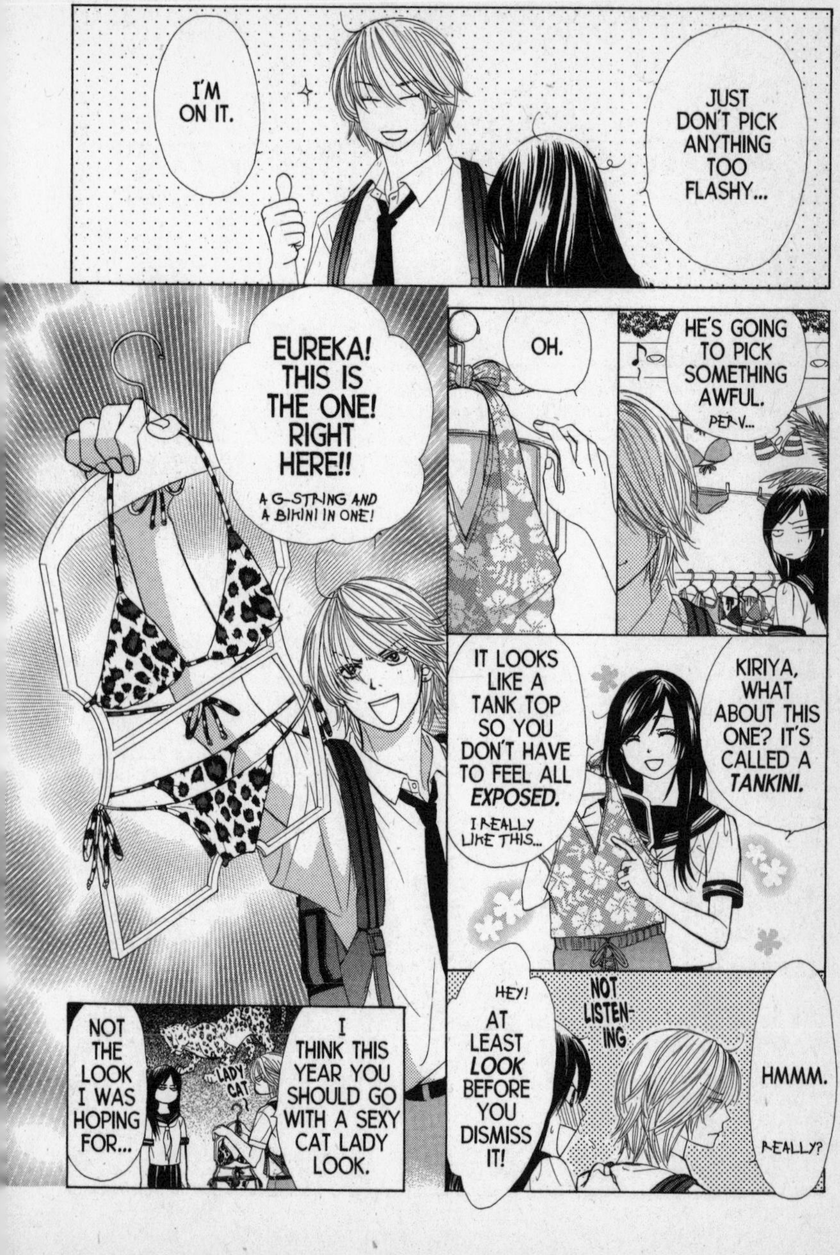
JUST DON'T PICK ANYTHING TOO FLASHY...
I'M ON IT.
HE'S GOING TO PICK SOMETHING AWFUL.
PERV...
OH.
KIRIYA, WHAT ABOUT THIS ONE? IT'S CALLED A *TANKINI.*
IT LOOKS LIKE A TANK TOP SO YOU DON'T HAVE TO FEEL ALL ***EXPOSED.***
I REALLY LIKE THIS...
HMMM.
REALLY?
NOT LISTEN-ING
HEY!
AT LEAST ***LOOK*** BEFORE YOU DISMISS IT!
EUREKA! THIS IS THE ONE! RIGHT HERE!!
A G-STRING AND A BIKINI IN ONE!
I THINK THIS YEAR YOU SHOULD GO WITH A SEXY CAT LADY LOOK.
LADY CAT
NOT THE LOOK I WAS HOPING FOR...

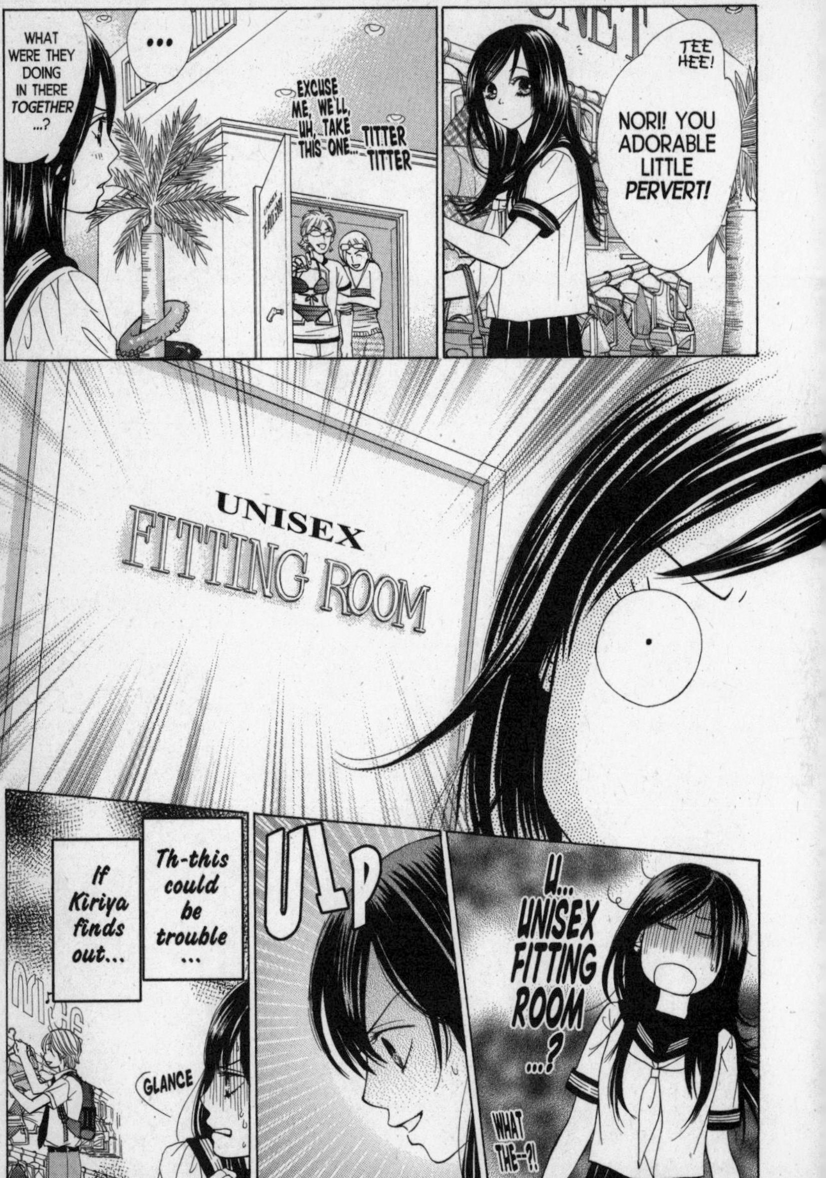
TEE HEE!
NORI! YOU ADORABLE LITTLE *PERVERT!*
EXCUSE ME, WE'LL, UH, TAKE THIS ONE...
TITTER TITTER
...
WHAT WERE THEY DOING IN THERE *TOGETHER* ...?
UNISEX
FITTING ROOM
U... UNISEX FITTING ROOM ...?
WHAT THE--?!
ULP
Th-this could be trouble...
If Kiriya finds out...
GLANCE
KARIN

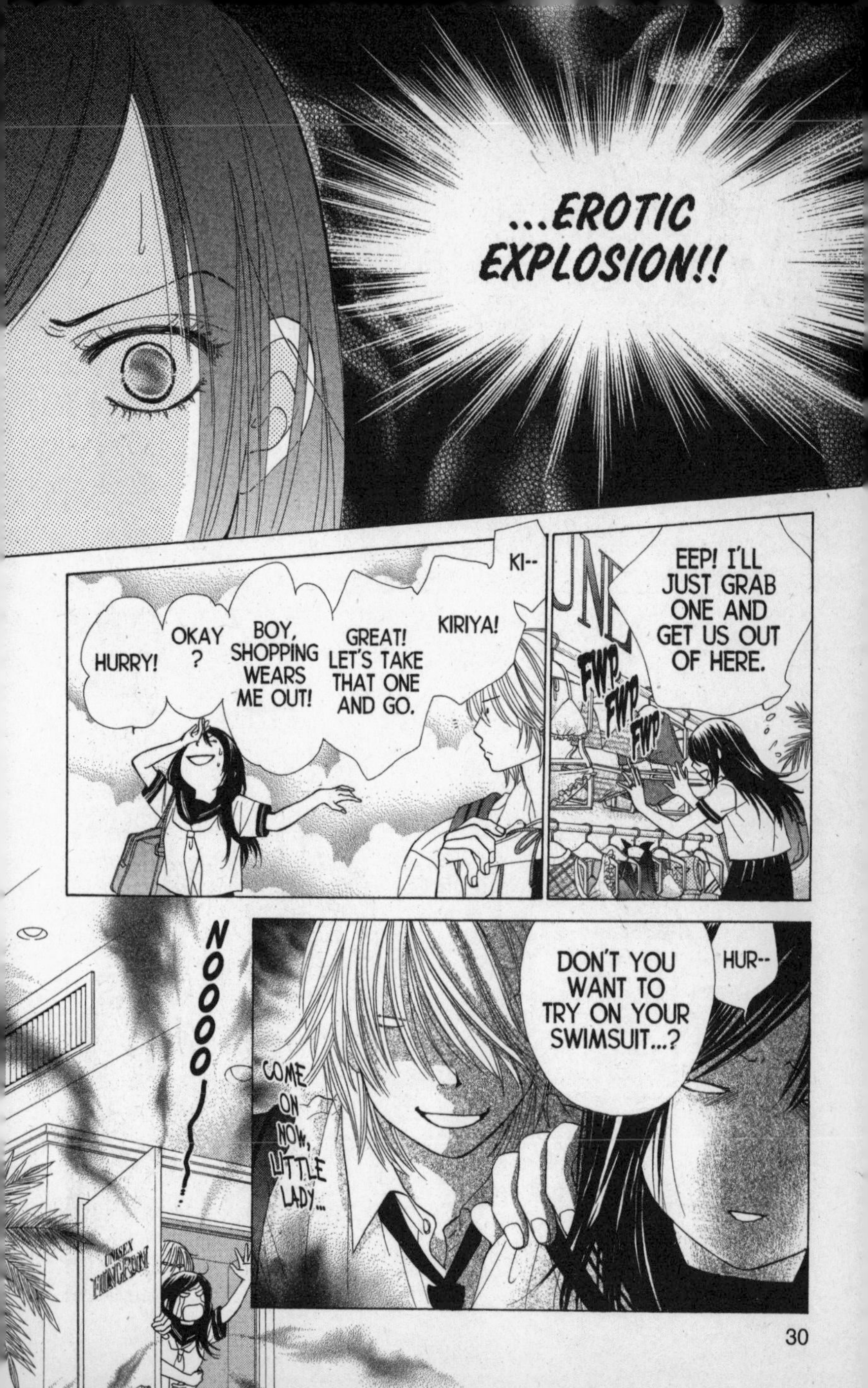
...EROTIC EXPLOSION!!
EEP! I'LL JUST GRAB ONE AND GET US OUT OF HERE.
FWP FWP FWP
KI--
KIRIYA!
GREAT! LET'S TAKE THAT ONE AND GO.
BOY, SHOPPING WEARS ME OUT!
OKAY?
HURRY!
HUR--
DON'T YOU WANT TO TRY ON YOUR SWIMSUIT...?
COME ON NOW, LITTLE LADY...
NOOOOO--!
UNISEX

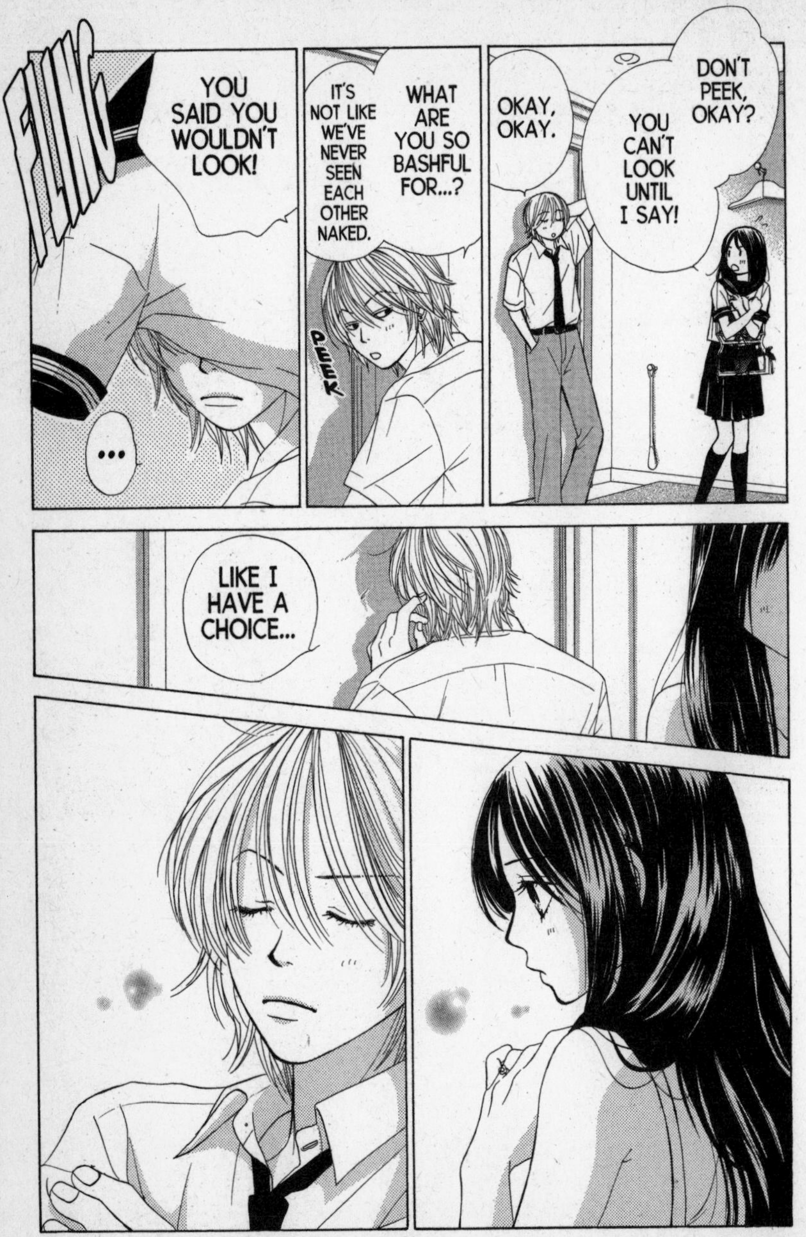
DON'T PEEK, OKAY?
YOU CAN'T LOOK UNTIL I SAY!
OKAY, OKAY.
WHAT ARE YOU SO BASHFUL FOR...?
IT'S NOT LIKE WE'VE NEVER SEEN EACH OTHER NAKED.
PEEK
FLING
YOU SAID YOU WOULDN'T LOOK!
...
LIKE I HAVE A CHOICE...

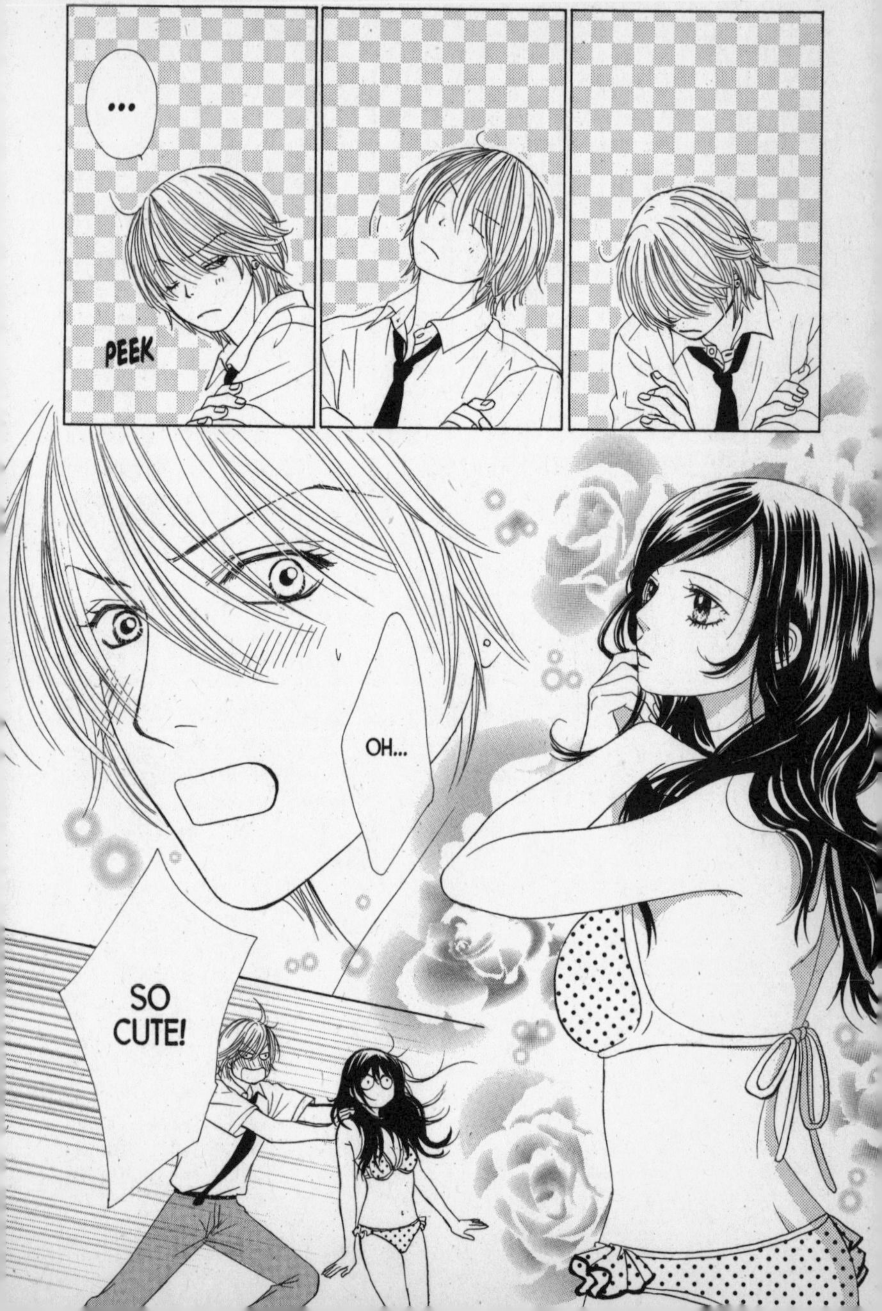
...
PEEK
OH...
SO CUTE!

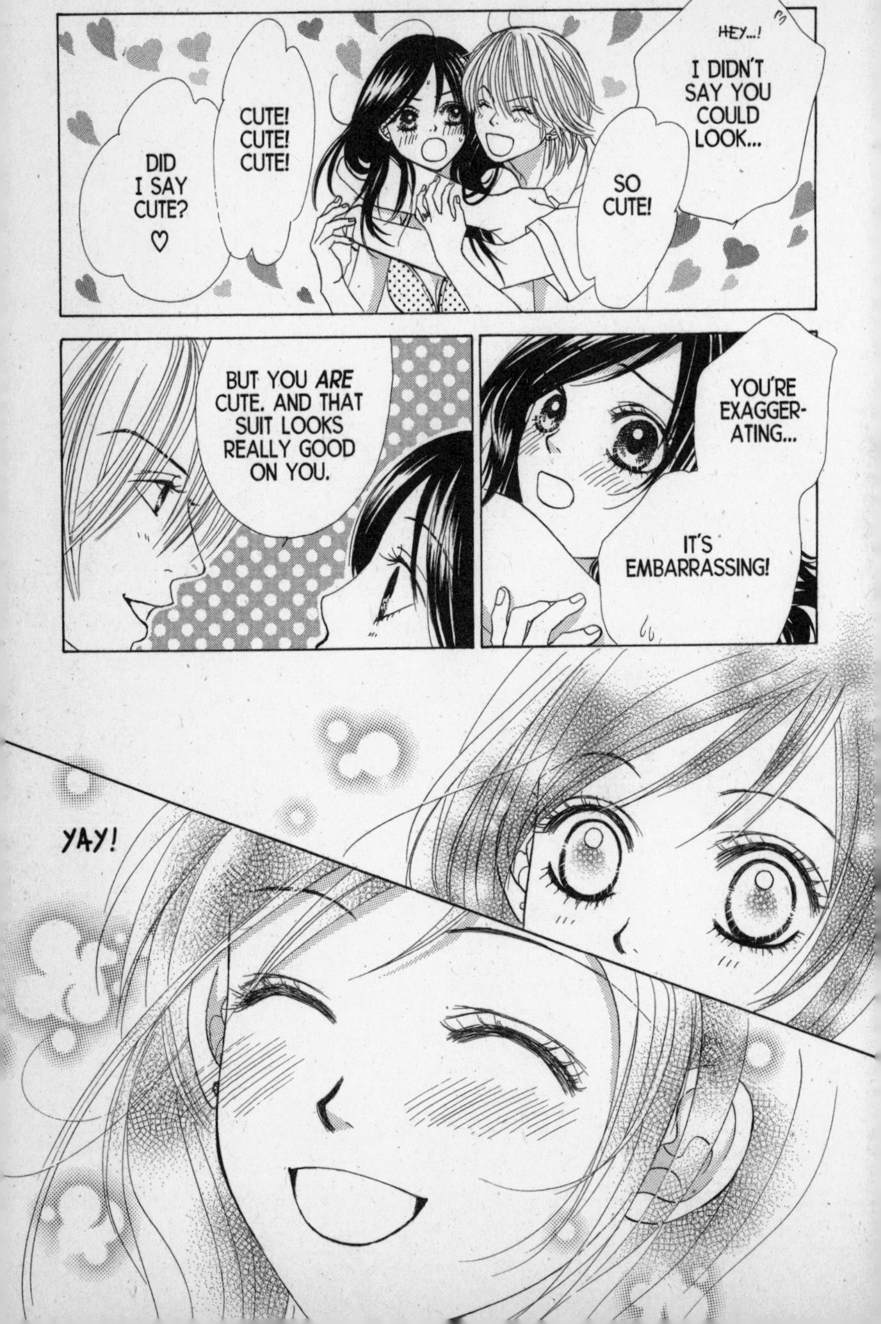
HEY...!
I DIDN'T SAY YOU COULD LOOK...
SO CUTE!
CUTE! CUTE! CUTE!
DID I SAY CUTE? ♡
YOU'RE EXAGGER-ATING...
IT'S EMBARRASSING!
BUT YOU *ARE* CUTE. AND THAT SUIT LOOKS REALLY GOOD ON YOU.
YAY!

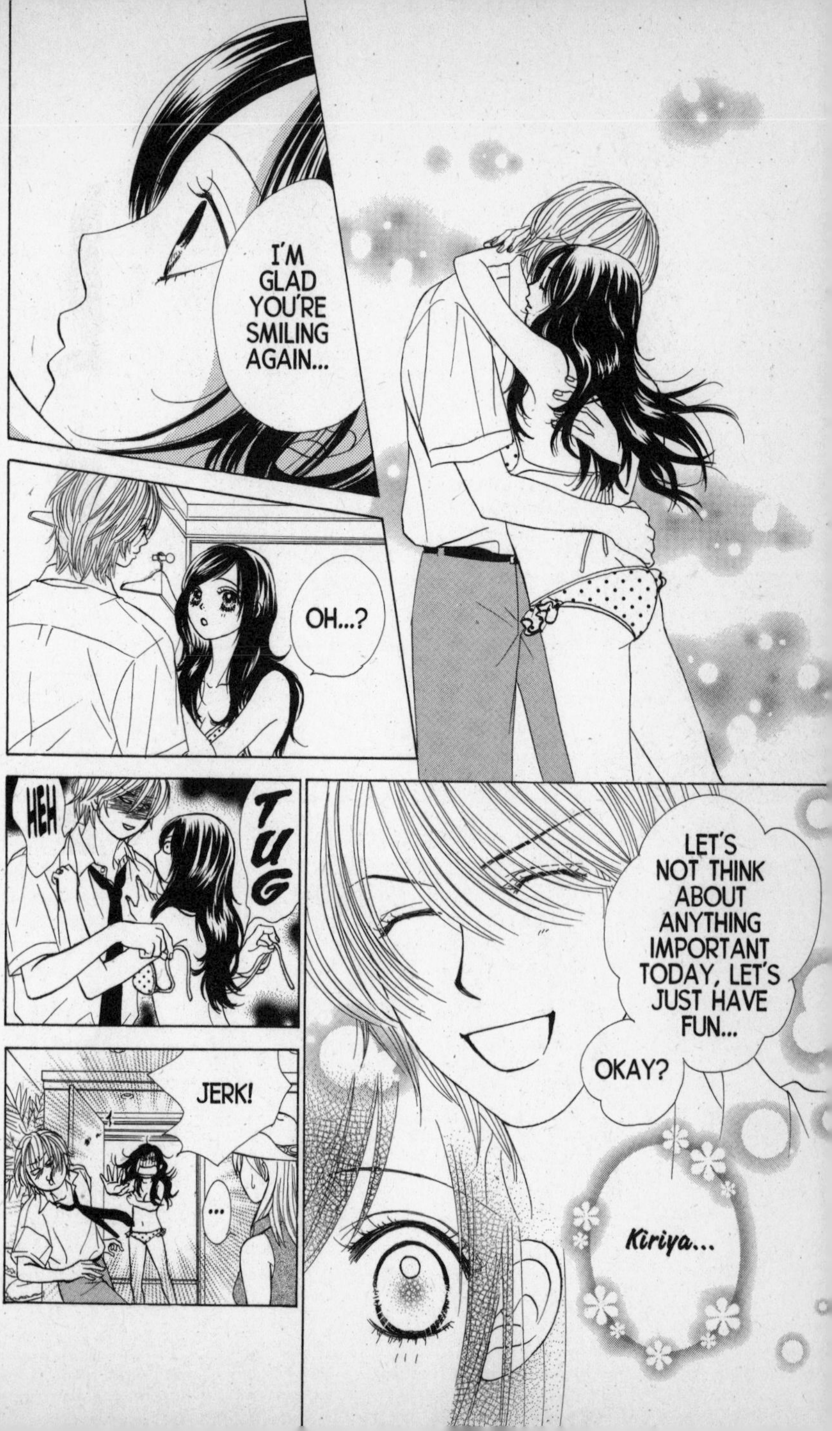

I'M GLAD YOU'RE SMILING AGAIN...
OH...?
LET'S NOT THINK ABOUT ANYTHING IMPORTANT TODAY, LET'S JUST HAVE FUN...
OKAY?
Kiriya...
TUG
HEH
JERK!
...

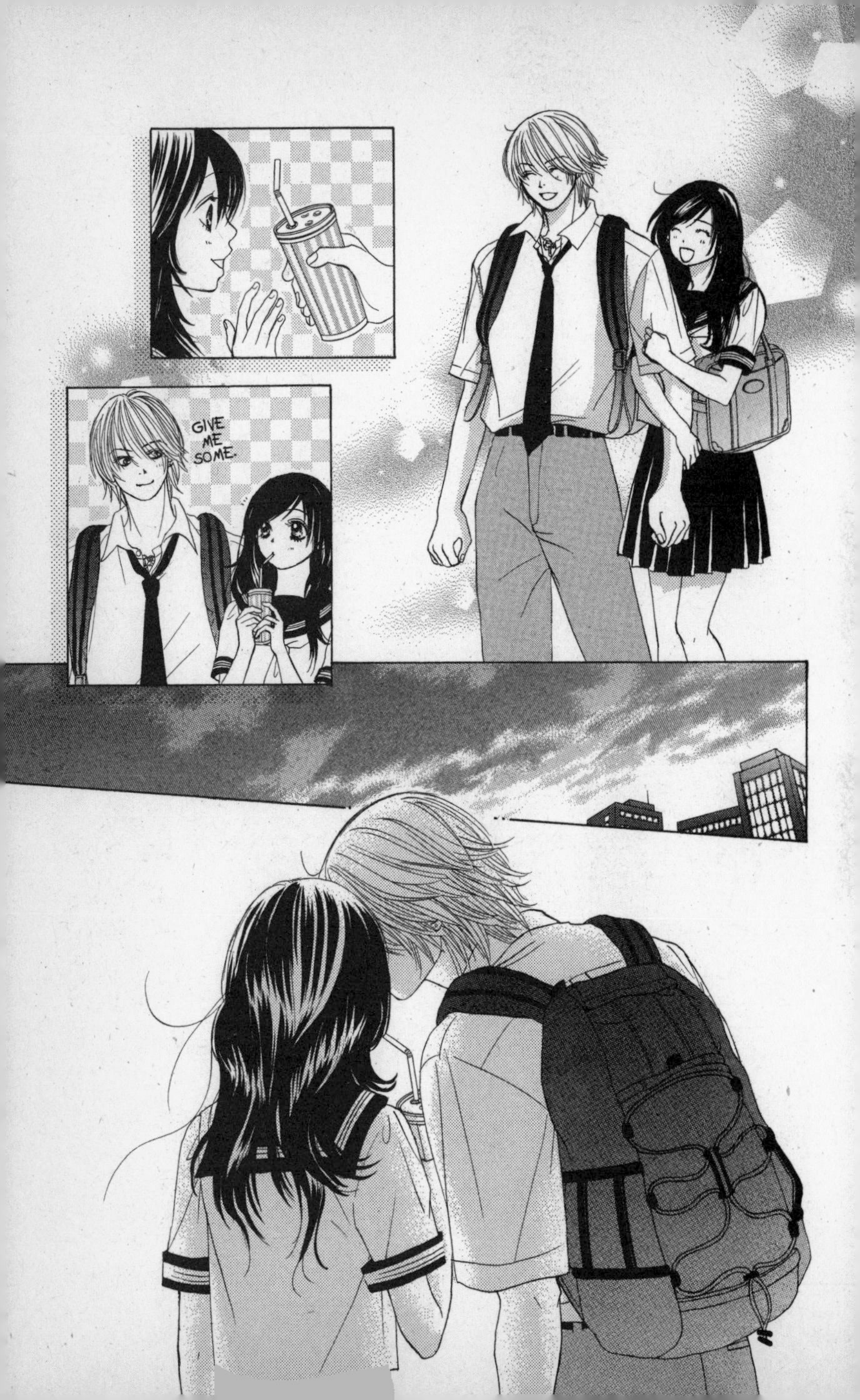
GIVE ME SOME.

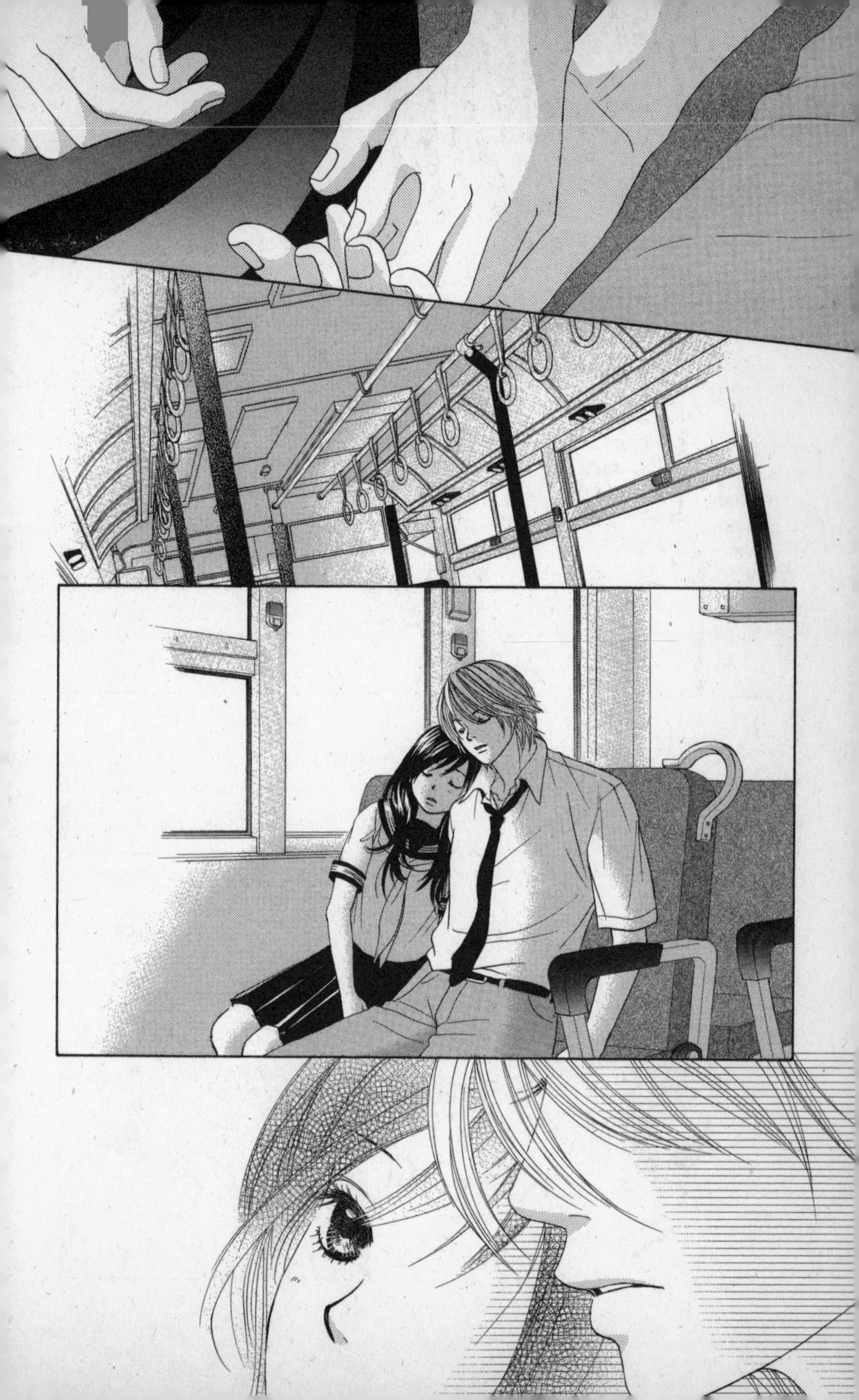

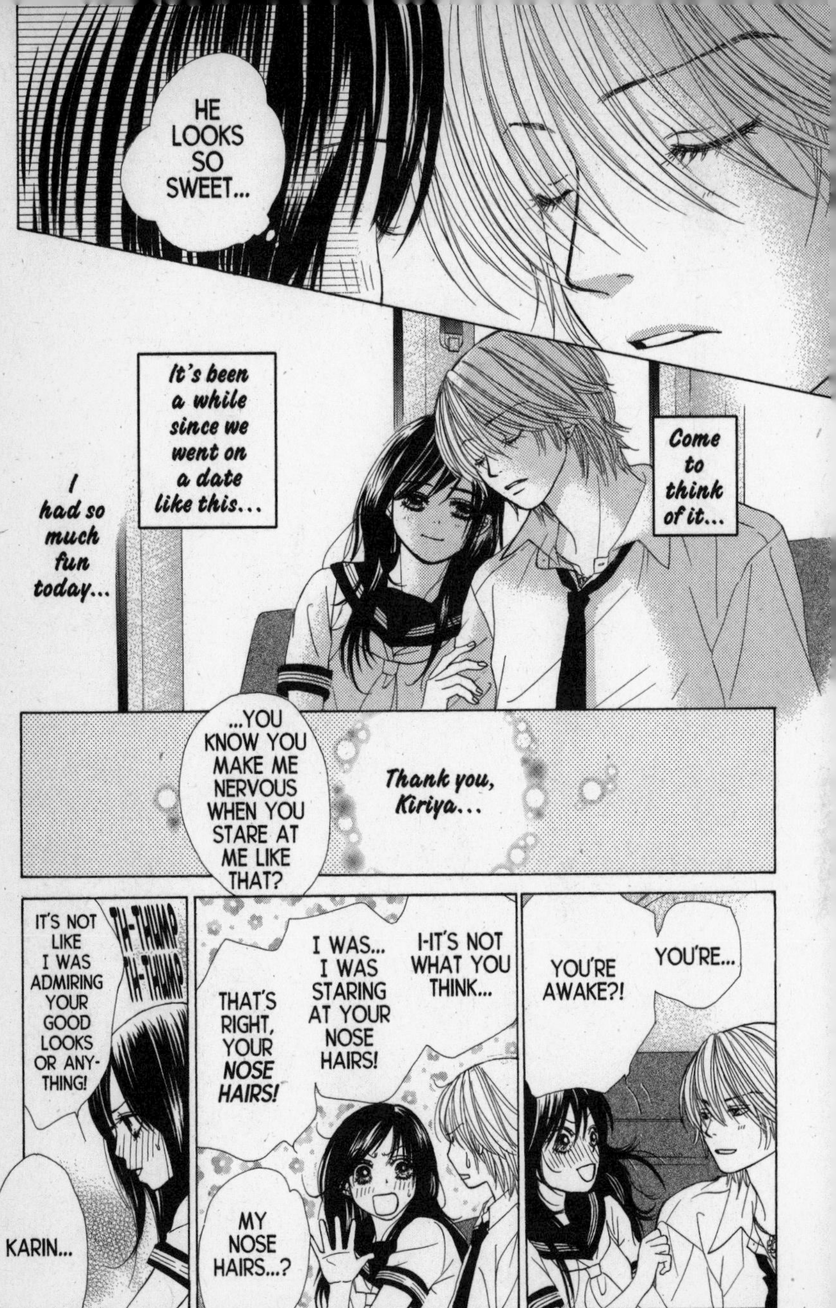
HE LOOKS SO SWEET...
Come to think of it...
It's been a while since we went on a date like this...
I had so much fun today...
Thank you, Kiriya...
...YOU KNOW YOU MAKE ME NERVOUS WHEN YOU STARE AT ME LIKE THAT?
YOU'RE...
YOU'RE AWAKE?!
I-IT'S NOT WHAT YOU THINK...
I WAS... I WAS STARING AT YOUR NOSE HAIRS!
THAT'S RIGHT, YOUR *NOSE HAIRS!*
MY NOSE HAIRS...?
TH-THUMP TH-THUMP
IT'S NOT LIKE I WAS ADMIRING YOUR GOOD LOOKS OR ANY-THING!
KARIN...

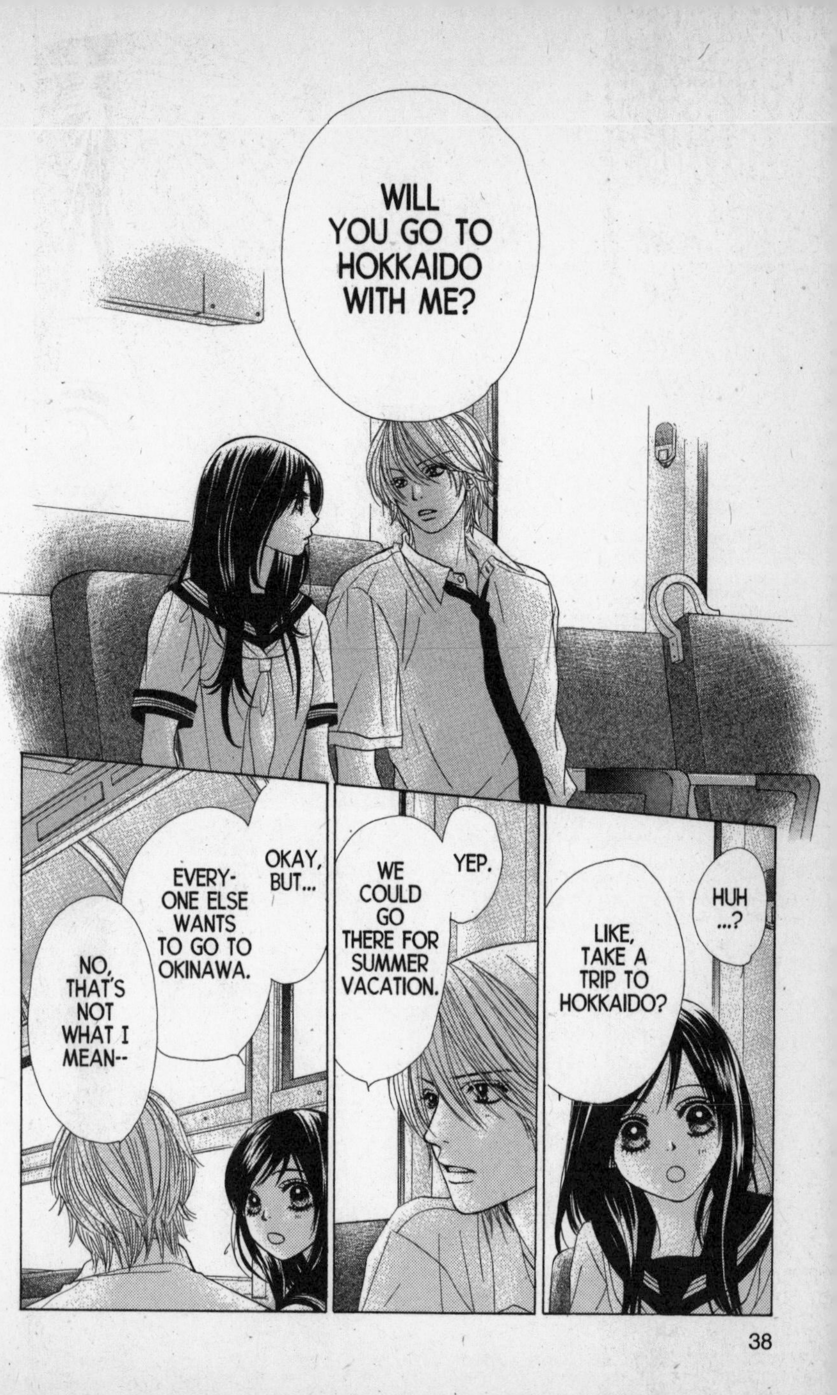
WILL YOU GO TO HOKKAIDO WITH ME?
HUH ...?
LIKE, TAKE A TRIP TO HOKKAIDO?
YEP.
WE COULD GO THERE FOR SUMMER VACATION.
OKAY, BUT...
EVERY-ONE ELSE WANTS TO GO TO OKINAWA.
NO, THAT'S NOT WHAT I MEAN--

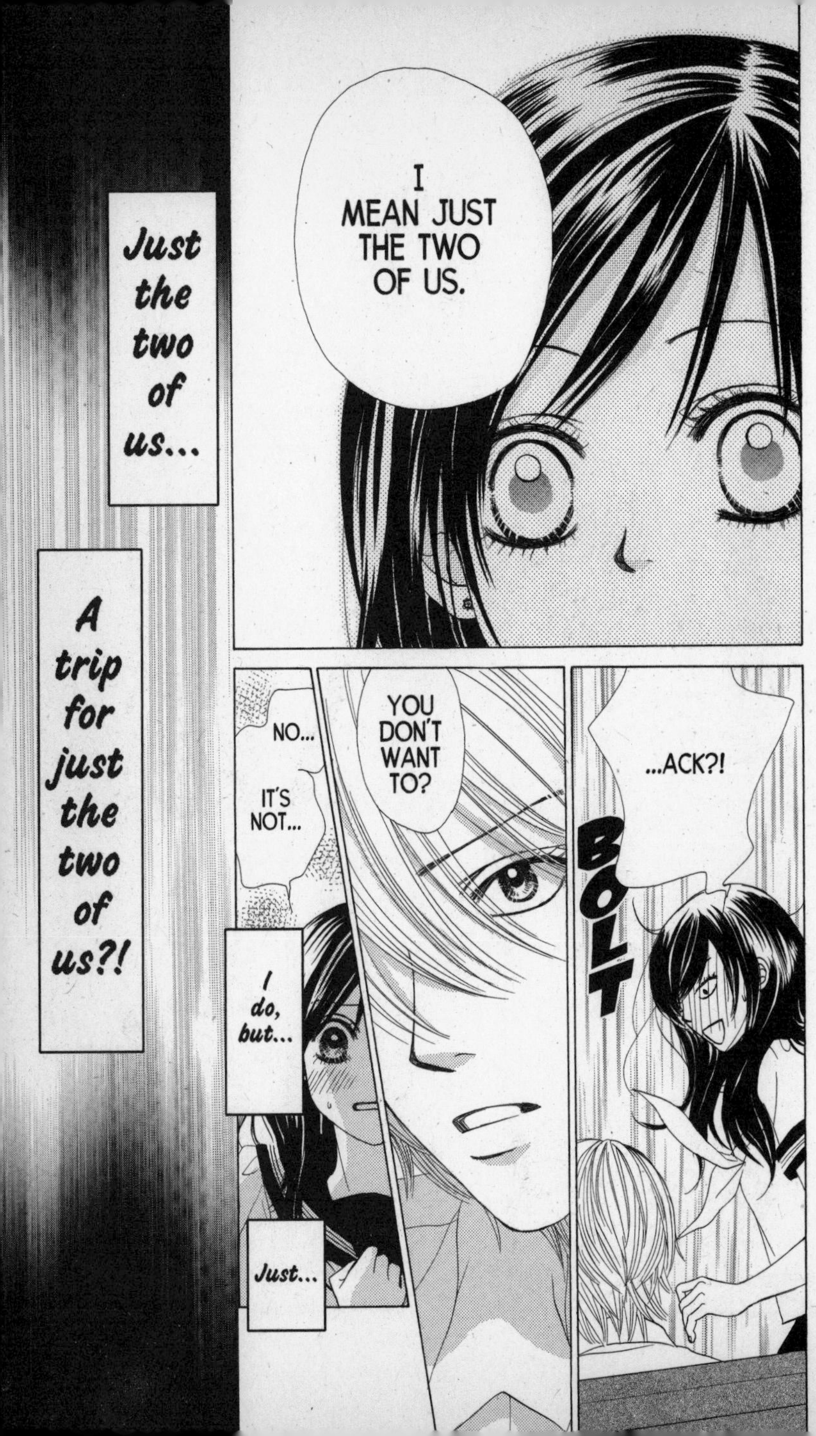
I MEAN JUST THE TWO OF US.
...ACK?!
BOLT
YOU DON'T WANT TO?
NO...
IT'S NOT...
I do, but...
Just...
Just the two of us...
A trip for just the two of us?!

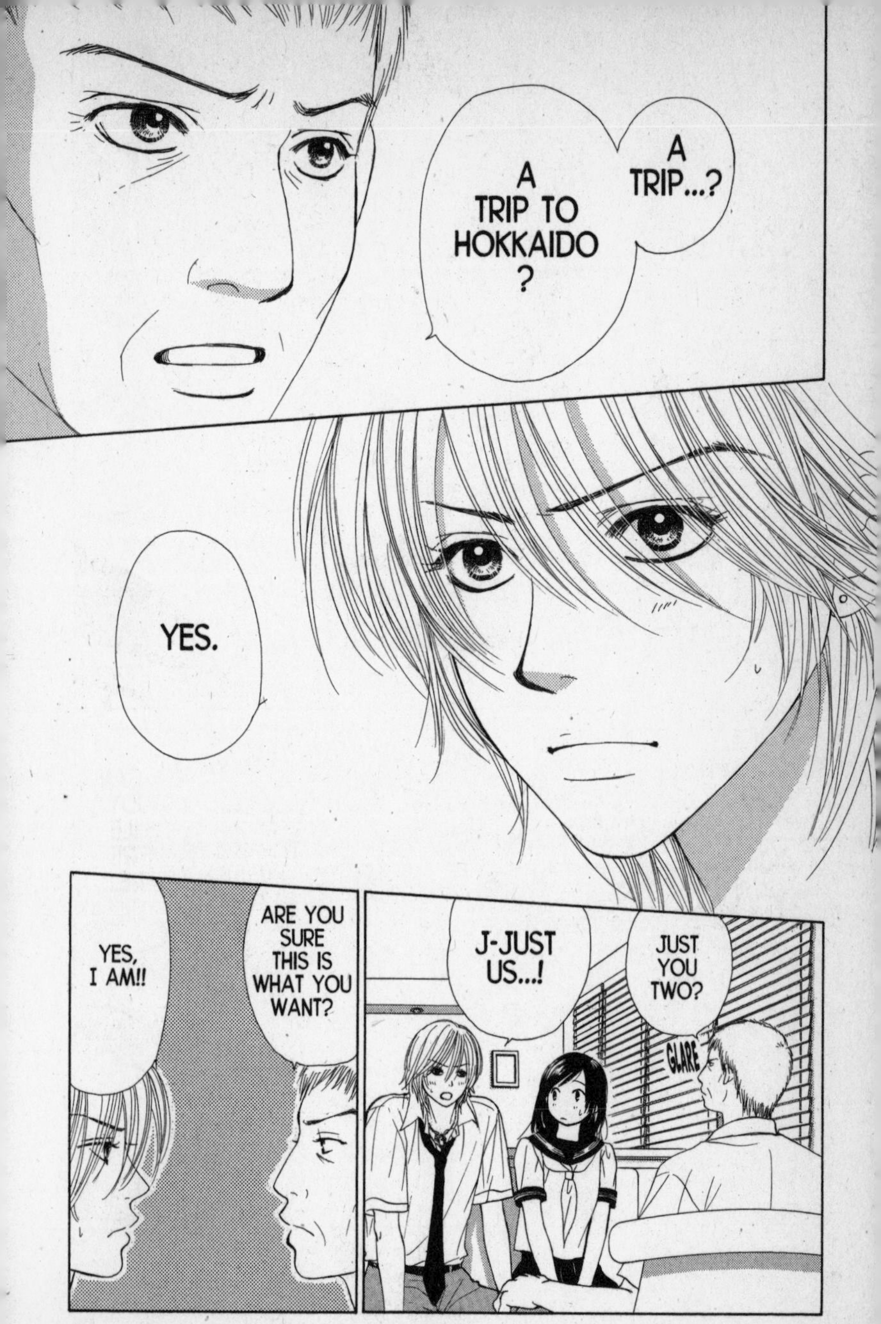
A TRIP...?
A TRIP TO HOKKAIDO ?
YES.
JUST YOU TWO?
J-JUST US...!
GLARE
ARE YOU SURE THIS IS WHAT YOU WANT?
YES, I AM!!

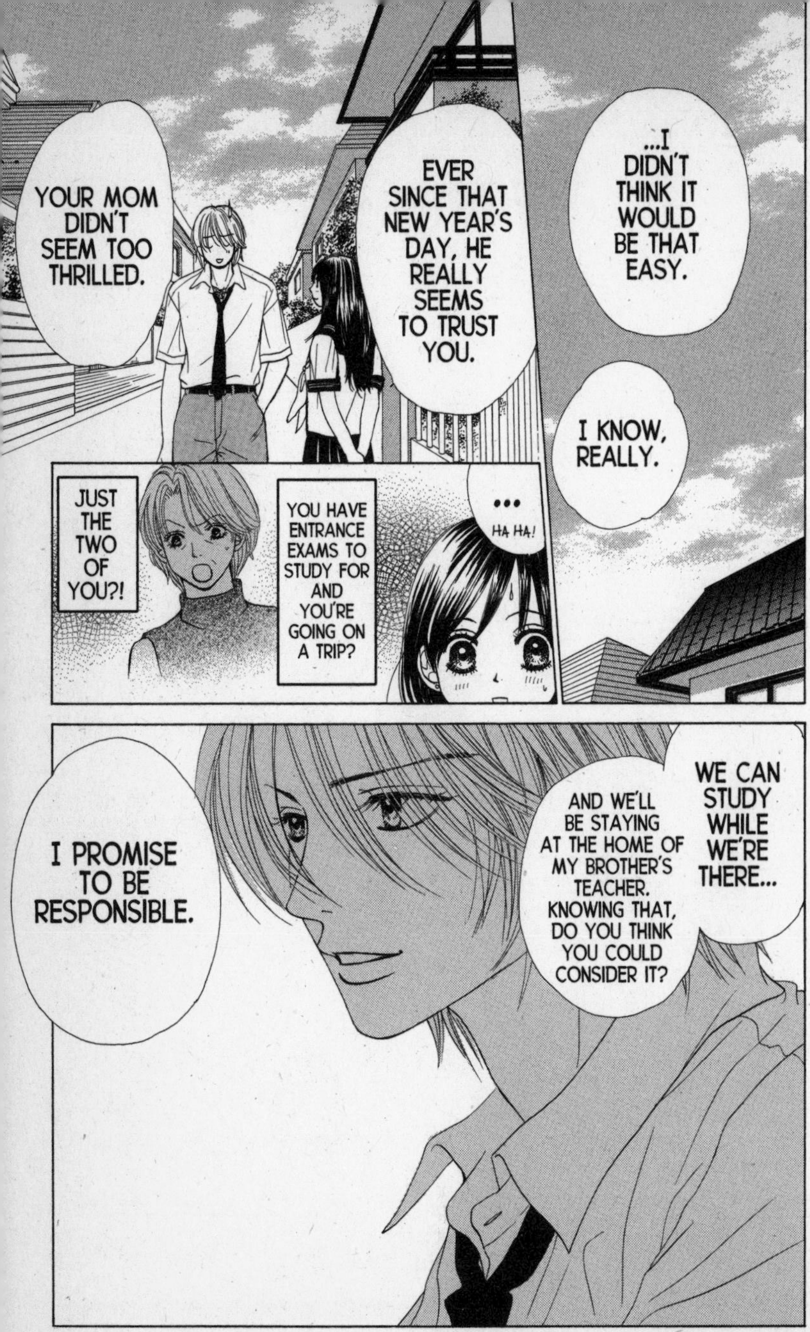
...I DIDN'T THINK IT WOULD BE THAT EASY.
EVER SINCE THAT NEW YEAR'S DAY, HE REALLY SEEMS TO TRUST YOU.
YOUR MOM DIDN'T SEEM TOO THRILLED.
I KNOW, REALLY.
...
HA HA!
YOU HAVE ENTRANCE EXAMS TO STUDY FOR AND YOU'RE GOING ON A TRIP?
JUST THE TWO OF YOU?!
WE CAN STUDY WHILE WE'RE THERE...
AND WE'LL BE STAYING AT THE HOME OF MY BROTHER'S TEACHER. KNOWING THAT, DO YOU THINK YOU COULD CONSIDER IT?
I PROMISE TO BE RESPONSIBLE.

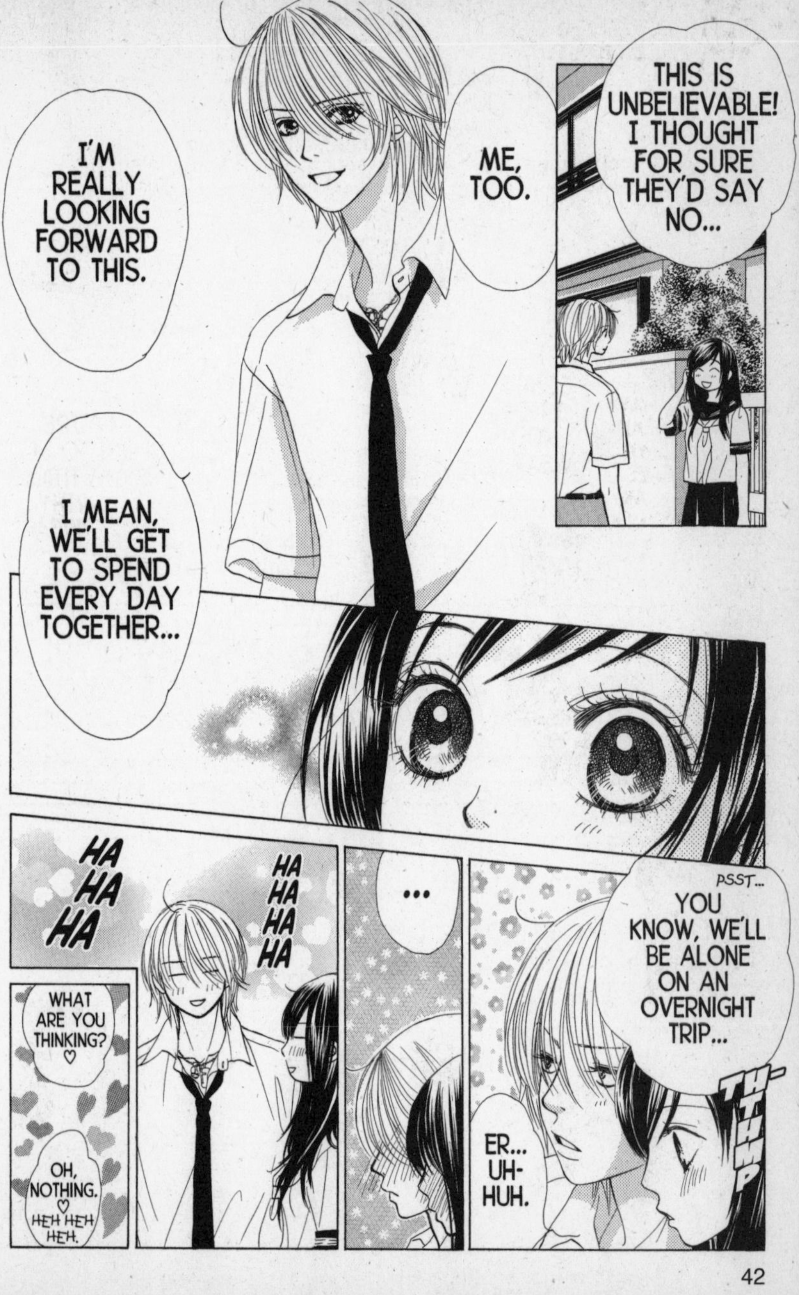
THIS IS UNBELIEVABLE! I THOUGHT FOR SURE THEY'D SAY NO...
ME, TOO.
I'M REALLY LOOKING FORWARD TO THIS.
I MEAN, WE'LL GET TO SPEND EVERY DAY TOGETHER...
PSST... YOU KNOW, WE'LL BE ALONE ON AN OVERNIGHT TRIP...
TH-THUMP
ER... UH-HUH.
...
HA HA HA HA
HA HA HA
WHAT ARE YOU THINKING? ♡
OH, NOTHING. ♡ HEH HEH HEH.

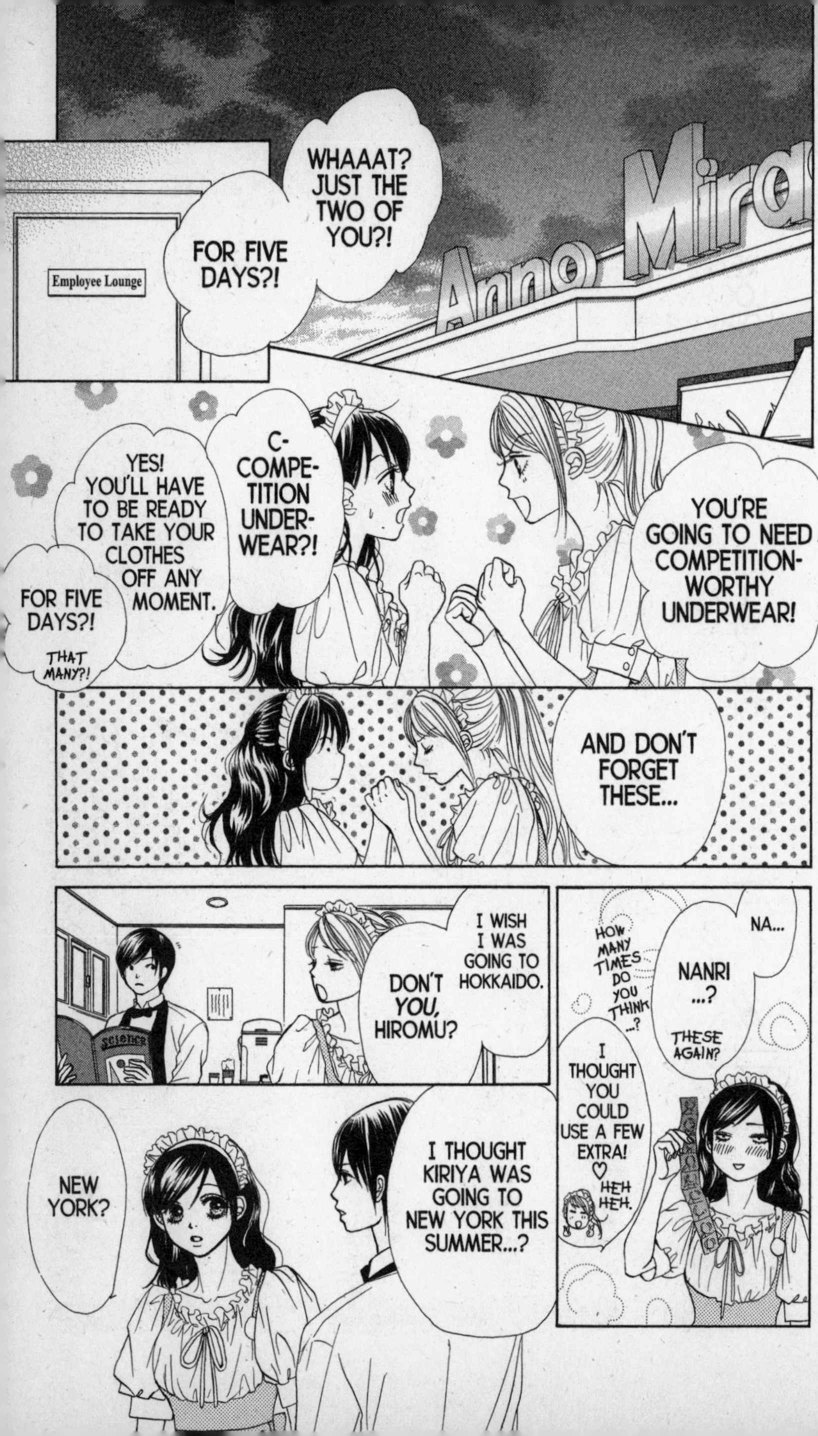

WHAAAT? JUST THE TWO OF YOU?!
FOR FIVE DAYS?!
Anno Mira
Employee Lounge
YOU'RE GOING TO NEED COMPETITION-WORTHY UNDERWEAR!
C-COMPETITION UNDERWEAR?!
YES! YOU'LL HAVE TO BE READY TO TAKE YOUR CLOTHES OFF ANY MOMENT.
FOR FIVE DAYS?!
THAT MANY?!
AND DON'T FORGET THESE...
NA...
NANRI ...?
HOW MANY TIMES DO YOU THINK ...?
THESE AGAIN?
I THOUGHT YOU COULD USE A FEW EXTRA! ♥
HEH HEH.
I WISH I WAS GOING TO HOKKAIDO.
DON'T *YOU*, HIROMU?
Science
I THOUGHT KIRIYA WAS GOING TO NEW YORK THIS SUMMER...?
NEW YORK?

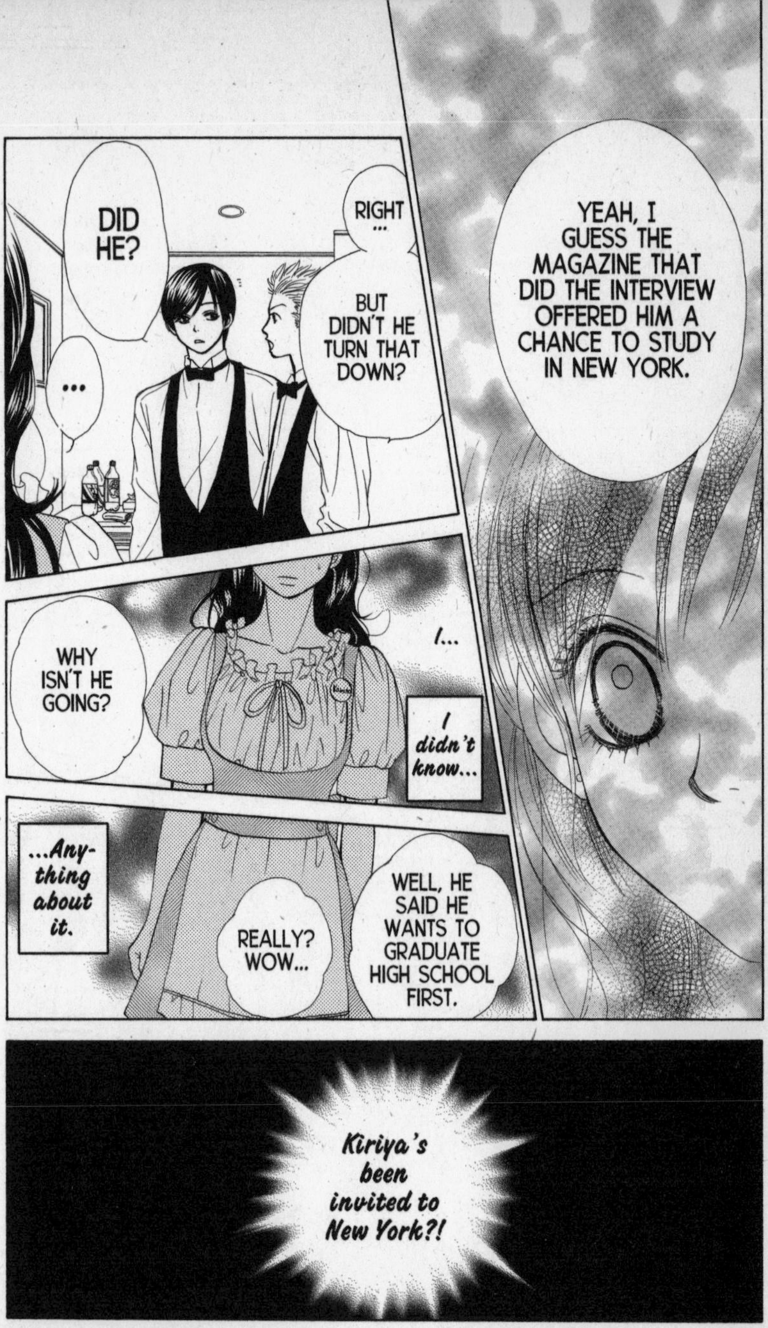
YEAH, I GUESS THE MAGAZINE THAT DID THE INTERVIEW OFFERED HIM A CHANCE TO STUDY IN NEW YORK.
RIGHT...
BUT DIDN'T HE TURN THAT DOWN?
DID HE?
...
I...
I didn't know...
WHY ISN'T HE GOING?
WELL, HE SAID HE WANTS TO GRADUATE HIGH SCHOOL FIRST.
REALLY? WOW...
...Anything about it.
Kiriya's been invited to New York?!

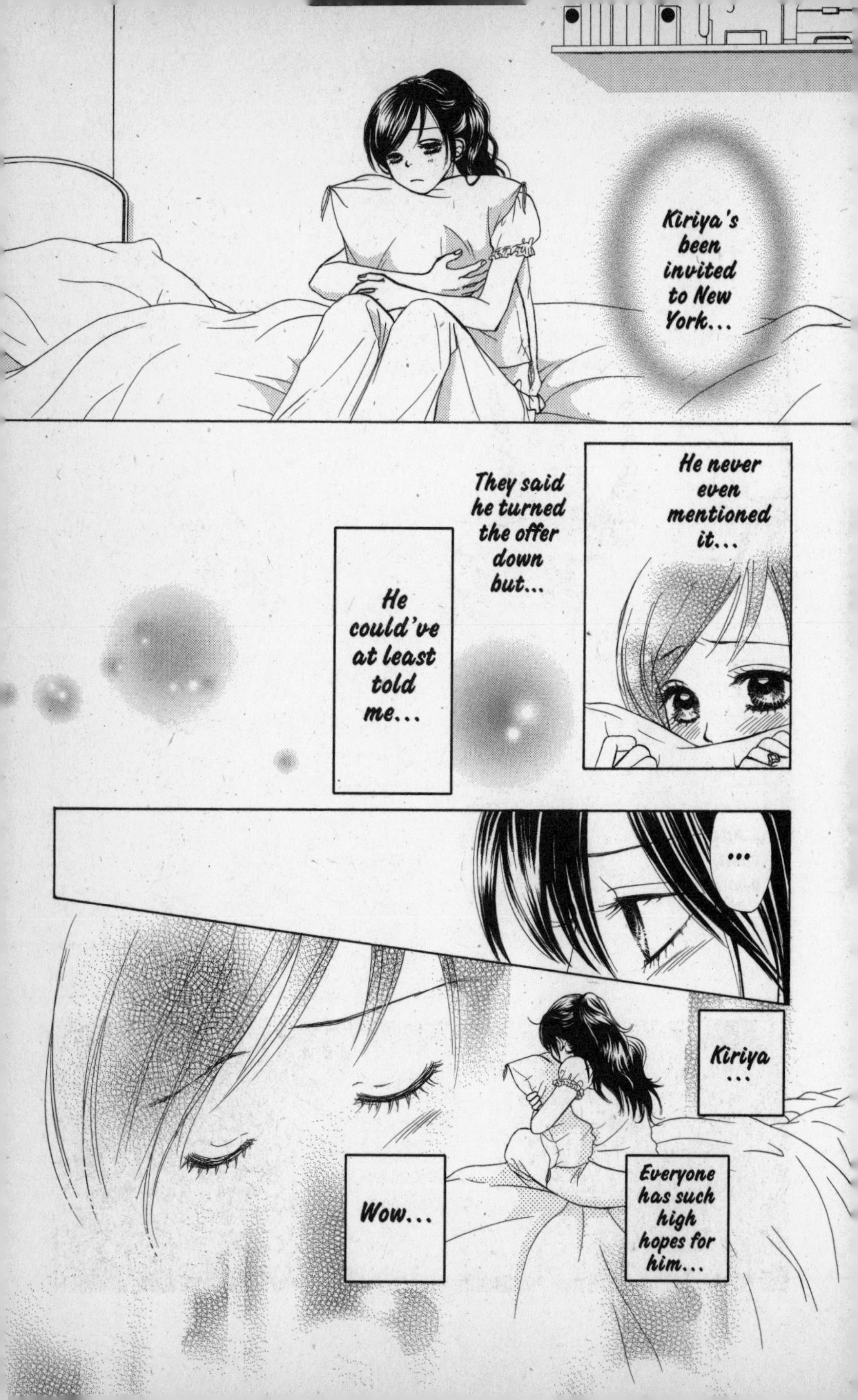
Kiriya's been invited to New York...
He never even mentioned it...
They said he turned the offer down but...
He could've at least told me...
...
Kiriya...
Everyone has such high hopes for him...
Wow...

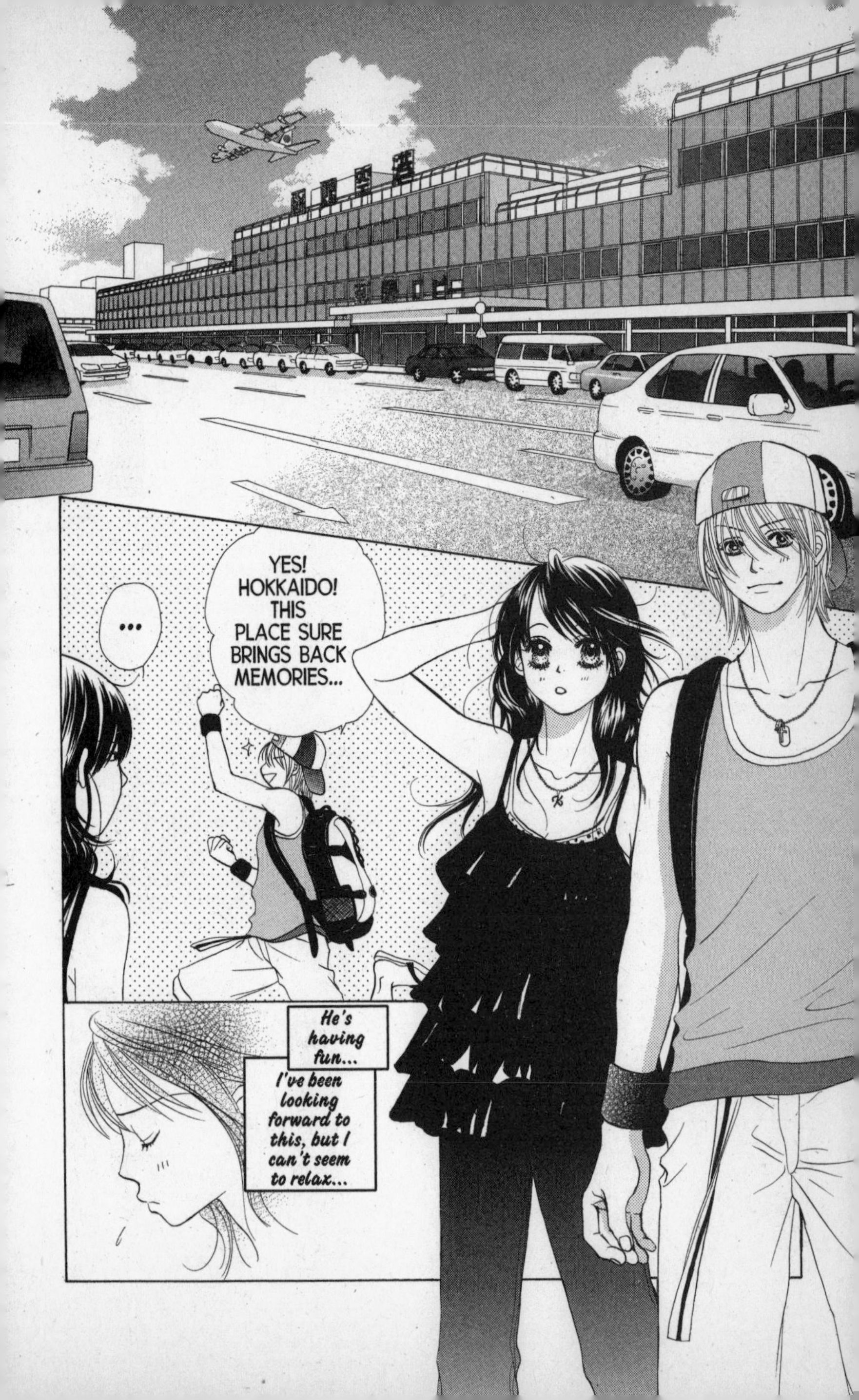
YES! HOKKAIDO! THIS PLACE SURE BRINGS BACK MEMORIES...
...
He's having fun...
I've been looking forward to this, but I can't seem to relax...

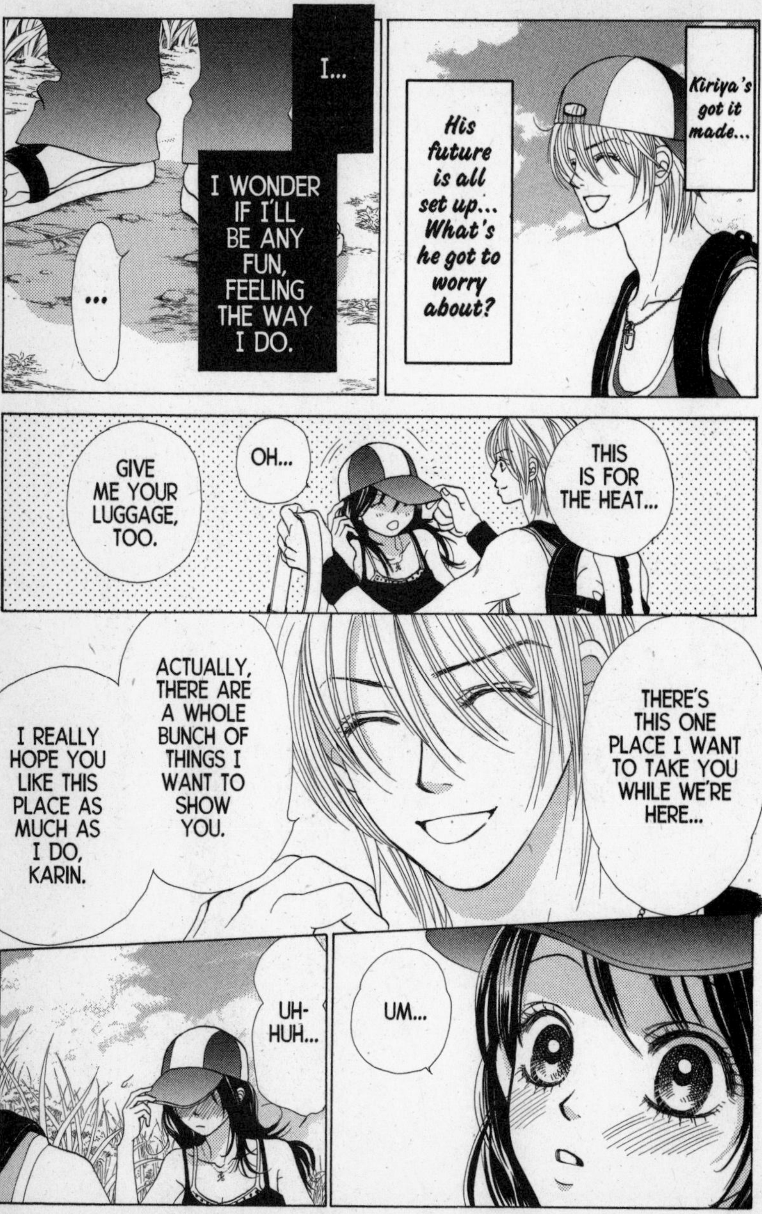
Kiriya's got it made...
His future is all set up... What's he got to worry about?
I...
I WONDER IF I'LL BE ANY FUN, FEELING THE WAY I DO.
...
THIS IS FOR THE HEAT...
OH...
GIVE ME YOUR LUGGAGE, TOO.
THERE'S THIS ONE PLACE I WANT TO TAKE YOU WHILE WE'RE HERE...
ACTUALLY, THERE ARE A WHOLE BUNCH OF THINGS I WANT TO SHOW YOU.
I REALLY HOPE YOU LIKE THIS PLACE AS MUCH AS I DO, KARIN.
UM...
UH-HUH...

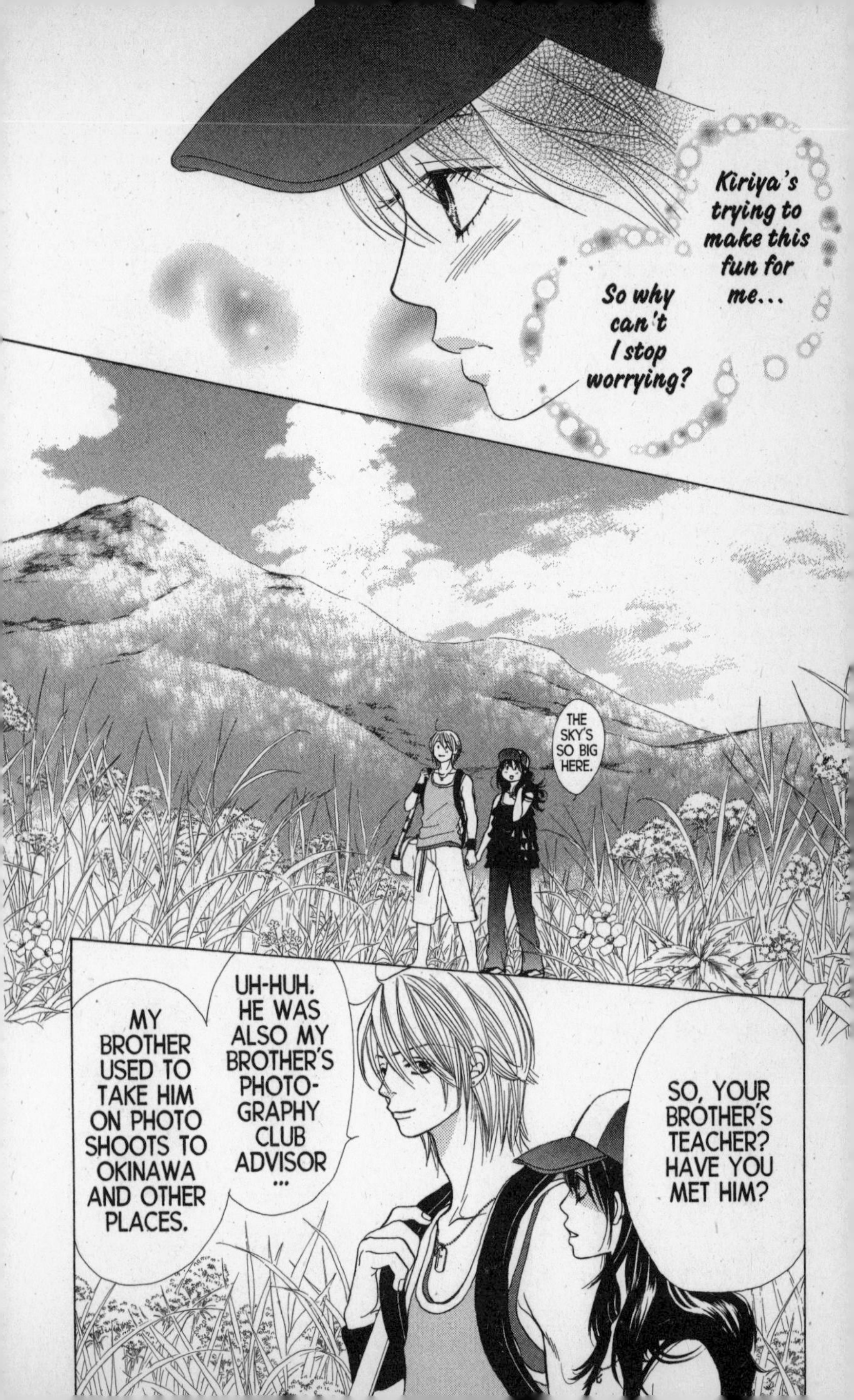
Kiriya's trying to make this fun for me...
So why can't I stop worrying?
THE SKY'S SO BIG HERE.
SO, YOUR BROTHER'S TEACHER? HAVE YOU MET HIM?
UH-HUH. HE WAS ALSO MY BROTHER'S PHOTOGRAPHY CLUB ADVISOR...
MY BROTHER USED TO TAKE HIM ON PHOTO SHOOTS TO OKINAWA AND OTHER PLACES.

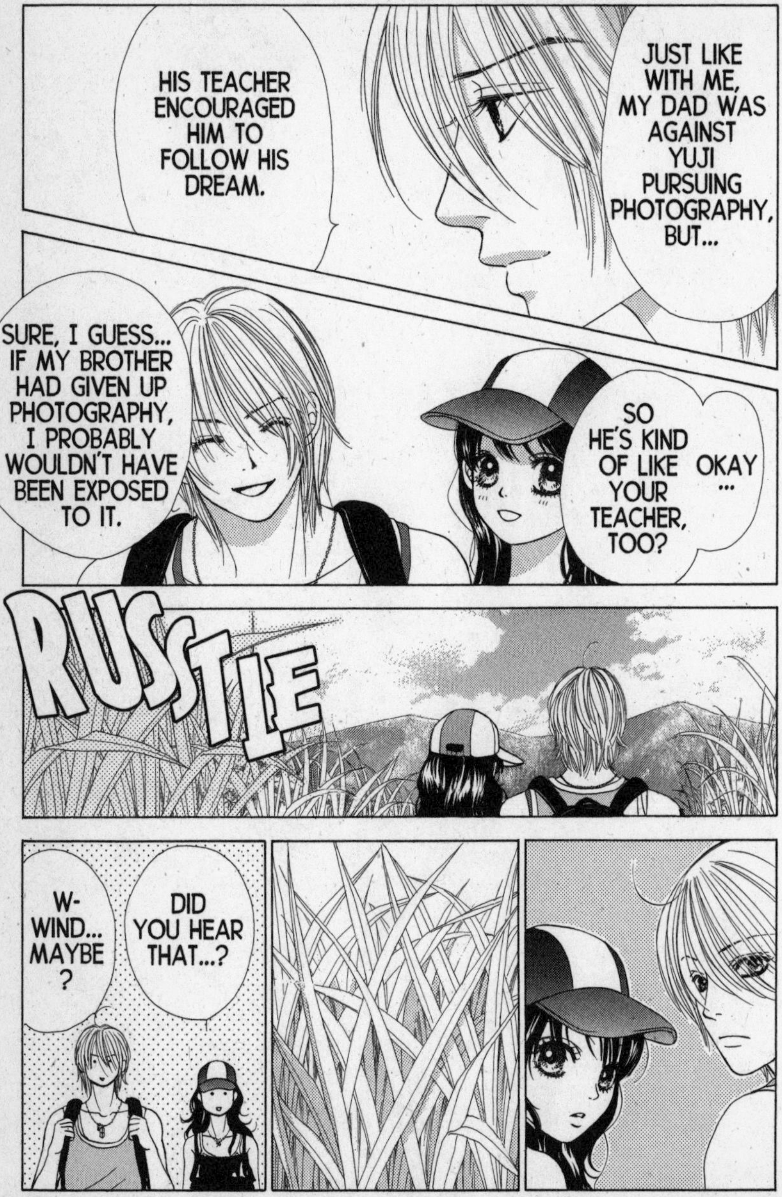
JUST LIKE WITH ME, MY DAD WAS AGAINST YUJI PURSUING PHOTOGRAPHY, BUT...
HIS TEACHER ENCOURAGED HIM TO FOLLOW HIS DREAM.
OKAY ...
SO HE'S KIND OF LIKE YOUR TEACHER, TOO?
SURE, I GUESS... IF MY BROTHER HAD GIVEN UP PHOTOGRAPHY, I PROBABLY WOULDN'T HAVE BEEN EXPOSED TO IT.
RUSTLE
DID YOU HEAR THAT...?
W-WIND... MAYBE ?

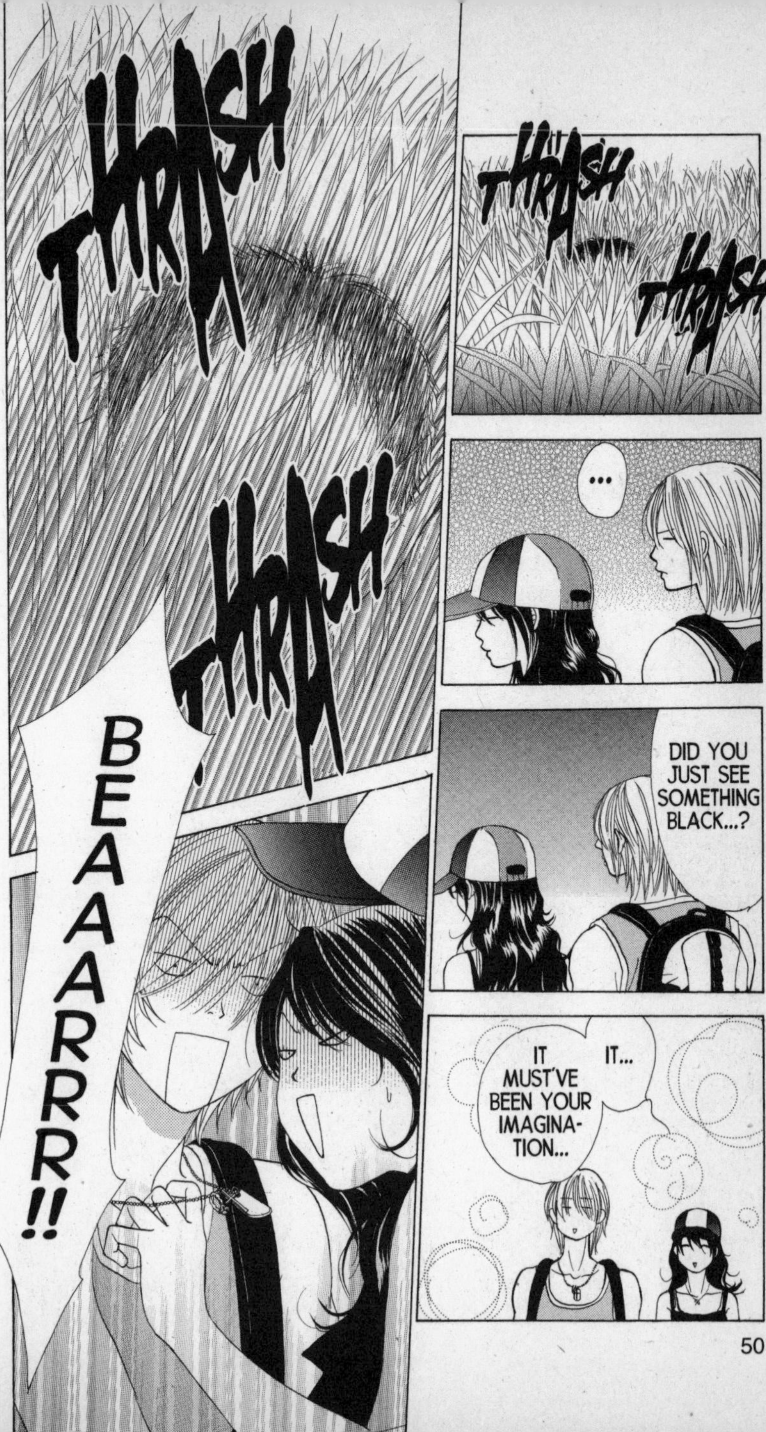
THRASH
THRASH
...
DID YOU JUST SEE SOMETHING BLACK...?
IT... IT MUST'VE BEEN YOUR IMAGINATION...
THRASH
THRASH
BEAAAARRRR!!

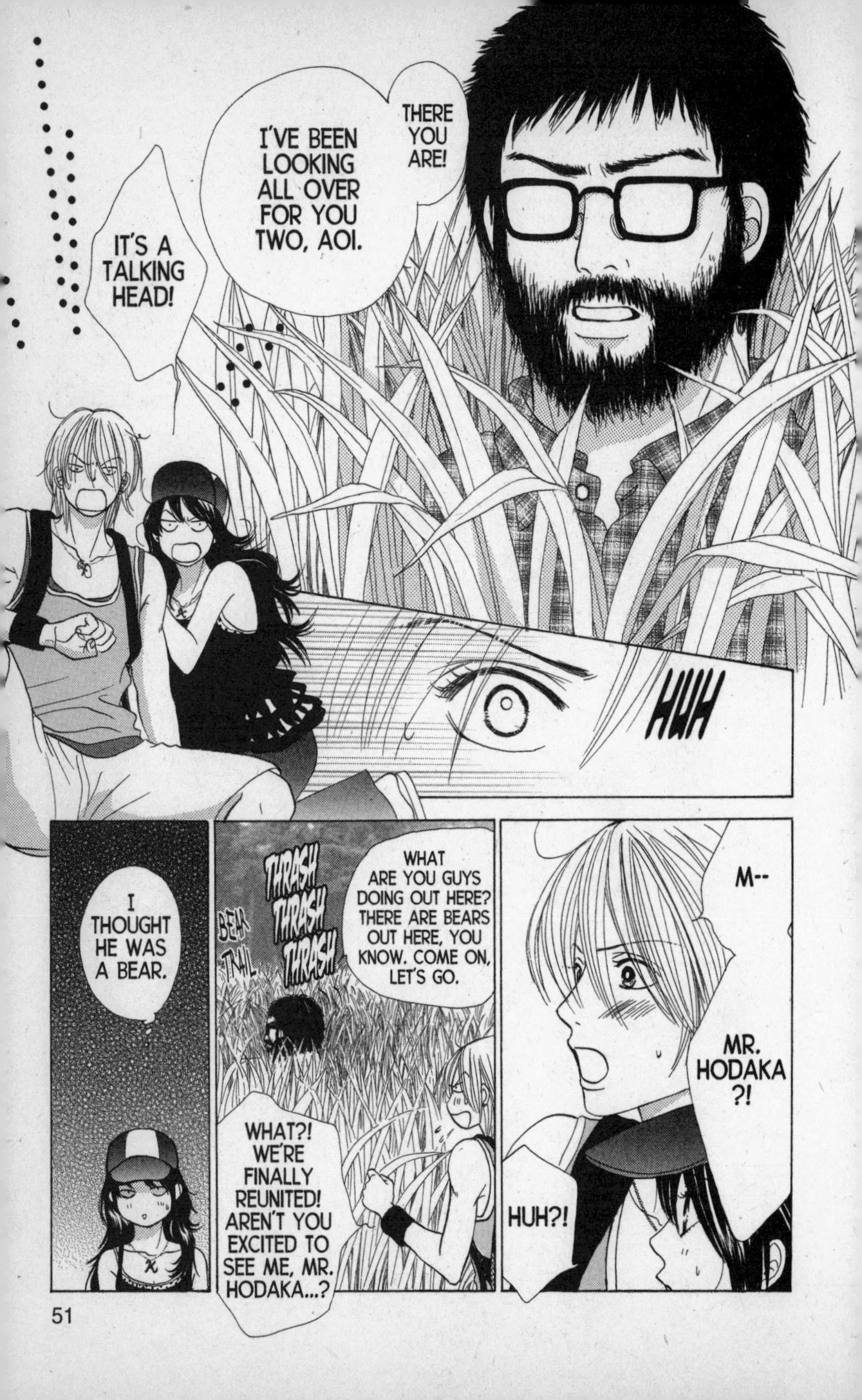
THERE YOU ARE!
I'VE BEEN LOOKING ALL OVER FOR YOU TWO, AOI.
IT'S A TALKING HEAD!
HUH
M--
MR. HODAKA?!
HUH?!
WHAT ARE YOU GUYS DOING OUT HERE? THERE ARE BEARS OUT HERE, YOU KNOW. COME ON, LET'S GO.
THRASH THRASH THRASH
BEAR TRAIL
WHAT?! WE'RE FINALLY REUNITED! AREN'T YOU EXCITED TO SEE ME, MR. HODAKA...?
I THOUGHT HE WAS A BEAR.

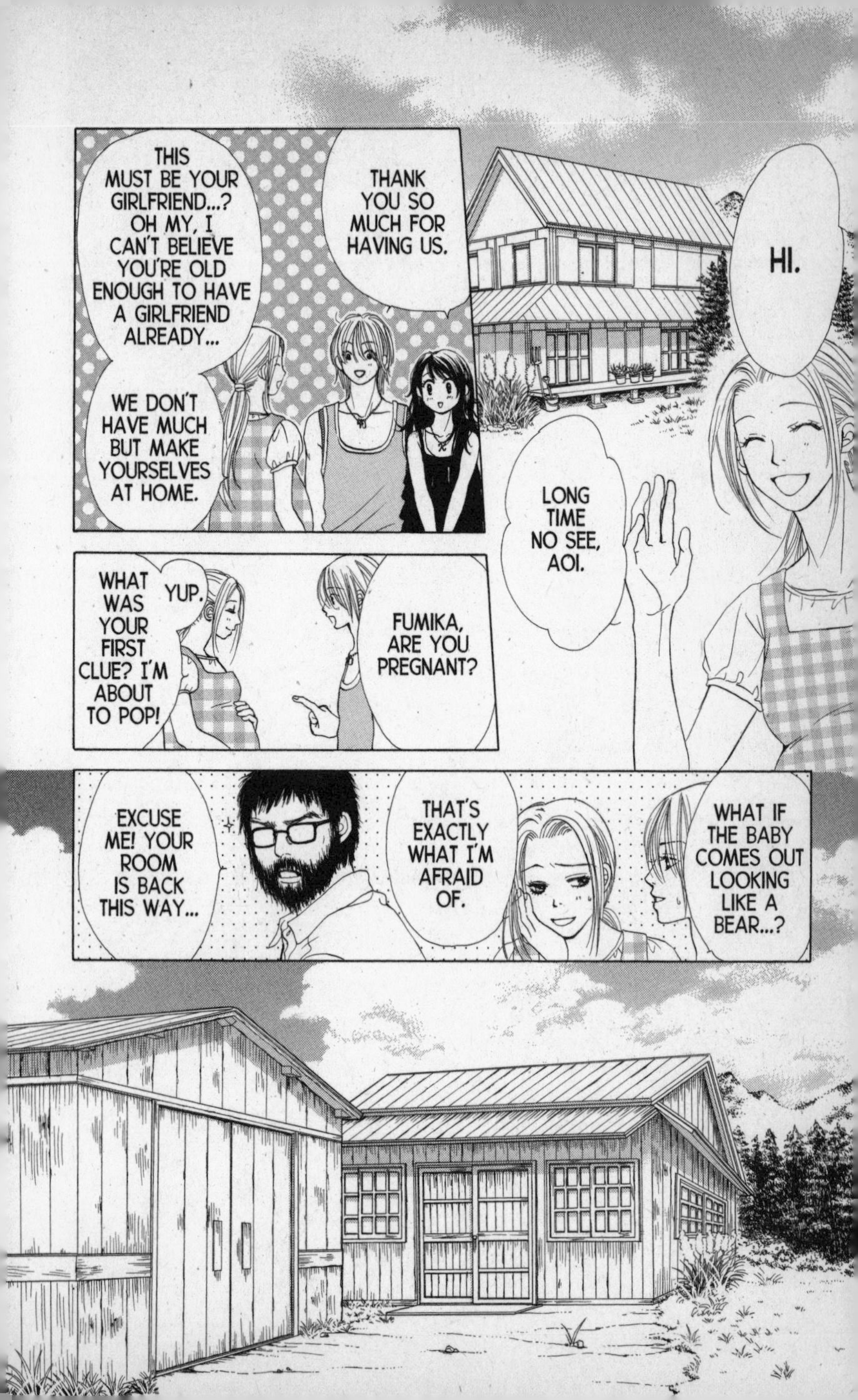
HI.
LONG TIME NO SEE, AOI.
THANK YOU SO MUCH FOR HAVING US.
THIS MUST BE YOUR GIRLFRIEND...? OH MY, I CAN'T BELIEVE YOU'RE OLD ENOUGH TO HAVE A GIRLFRIEND ALREADY...
WE DON'T HAVE MUCH BUT MAKE YOURSELVES AT HOME.
FUMIKA, ARE YOU PREGNANT?
YUP.
WHAT WAS YOUR FIRST CLUE? I'M ABOUT TO POP!
WHAT IF THE BABY COMES OUT LOOKING LIKE A BEAR...?
THAT'S EXACTLY WHAT I'M AFRAID OF.
EXCUSE ME! YOUR ROOM IS BACK THIS WAY...

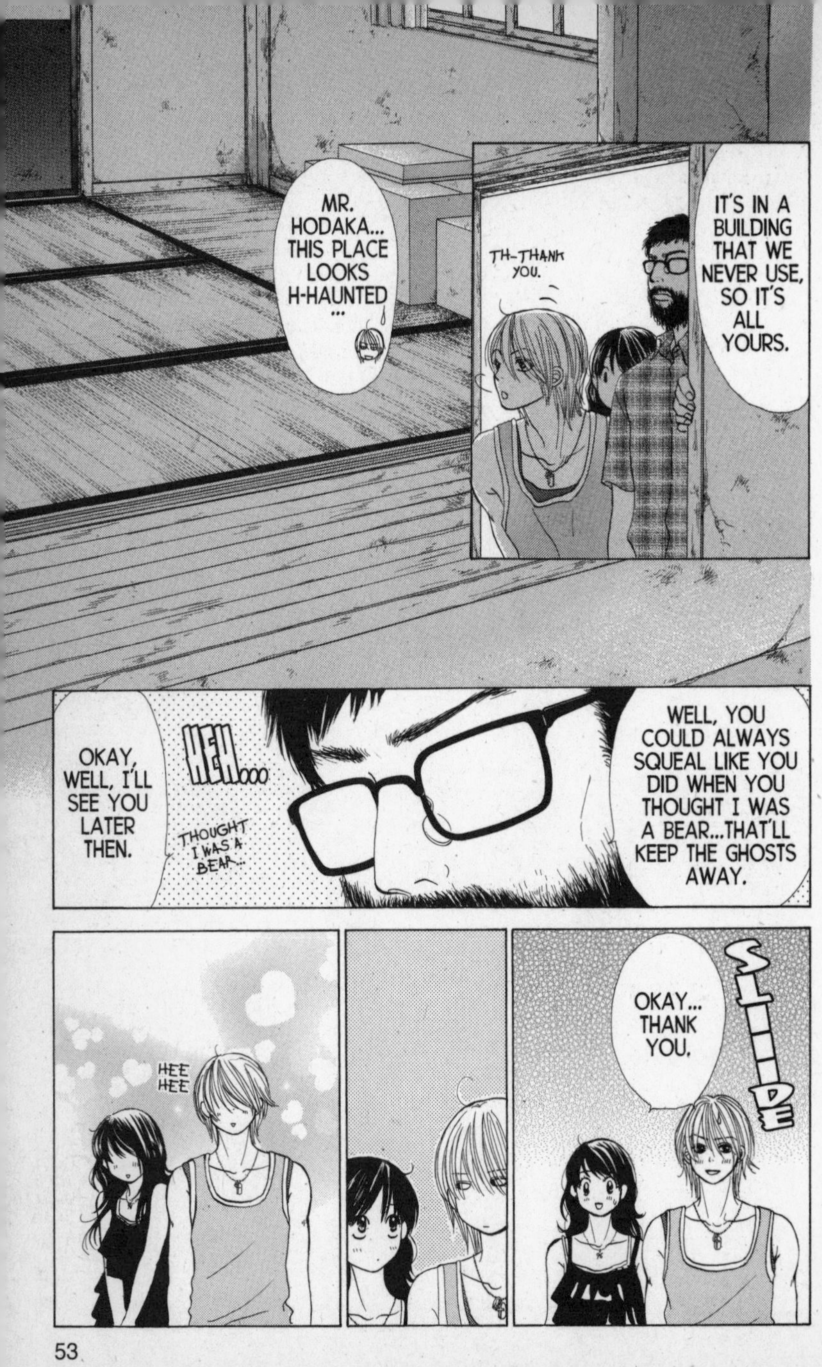
IT'S IN A BUILDING THAT WE NEVER USE, SO IT'S ALL YOURS.
TH-THANK YOU.
MR. HODAKA... THIS PLACE LOOKS H-HAUNTED...
WELL, YOU COULD ALWAYS SQUEAL LIKE YOU DID WHEN YOU THOUGHT I WAS A BEAR...THAT'LL KEEP THE GHOSTS AWAY.
THOUGHT I WAS A BEAR...
HEH...
OKAY, WELL, I'LL SEE YOU LATER THEN.
SLIIIDE
OKAY... THANK YOU.
HEE HEE

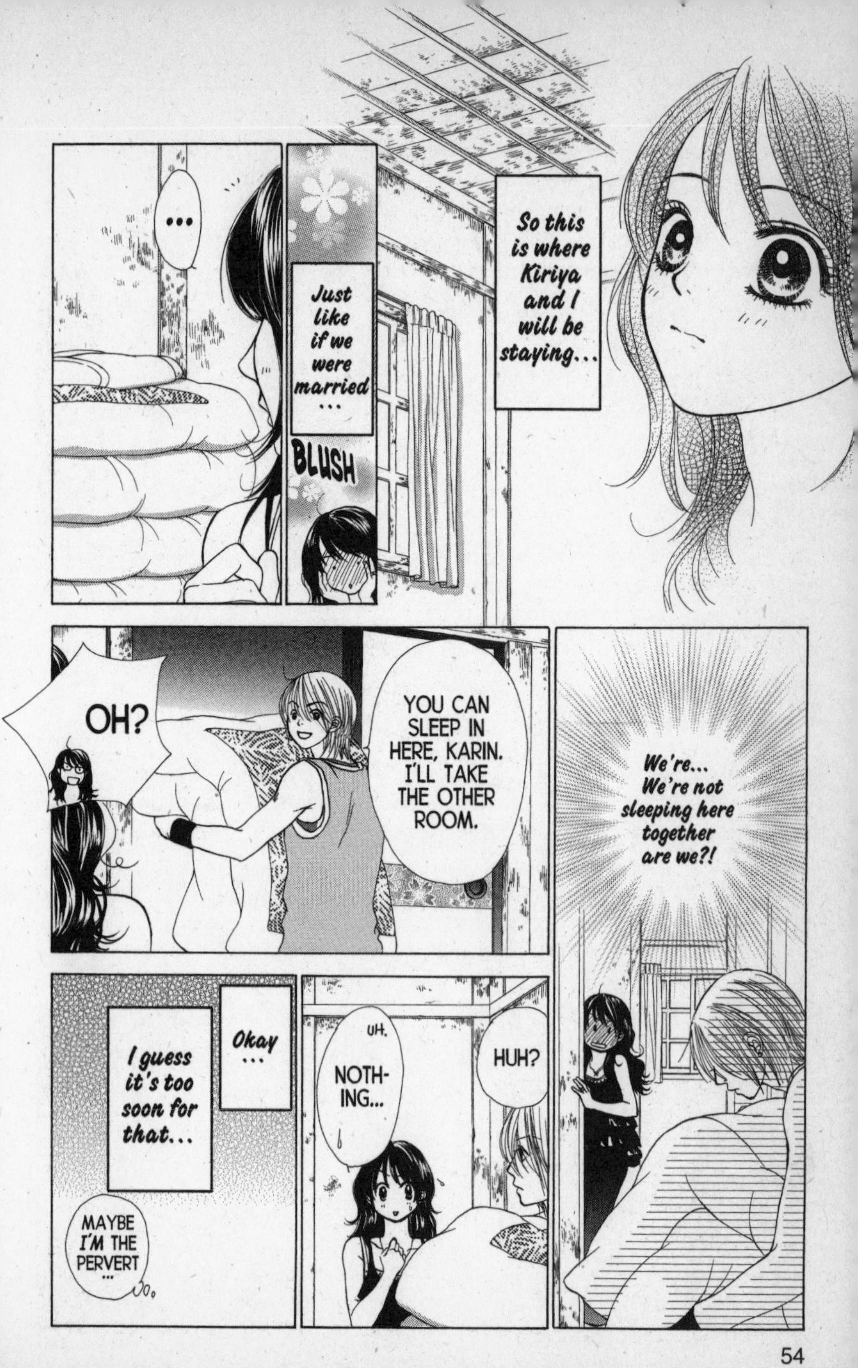
So this is where Kiriya and I will be staying...
Just like if we were married...
BLUSH
...
We're... We're not sleeping here together are we?!
YOU CAN SLEEP IN HERE, KARIN. I'LL TAKE THE OTHER ROOM.
OH?
HUH?
UH, NOTHING...
Okay...
I guess it's too soon for that...
MAYBE I'M THE PERVERT...

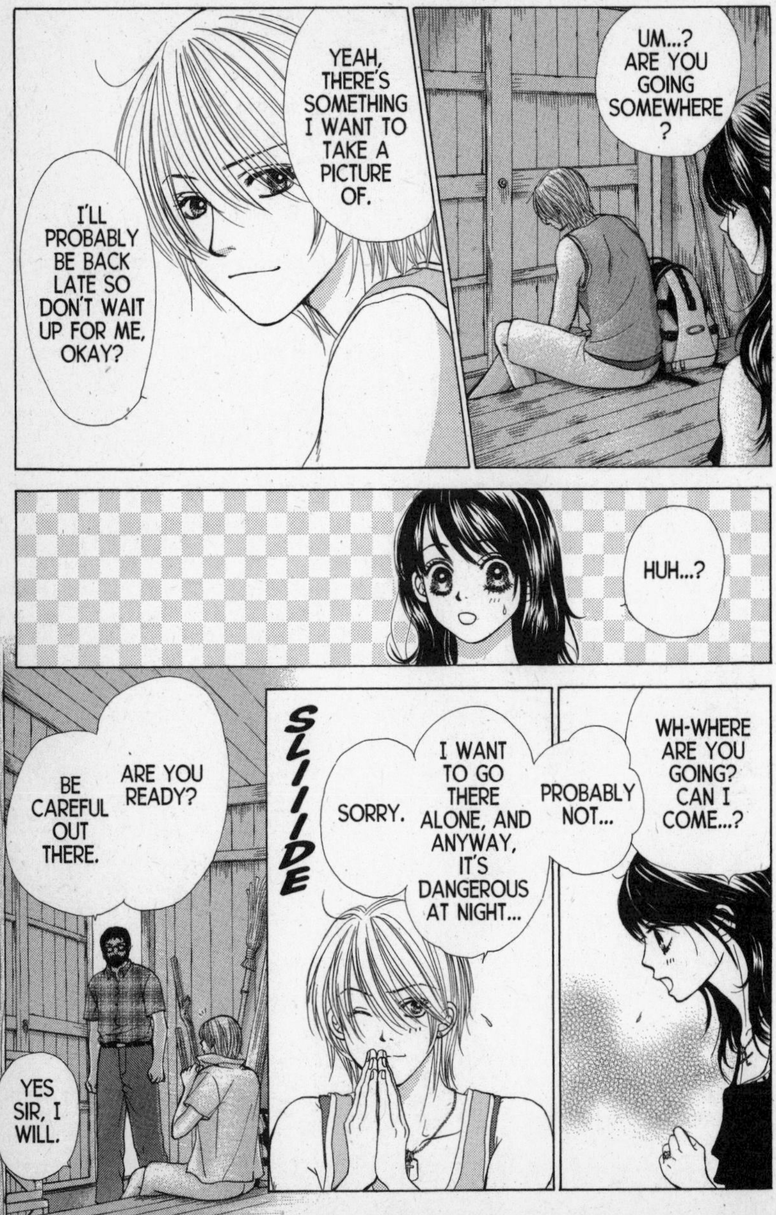
UM...? ARE YOU GOING SOMEWHERE?
YEAH, THERE'S SOMETHING I WANT TO TAKE A PICTURE OF.
I'LL PROBABLY BE BACK LATE SO DON'T WAIT UP FOR ME, OKAY?
HUH...?
WH-WHERE ARE YOU GOING? CAN I COME...?
PROBABLY NOT...
I WANT TO GO THERE ALONE, AND ANYWAY, IT'S DANGEROUS AT NIGHT...
SORRY.
SLIIIDE
ARE YOU READY?
BE CAREFUL OUT THERE.
YES SIR, I WILL.

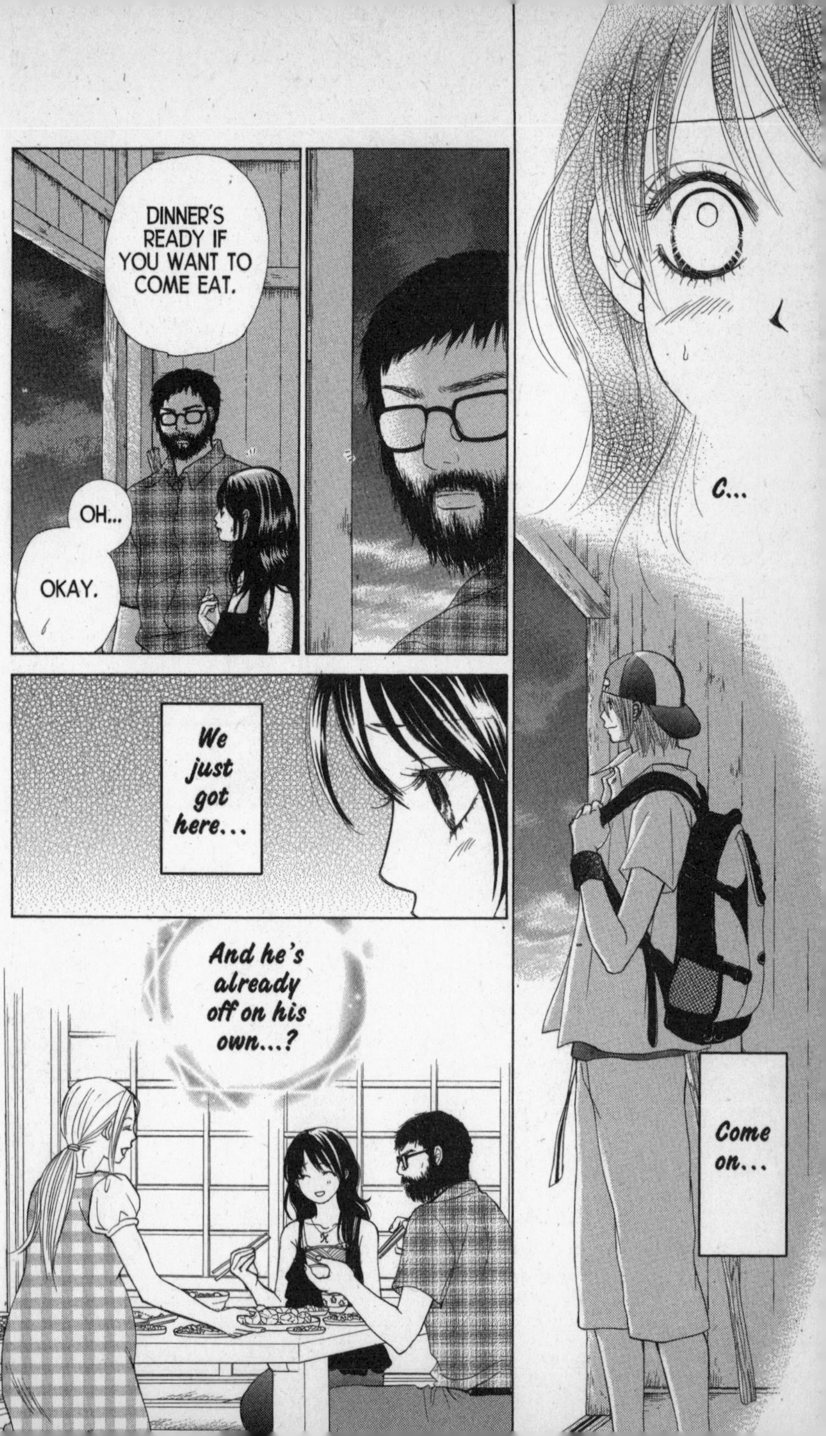
C...
Come on...
DINNER'S READY IF YOU WANT TO COME EAT.
OH...
OKAY.
We just got here...
And he's already off on his own...?

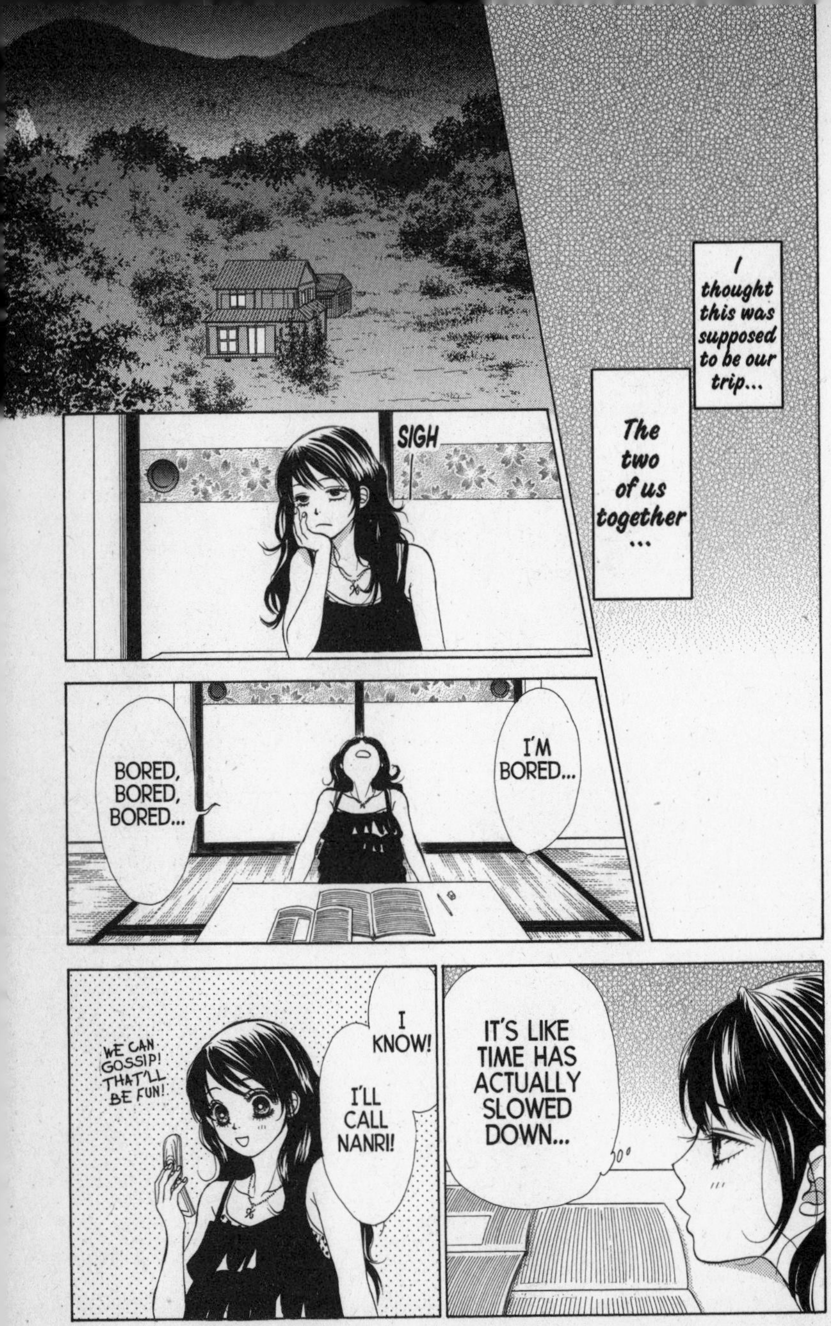
I thought this was supposed to be our trip...
The two of us together...
SIGH
I'M BORED...
BORED, BORED, BORED...
IT'S LIKE TIME HAS ACTUALLY SLOWED DOWN...
I KNOW!
I'LL CALL NANRI!
WE CAN GOSSIP! THAT'LL BE FUN!

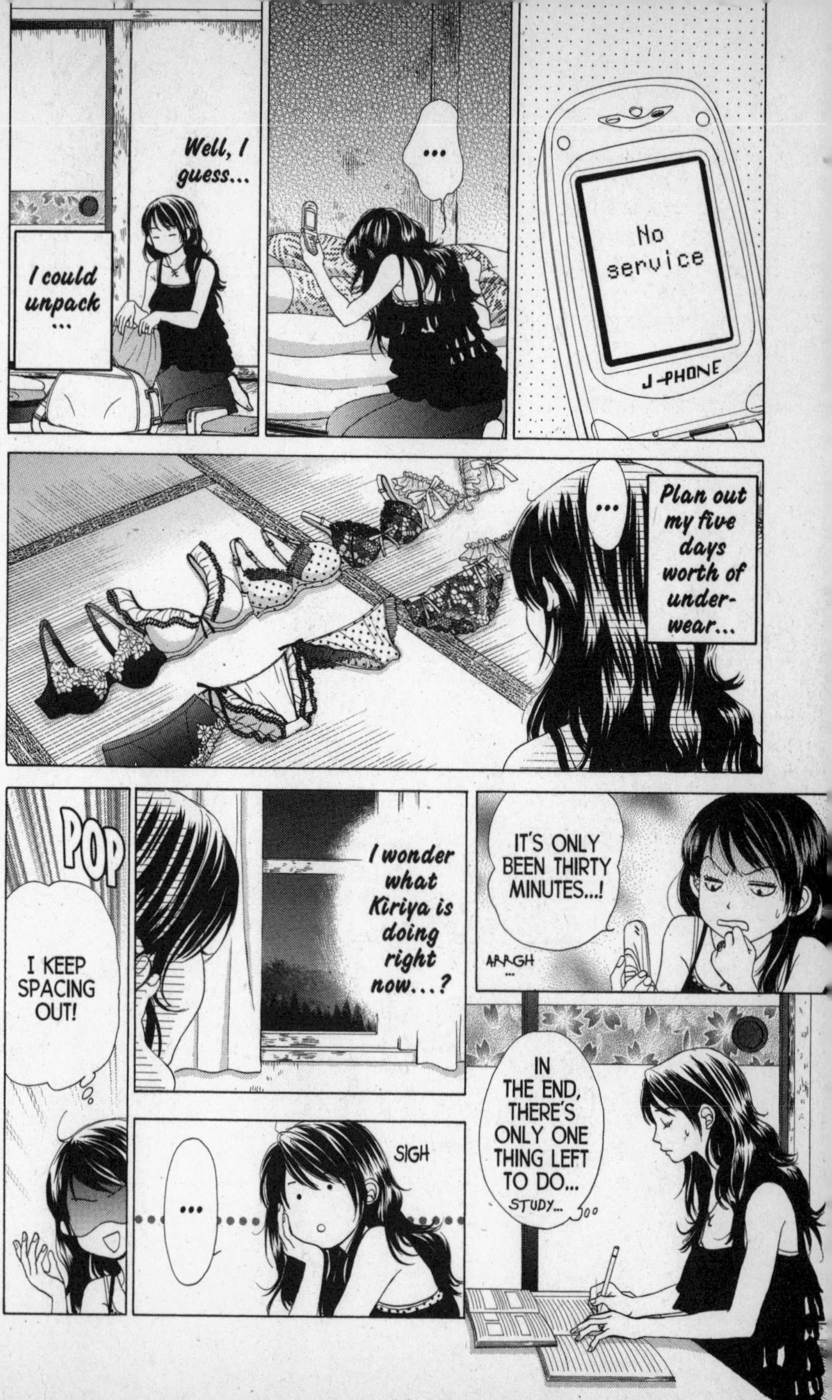
No service
J-PHONE
...
Well, I guess...
I could unpack...
Plan out my five days worth of under-wear...
...
IT'S ONLY BEEN THIRTY MINUTES...!
ARRGH...
IN THE END, THERE'S ONLY ONE THING LEFT TO DO...
STUDY...
I wonder what Kiriya is doing right now...?
SIGH
...
POP
I KEEP SPACING OUT!

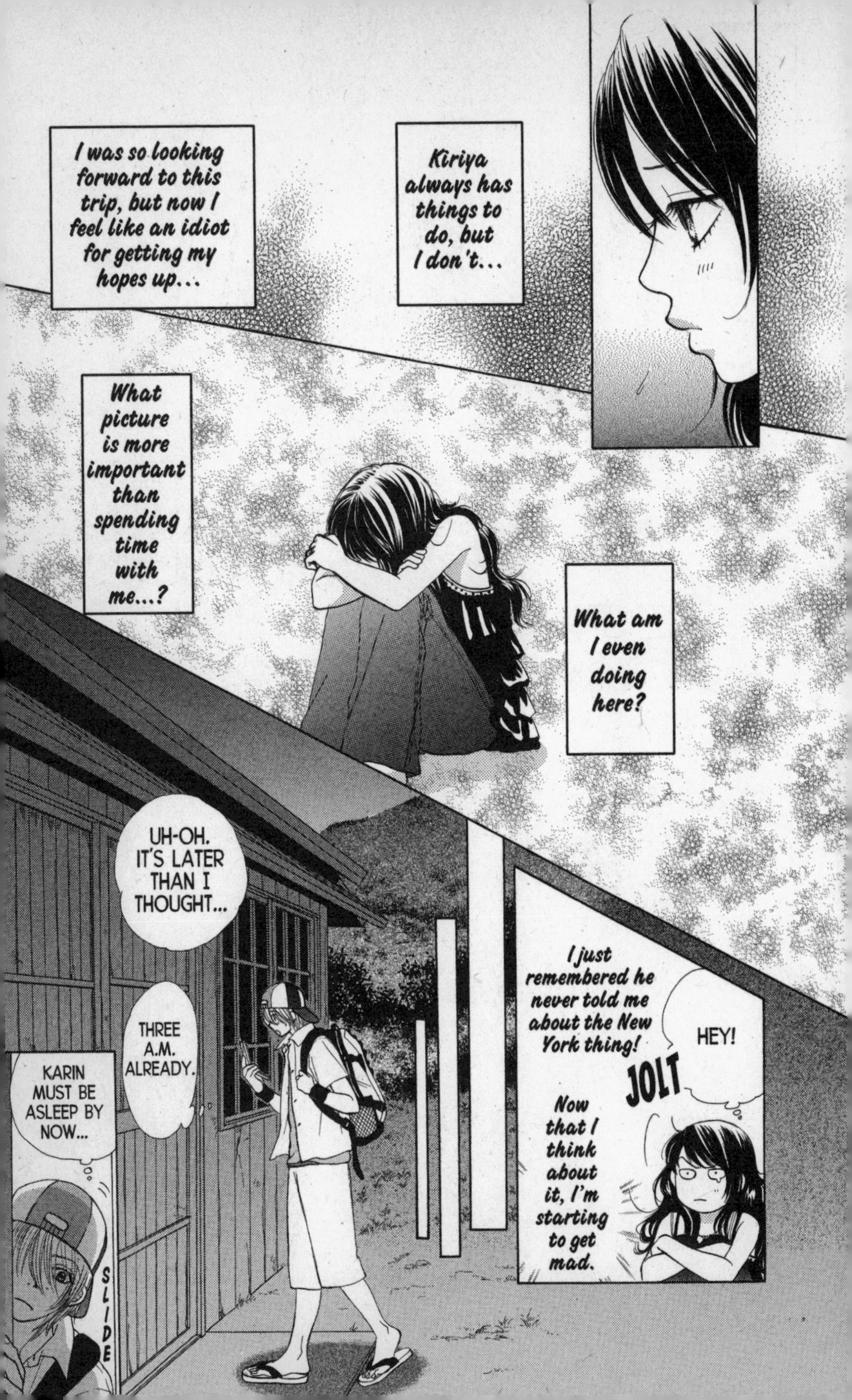
Kiriya always has things to do, but I don't...
I was so looking forward to this trip, but now I feel like an idiot for getting my hopes up...
What picture is more important than spending time with me...?
What am I even doing here?
I just remembered he never told me about the New York thing!
HEY!
JOLT
Now that I think about it, I'm starting to get mad.
UH-OH. IT'S LATER THAN I THOUGHT...
THREE A.M. ALREADY.
KARIN MUST BE ASLEEP BY NOW...
SLIDE

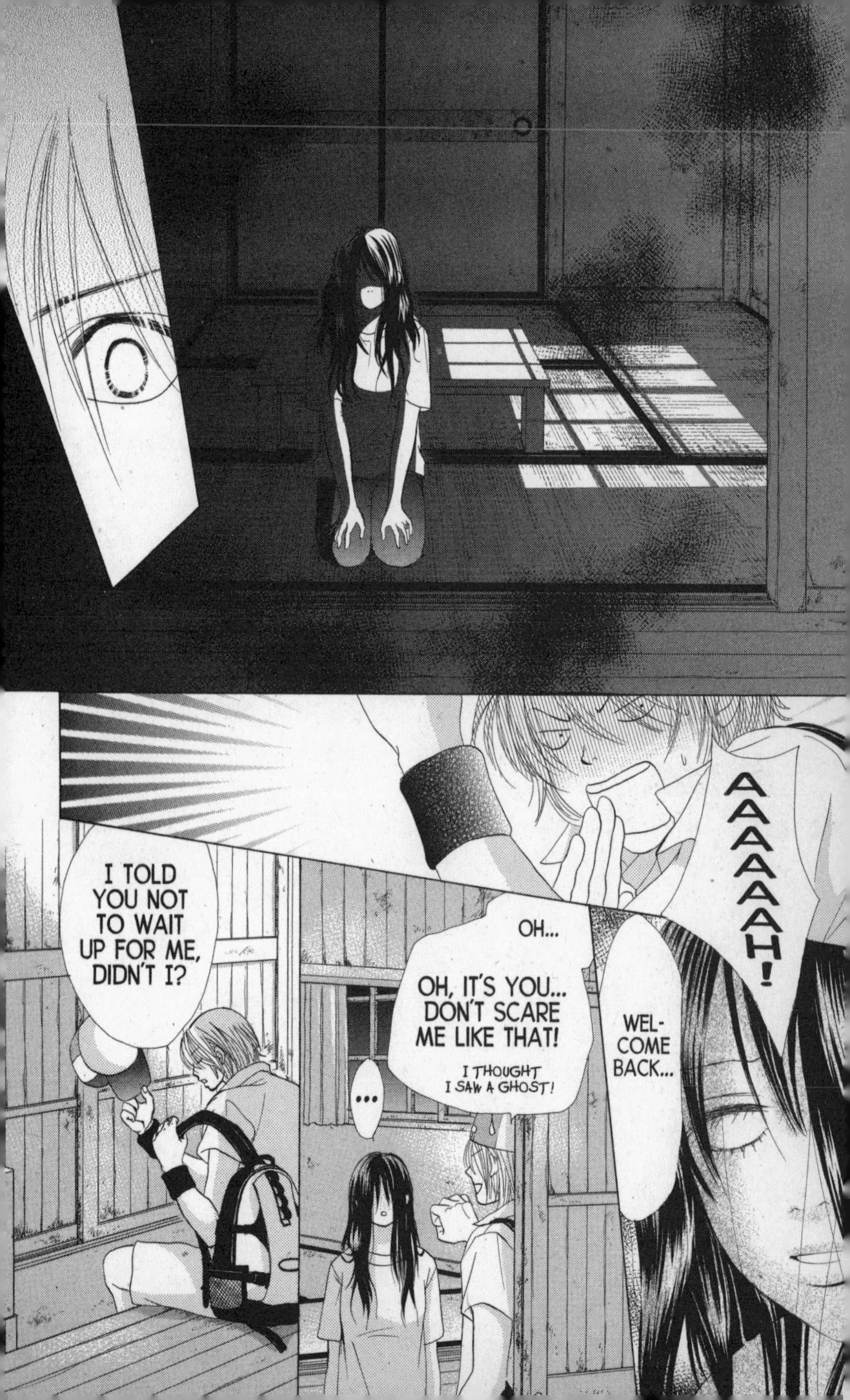
AAAAAAH!
WEL-COME BACK...
OH...
OH, IT'S YOU... DON'T SCARE ME LIKE THAT!
I THOUGHT I SAW A GHOST!
...
I TOLD YOU NOT TO WAIT UP FOR ME, DIDN'T I?

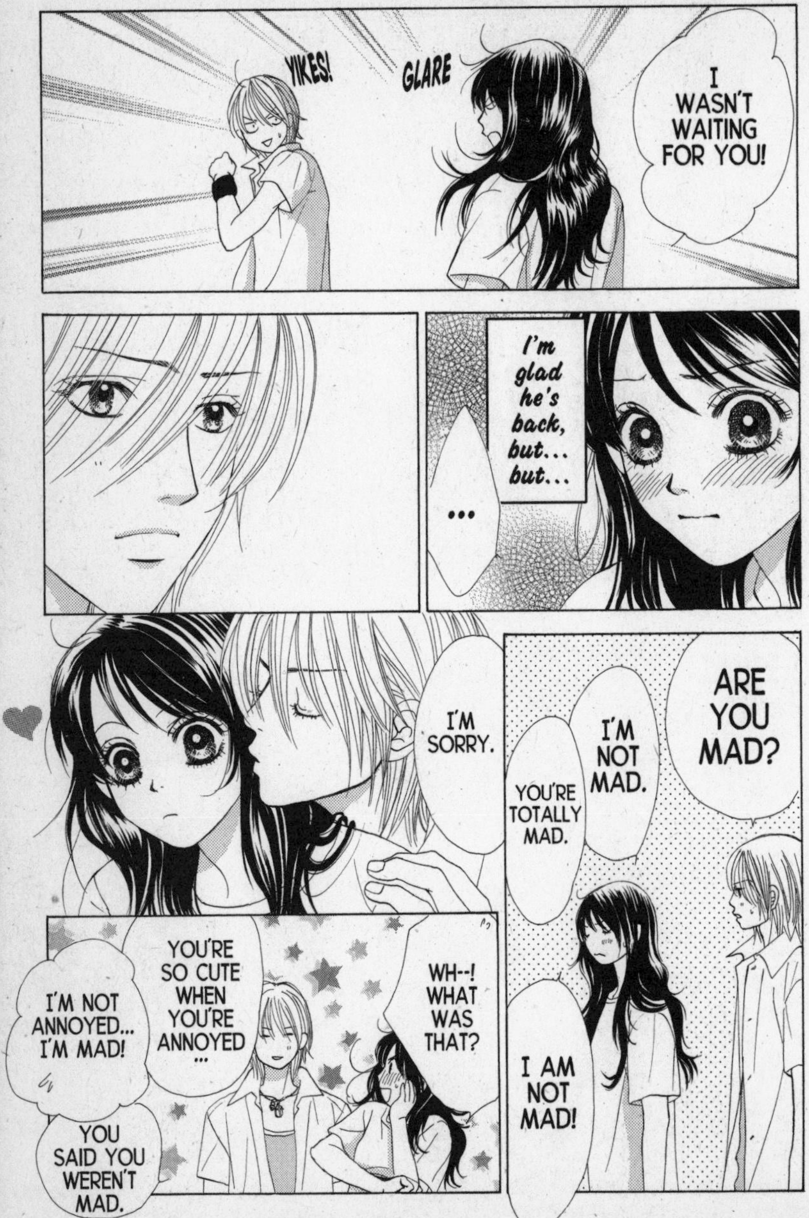
I WASN'T WAITING FOR YOU!
GLARE
YIKES!
I'm glad he's back, but... but...
...
ARE YOU MAD?
I'M NOT MAD.
YOU'RE TOTALLY MAD.
I AM NOT MAD!
I'M SORRY.
WH--! WHAT WAS THAT?
YOU'RE SO CUTE WHEN YOU'RE ANNOYED...
I'M NOT ANNOYED... I'M MAD!
YOU SAID YOU WEREN'T MAD.

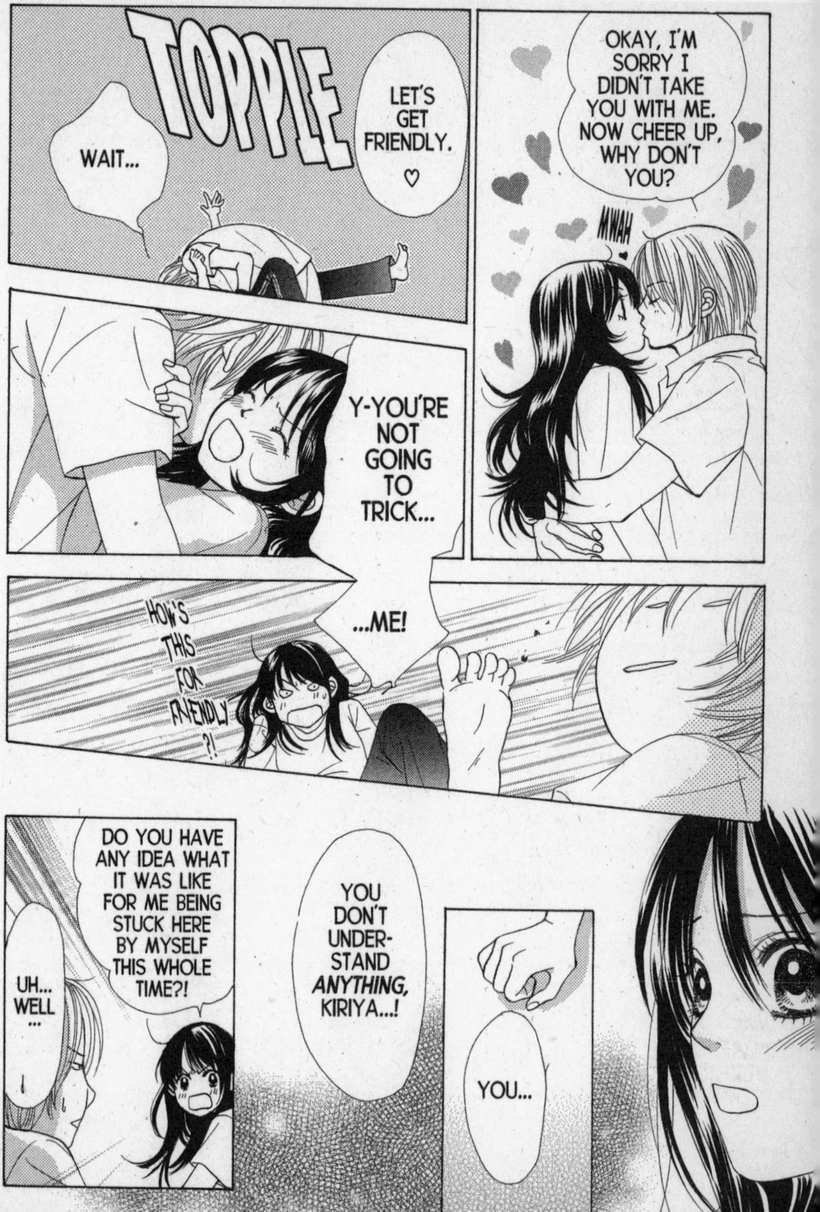
OKAY, I'M SORRY I DIDN'T TAKE YOU WITH ME. NOW CHEER UP, WHY DON'T YOU?
MWAH
LET'S GET FRIENDLY. ♡
TOPPLE
WAIT...
Y-YOU'RE NOT GOING TO TRICK...
...ME!
HOW'S THIS FOR FRIENDLY?!
YOU...
YOU DON'T UNDERSTAND ANYTHING, KIRIYA...!
DO YOU HAVE ANY IDEA WHAT IT WAS LIKE FOR ME BEING STUCK HERE BY MYSELF THIS WHOLE TIME?!
UH... WELL...

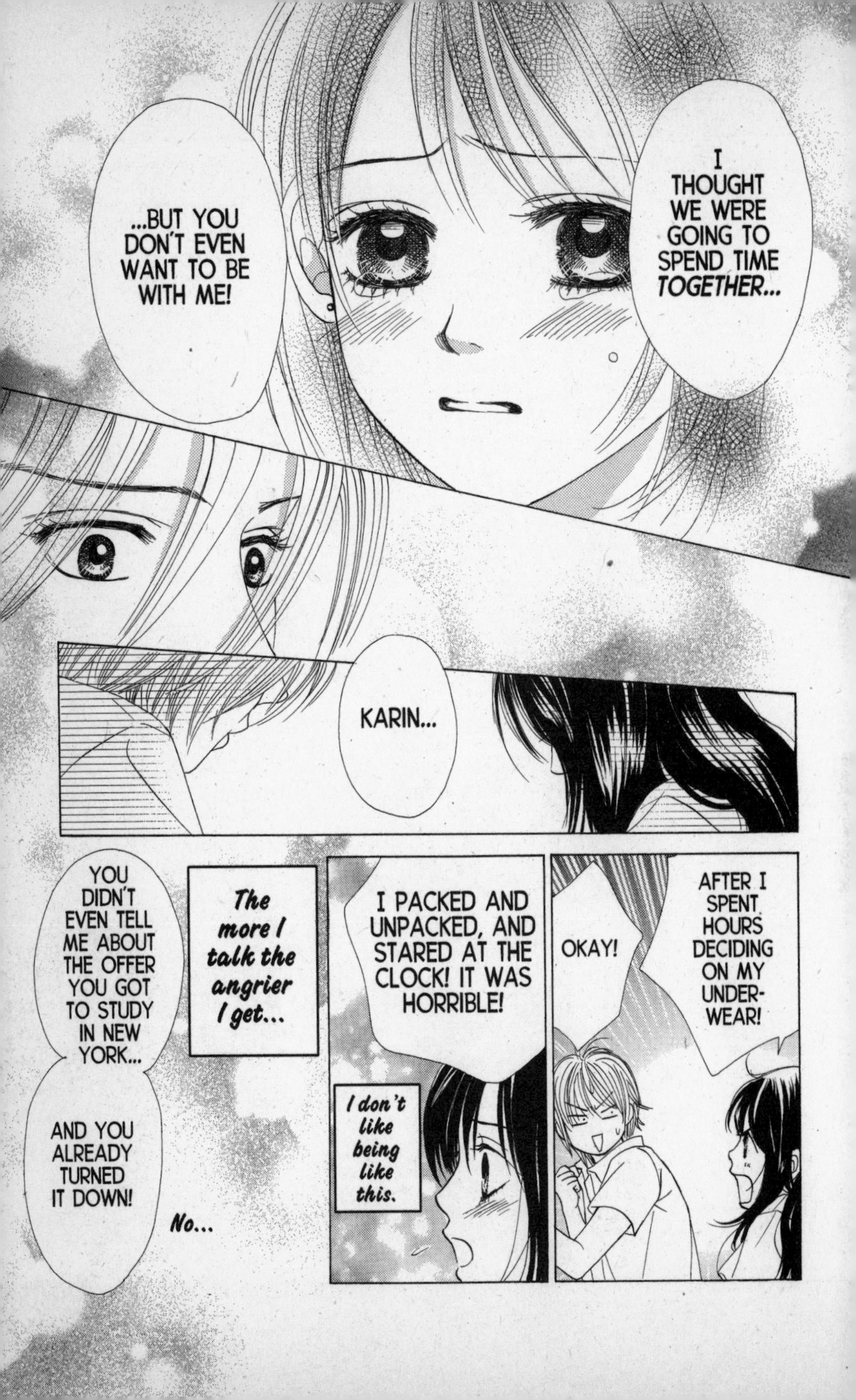
I THOUGHT WE WERE GOING TO SPEND TIME *TOGETHER...*
...BUT YOU DON'T EVEN WANT TO BE WITH ME!
KARIN...
AFTER I SPENT HOURS DECIDING ON MY UNDER-WEAR!
OKAY!
I PACKED AND UNPACKED, AND STARED AT THE CLOCK! IT WAS HORRIBLE!
*I don't like being like this.*
*The more I talk the angrier I get...*
YOU DIDN'T EVEN TELL ME ABOUT THE OFFER YOU GOT TO STUDY IN NEW YORK...
AND YOU ALREADY TURNED IT DOWN!
*No...*

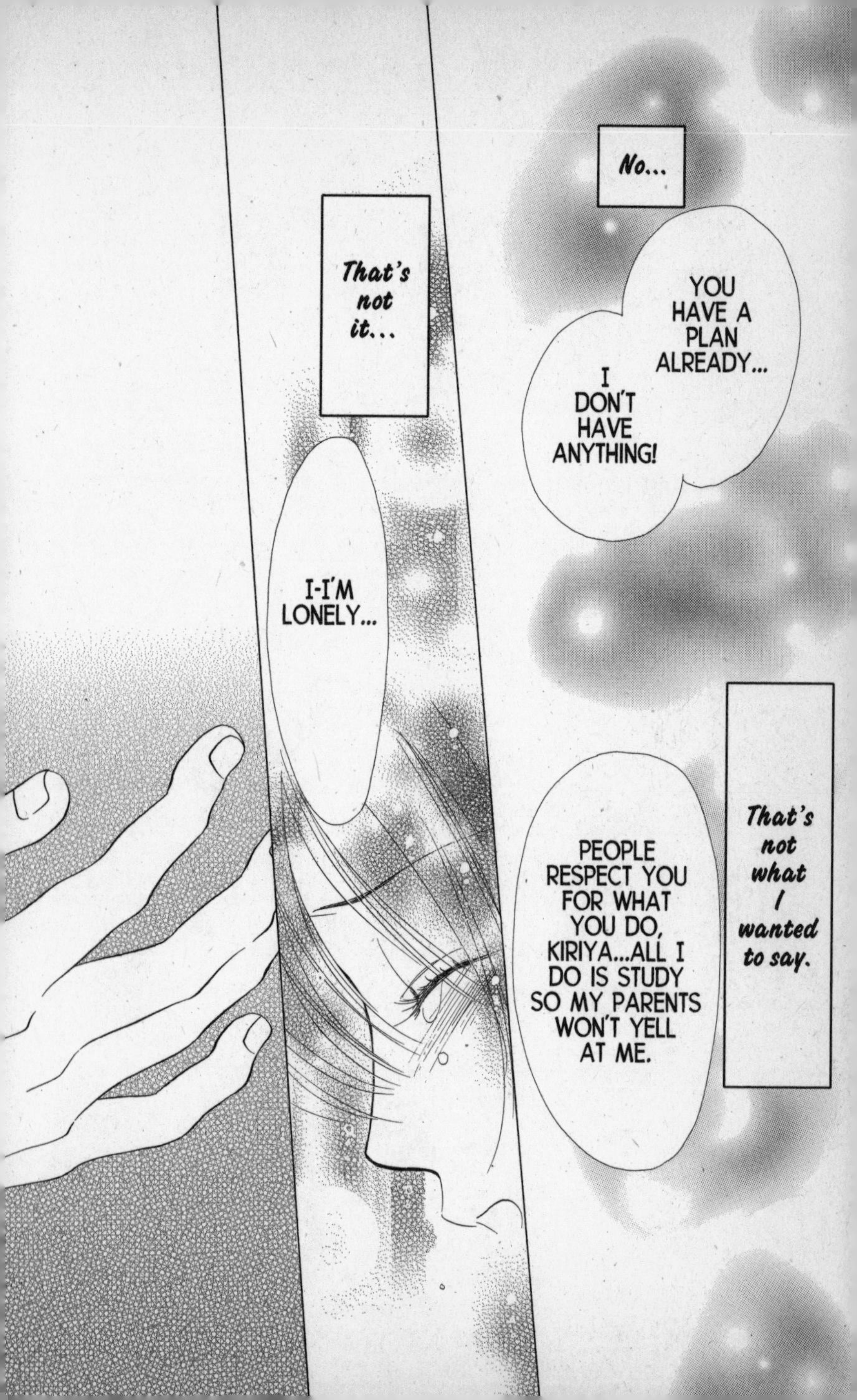
No...
YOU HAVE A PLAN ALREADY...
I DON'T HAVE ANYTHING!
That's not what I wanted to say.
PEOPLE RESPECT YOU FOR WHAT YOU DO, KIRIYA...ALL I DO IS STUDY SO MY PARENTS WON'T YELL AT ME.
That's not it...
I-I'M LONELY...

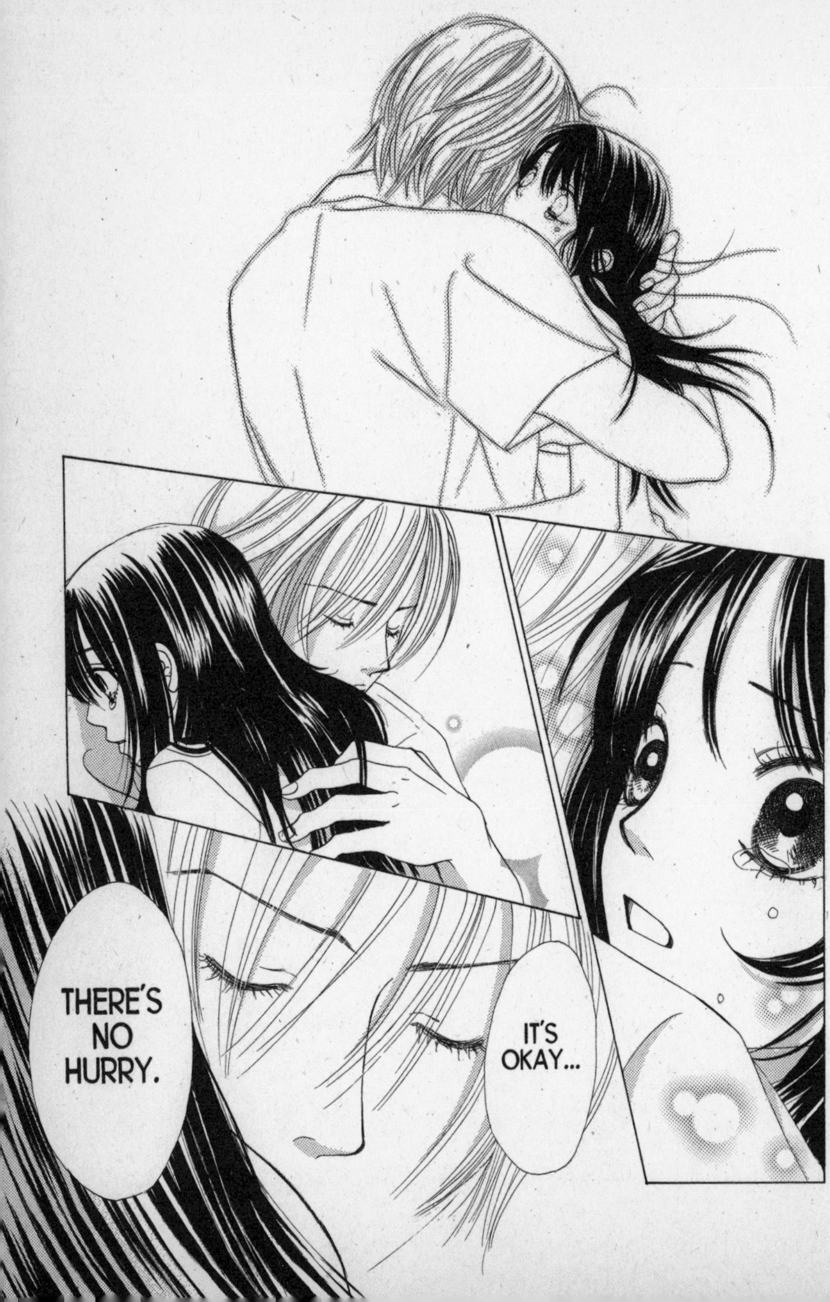
IT'S OKAY...
THERE'S NO HURRY.

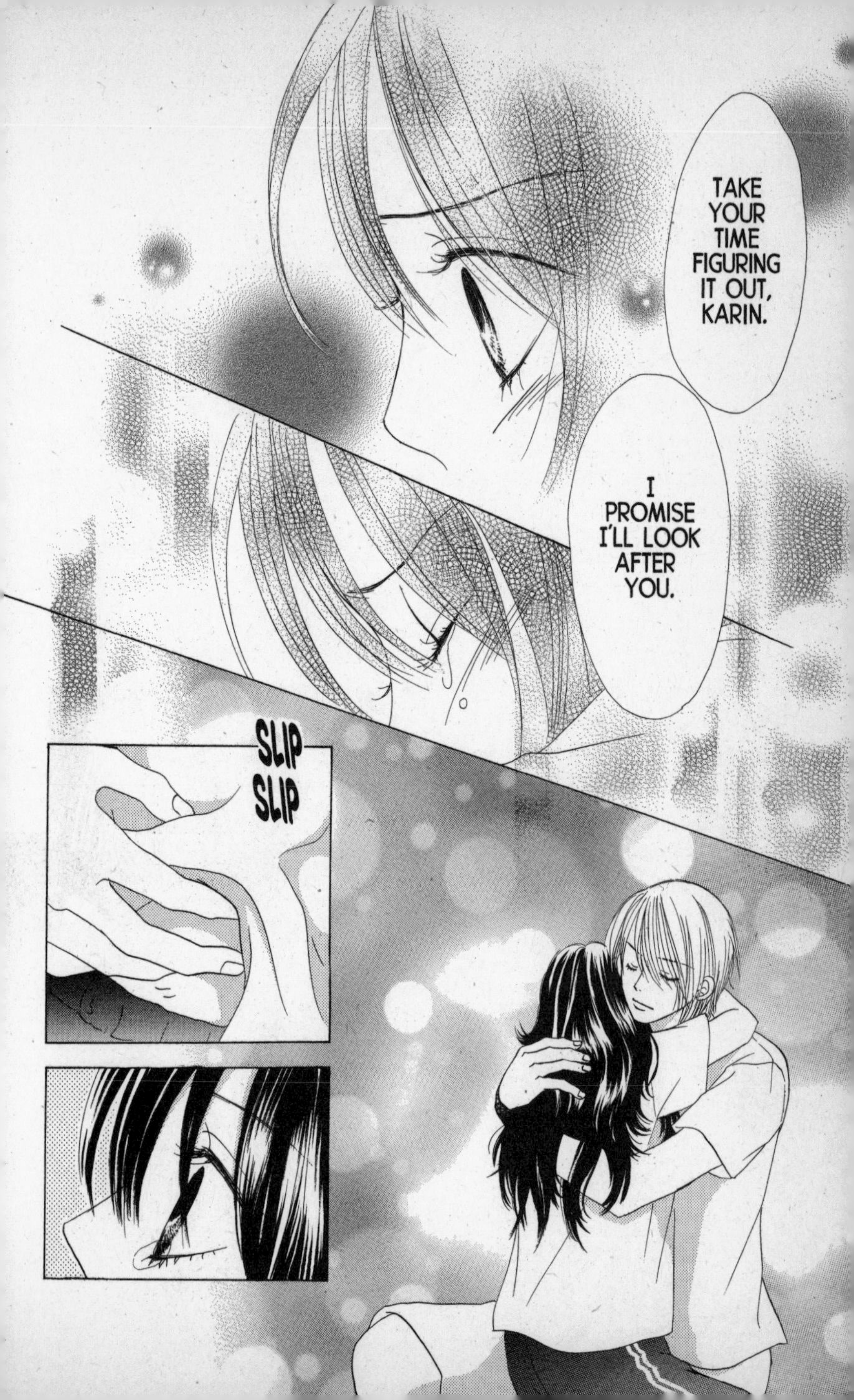
TAKE YOUR TIME FIGURING IT OUT, KARIN.
I PROMISE I'LL LOOK AFTER YOU.
SLIP SLIP

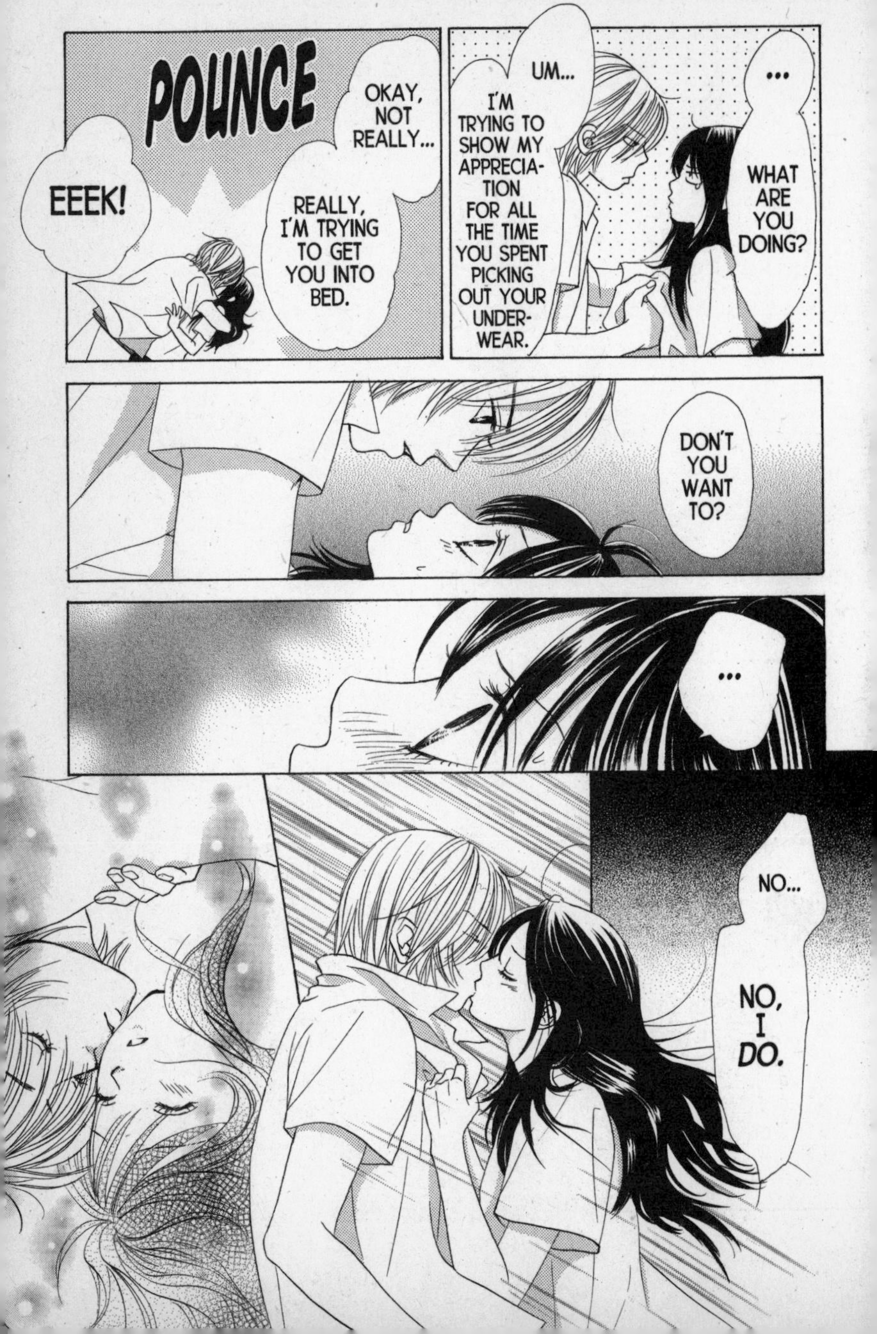
...
WHAT ARE YOU DOING?
UM...
I'M TRYING TO SHOW MY APPRECIA-TION FOR ALL THE TIME YOU SPENT PICKING OUT YOUR UNDER-WEAR.
OKAY, NOT REALLY...
REALLY, I'M TRYING TO GET YOU INTO BED.
POUNCE
EEEK!
DON'T YOU WANT TO?
...
NO...
NO, I DO.

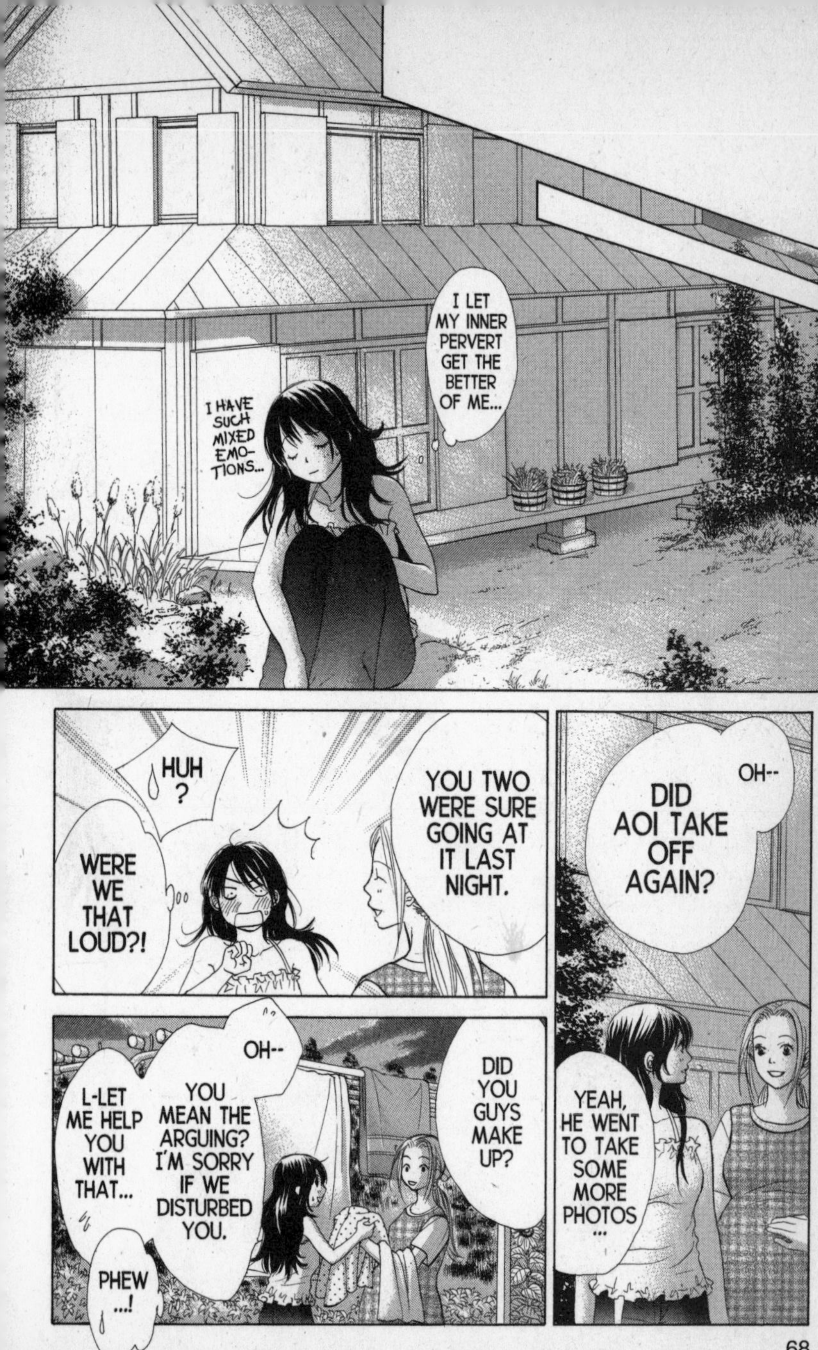
I LET MY INNER PERVERT GET THE BETTER OF ME...
I HAVE SUCH MIXED EMO-TIONS...
OH--
DID AOI TAKE OFF AGAIN?
YEAH, HE WENT TO TAKE SOME MORE PHOTOS...
YOU TWO WERE SURE GOING AT IT LAST NIGHT.
HUH?
WERE WE THAT LOUD?!
DID YOU GUYS MAKE UP?
OH--
YOU MEAN THE ARGUING? I'M SORRY IF WE DISTURBED YOU.
L-LET ME HELP YOU WITH THAT...
PHEW...!

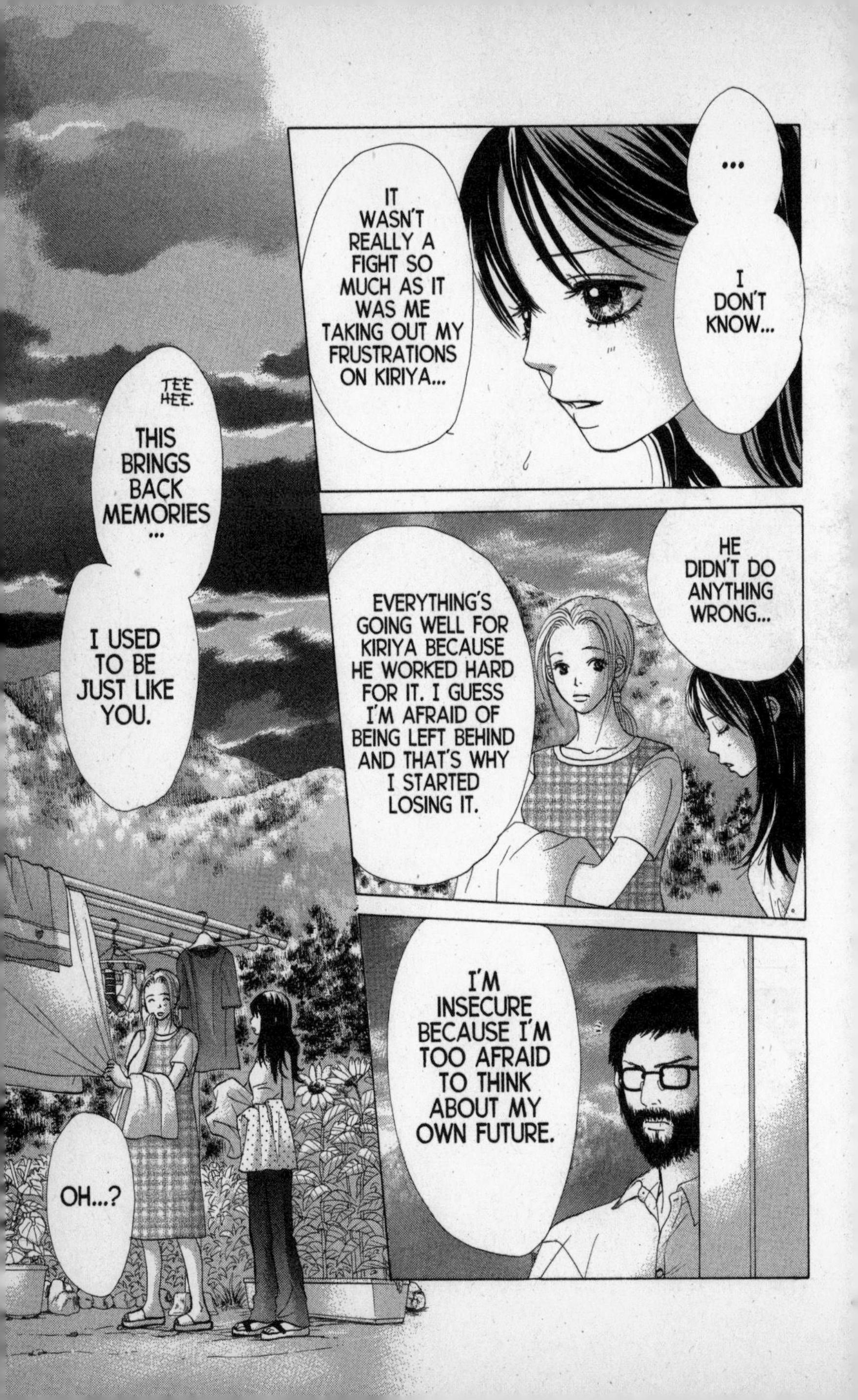
...
I DON'T KNOW...
IT WASN'T REALLY A FIGHT SO MUCH AS IT WAS ME TAKING OUT MY FRUSTRATIONS ON KIRIYA...
HE DIDN'T DO ANYTHING WRONG...
EVERYTHING'S GOING WELL FOR KIRIYA BECAUSE HE WORKED HARD FOR IT. I GUESS I'M AFRAID OF BEING LEFT BEHIND AND THAT'S WHY I STARTED LOSING IT.
I'M INSECURE BECAUSE I'M TOO AFRAID TO THINK ABOUT MY OWN FUTURE.
TEE HEE.
THIS BRINGS BACK MEMORIES...
I USED TO BE JUST LIKE YOU.
OH...?

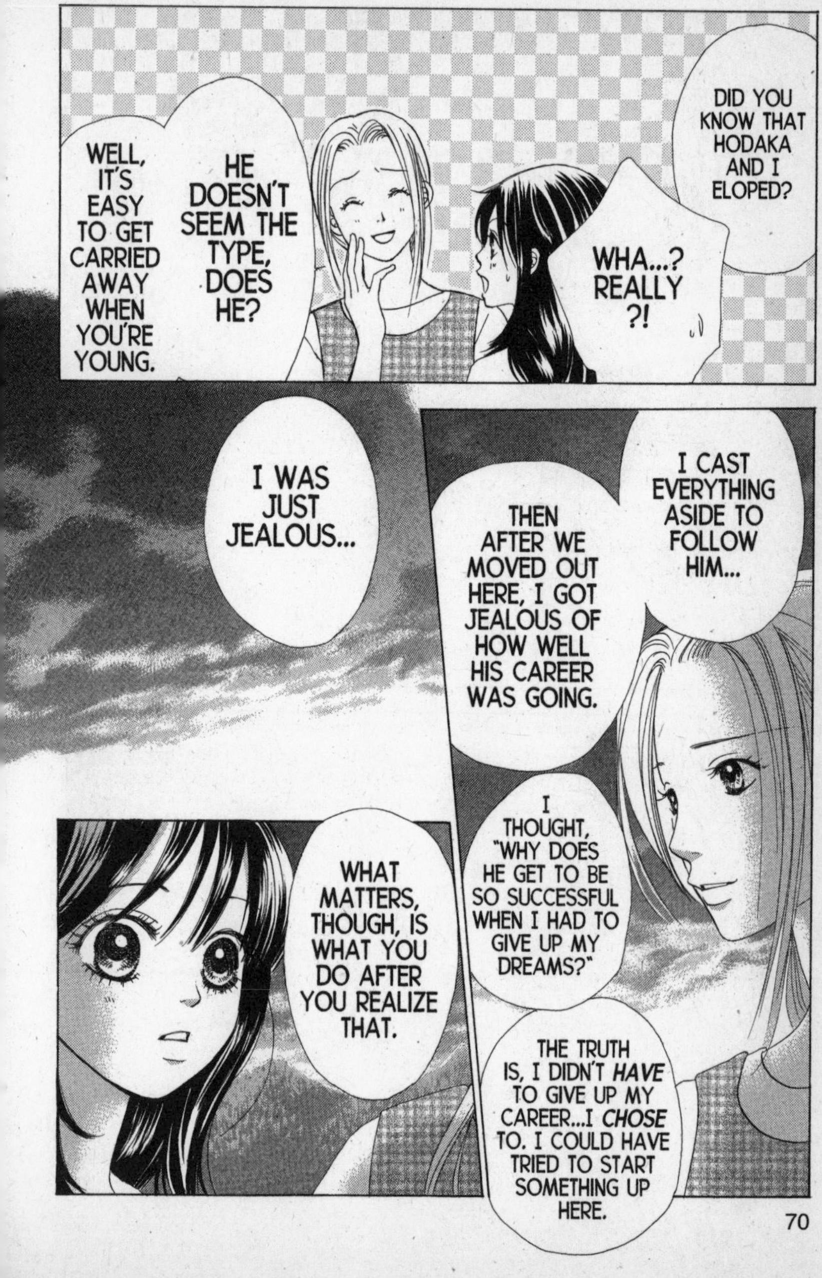
DID YOU KNOW THAT HODAKA AND I ELOPED?
WHA...? REALLY ?!
HE DOESN'T SEEM THE TYPE, DOES HE?
WELL, IT'S EASY TO GET CARRIED AWAY WHEN YOU'RE YOUNG.
I CAST EVERYTHING ASIDE TO FOLLOW HIM...
THEN AFTER WE MOVED OUT HERE, I GOT JEALOUS OF HOW WELL HIS CAREER WAS GOING.
I THOUGHT, "WHY DOES HE GET TO BE SO SUCCESSFUL WHEN I HAD TO GIVE UP MY DREAMS?"
THE TRUTH IS, I DIDN'T *HAVE* TO GIVE UP MY CAREER...I *CHOSE* TO. I COULD HAVE TRIED TO START SOMETHING UP HERE.
I WAS JUST JEALOUS...
WHAT MATTERS, THOUGH, IS WHAT YOU DO AFTER YOU REALIZE THAT.

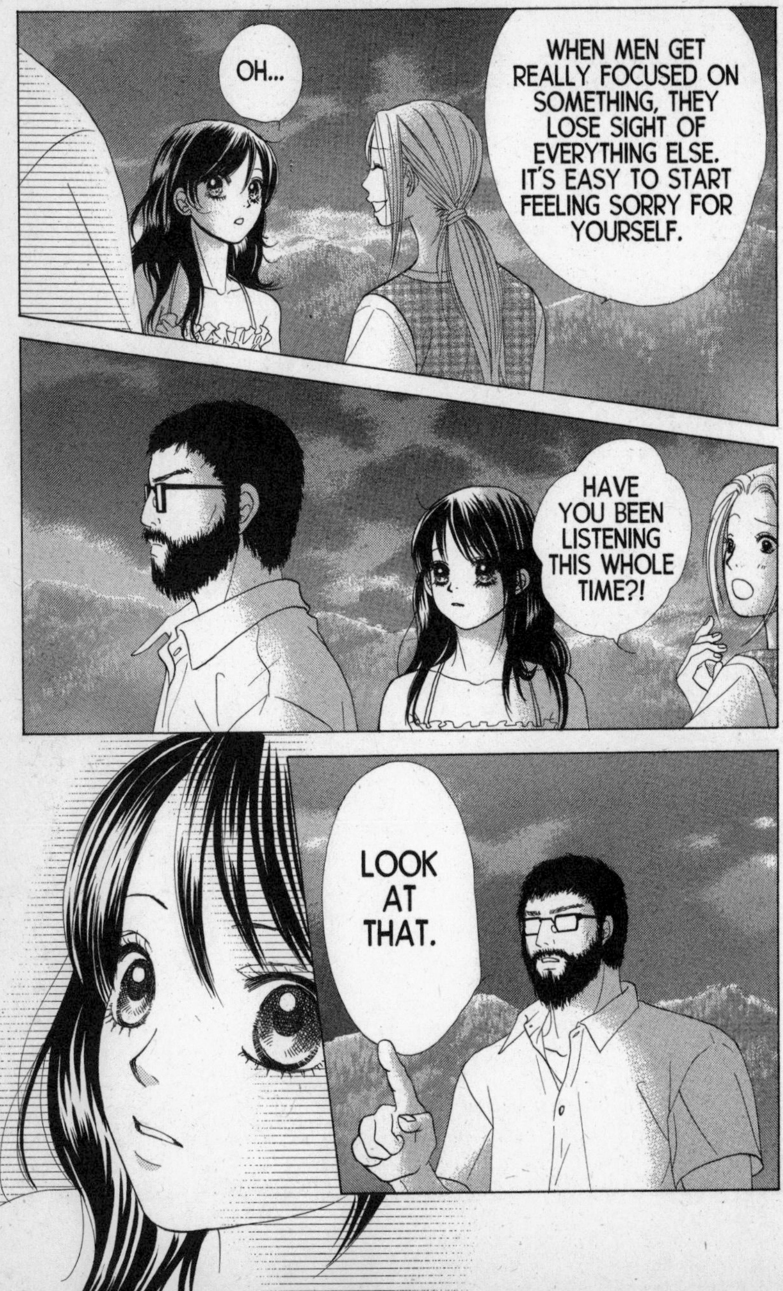
WHEN MEN GET REALLY FOCUSED ON SOMETHING, THEY LOSE SIGHT OF EVERYTHING ELSE. IT'S EASY TO START FEELING SORRY FOR YOURSELF.
OH...
HAVE YOU BEEN LISTENING THIS WHOLE TIME?!
LOOK AT THAT.

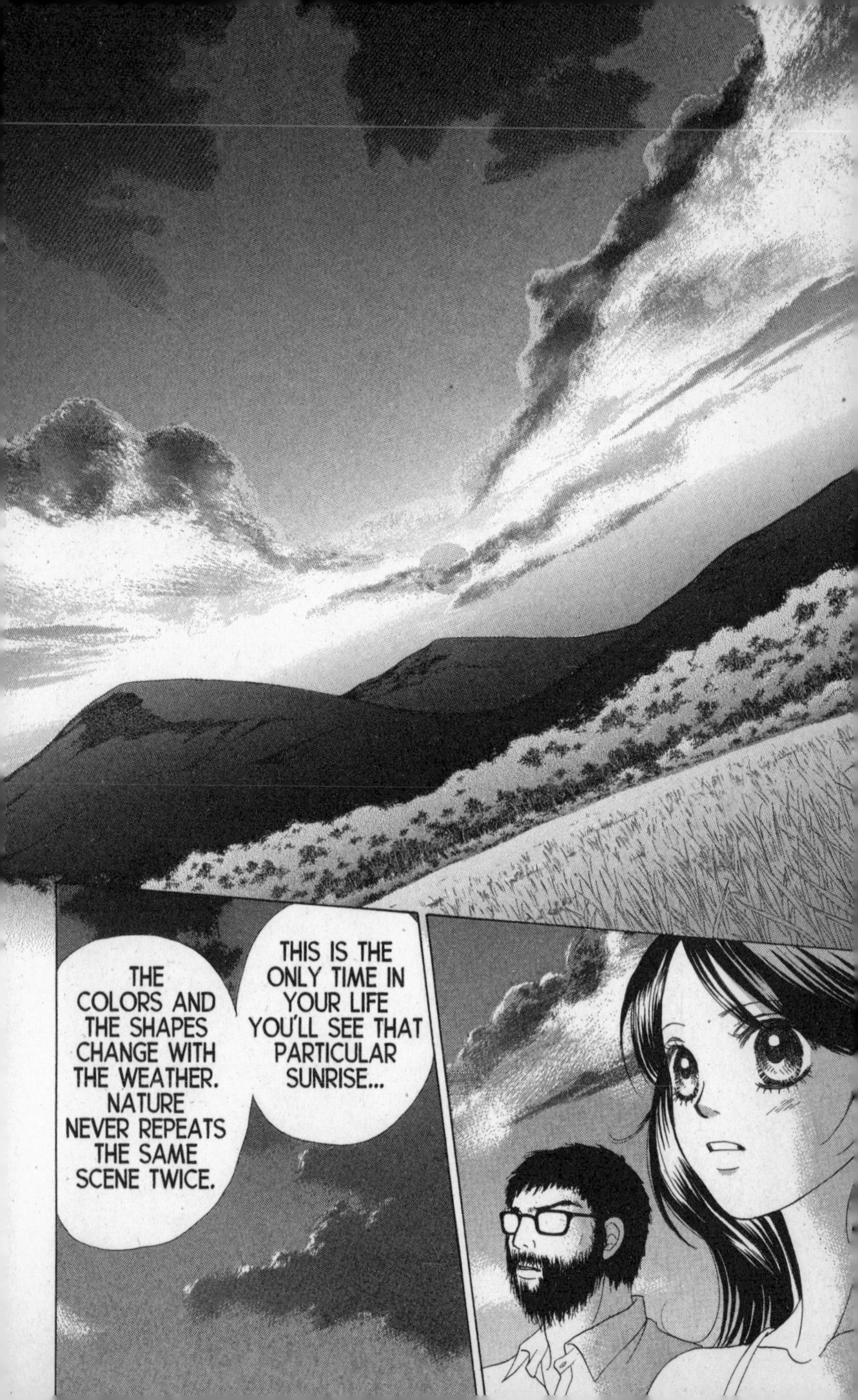
THIS IS THE ONLY TIME IN YOUR LIFE YOU'LL SEE THAT PARTICULAR SUNRISE...
THE COLORS AND THE SHAPES CHANGE WITH THE WEATHER. NATURE NEVER REPEATS THE SAME SCENE TWICE.

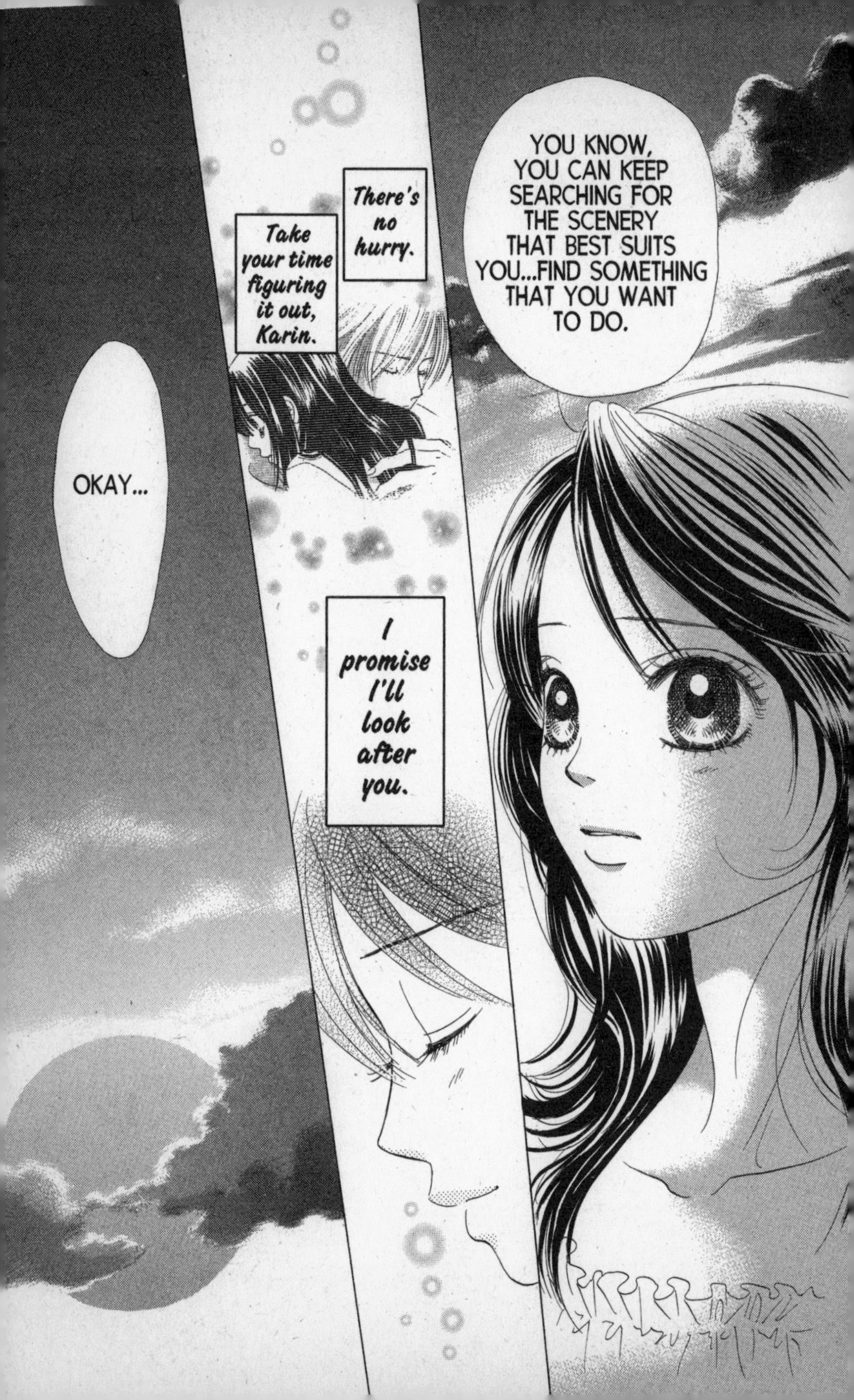
YOU KNOW, YOU CAN KEEP SEARCHING FOR THE SCENERY THAT BEST SUITS YOU...FIND SOMETHING THAT YOU WANT TO DO.
There's no hurry.
Take your time figuring it out, Karin.
I promise I'll look after you.
OKAY...

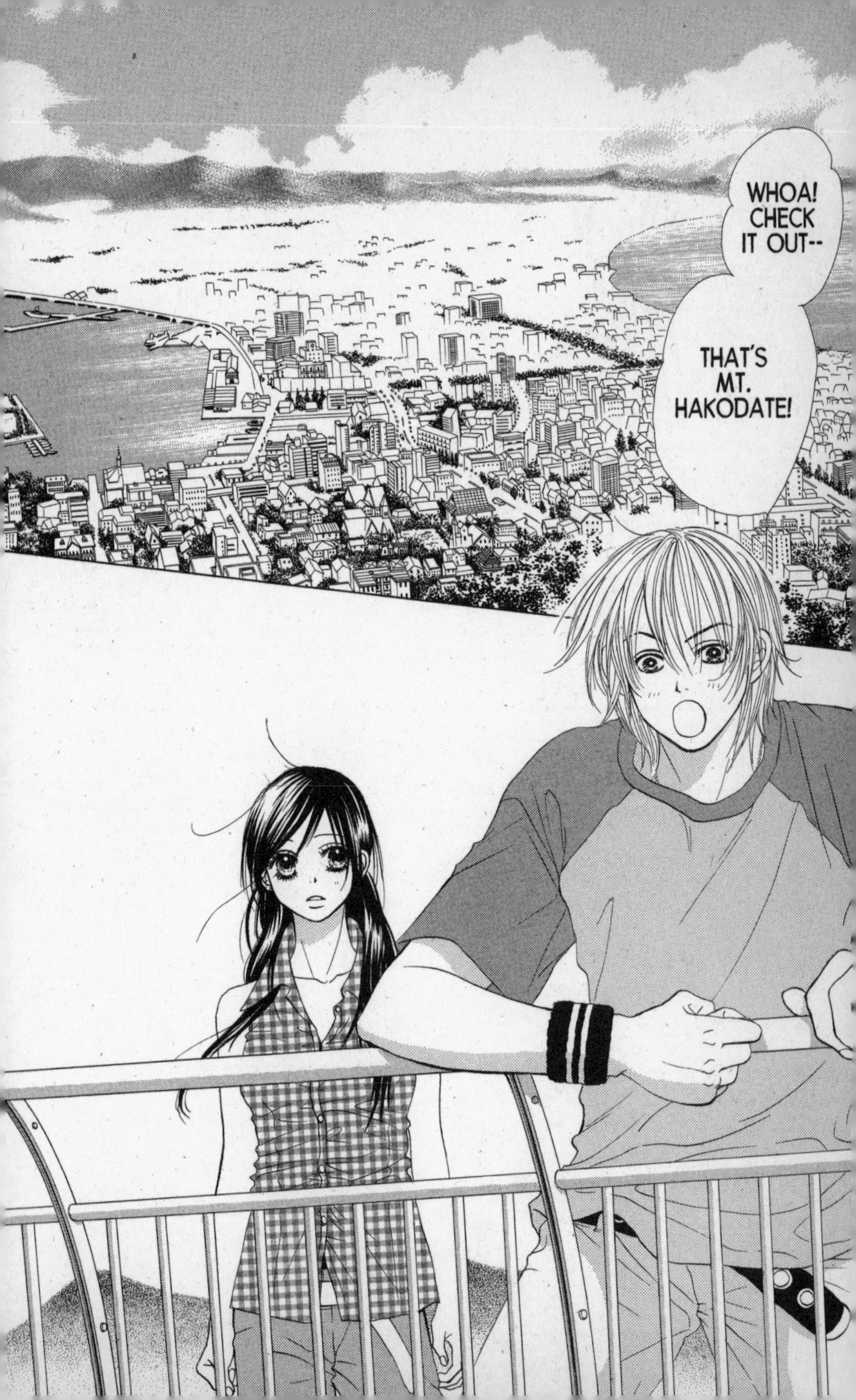
WHOA! CHECK IT OUT--
THAT'S MT. HAKODATE!

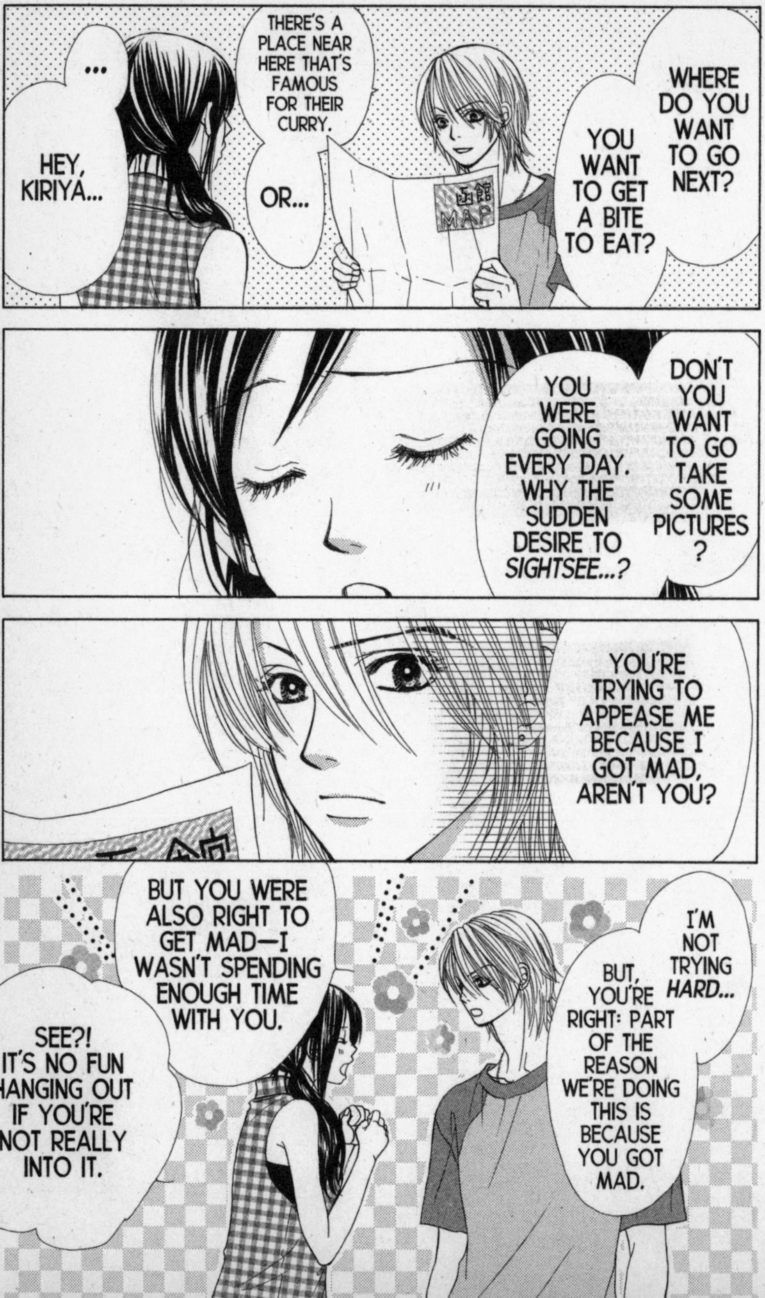
WHERE DO YOU WANT TO GO NEXT?
YOU WANT TO GET A BITE TO EAT?
THERE'S A PLACE NEAR HERE THAT'S FAMOUS FOR THEIR CURRY.
OR...
函館 MAP
...
HEY, KIRIYA...
DON'T YOU WANT TO GO TAKE SOME PICTURES?
YOU WERE GOING EVERY DAY. WHY THE SUDDEN DESIRE TO *SIGHTSEE*...?
YOU'RE TRYING TO APPEASE ME BECAUSE I GOT MAD, AREN'T YOU?
I'M NOT TRYING *HARD*...
BUT, YOU'RE RIGHT: PART OF THE REASON WE'RE DOING THIS IS BECAUSE YOU GOT MAD.
BUT YOU WERE ALSO RIGHT TO GET MAD—I WASN'T SPENDING ENOUGH TIME WITH YOU.
SEE?! IT'S NO FUN HANGING OUT IF YOU'RE NOT REALLY INTO IT.

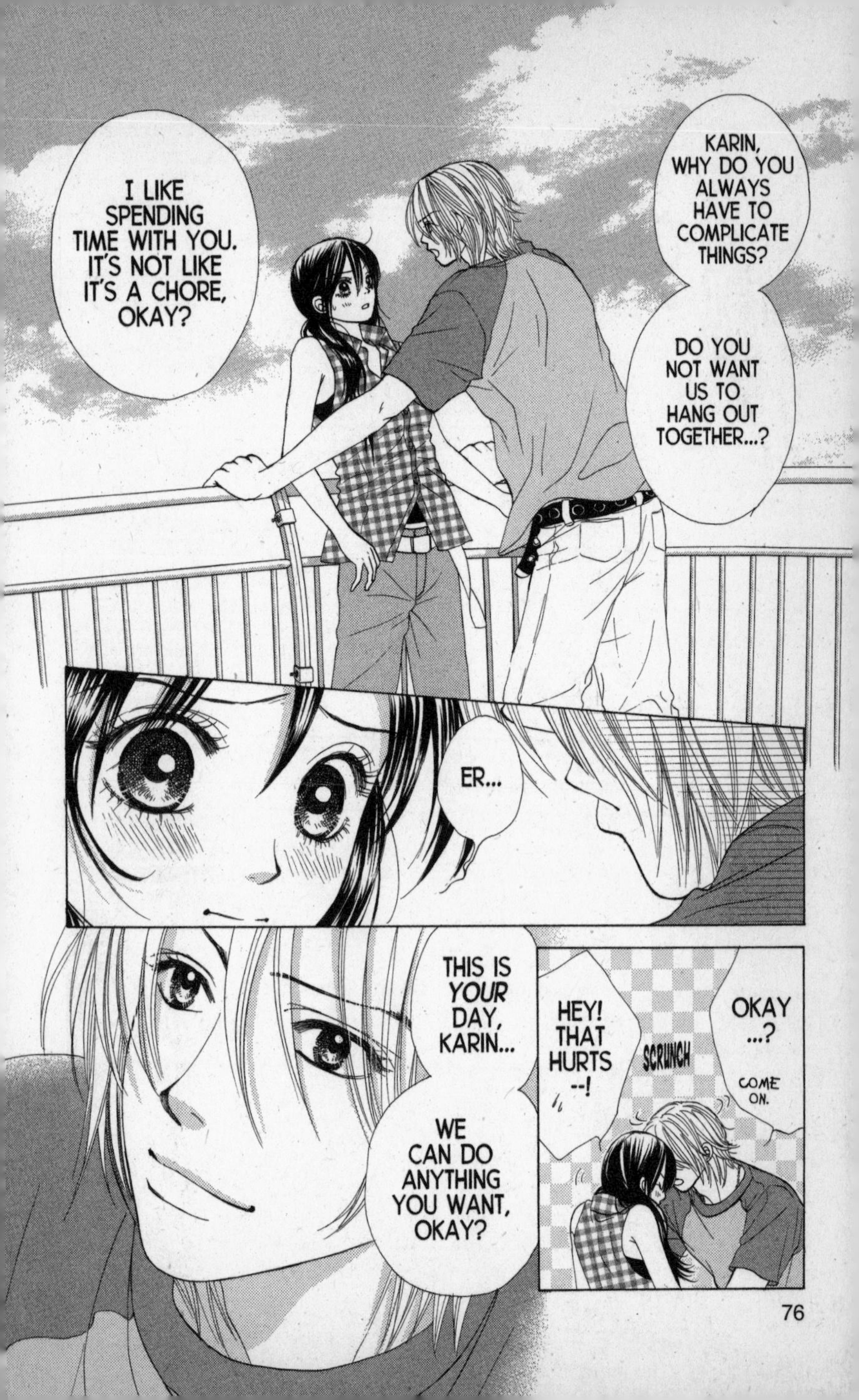
KARIN, WHY DO YOU ALWAYS HAVE TO COMPLICATE THINGS?
DO YOU NOT WANT US TO HANG OUT TOGETHER...?
I LIKE SPENDING TIME WITH YOU. IT'S NOT LIKE IT'S A CHORE, OKAY?
ER...
OKAY ...?
COME ON.
SCRUNCH
HEY! THAT HURTS --!
THIS IS *YOUR* DAY, KARIN...
WE CAN DO ANYTHING YOU WANT, OKAY?

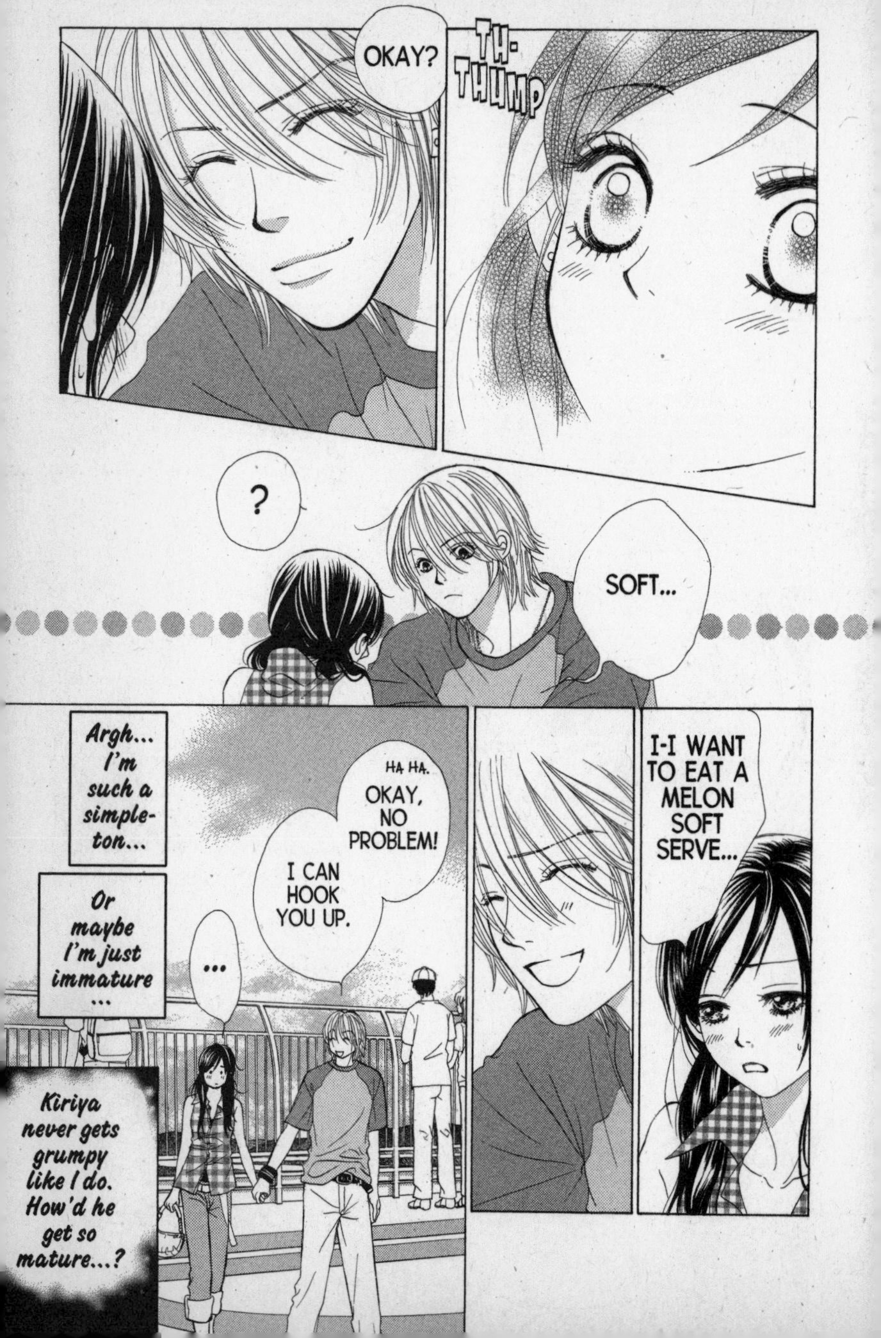
OKAY?
TH-THUMP
SOFT...
?
I-I WANT TO EAT A MELON SOFT SERVE...
HA HA.
OKAY, NO PROBLEM!
I CAN HOOK YOU UP.
...
Argh... I'm such a simpleton...
Or maybe I'm just immature...
Kiriya never gets grumpy like I do. How'd he get so mature...?

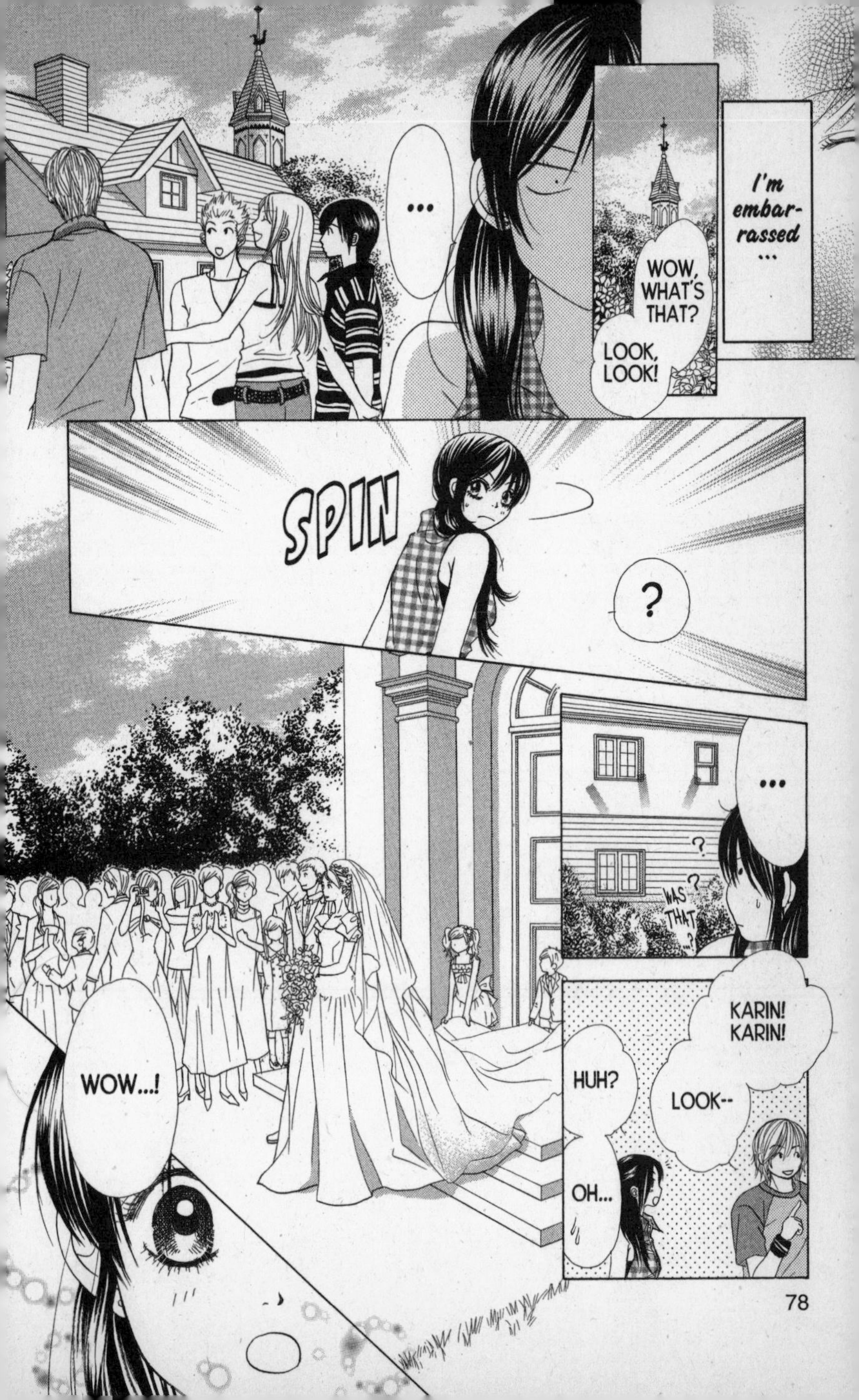

I'm embarrassed...
WOW, WHAT'S THAT?
LOOK, LOOK!
...
SPIN
?
...
WAS THAT ?
KARIN! KARIN!
LOOK--
HUH?
OH...
WOW...!

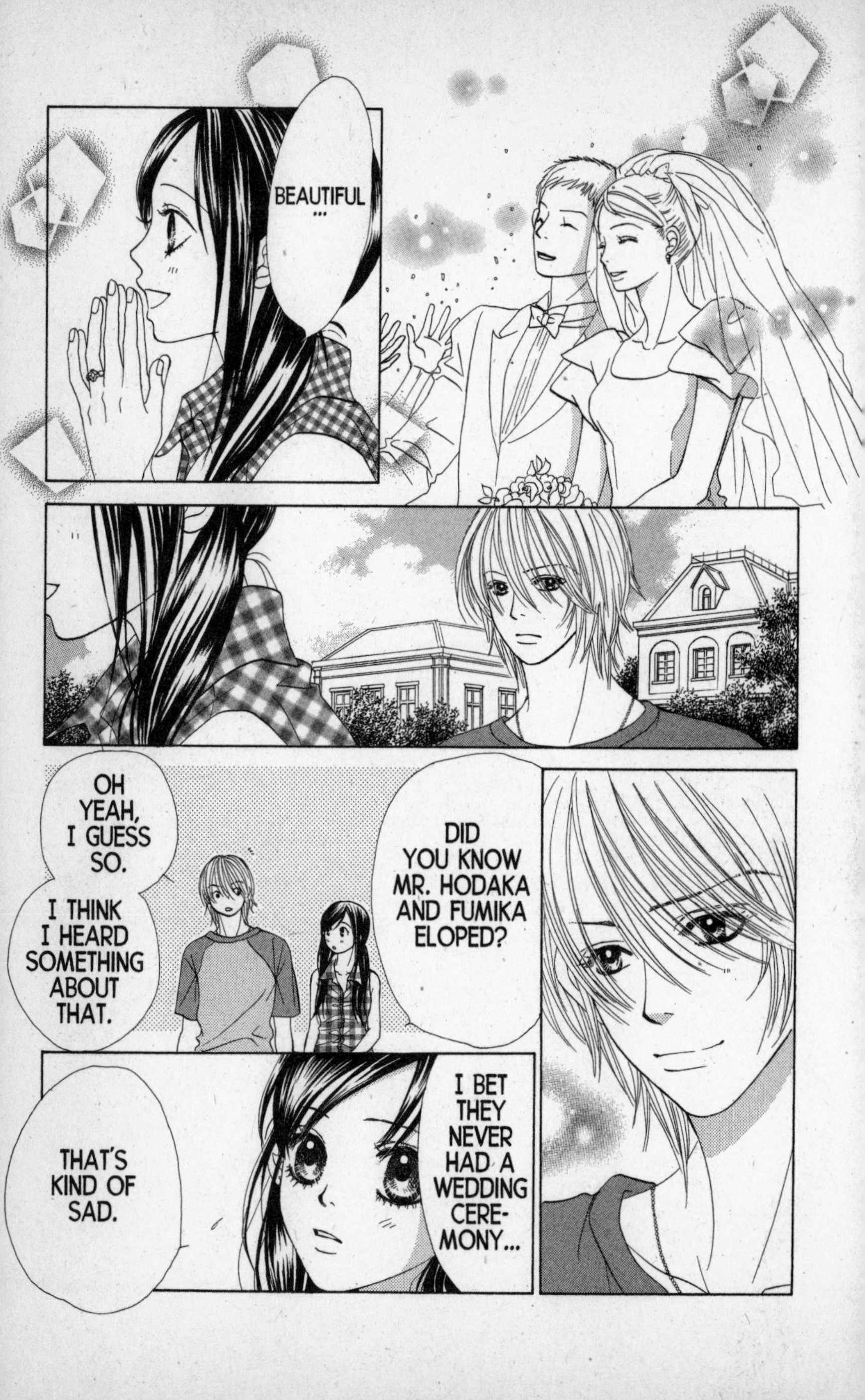
BEAUTIFUL ...
DID YOU KNOW MR. HODAKA AND FUMIKA ELOPED?
OH YEAH, I GUESS SO.
I THINK I HEARD SOMETHING ABOUT THAT.
I BET THEY NEVER HAD A WEDDING CERE-MONY...
THAT'S KIND OF SAD.

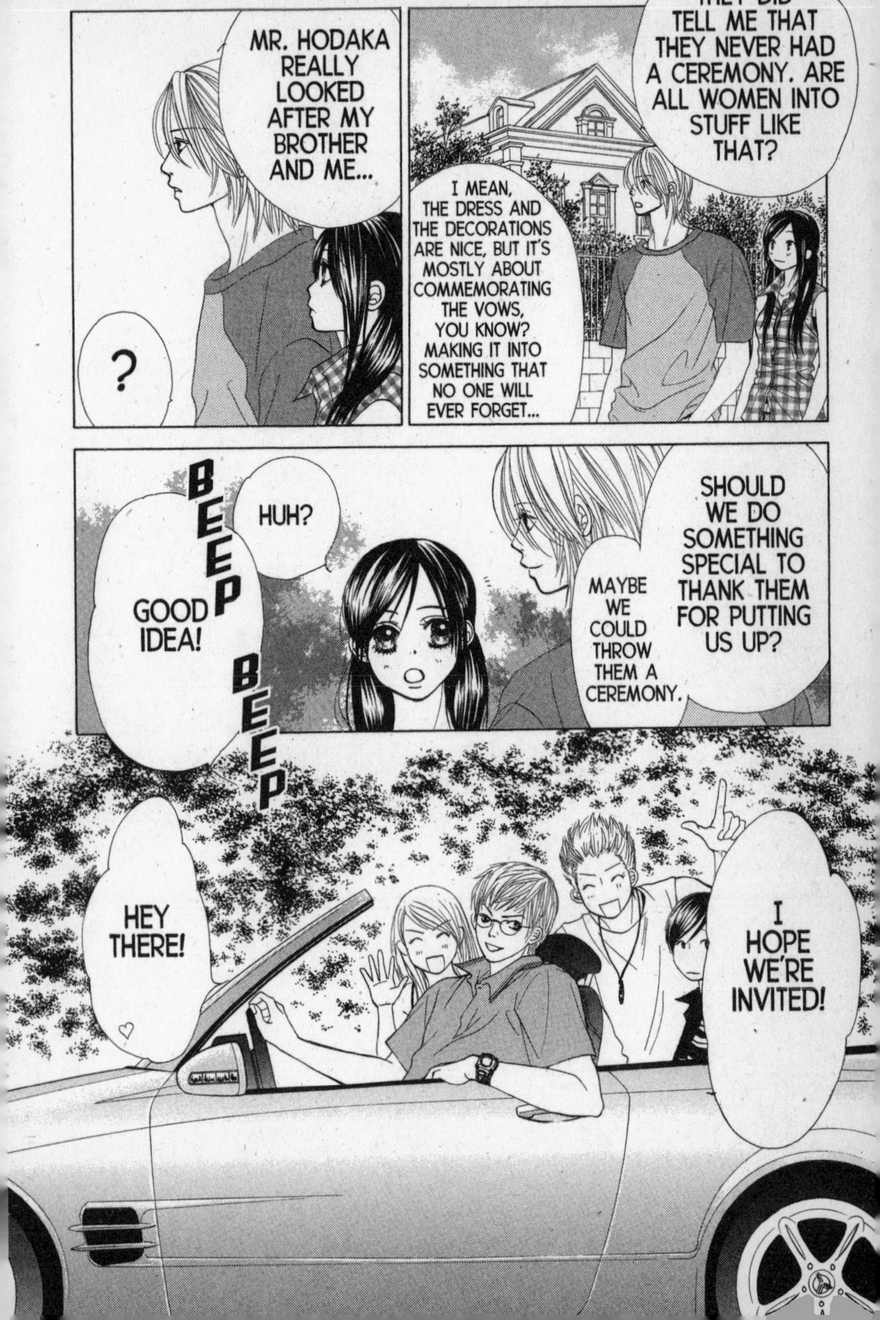
THEY DID TELL ME THAT THEY NEVER HAD A CEREMONY. ARE ALL WOMEN INTO STUFF LIKE THAT?
I MEAN, THE DRESS AND THE DECORATIONS ARE NICE, BUT IT'S MOSTLY ABOUT COMMEMORATING THE VOWS, YOU KNOW? MAKING IT INTO SOMETHING THAT NO ONE WILL EVER FORGET...
MR. HODAKA REALLY LOOKED AFTER MY BROTHER AND ME...
?
SHOULD WE DO SOMETHING SPECIAL TO THANK THEM FOR PUTTING US UP?
MAYBE WE COULD THROW THEM A CEREMONY.
HUH?
GOOD IDEA!
BEEP
BEEP
I HOPE WE'RE INVITED!
HEY THERE! ♡

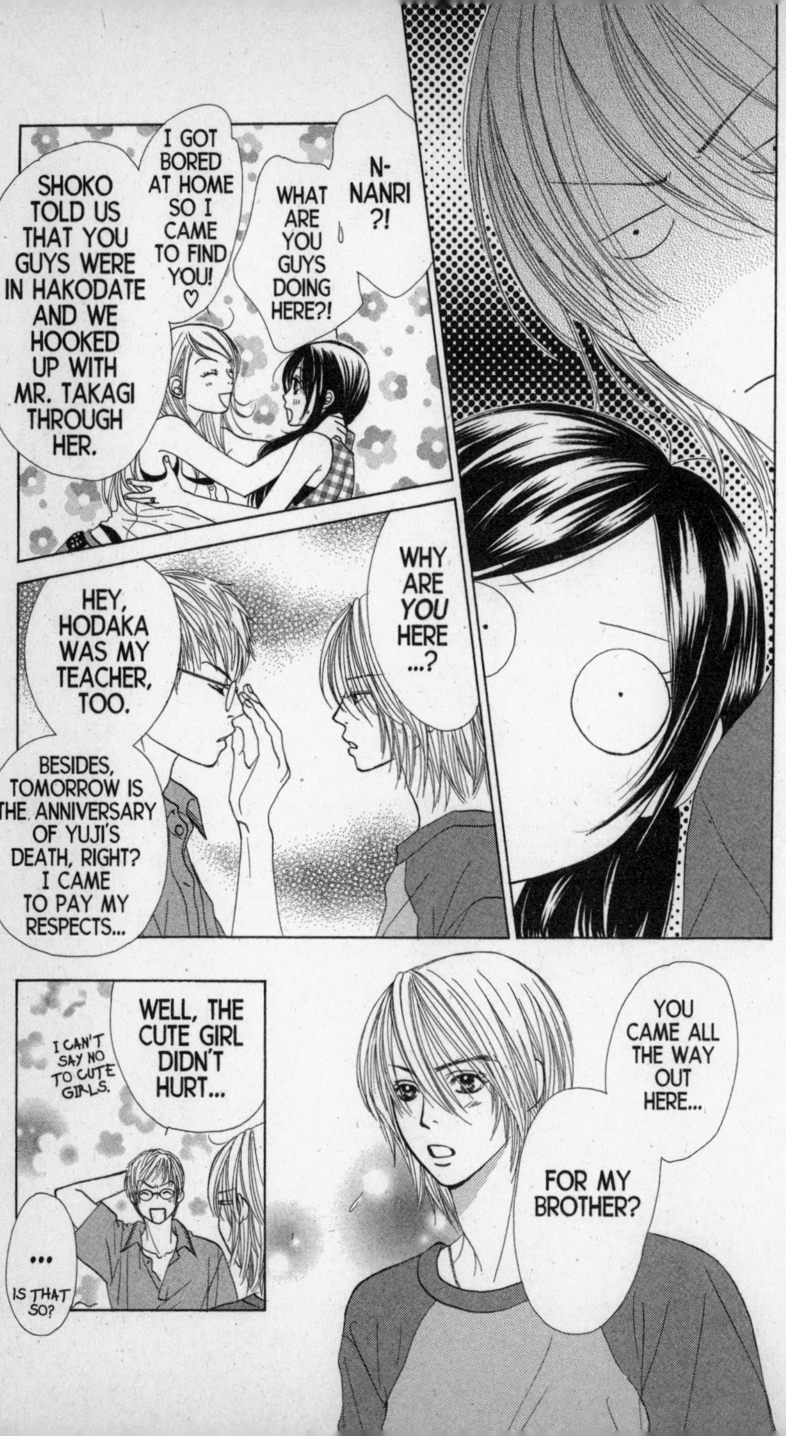
N-NANRI?!
WHAT ARE YOU GUYS DOING HERE?!
I GOT BORED AT HOME SO I CAME TO FIND YOU! ♡
SHOKO TOLD US THAT YOU GUYS WERE IN HAKODATE AND WE HOOKED UP WITH MR. TAKAGI THROUGH HER.
WHY ARE *YOU* HERE...?
HEY, HODAKA WAS MY TEACHER, TOO.
BESIDES, TOMORROW IS THE ANNIVERSARY OF YUJI'S DEATH, RIGHT? I CAME TO PAY MY RESPECTS...
YOU CAME ALL THE WAY OUT HERE...
FOR MY BROTHER?
WELL, THE CUTE GIRL DIDN'T HURT...
I CAN'T SAY NO TO CUTE GIRLS.
...
IS THAT SO?

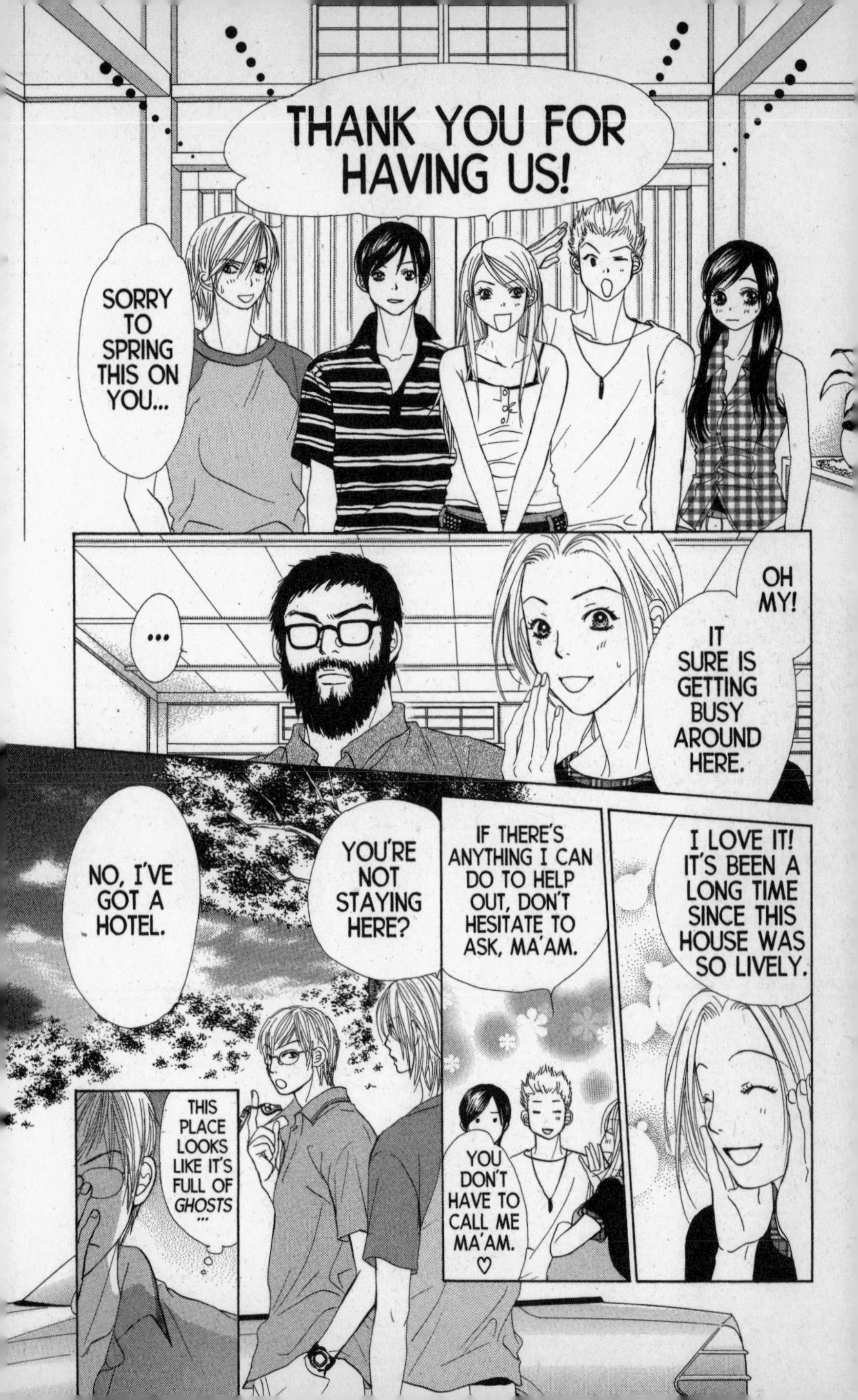
THANK YOU FOR HAVING US!
SORRY TO SPRING THIS ON YOU...
OH MY! IT SURE IS GETTING BUSY AROUND HERE.
...
I LOVE IT! IT'S BEEN A LONG TIME SINCE THIS HOUSE WAS SO LIVELY.
IF THERE'S ANYTHING I CAN DO TO HELP OUT, DON'T HESITATE TO ASK, MA'AM.
YOU DON'T HAVE TO CALL ME MA'AM. ♡
YOU'RE NOT STAYING HERE?
NO, I'VE GOT A HOTEL.
THIS PLACE LOOKS LIKE IT'S FULL OF *GHOSTS*...

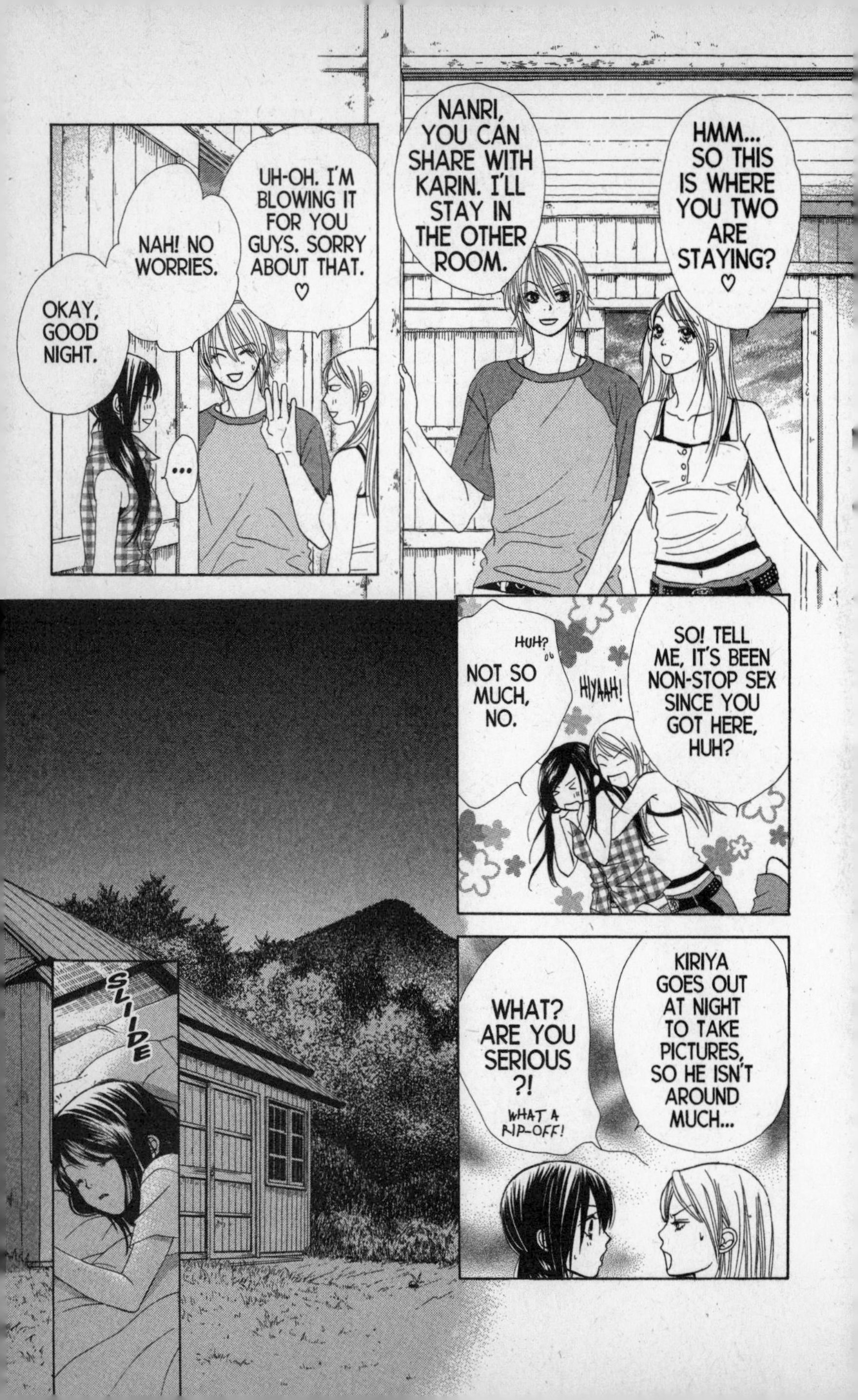
HMM... SO THIS IS WHERE YOU TWO ARE STAYING? ♡
NANRI, YOU CAN SHARE WITH KARIN. I'LL STAY IN THE OTHER ROOM.
UH-OH. I'M BLOWING IT FOR YOU GUYS. SORRY ABOUT THAT. ♡
NAH! NO WORRIES.
OKAY, GOOD NIGHT.
...
SO! TELL ME, IT'S BEEN NON-STOP SEX SINCE YOU GOT HERE, HUH?
HIYAAH!
HUH?
NOT SO MUCH, NO.
KIRIYA GOES OUT AT NIGHT TO TAKE PICTURES, SO HE ISN'T AROUND MUCH...
WHAT? ARE YOU SERIOUS ?!
WHAT A RIP-OFF!
SLIDE

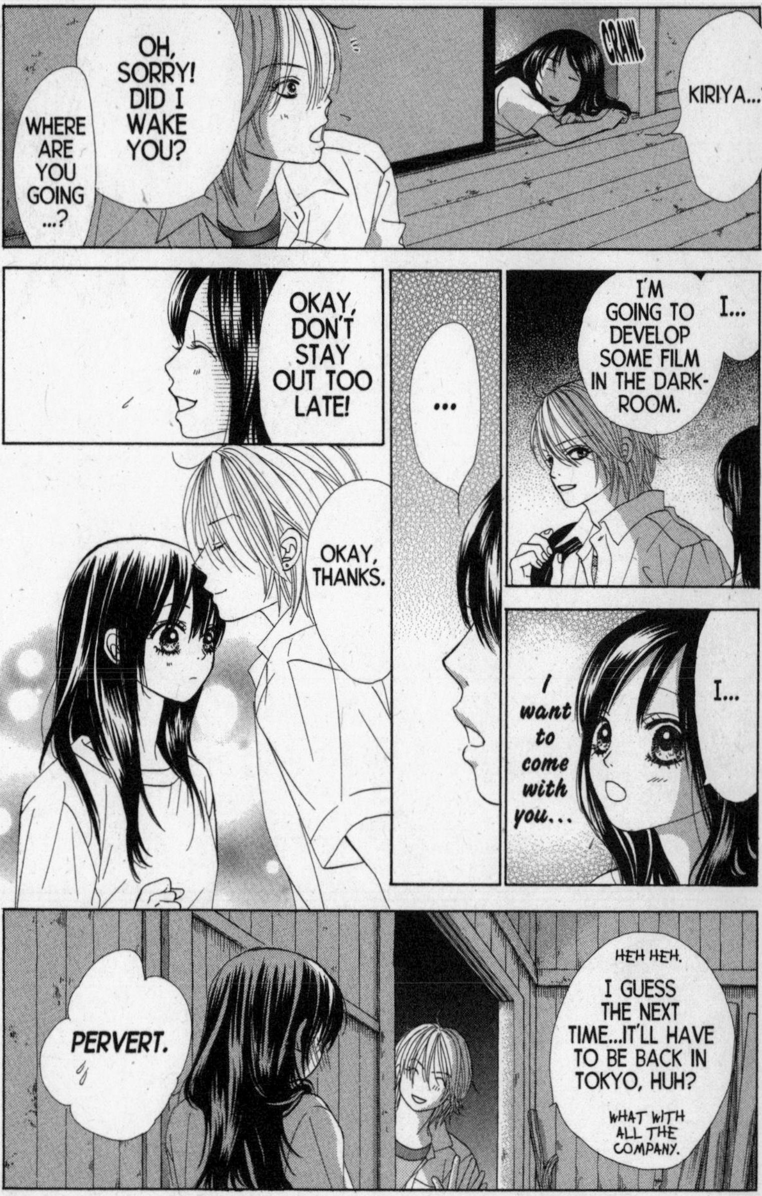
CRAWL
KIRIYA...?
OH, SORRY! DID I WAKE YOU?
WHERE ARE YOU GOING ...?
I...
I'M GOING TO DEVELOP SOME FILM IN THE DARK-ROOM.
I...
I want to come with you...
...
OKAY, DON'T STAY OUT TOO LATE!
OKAY, THANKS.
HEH HEH.
I GUESS THE NEXT TIME...IT'LL HAVE TO BE BACK IN TOKYO, HUH?
WHAT WITH ALL THE COMPANY.
PERVERT.

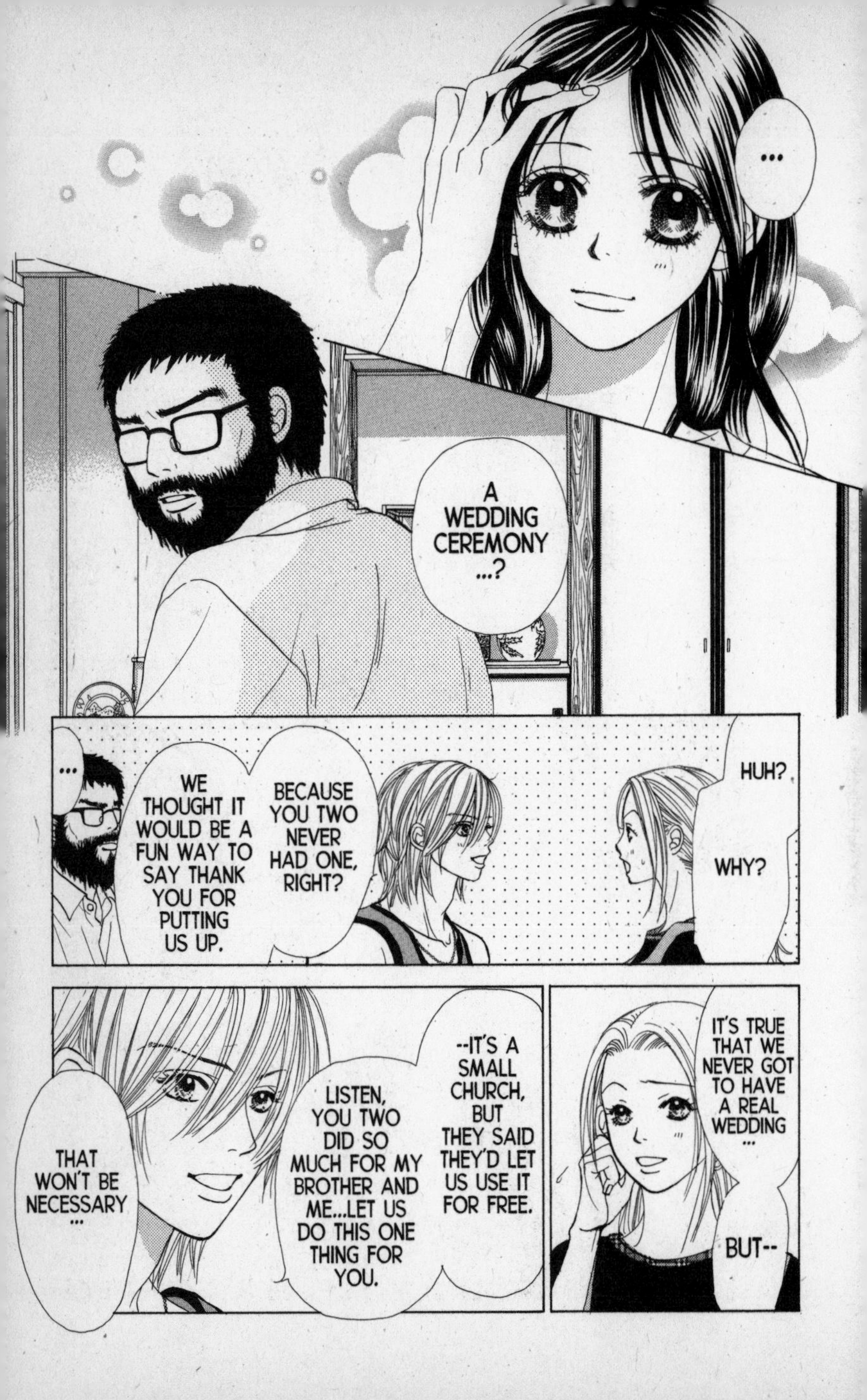
...
A WEDDING CEREMONY ...?
HUH?
WHY?
BECAUSE YOU TWO NEVER HAD ONE, RIGHT?
WE THOUGHT IT WOULD BE A FUN WAY TO SAY THANK YOU FOR PUTTING US UP.
...
IT'S TRUE THAT WE NEVER GOT TO HAVE A REAL WEDDING ...
BUT--
--IT'S A SMALL CHURCH, BUT THEY SAID THEY'D LET US USE IT FOR FREE.
LISTEN, YOU TWO DID SO MUCH FOR MY BROTHER AND ME...LET US DO THIS ONE THING FOR YOU.
THAT WON'T BE NECESSARY ...

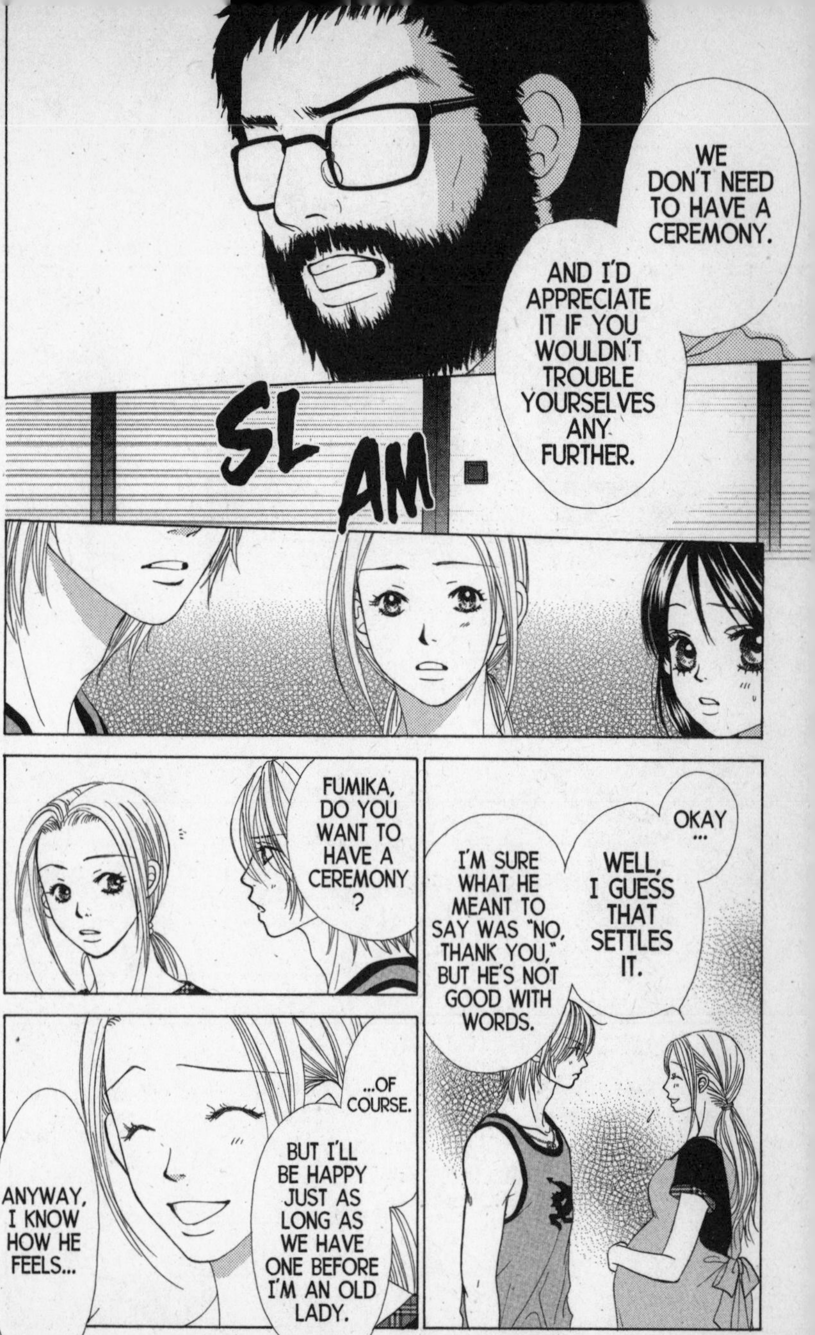
WE DON'T NEED TO HAVE A CEREMONY.
AND I'D APPRECIATE IT IF YOU WOULDN'T TROUBLE YOURSELVES ANY FURTHER.
SLAM.
OKAY...
WELL, I GUESS THAT SETTLES IT.
I'M SURE WHAT HE MEANT TO SAY WAS "NO, THANK YOU," BUT HE'S NOT GOOD WITH WORDS.
FUMIKA, DO YOU WANT TO HAVE A CEREMONY?
...OF COURSE.
BUT I'LL BE HAPPY JUST AS LONG AS WE HAVE ONE BEFORE I'M AN OLD LADY.
ANYWAY, I KNOW HOW HE FEELS...

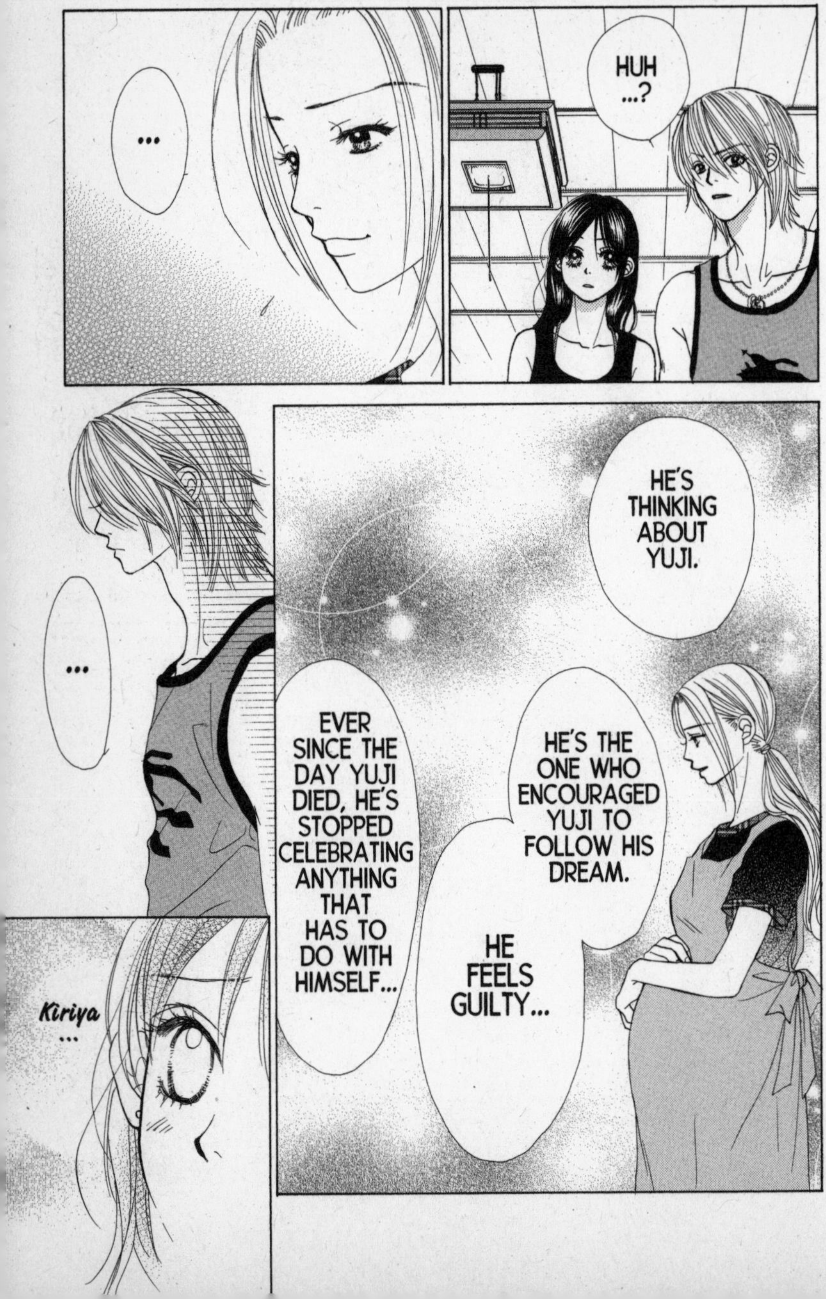
HUH ...?
...
HE'S THINKING ABOUT YUJI.
HE'S THE ONE WHO ENCOURAGED YUJI TO FOLLOW HIS DREAM.
HE FEELS GUILTY...
EVER SINCE THE DAY YUJI DIED, HE'S STOPPED CELEBRATING ANYTHING THAT HAS TO DO WITH HIMSELF...
...
Kiriya ...

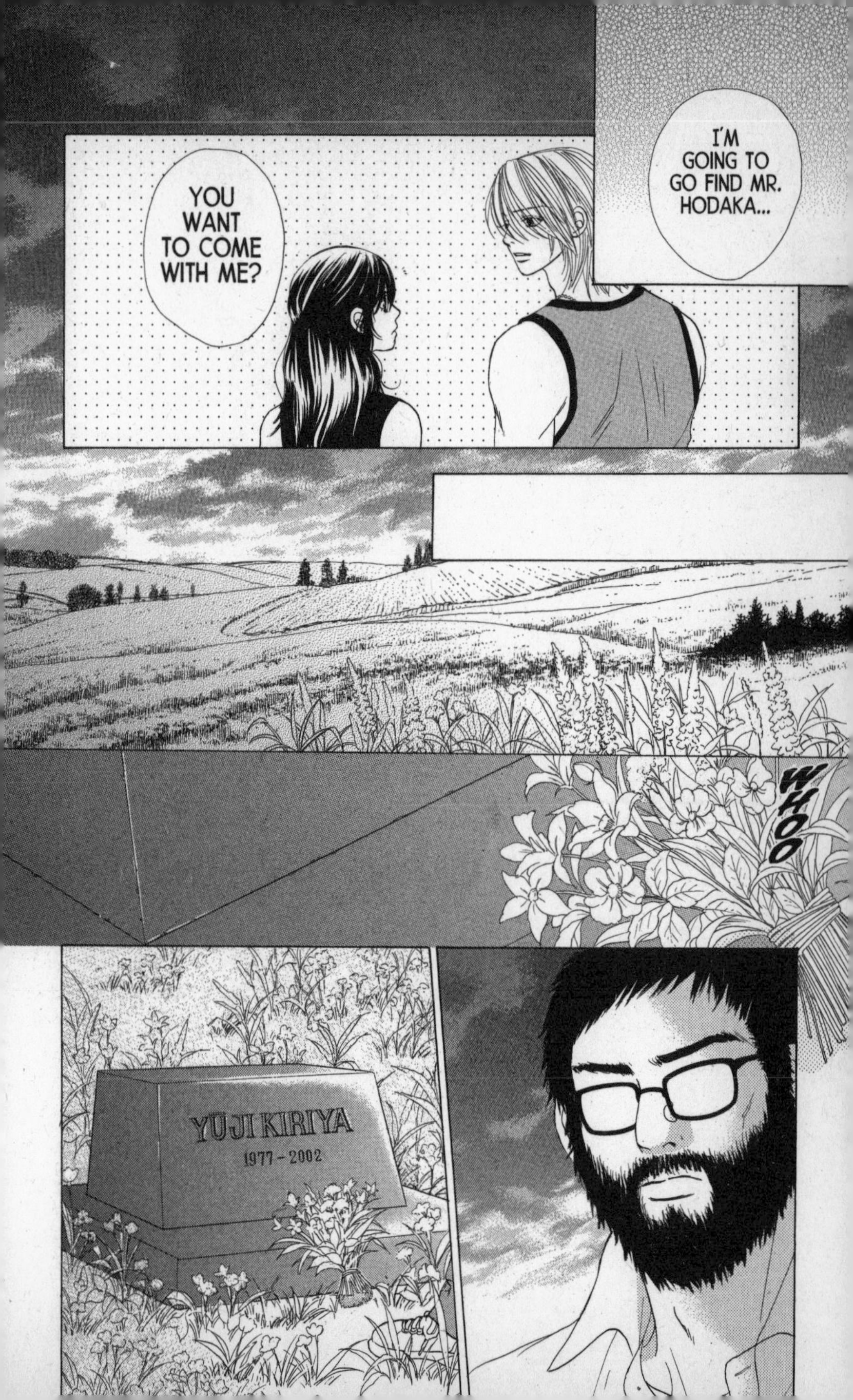
I'M GOING TO GO FIND MR. HODAKA...
YOU WANT TO COME WITH ME?
WHOO
YUJI KIRIYA
1977 - 2002

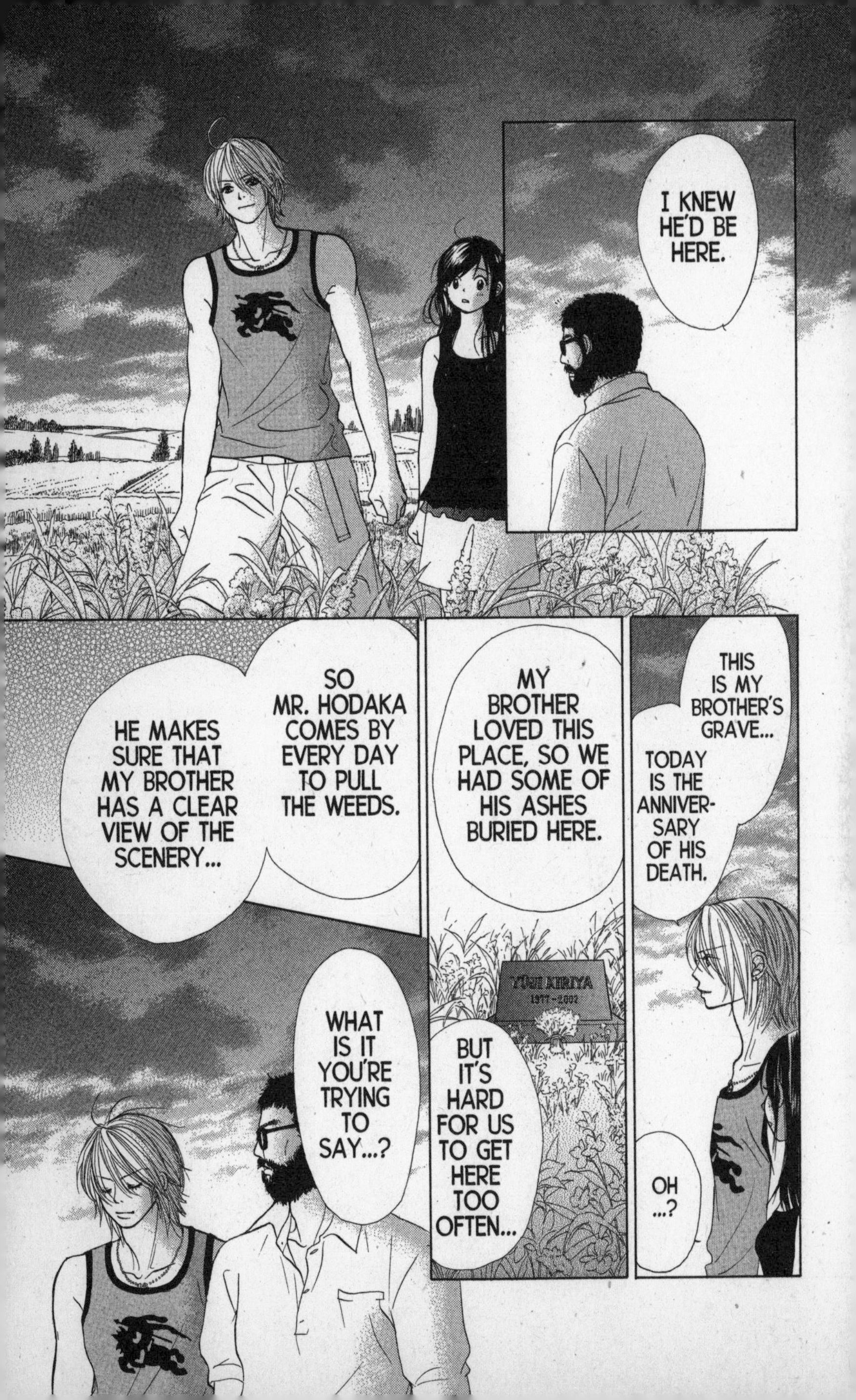
I KNEW HE'D BE HERE.
THIS IS MY BROTHER'S GRAVE...
TODAY IS THE ANNIVERSARY OF HIS DEATH.
OH ...?
MY BROTHER LOVED THIS PLACE, SO WE HAD SOME OF HIS ASHES BURIED HERE.
YUJI KIRIYA
BUT IT'S HARD FOR US TO GET HERE TOO OFTEN...
SO MR. HODAKA COMES BY EVERY DAY TO PULL THE WEEDS.
HE MAKES SURE THAT MY BROTHER HAS A CLEAR VIEW OF THE SCENERY...
WHAT IS IT YOU'RE TRYING TO SAY...?

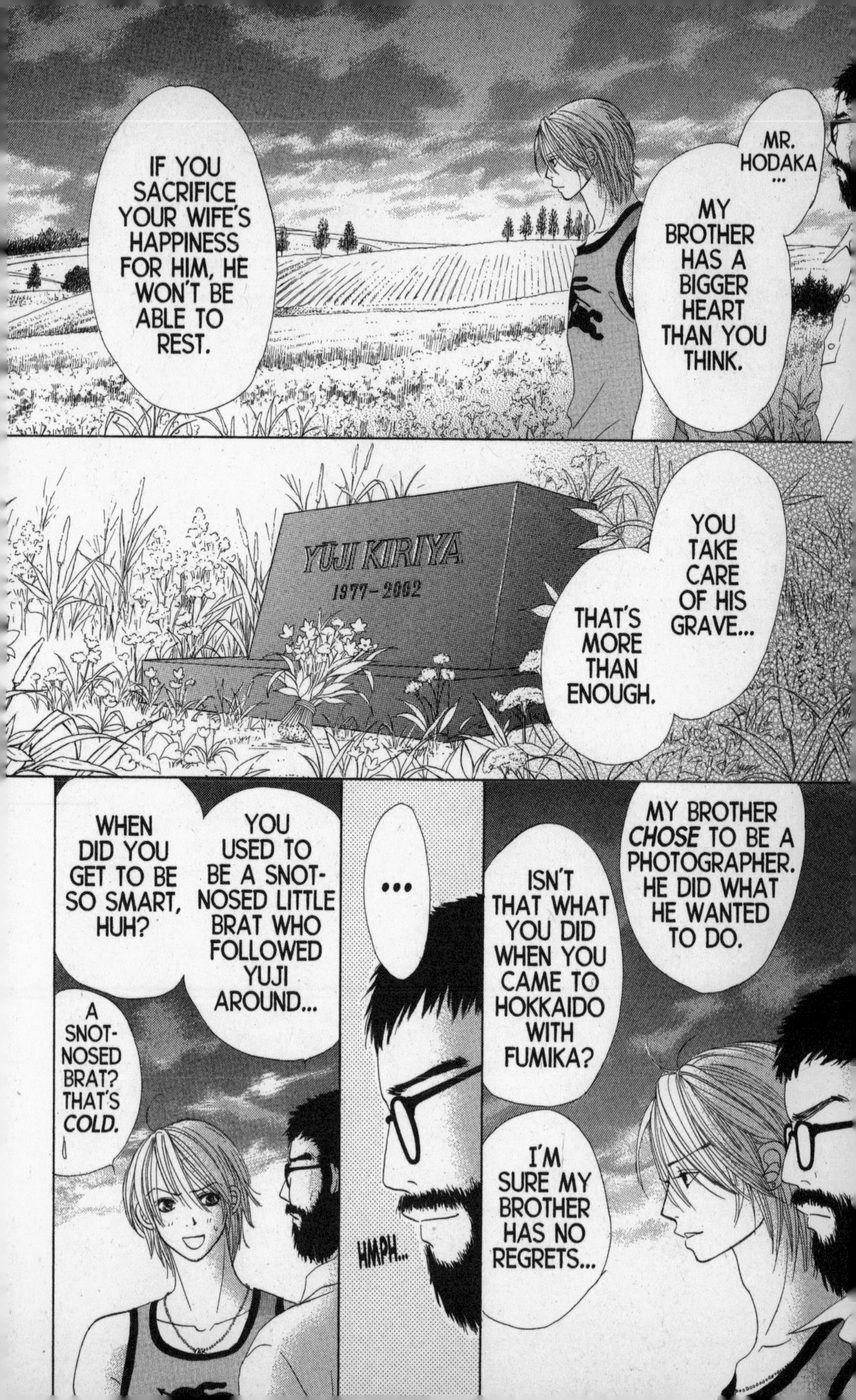
MR. HODAKA...
MY BROTHER HAS A BIGGER HEART THAN YOU THINK.
IF YOU SACRIFICE YOUR WIFE'S HAPPINESS FOR HIM, HE WON'T BE ABLE TO REST.
YUJI KIRIYA
1977-2002
YOU TAKE CARE OF HIS GRAVE...
THAT'S MORE THAN ENOUGH.
MY BROTHER *CHOSE* TO BE A PHOTOGRAPHER. HE DID WHAT HE WANTED TO DO.
ISN'T THAT WHAT YOU DID WHEN YOU CAME TO HOKKAIDO WITH FUMIKA?
I'M SURE MY BROTHER HAS NO REGRETS...
...
HMPH...
YOU USED TO BE A SNOT-NOSED LITTLE BRAT WHO FOLLOWED YUJI AROUND...
WHEN DID YOU GET TO BE SO SMART, HUH?
A SNOT-NOSED BRAT? THAT'S *COLD.*

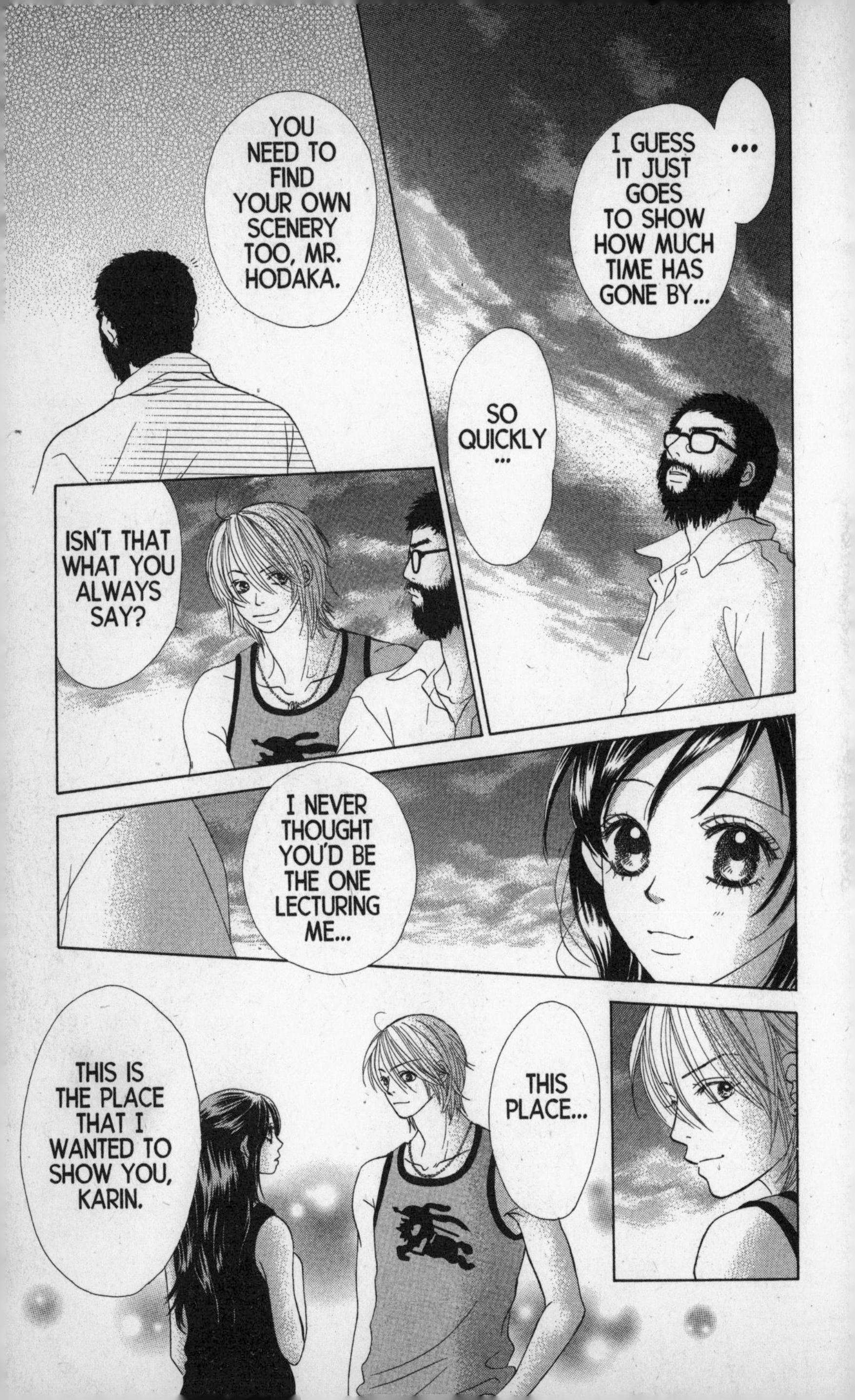
...
I GUESS IT JUST GOES TO SHOW HOW MUCH TIME HAS GONE BY...
SO QUICKLY ...
YOU NEED TO FIND YOUR OWN SCENERY TOO, MR. HODAKA.
ISN'T THAT WHAT YOU ALWAYS SAY?
I NEVER THOUGHT YOU'D BE THE ONE LECTURING ME...
THIS PLACE...
THIS IS THE PLACE THAT I WANTED TO SHOW YOU, KARIN.

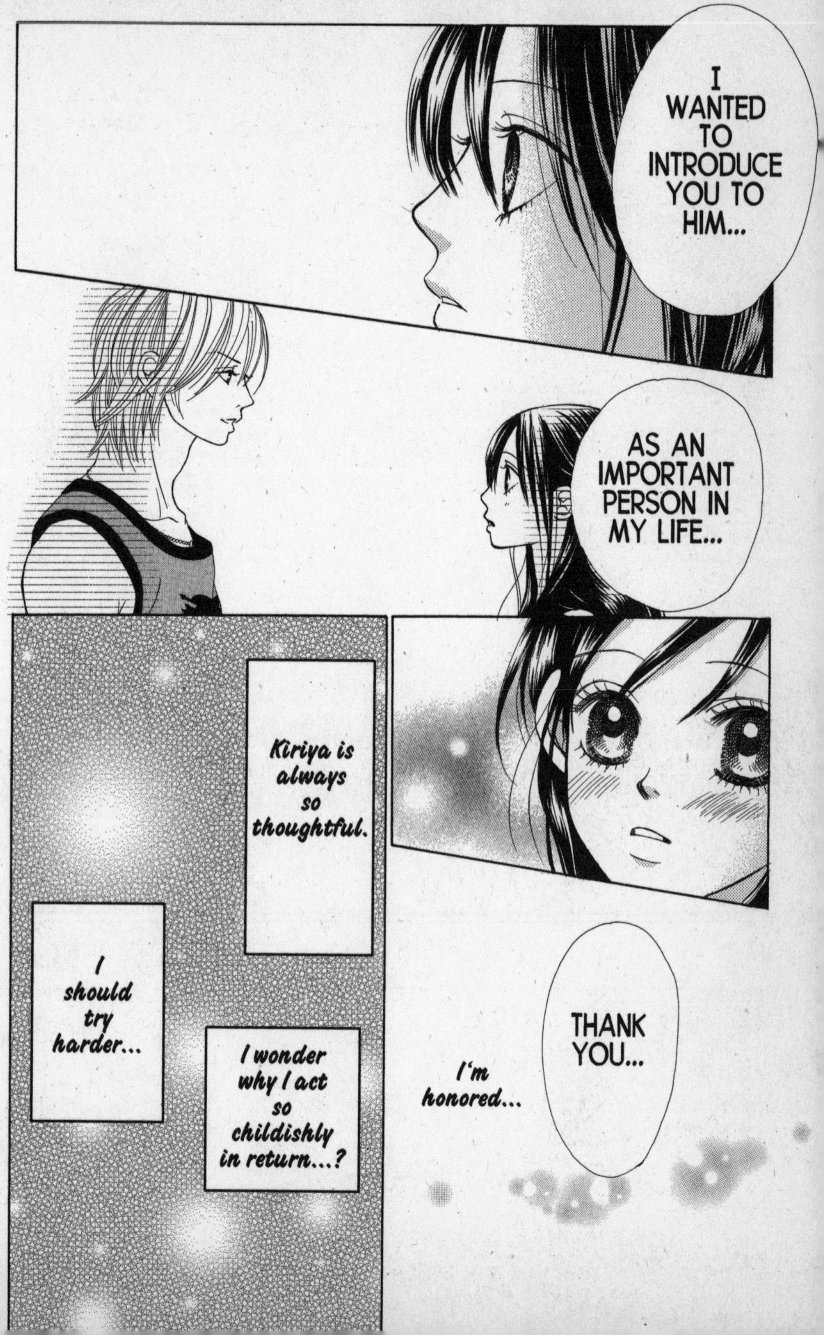
I WANTED TO INTRODUCE YOU TO HIM...
AS AN IMPORTANT PERSON IN MY LIFE...
THANK YOU...
I'm honored...
Kiriya is always so thoughtful.
I wonder why I act so childishly in return...?
I should try harder...

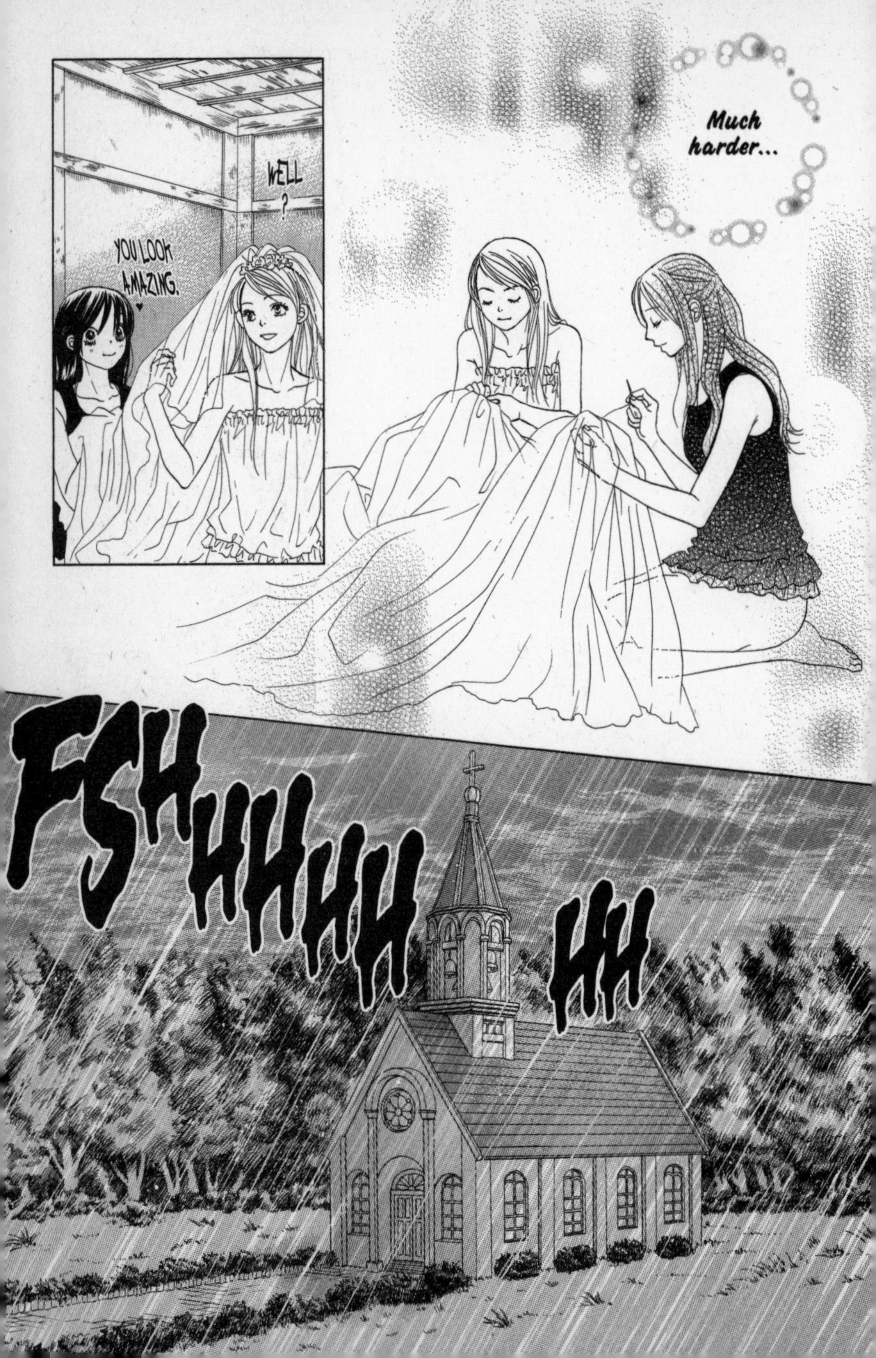
Much harder...
WELL?
YOU LOOK AMAZING.
FSHHHHHHHH

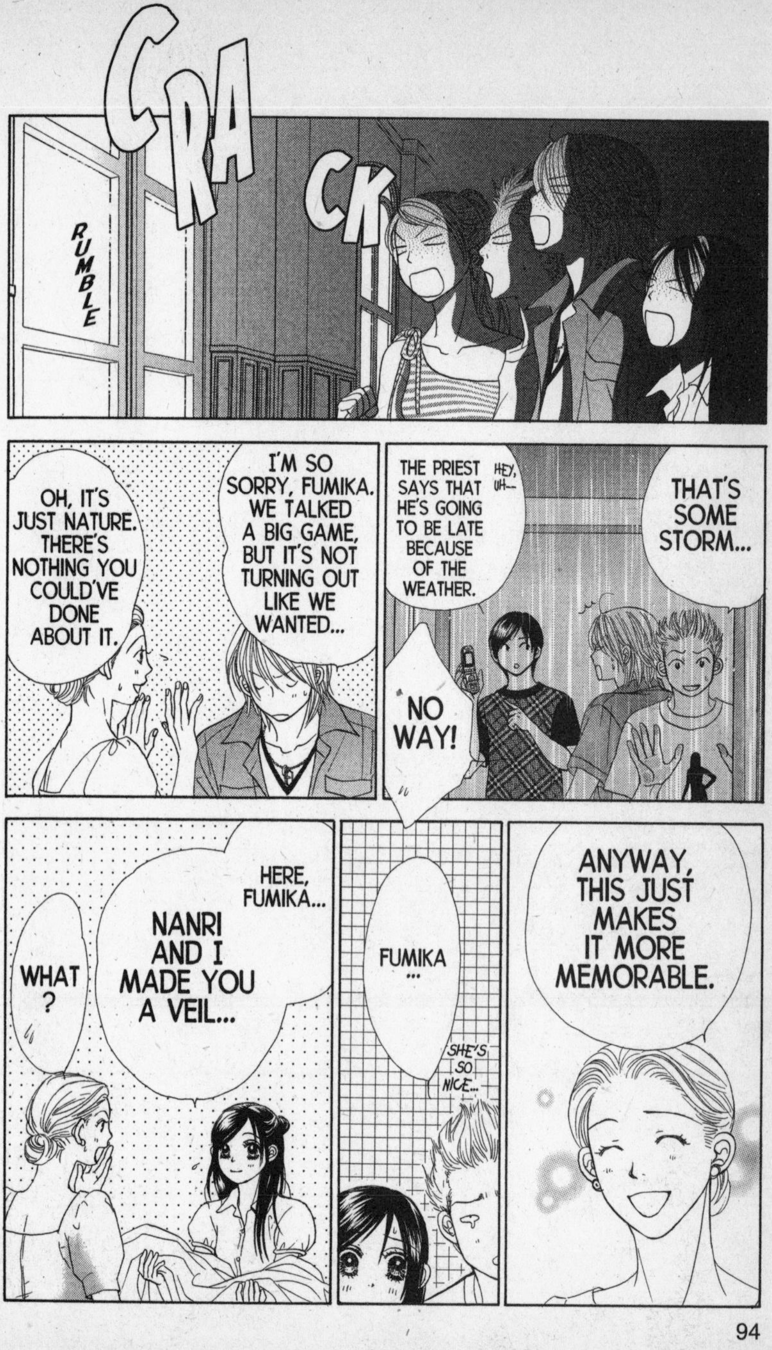
CRACK
RUMBLE
THAT'S SOME STORM...
HEY, UH--
THE PRIEST SAYS THAT HE'S GOING TO BE LATE BECAUSE OF THE WEATHER.
NO WAY!
I'M SO SORRY, FUMIKA. WE TALKED A BIG GAME, BUT IT'S NOT TURNING OUT LIKE WE WANTED...
OH, IT'S JUST NATURE. THERE'S NOTHING YOU COULD'VE DONE ABOUT IT.
ANYWAY, THIS JUST MAKES IT MORE MEMORABLE.
FUMIKA...
SHE'S SO NICE...
HERE, FUMIKA... NANRI AND I MADE YOU A VEIL...
WHAT?

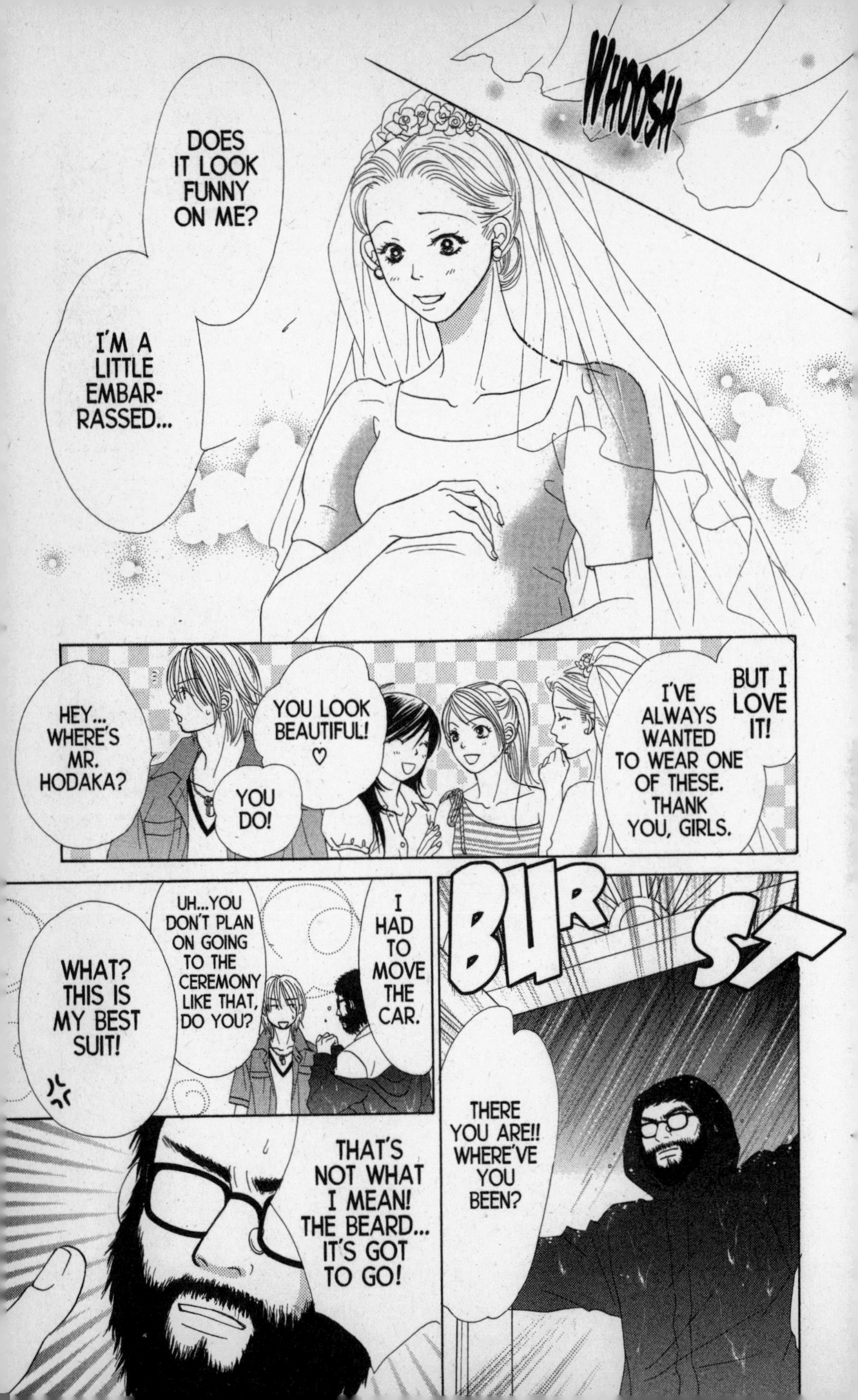
WHOOSH
DOES IT LOOK FUNNY ON ME?
I'M A LITTLE EMBARRASSED...
BUT I LOVE IT!
I'VE ALWAYS WANTED TO WEAR ONE OF THESE. THANK YOU, GIRLS.
YOU LOOK BEAUTIFUL! ♡
YOU DO!
HEY... WHERE'S MR. HODAKA?
BURST
THERE YOU ARE!! WHERE'VE YOU BEEN?
I HAD TO MOVE THE CAR.
UH...YOU DON'T PLAN ON GOING TO THE CEREMONY LIKE THAT, DO YOU?
WHAT? THIS IS MY BEST SUIT!
THAT'S NOT WHAT I MEAN! THE BEARD... IT'S GOT TO GO!

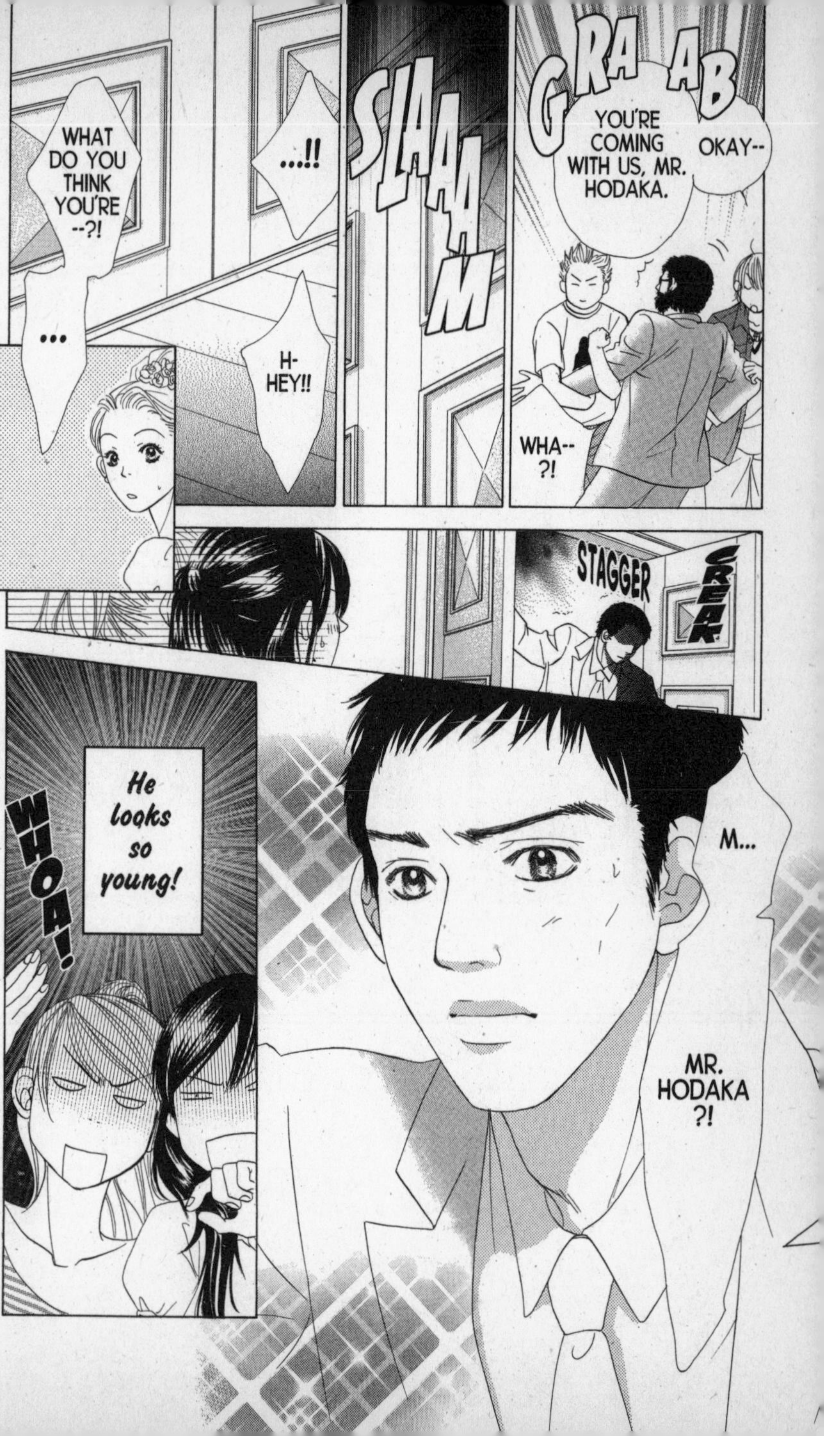
GRAAB
YOU'RE COMING WITH US, MR. HODAKA.
OKAY--
WHA--?!
SLAAAAM
...!!
WHAT DO YOU THINK YOU'RE --?!
H-HEY!!
...
CREAK
STAGGER
M...
MR. HODAKA ?!
WHOA!
He looks so young!

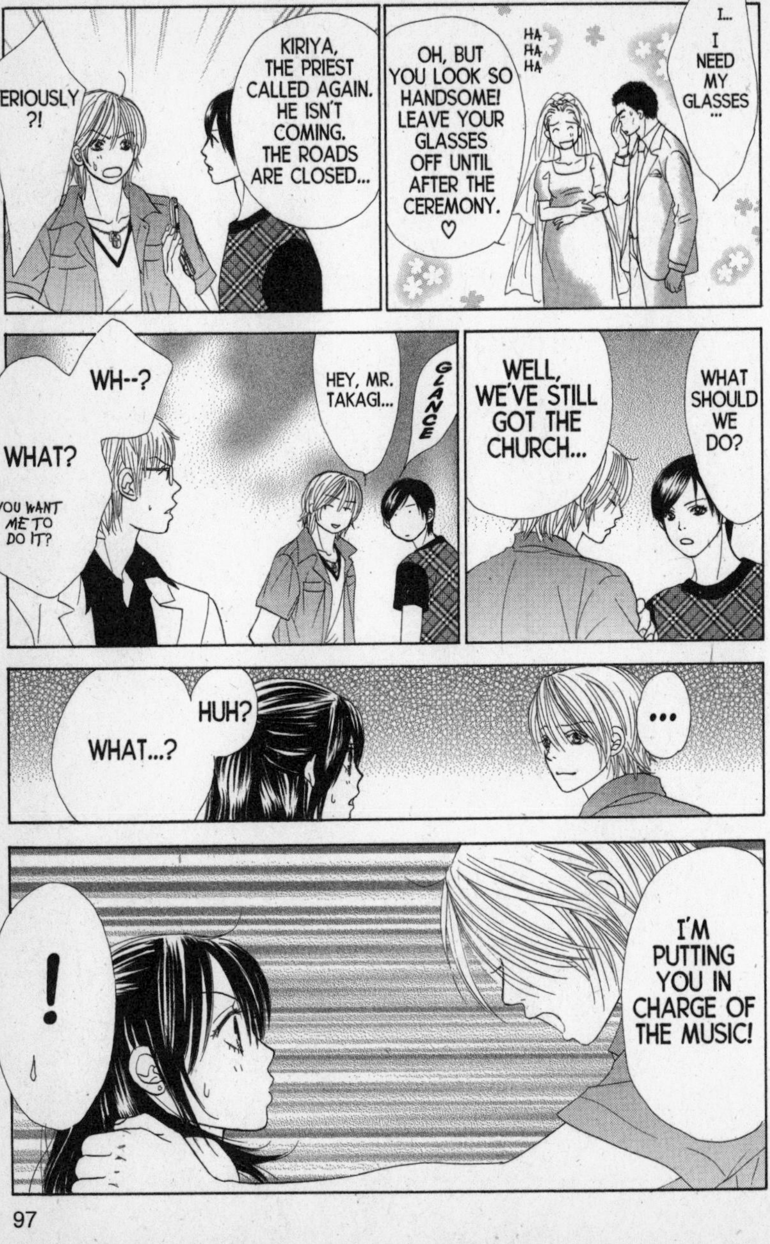
I... I NEED MY GLASSES...
HA HA HA
OH, BUT YOU LOOK SO HANDSOME! LEAVE YOUR GLASSES OFF UNTIL AFTER THE CEREMONY. ♡
KIRIYA, THE PRIEST CALLED AGAIN. HE ISN'T COMING. THE ROADS ARE CLOSED...
SERIOUSLY?!
WHAT SHOULD WE DO?
WELL, WE'VE STILL GOT THE CHURCH...
GLANCE
HEY, MR. TAKAGI...
WH--? WHAT? YOU WANT ME TO DO IT?
...
HUH? WHAT...?
I'M PUTTING YOU IN CHARGE OF THE MUSIC!
!

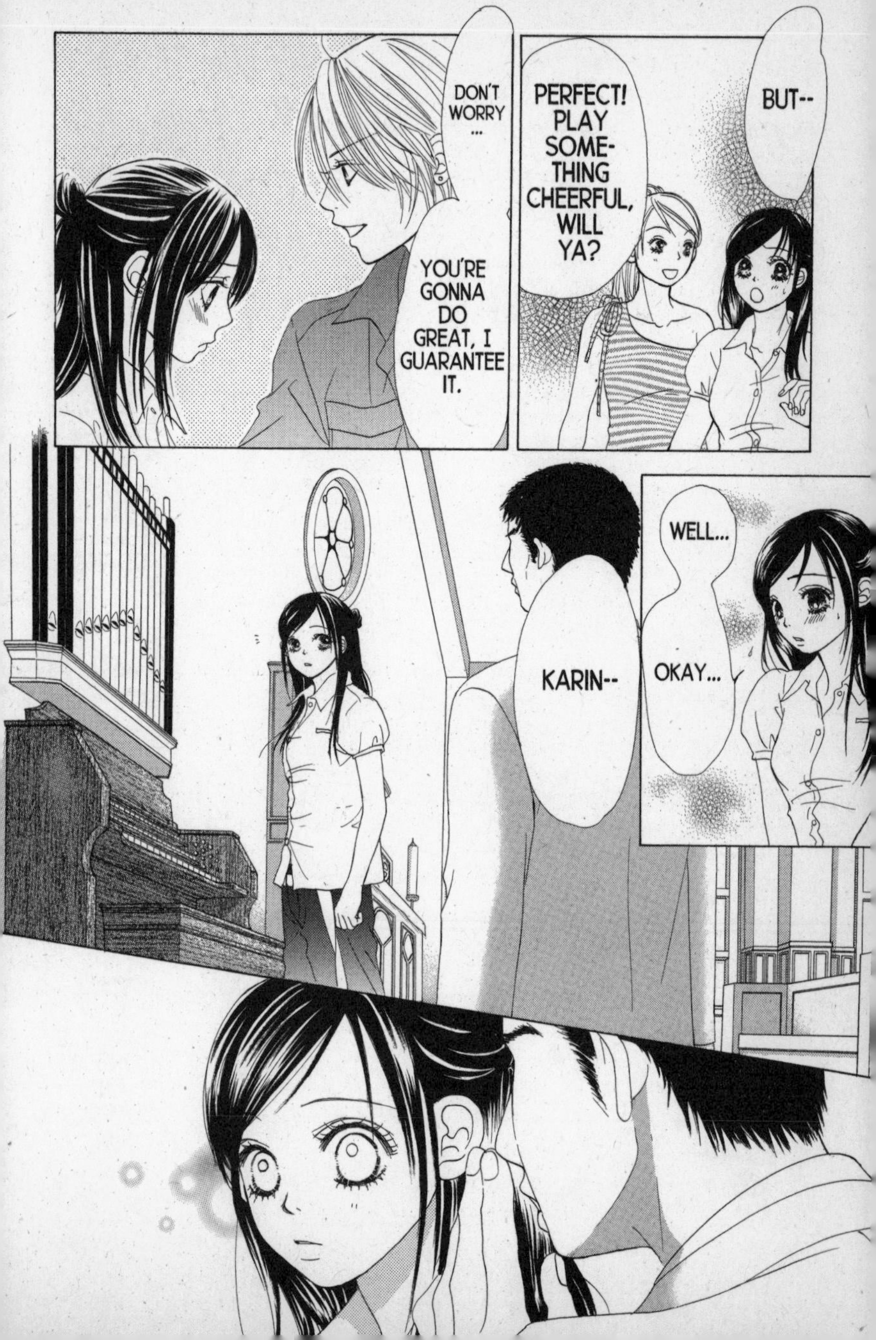
BUT--
PERFECT! PLAY SOME-THING CHEERFUL, WILL YA?
DON'T WORRY ...
YOU'RE GONNA DO GREAT, I GUARANTEE IT.
WELL...
OKAY...
KARIN--

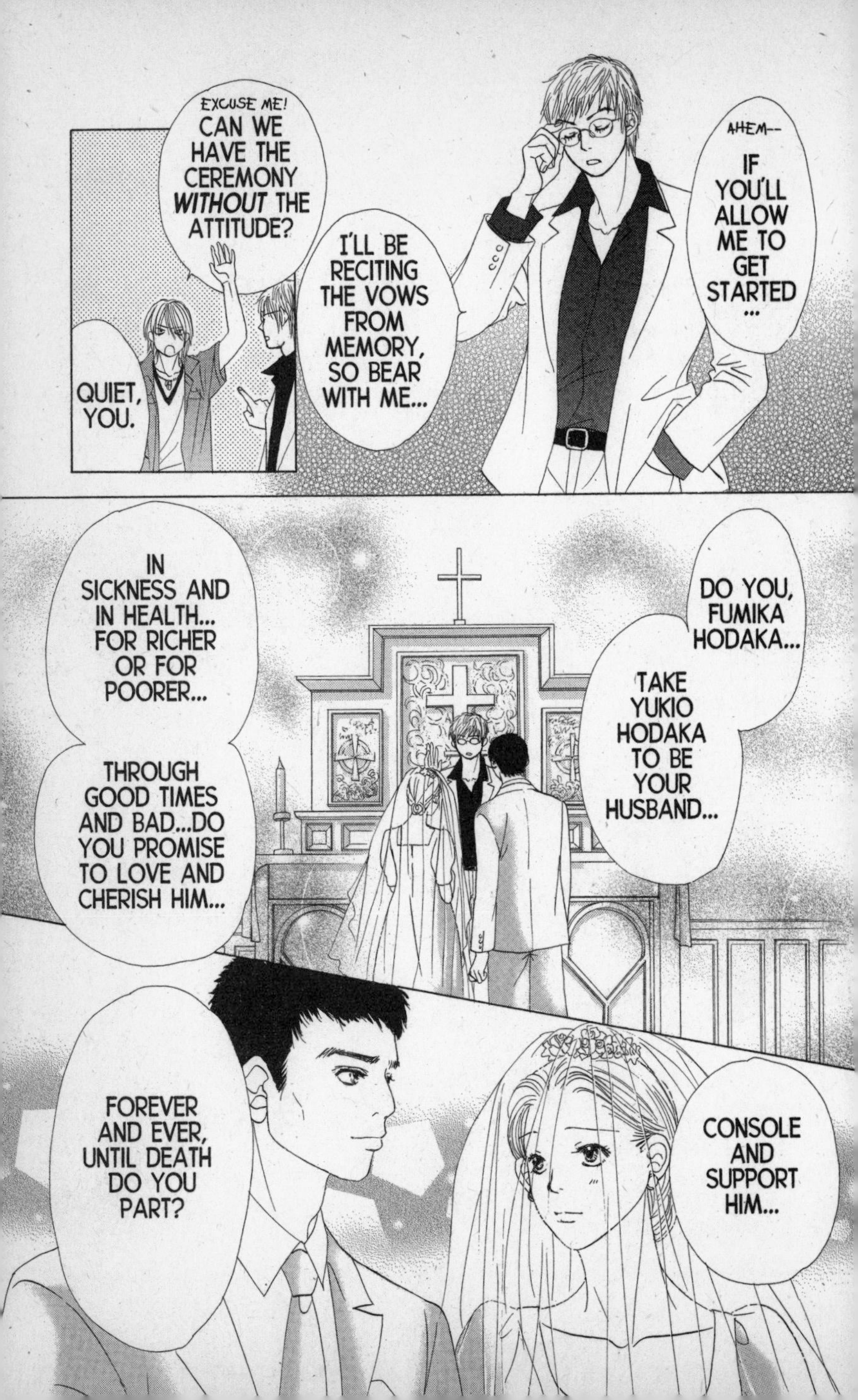
AHEM-- IF YOU'LL ALLOW ME TO GET STARTED...
I'LL BE RECITING THE VOWS FROM MEMORY, SO BEAR WITH ME...
EXCUSE ME! CAN WE HAVE THE CEREMONY *WITHOUT* THE ATTITUDE?
QUIET, YOU.
DO YOU, FUMIKA HODAKA...
TAKE YUKIO HODAKA TO BE YOUR HUSBAND...
IN SICKNESS AND IN HEALTH... FOR RICHER OR FOR POORER...
THROUGH GOOD TIMES AND BAD...DO YOU PROMISE TO LOVE AND CHERISH HIM...
CONSOLE AND SUPPORT HIM...
FOREVER AND EVER, UNTIL DEATH DO YOU PART?

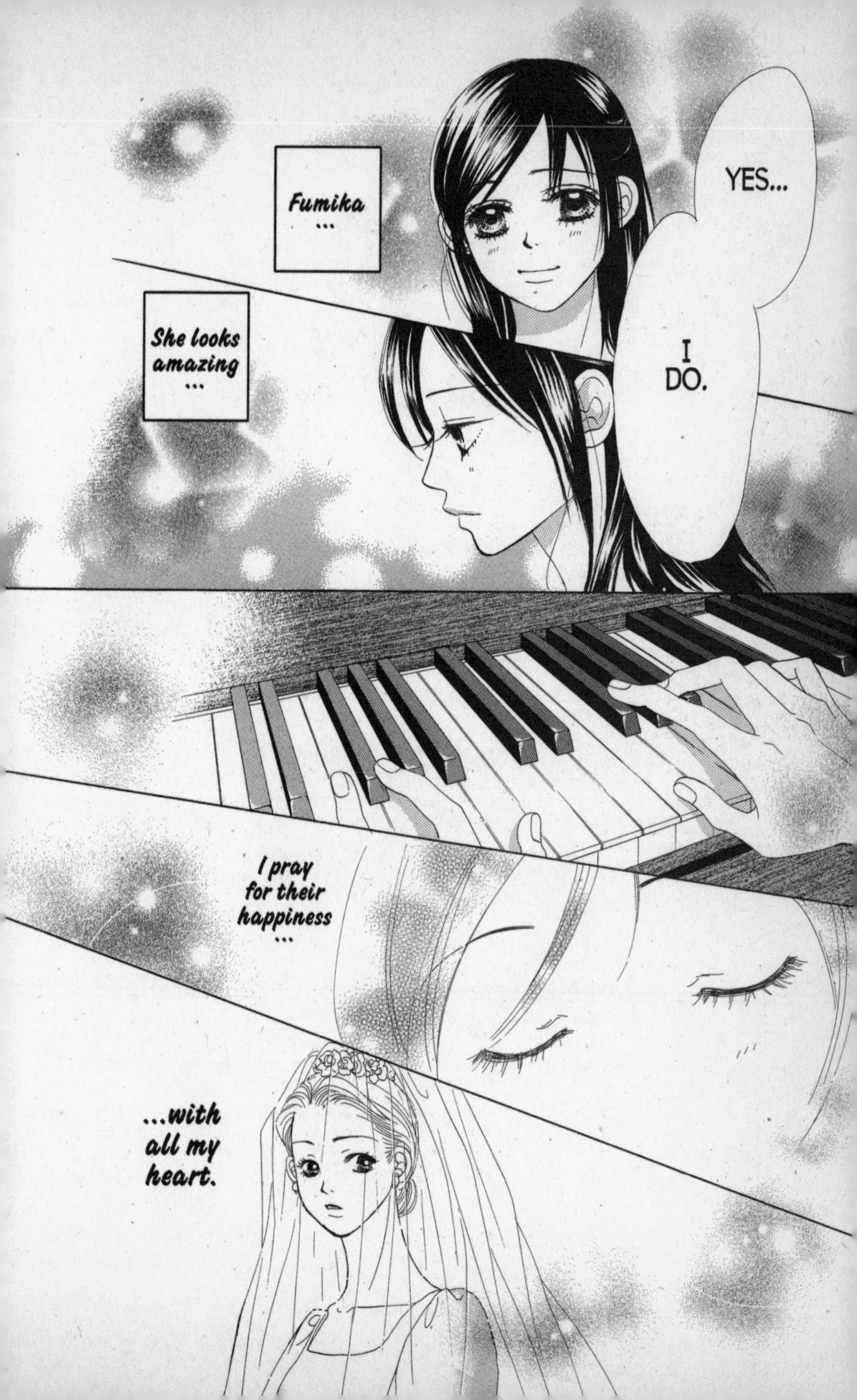
YES...
Fumika ...
I DO.
She looks amazing ...
I pray for their happiness ...
...with all my heart.

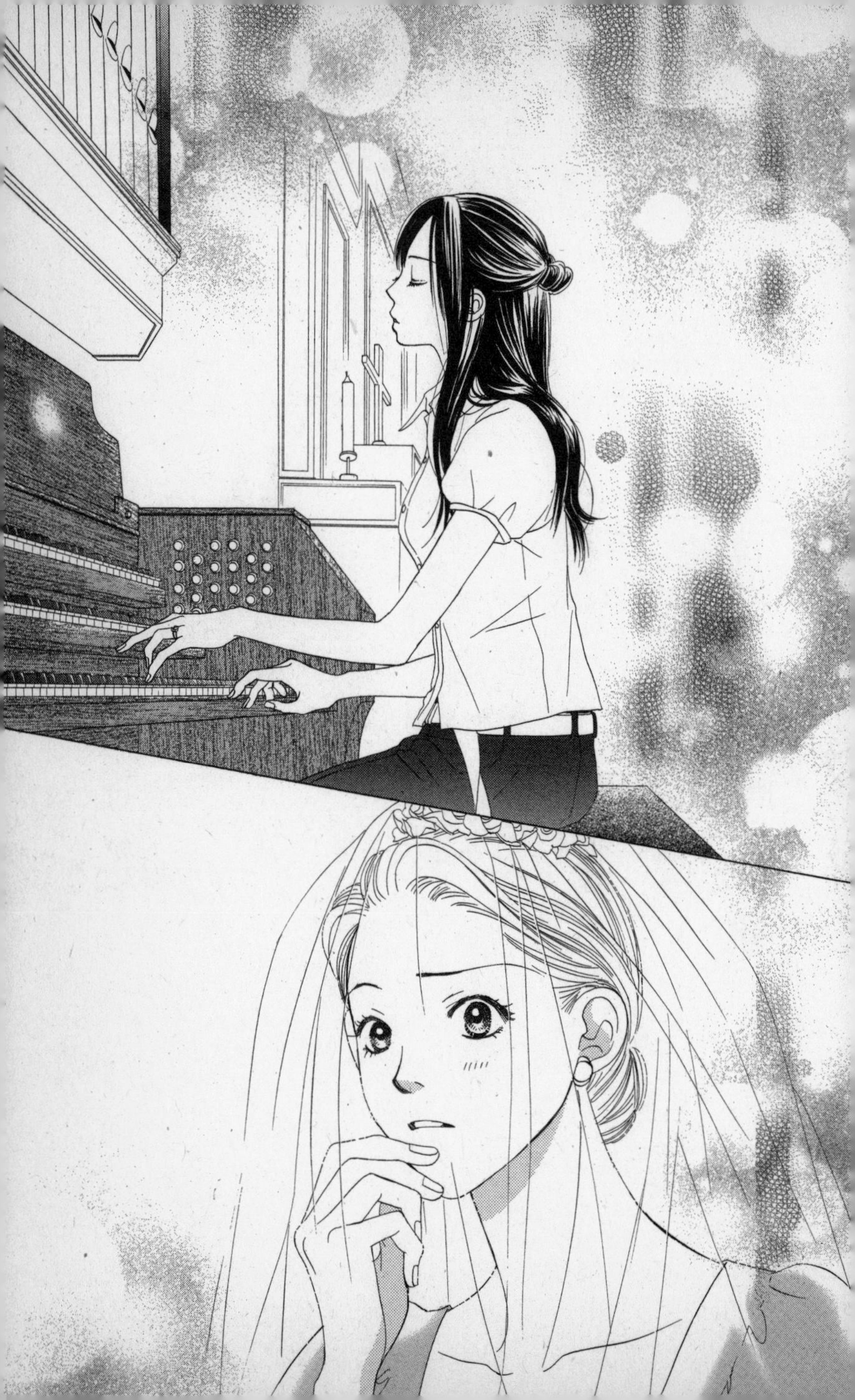

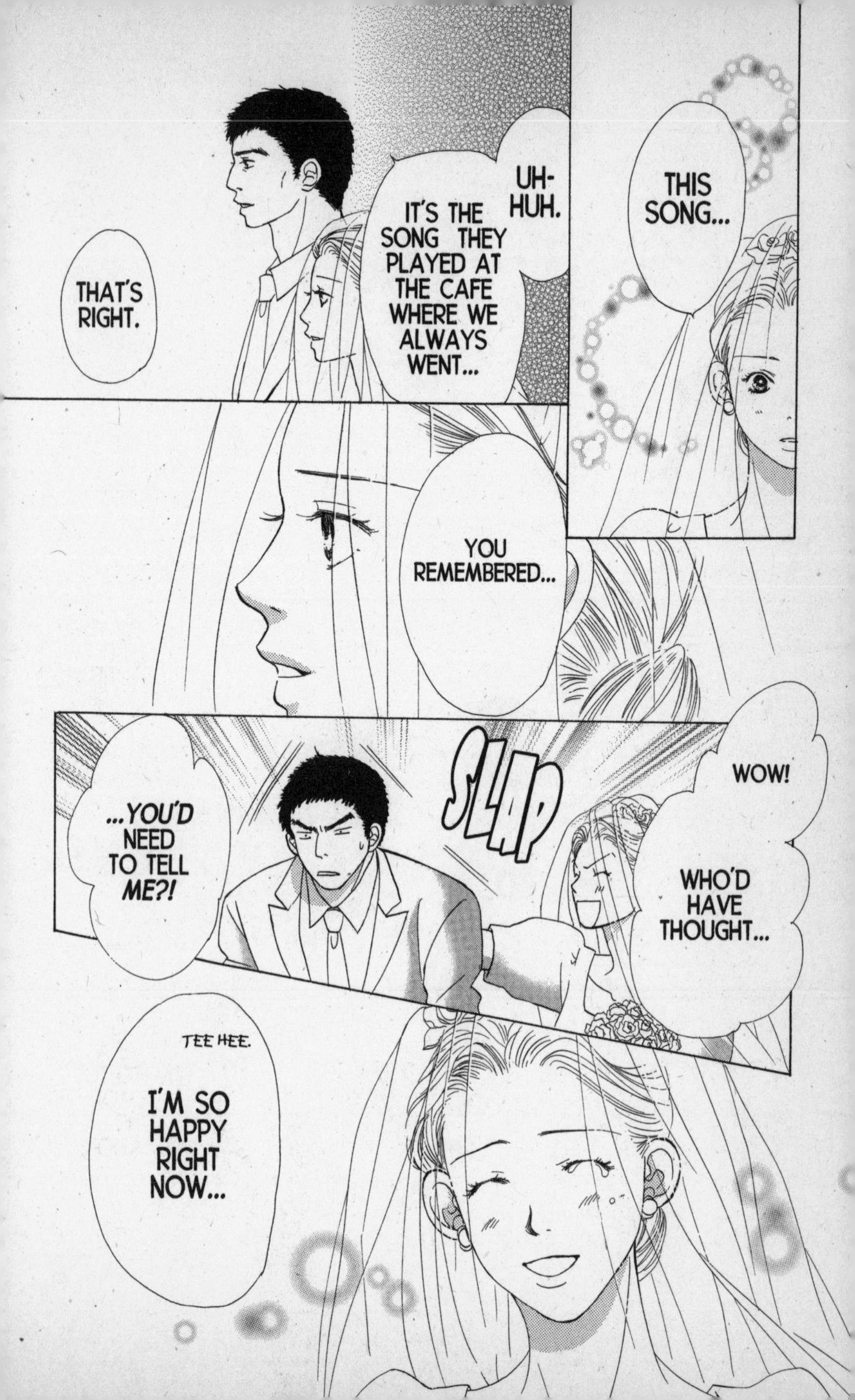
THIS SONG...
UH-HUH.
IT'S THE SONG THEY PLAYED AT THE CAFE WHERE WE ALWAYS WENT...
THAT'S RIGHT.
YOU REMEMBERED...
WOW!
WHO'D HAVE THOUGHT...
SLAP
...YOU'D NEED TO TELL ME?!
TEE HEE.
I'M SO HAPPY RIGHT NOW...

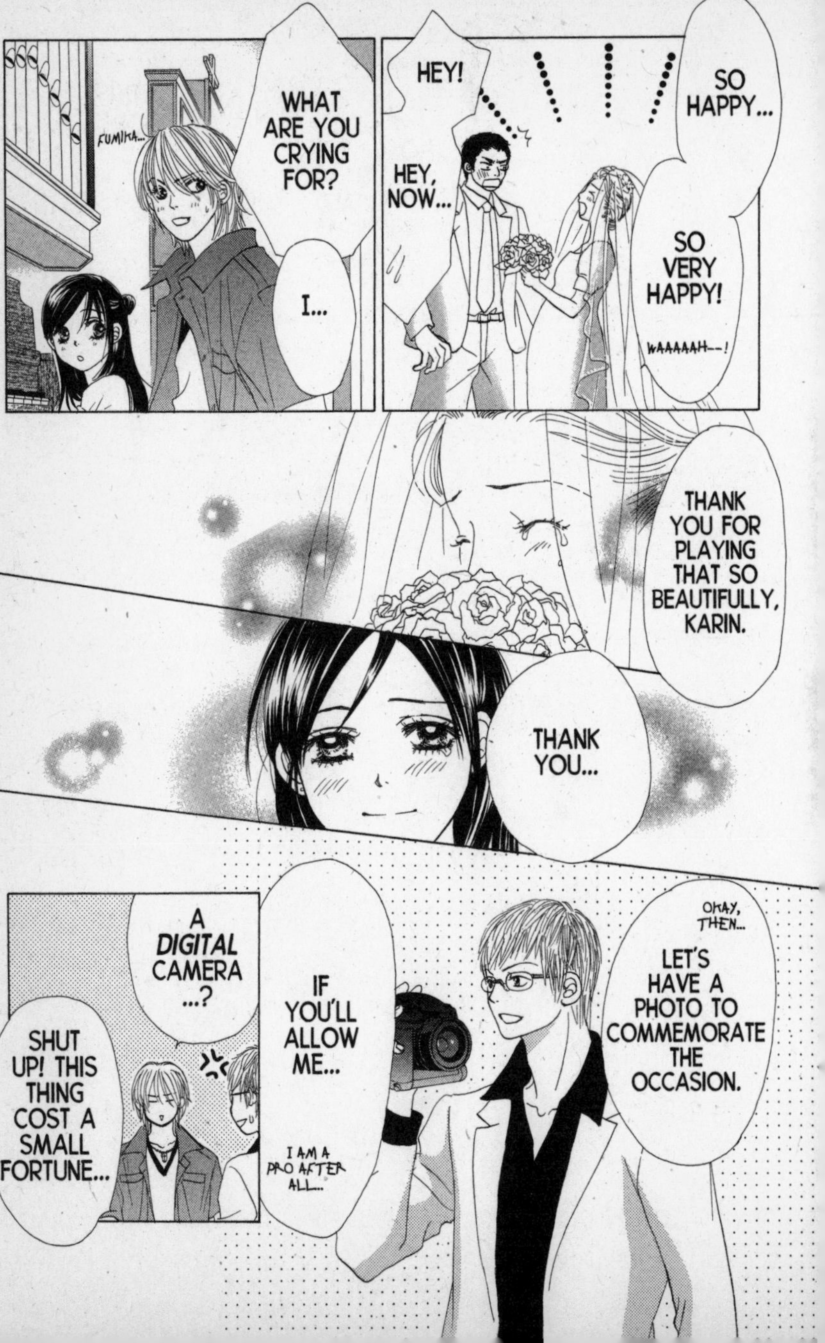
SO HAPPY...
. . .
HEY!
HEY, NOW...
SO VERY HAPPY!
WAAAAAH—!
FUMIKA...
WHAT ARE YOU CRYING FOR?
I...
THANK YOU FOR PLAYING THAT SO BEAUTIFULLY, KARIN.
THANK YOU...
OKAY, THEN...
LET'S HAVE A PHOTO TO COMMEMORATE THE OCCASION.
IF YOU'LL ALLOW ME...
I AM A PRO AFTER ALL...
A *DIGITAL* CAMERA ...?
SHUT UP! THIS THING COST A SMALL FORTUNE...

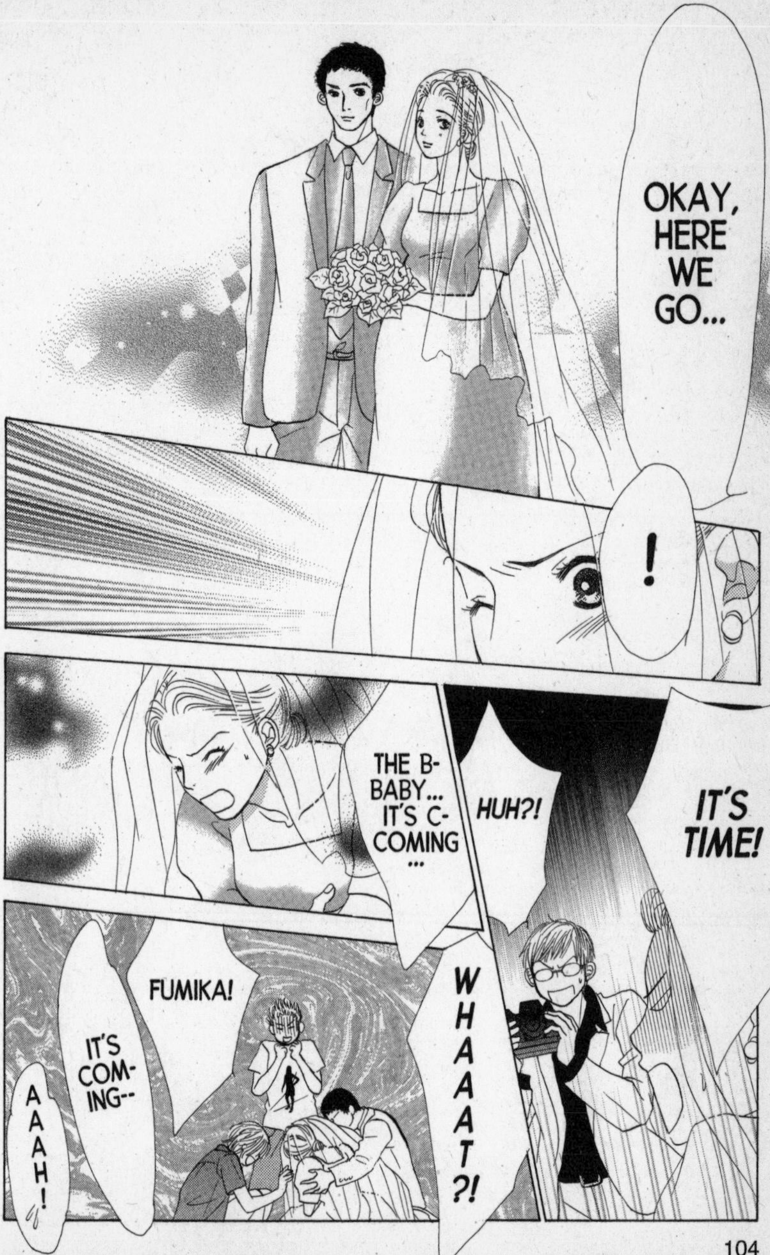
OKAY, HERE WE GO...
!
IT'S TIME!
HUH?!
WHAAAAT?!
THE B-BABY... IT'S C-COMING...
FUMIKA!
IT'S COMING--
AAAH!

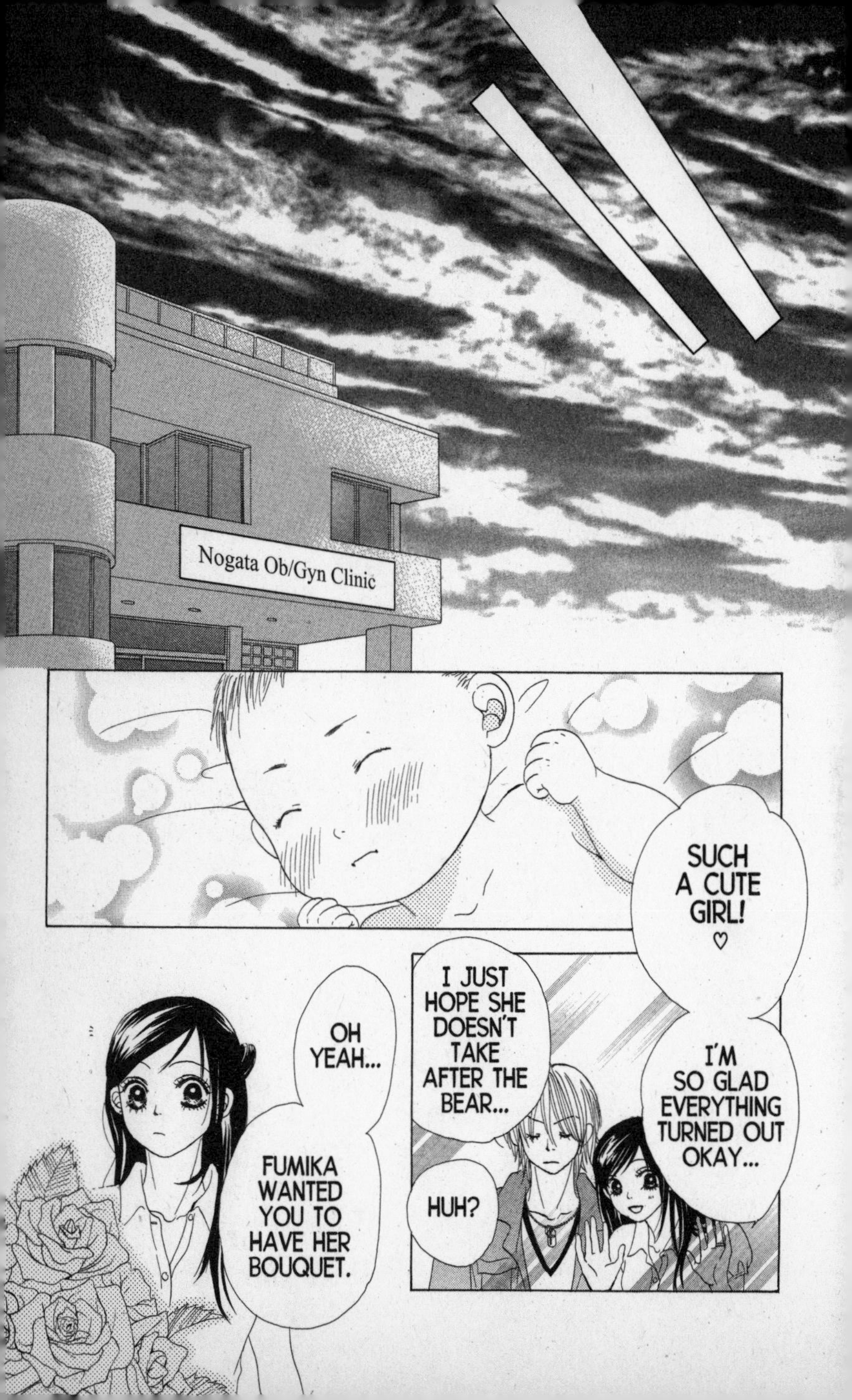
Nogata Ob/Gyn Clinic
SUCH A CUTE GIRL! ♡
I'M SO GLAD EVERYTHING TURNED OUT OKAY...
I JUST HOPE SHE DOESN'T TAKE AFTER THE BEAR...
HUH?
OH YEAH...
FUMIKA WANTED YOU TO HAVE HER BOUQUET.

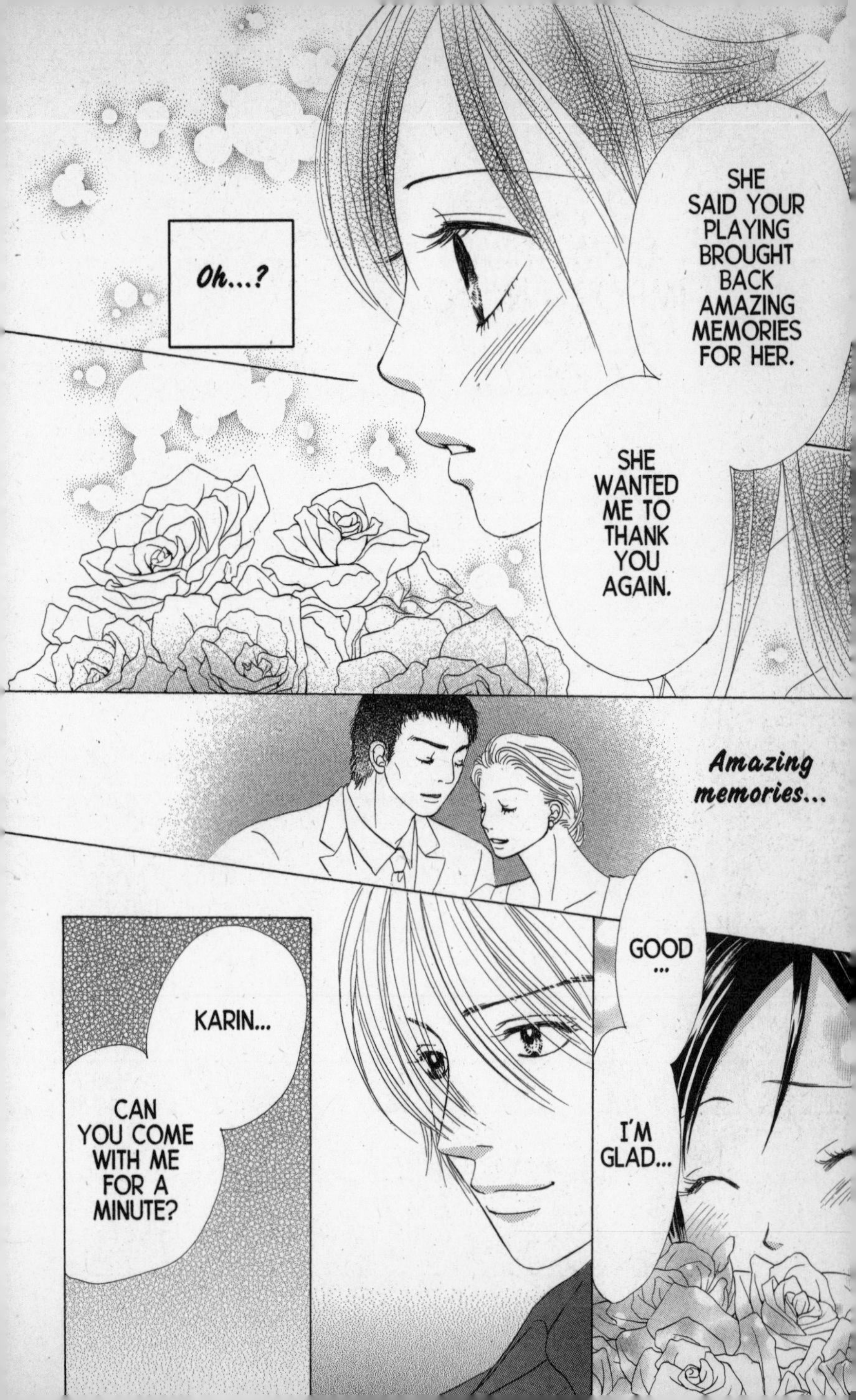
SHE SAID YOUR PLAYING BROUGHT BACK AMAZING MEMORIES FOR HER.
SHE WANTED ME TO THANK YOU AGAIN.
Oh...?
Amazing memories...
GOOD...
I'M GLAD...
KARIN...
CAN YOU COME WITH ME FOR A MINUTE?

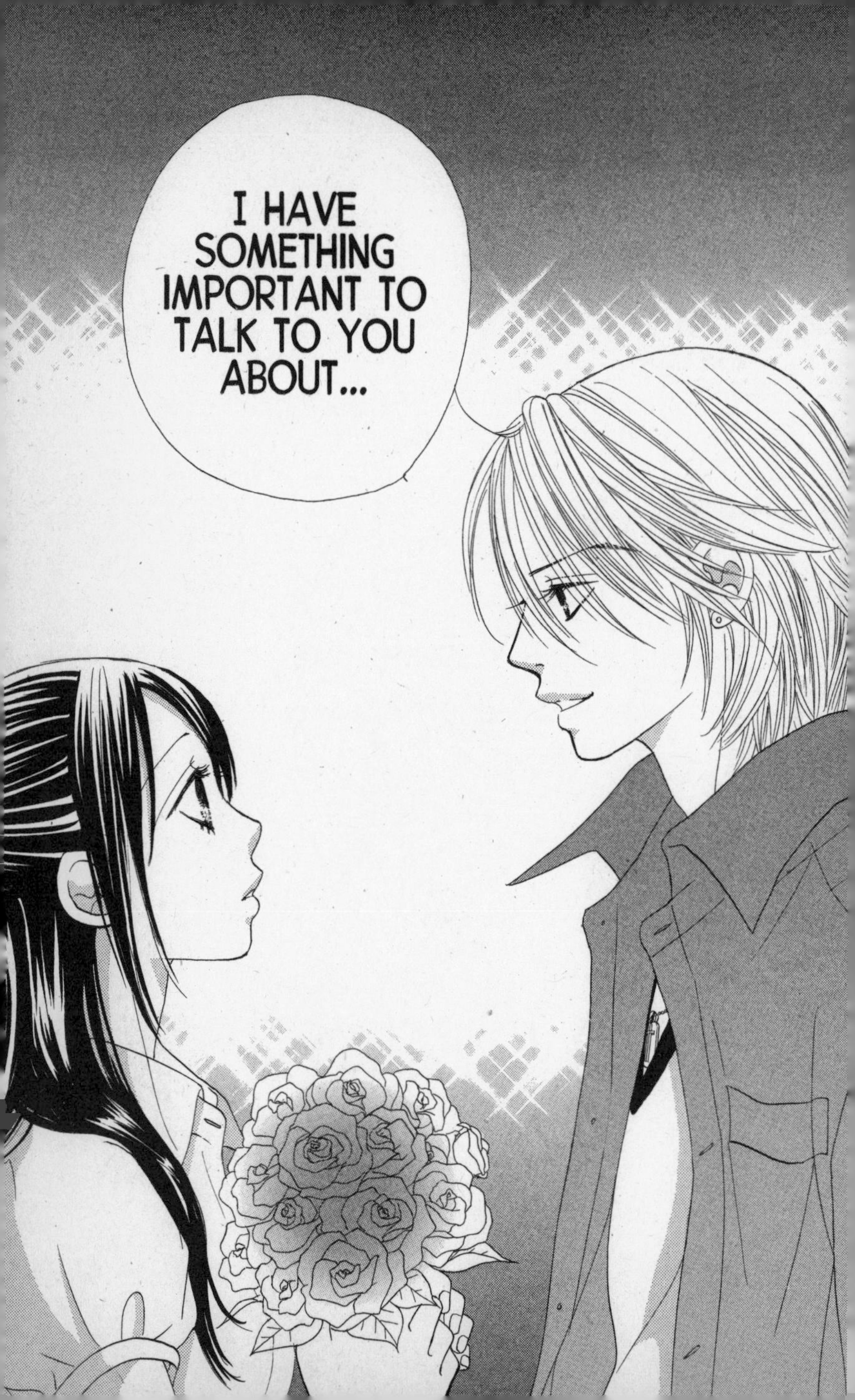
I HAVE SOMETHING IMPORTANT TO TALK TO YOU ABOUT...

彼 KARE
First Love

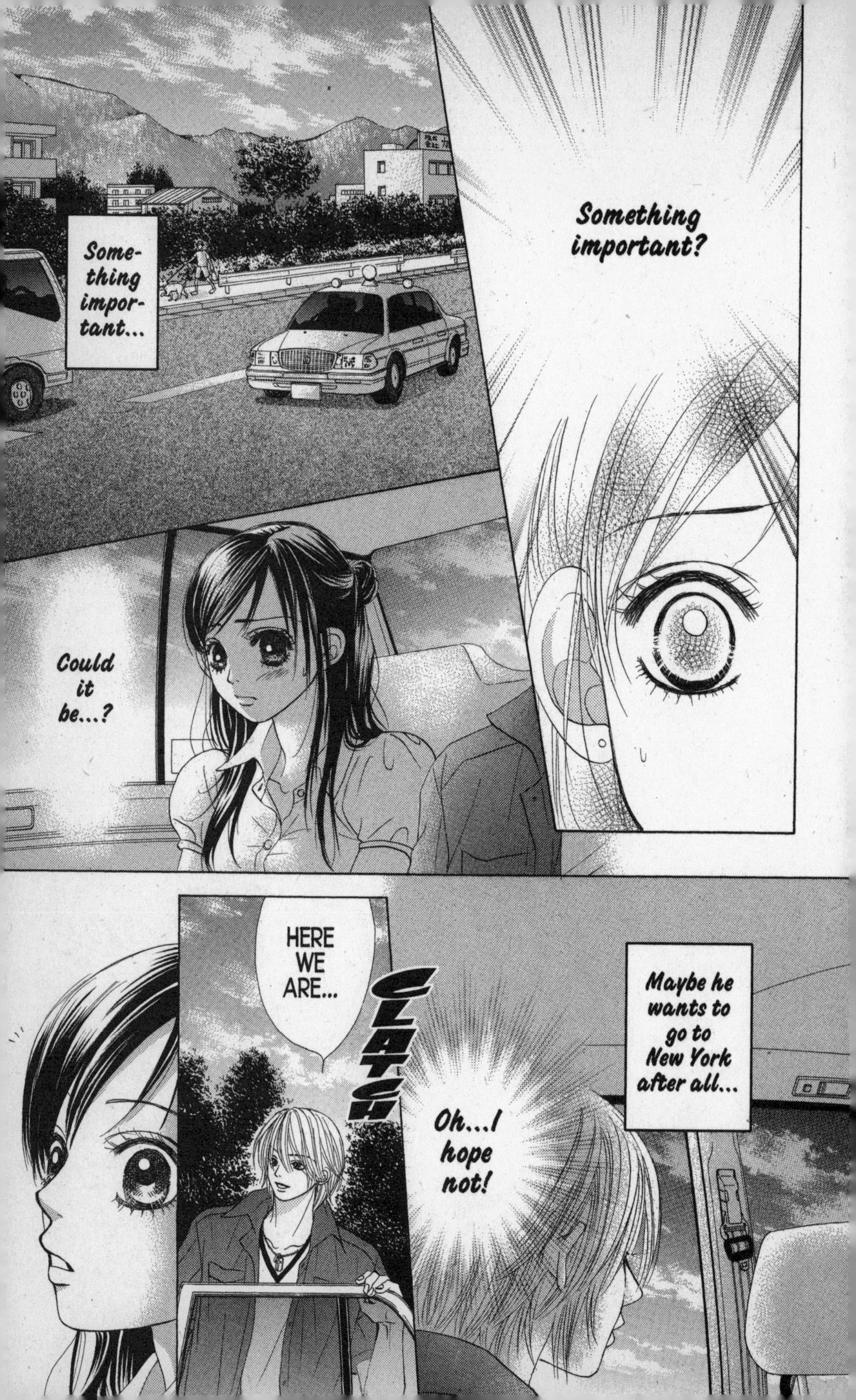
Something important?
Something important...
Could it be...?
Maybe he wants to go to New York after all...
Oh...I hope not!
CLATCH
HERE WE ARE...

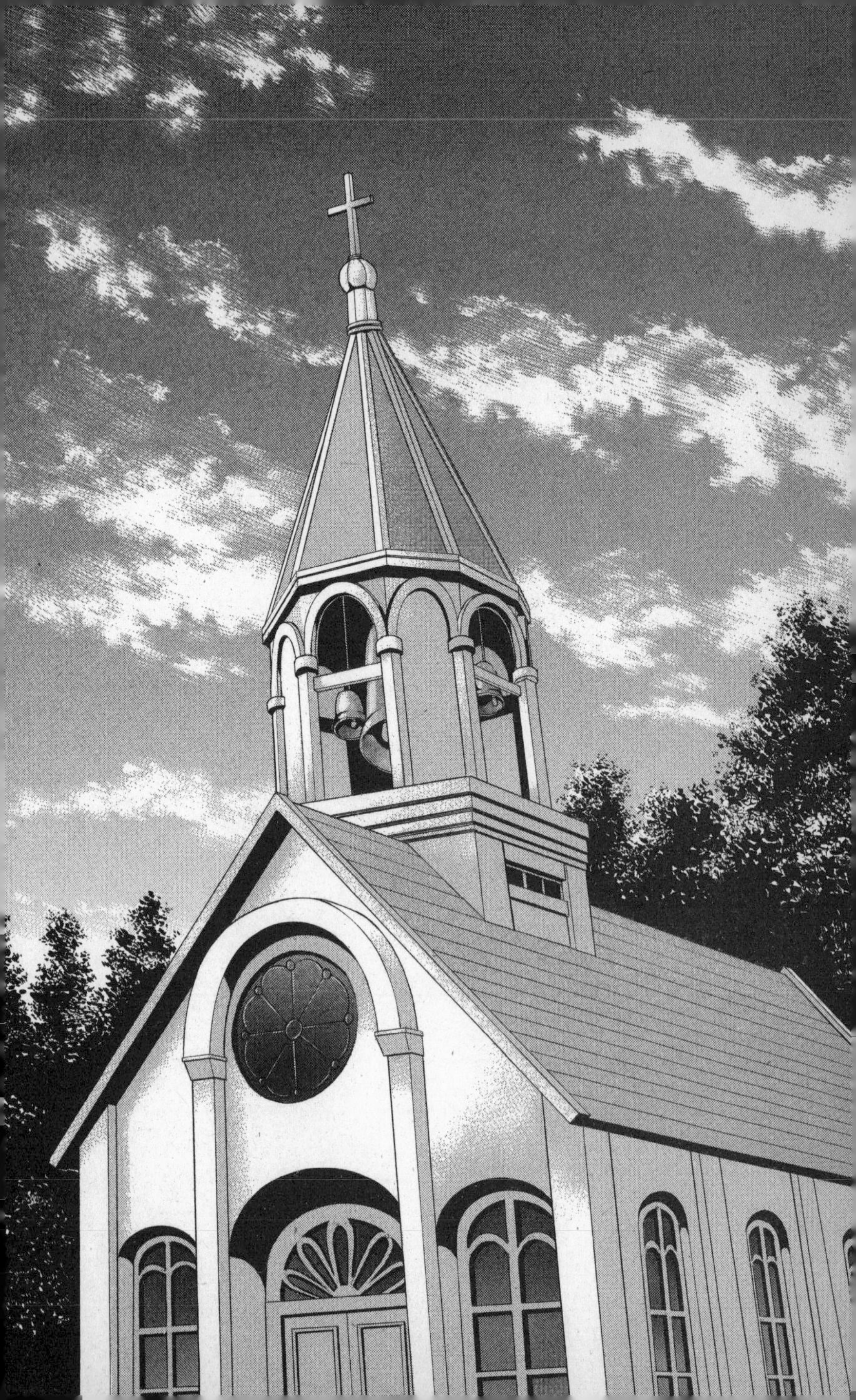

THIS IS THE CHURCH WHERE FUMIKA AND MR. HODAKA HAD THEIR WEDDING...
What's this about?
IN HERE...
THIS WAY...

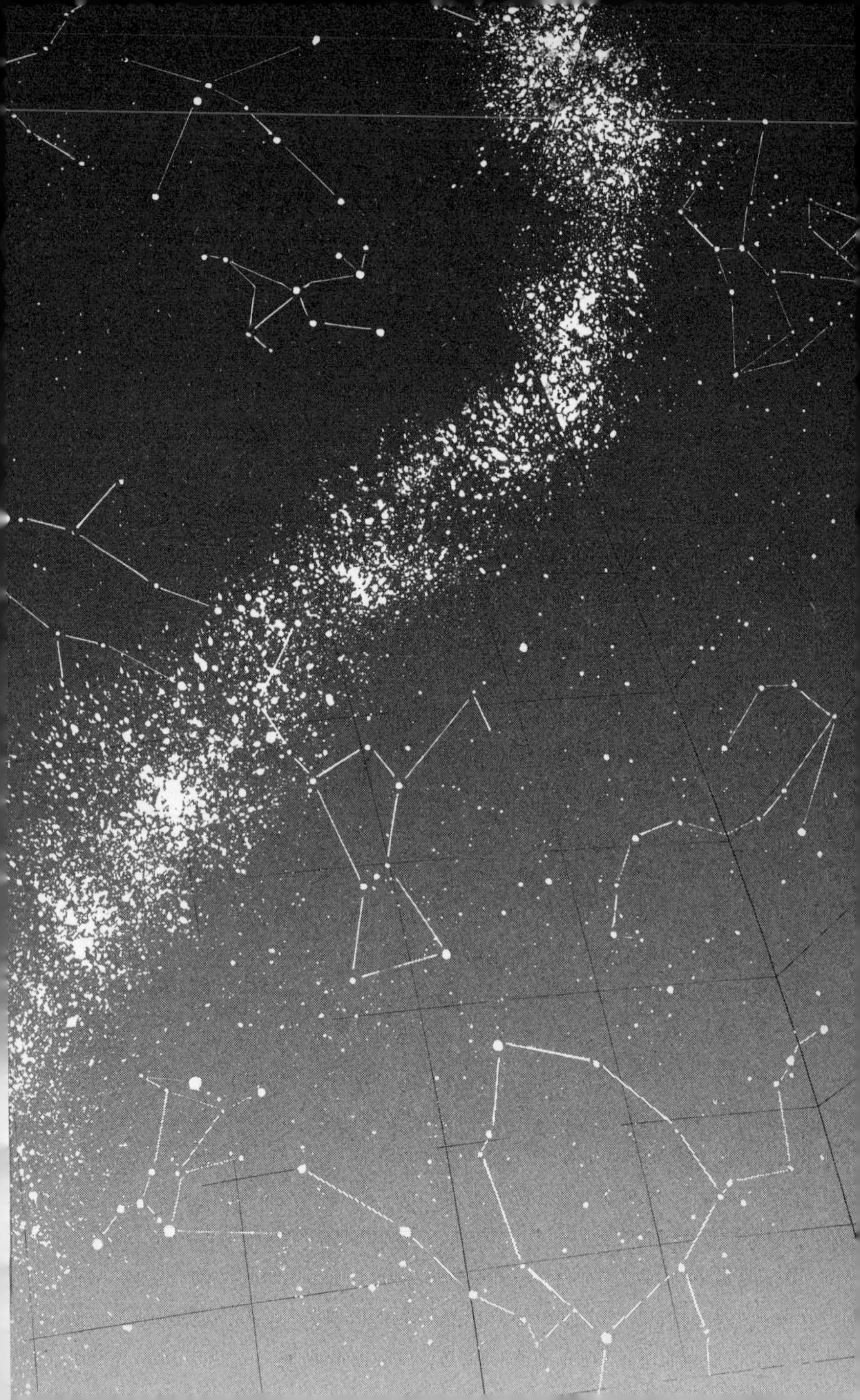

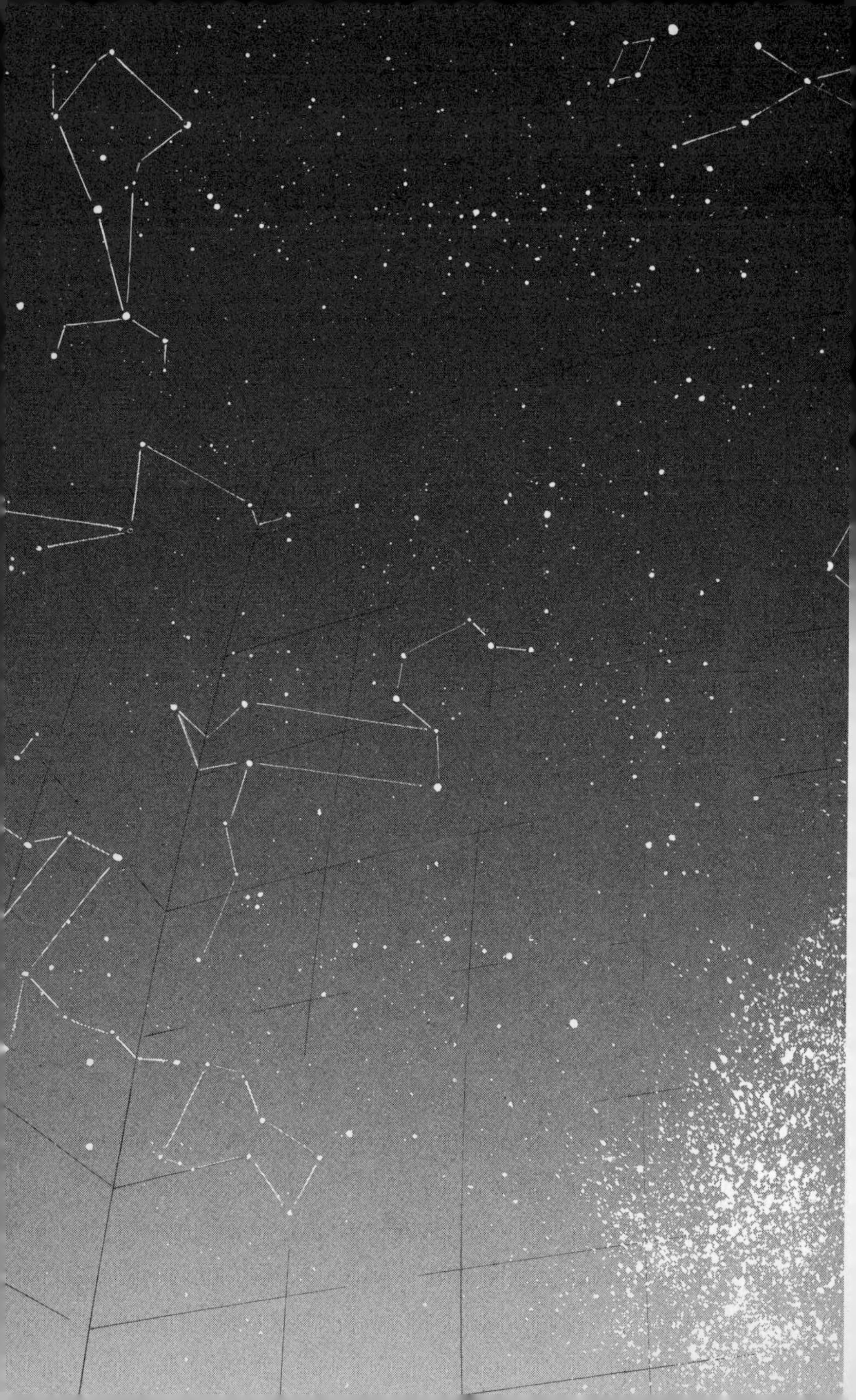

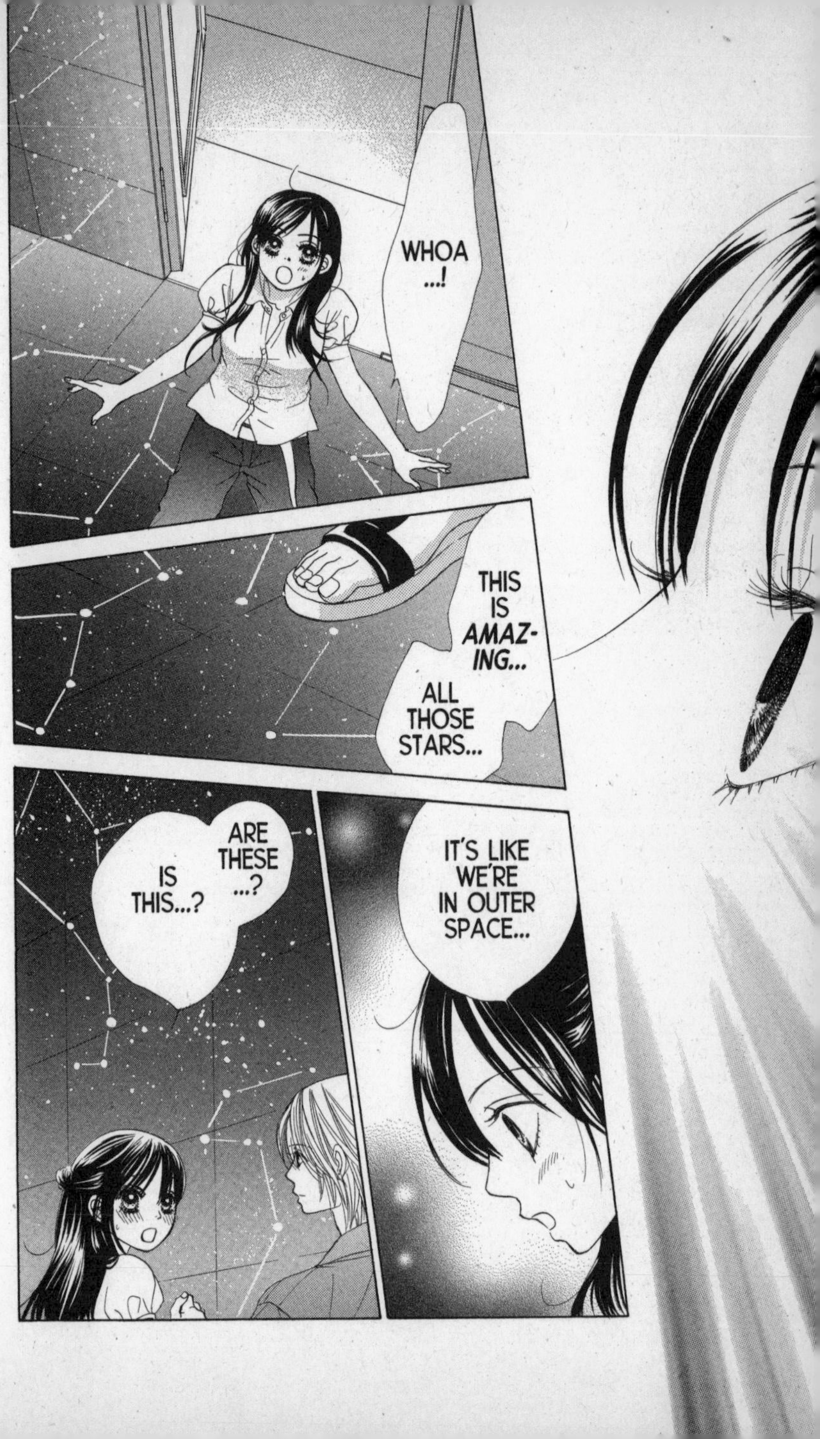
WHOA ...!
THIS IS *AMAZING...*
ALL THOSE STARS...
IT'S LIKE WE'RE IN OUTER SPACE...
ARE THESE ...?
IS THIS...?

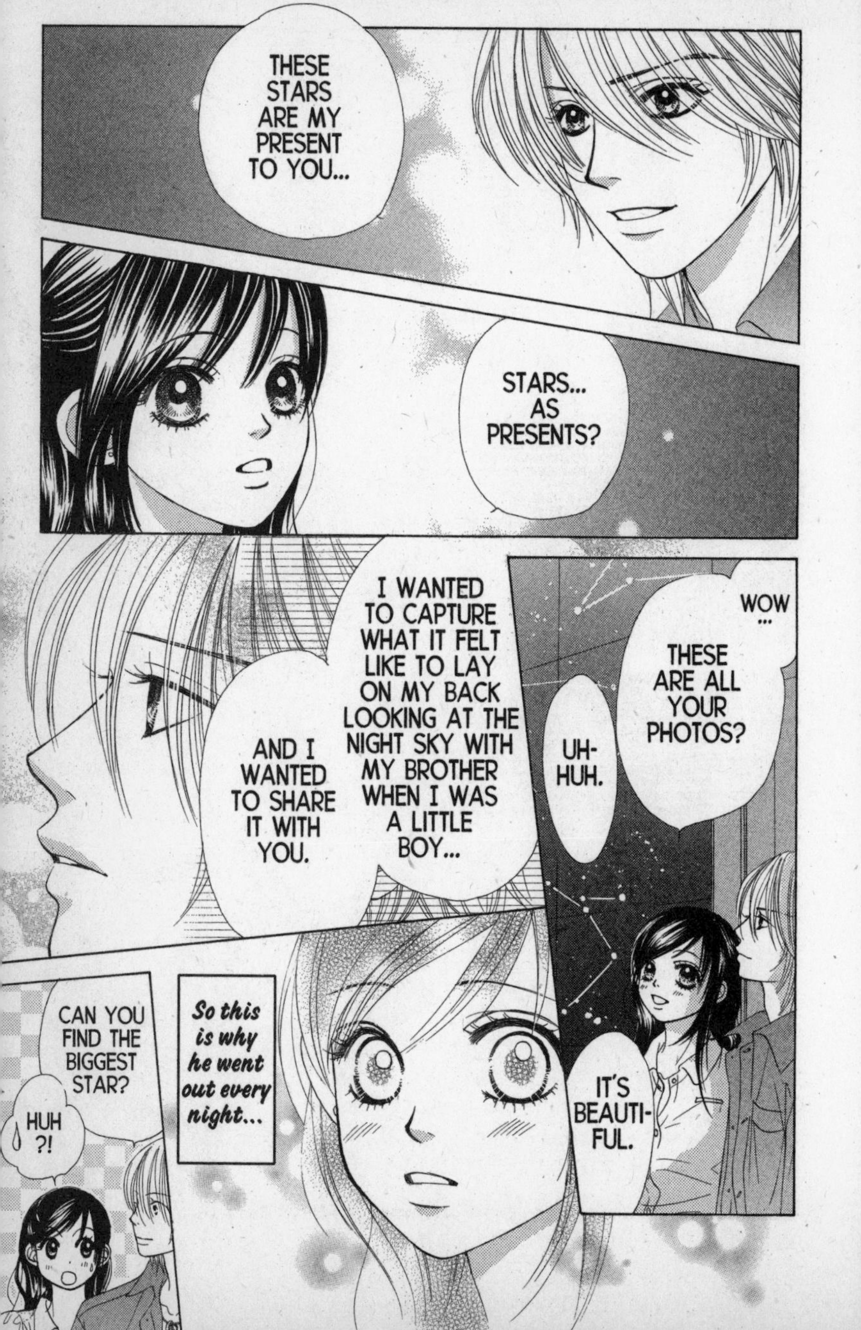
THESE STARS ARE MY PRESENT TO YOU...
STARS... AS PRESENTS?
WOW...
THESE ARE ALL YOUR PHOTOS?
UH-HUH.
IT'S BEAUTIFUL.
I WANTED TO CAPTURE WHAT IT FELT LIKE TO LAY ON MY BACK LOOKING AT THE NIGHT SKY WITH MY BROTHER WHEN I WAS A LITTLE BOY...
AND I WANTED TO SHARE IT WITH YOU.
So this is why he went out every night...
CAN YOU FIND THE BIGGEST STAR?
HUH ?!

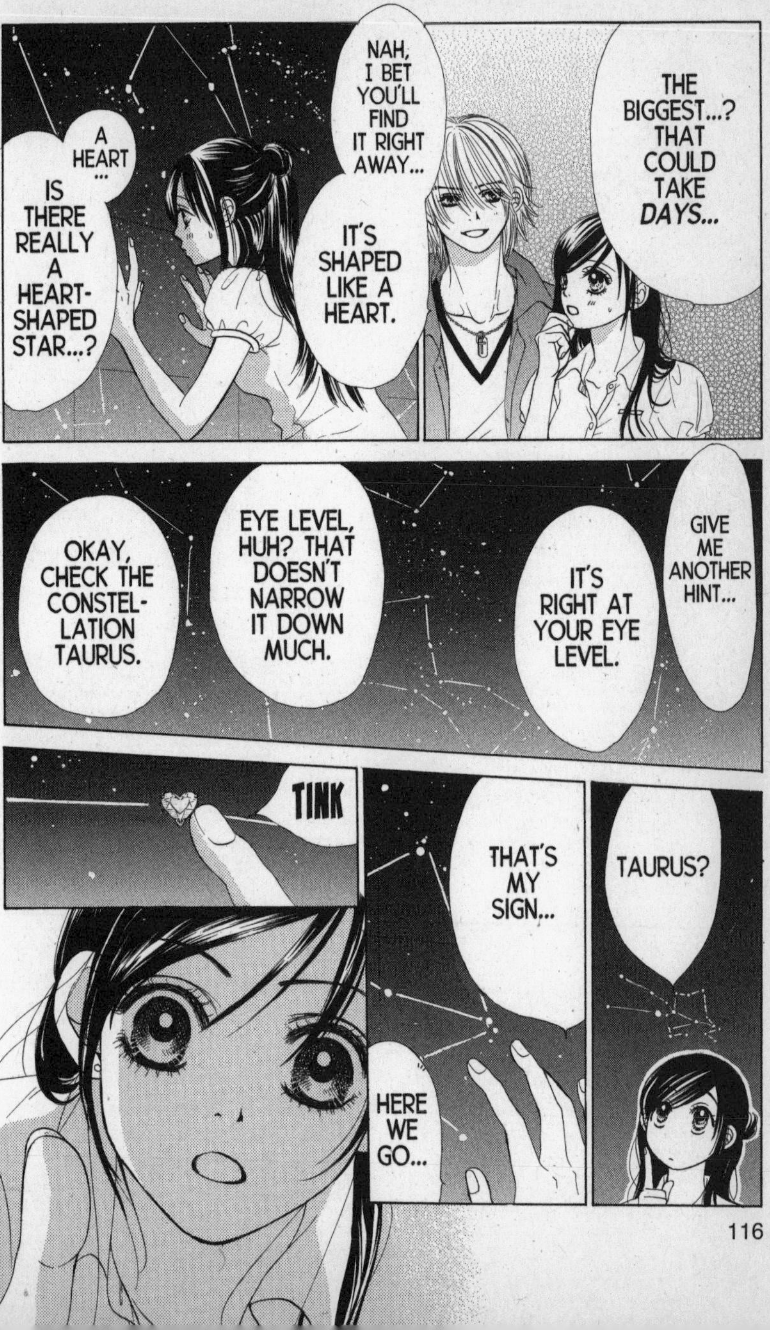
THE BIGGEST...? THAT COULD TAKE *DAYS*...
NAH, I BET YOU'LL FIND IT RIGHT AWAY...
IT'S SHAPED LIKE A HEART.
A HEART...
IS THERE REALLY A HEART-SHAPED STAR...?
GIVE ME ANOTHER HINT...
IT'S RIGHT AT YOUR EYE LEVEL.
EYE LEVEL, HUH? THAT DOESN'T NARROW IT DOWN MUCH.
OKAY, CHECK THE CONSTEL-LATION TAURUS.
TAURUS?
THAT'S MY SIGN...
HERE WE GO...
TINK

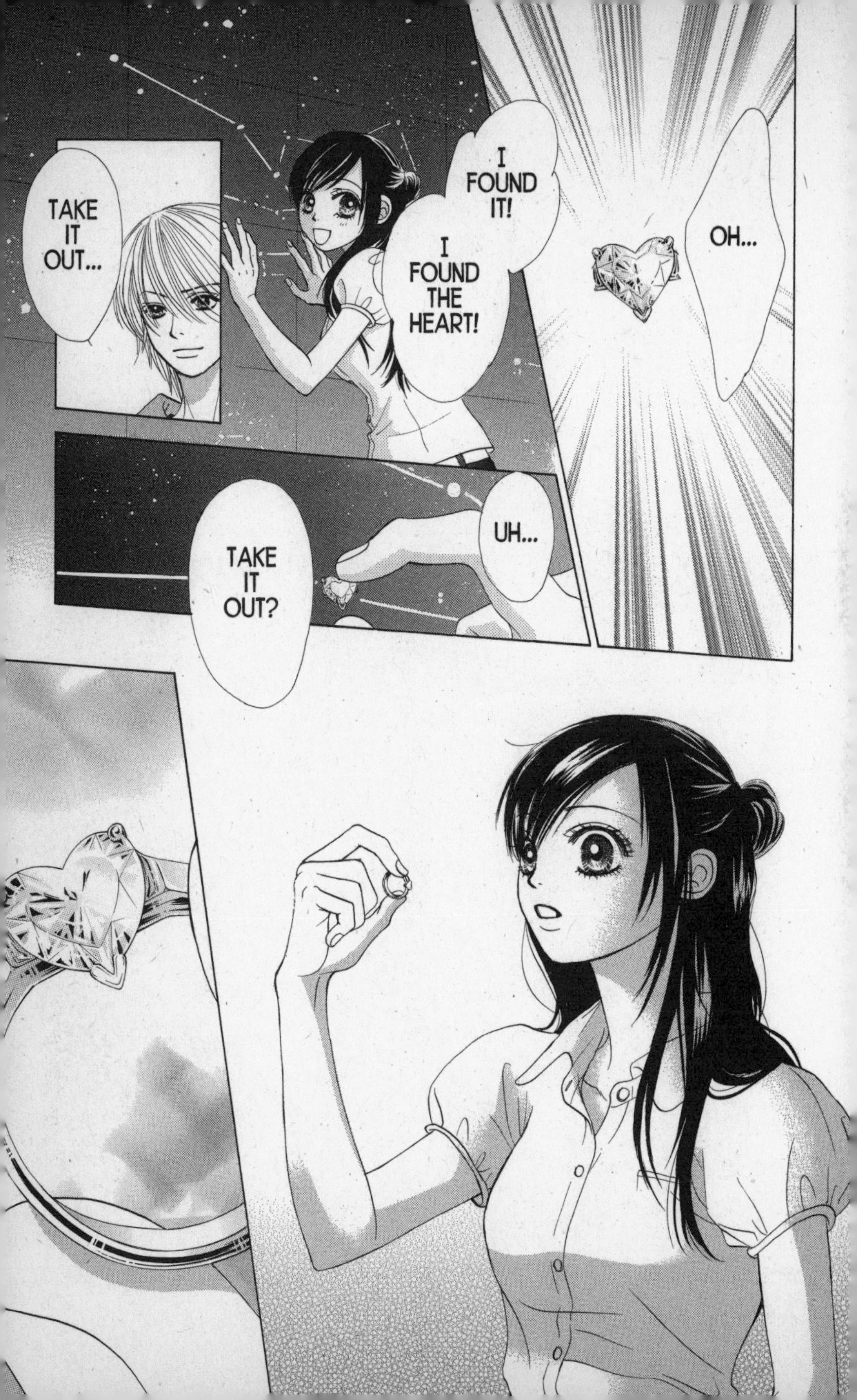
OH...
I FOUND IT!
I FOUND THE HEART!
TAKE IT OUT...
UH...
TAKE IT OUT?

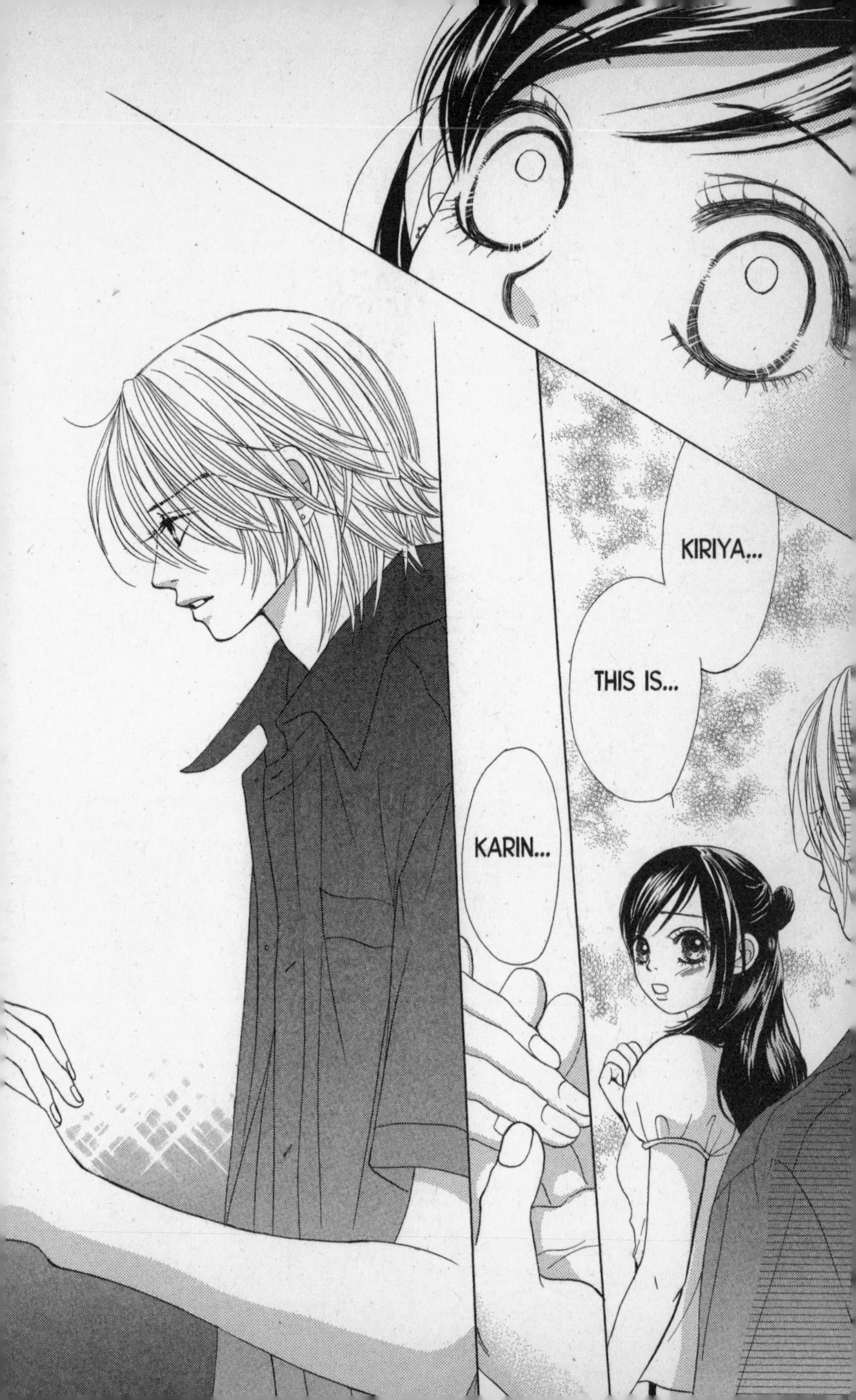
KIRIYA...
THIS IS...
KARIN...

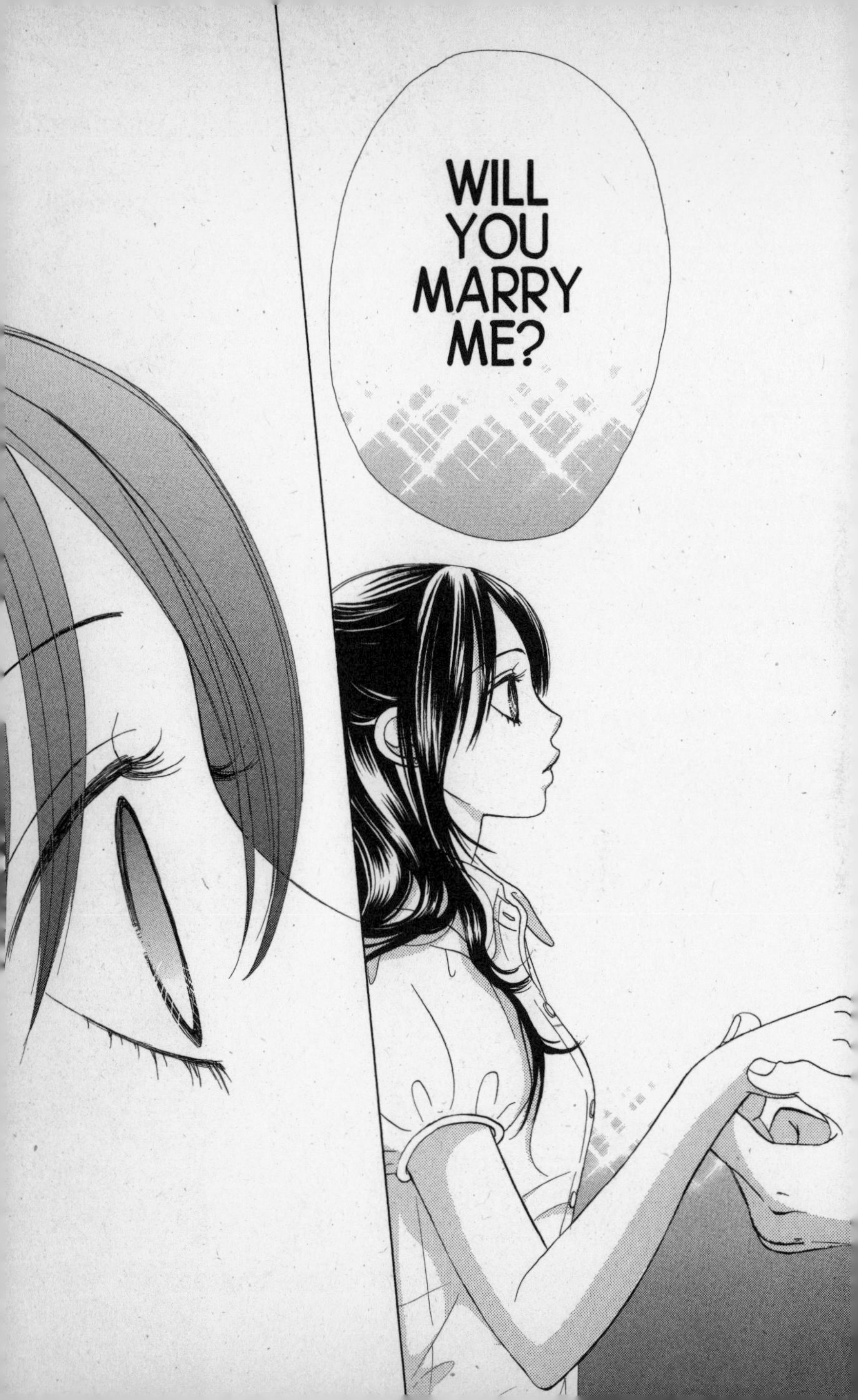
WILL YOU MARRY ME?

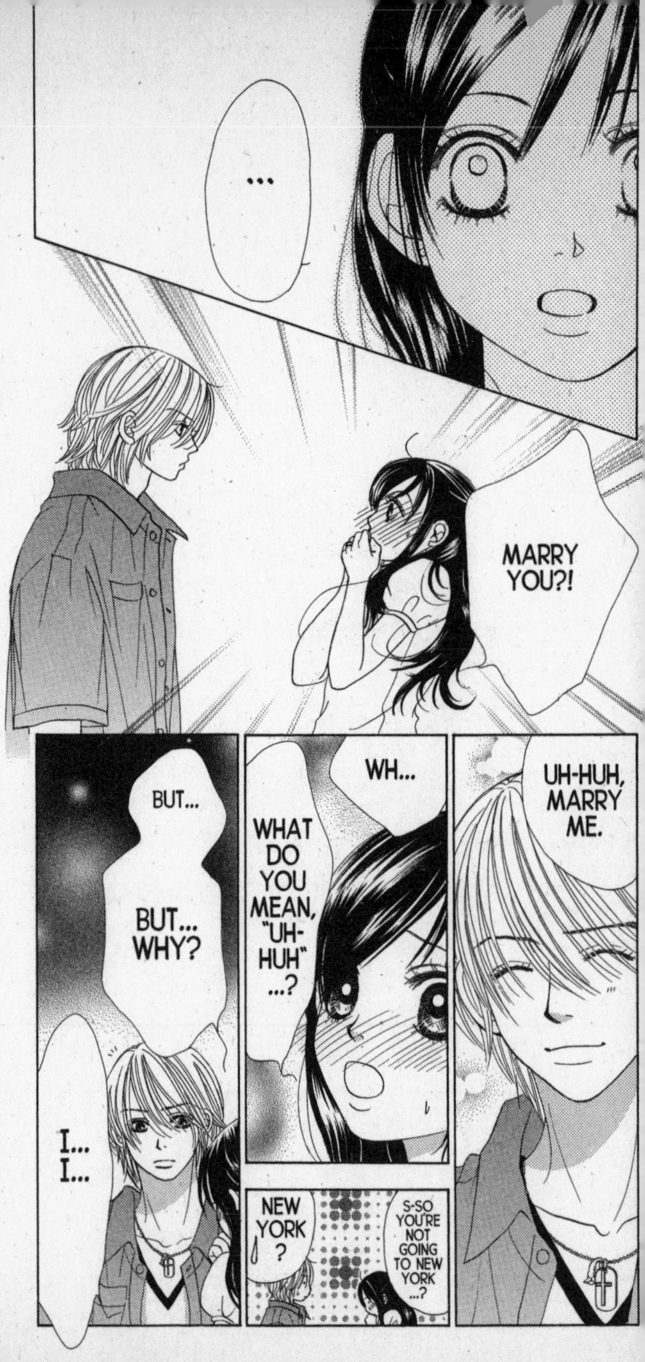
...
MARRY YOU?!
UH-HUH, MARRY ME.
WH...
WHAT DO YOU MEAN, "UH-HUH" ...?
S-SO YOU'RE NOT GOING TO NEW YORK ...?
NEW YORK ?
BUT...
BUT... WHY?
I... I...

I'M NOT A VERY GOOD COOK...
YOU'LL LEARN. JUST TAKE IT ONE STEP AT A TIME.
AND I'M REALLY IMMATURE!
UH-HUH. I LIKE THAT ABOUT YOU.
BUT I YELL AT YOU!
I KNOW.
I'M ALWAYS CAUSING YOU TROUBLE...
I'VE BEEN JUST AS MUCH TROUBLE TO YOU...
I-I'M SELF CENTERED--
SOME-TIMES. BUT WE'RE ALL LIKE THAT SOMETIMES.
KARIN, NONE OF THAT MATTERS...
I'M NEVER AS COMFORTABLE AND HAPPY AS I AM WITH YOU. I'VE KNOWN I WANTED TO MARRY YOU FOR A LONG TIME...
AND IF YOU'LL LET ME, I PROMISE YOU'LL NEVER REGRET IT.

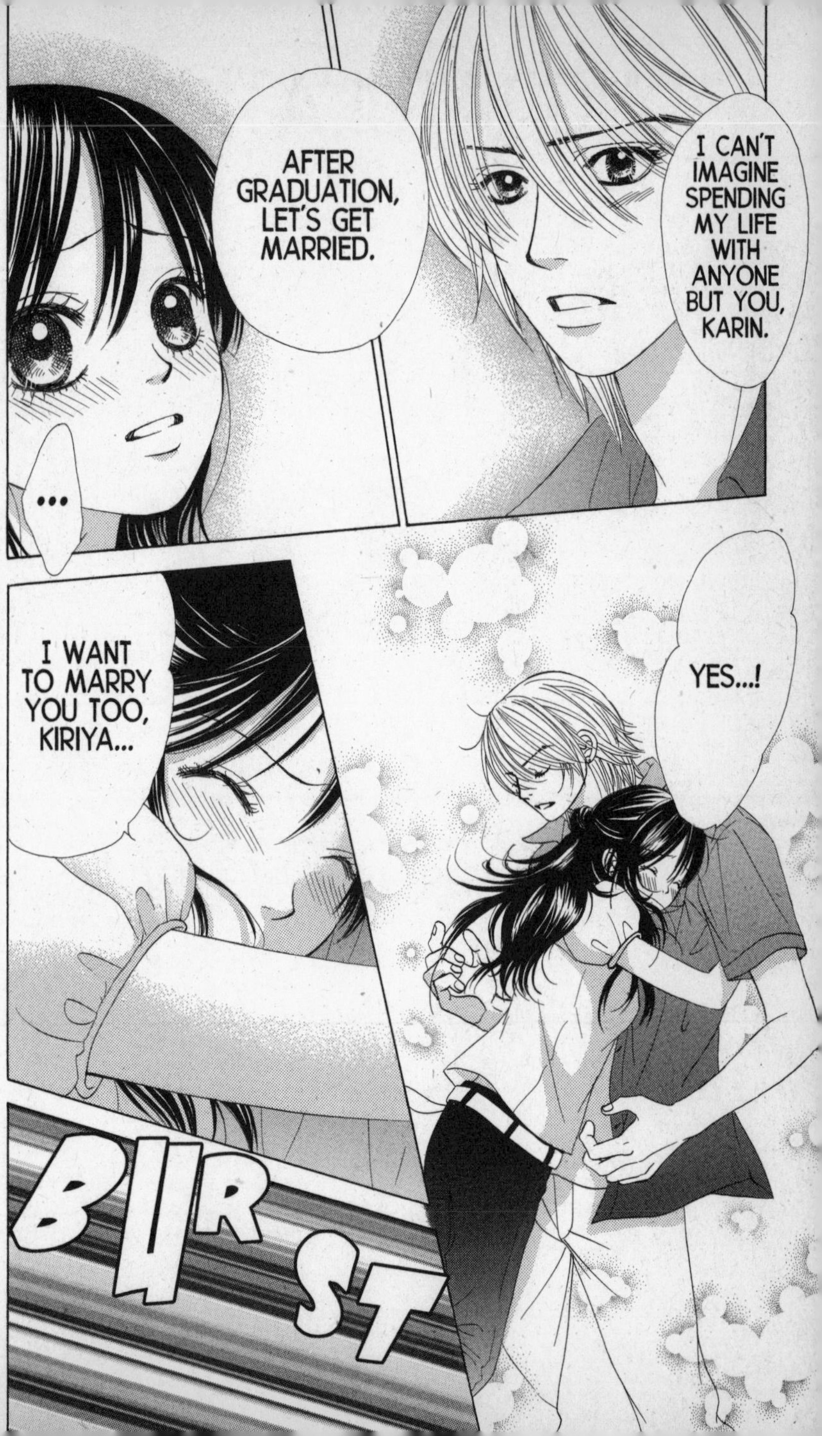
AFTER GRADUATION, LET'S GET MARRIED.
I CAN'T IMAGINE SPENDING MY LIFE WITH ANYONE BUT YOU, KARIN.
...
YES...!
I WANT TO MARRY YOU TOO, KIRIYA...
BURST

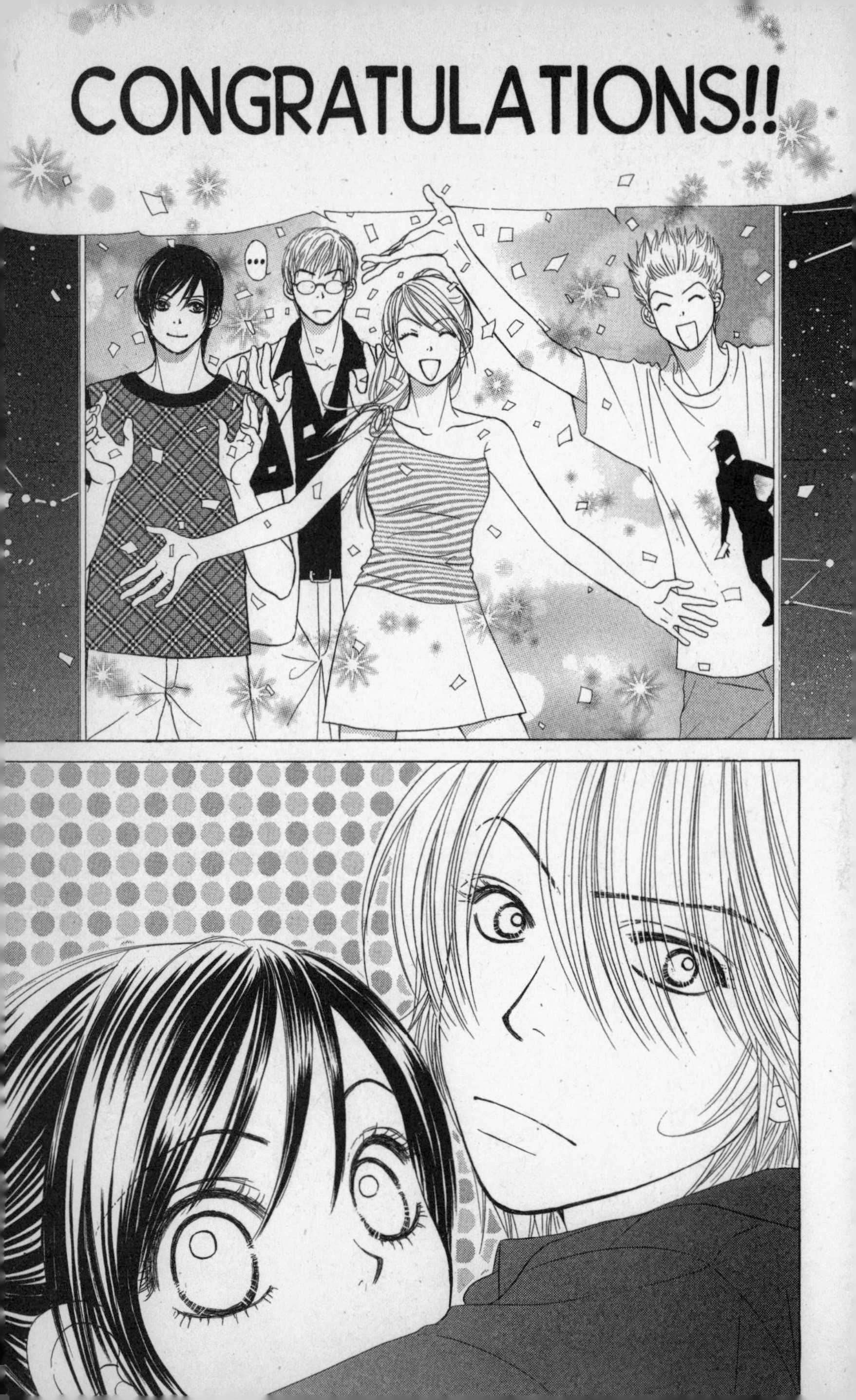
CONGRATULATIONS!!
...

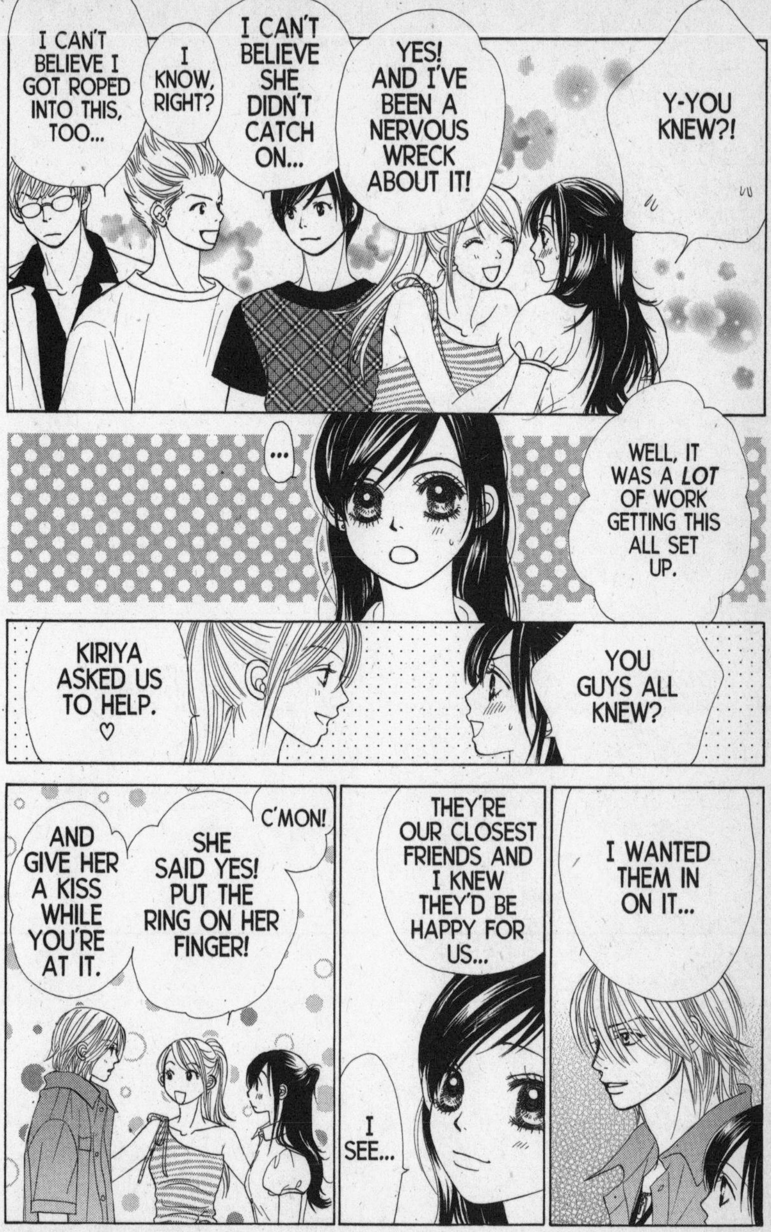
Y-YOU KNEW?!
YES! AND I'VE BEEN A NERVOUS WRECK ABOUT IT!
I CAN'T BELIEVE SHE DIDN'T CATCH ON...
I KNOW, RIGHT?
I CAN'T BELIEVE I GOT ROPED INTO THIS, TOO...
WELL, IT WAS A *LOT* OF WORK GETTING THIS ALL SET UP.
...
YOU GUYS ALL KNEW?
KIRIYA ASKED US TO HELP. ♡
I WANTED THEM IN ON IT...
THEY'RE OUR CLOSEST FRIENDS AND I KNEW THEY'D BE HAPPY FOR US...
I SEE...
C'MON!
SHE SAID YES! PUT THE RING ON HER FINGER!
AND GIVE HER A KISS WHILE YOU'RE AT IT.

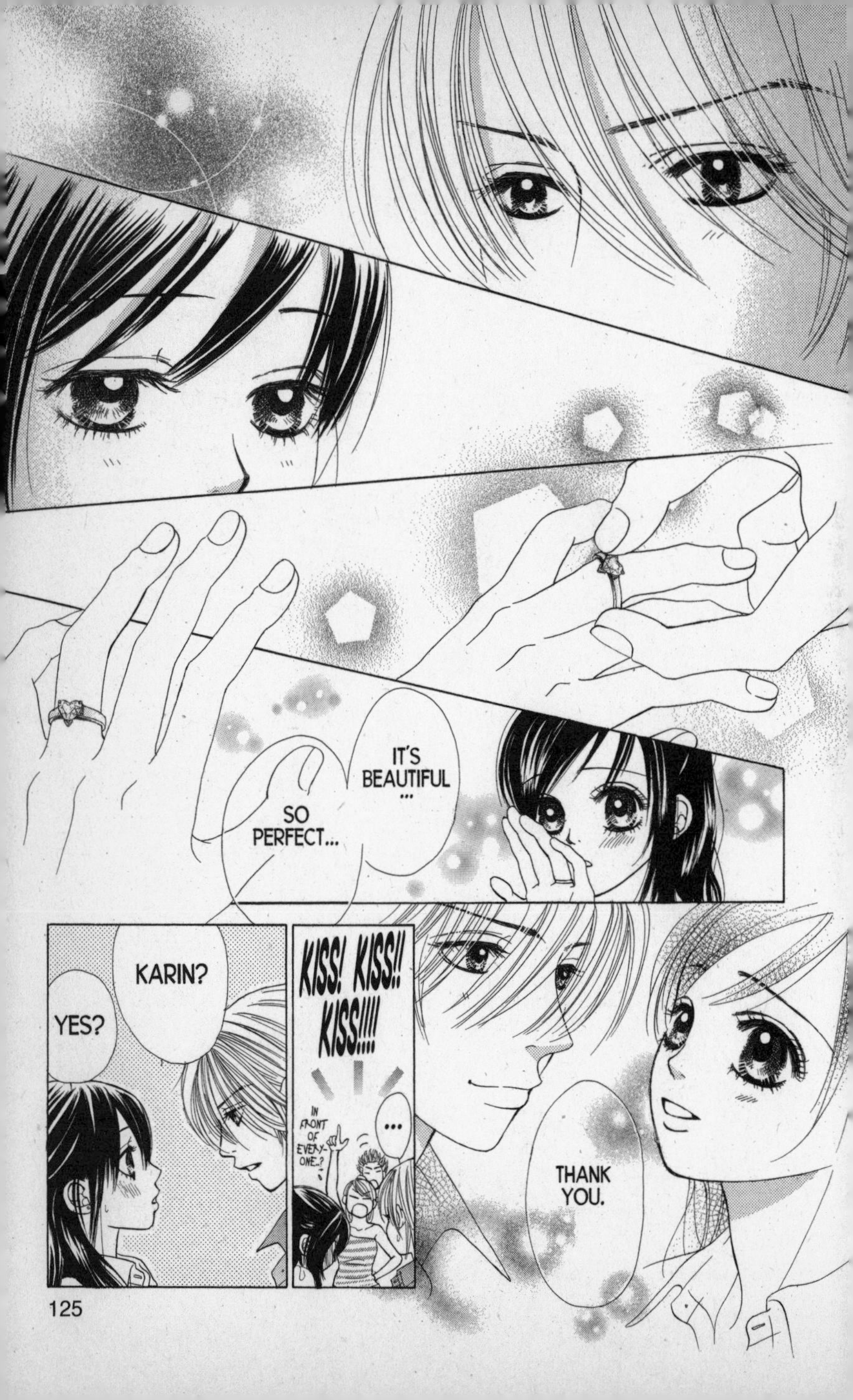
IT'S BEAUTIFUL ...
SO PERFECT...
THANK YOU.
KISS! KISS!! KISS!!!!
...
IN FRONT OF EVERY-ONE..?
KARIN?
YES?

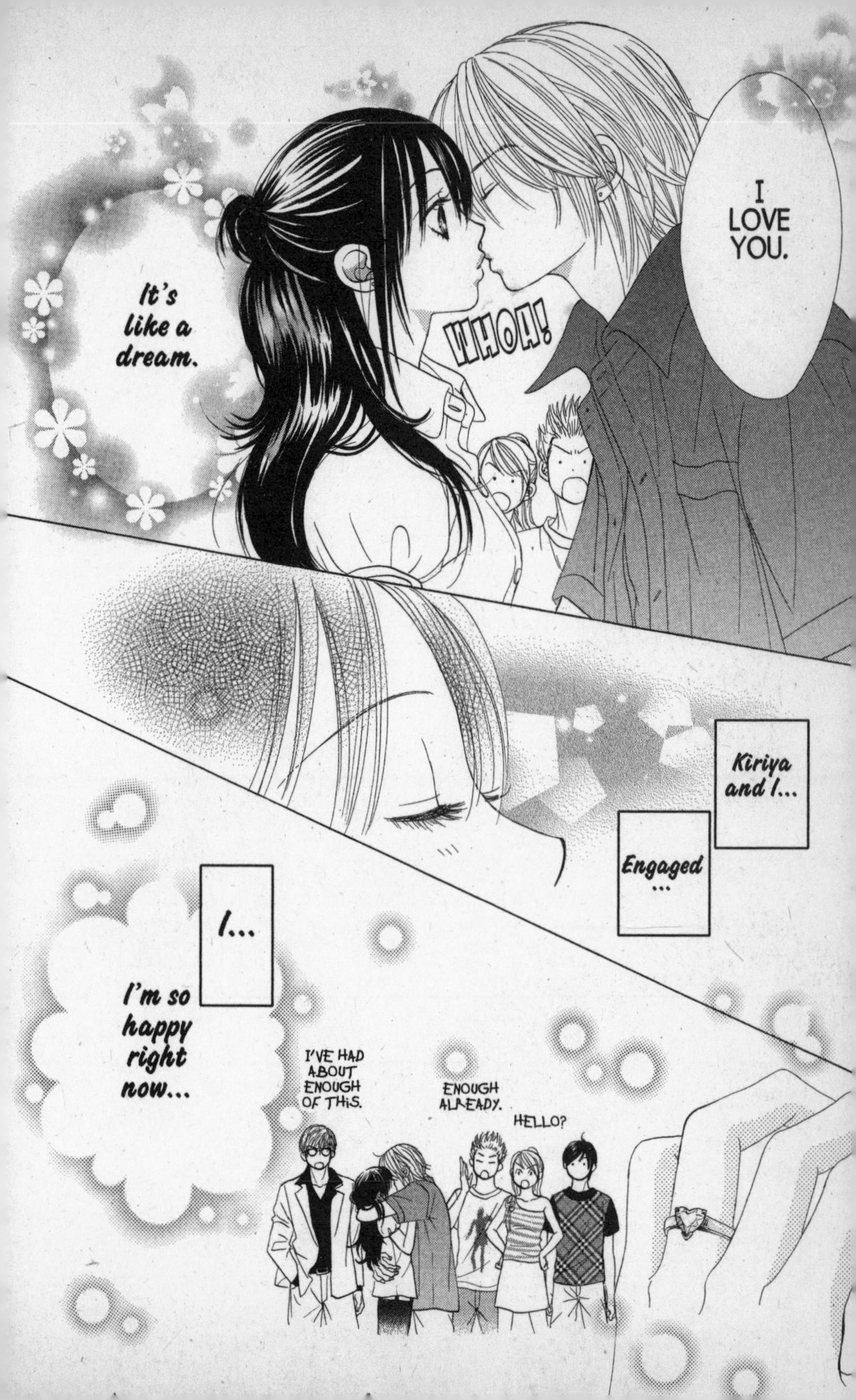
I LOVE YOU.
WHOA!
It's like a dream.
Kiriya and I...
Engaged...
I...
I'm so happy right now...
HELLO?
ENOUGH ALREADY.
I'VE HAD ABOUT ENOUGH OF THIS.

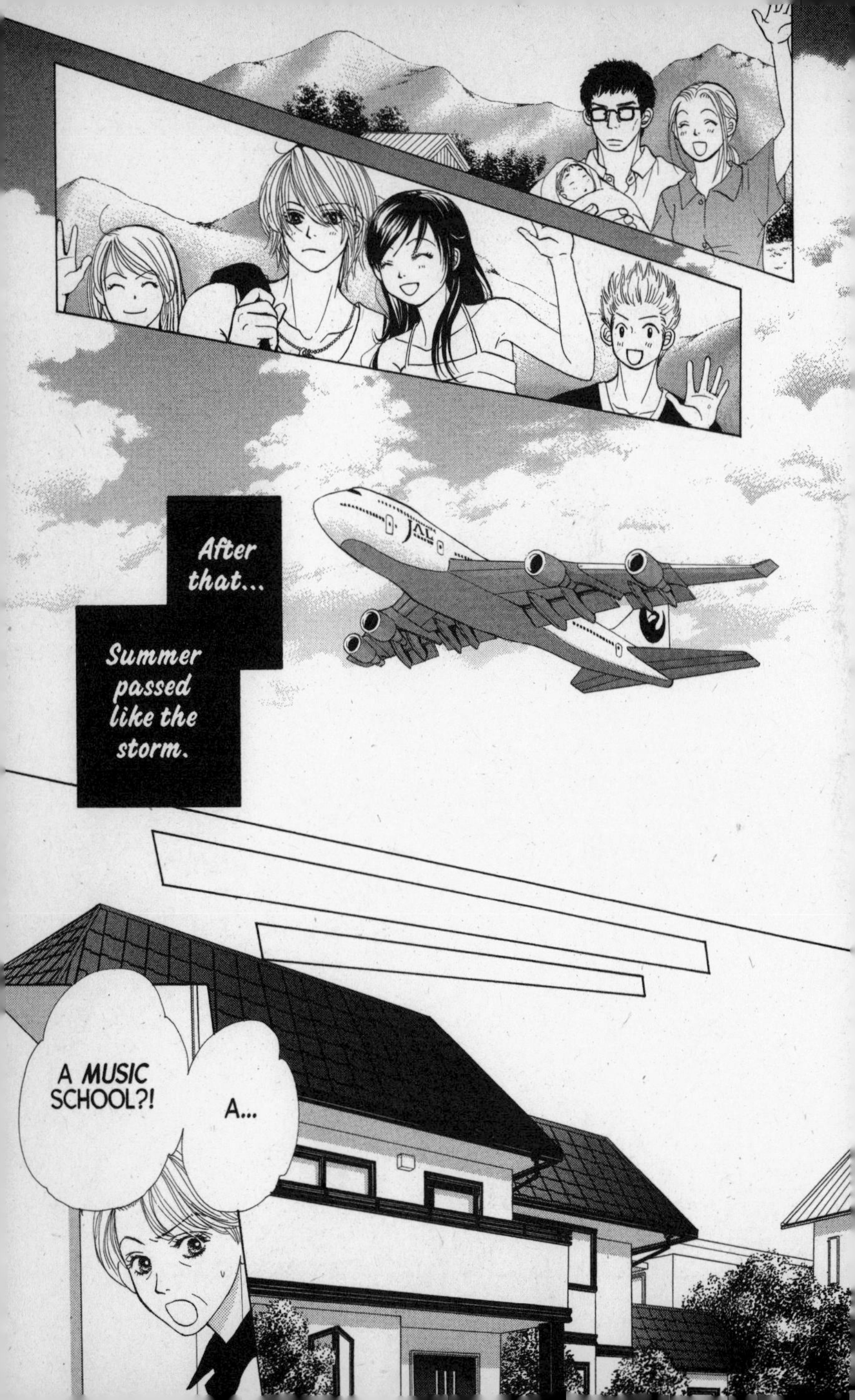
After that...
Summer passed like the storm.
A...
A MUSIC SCHOOL?!

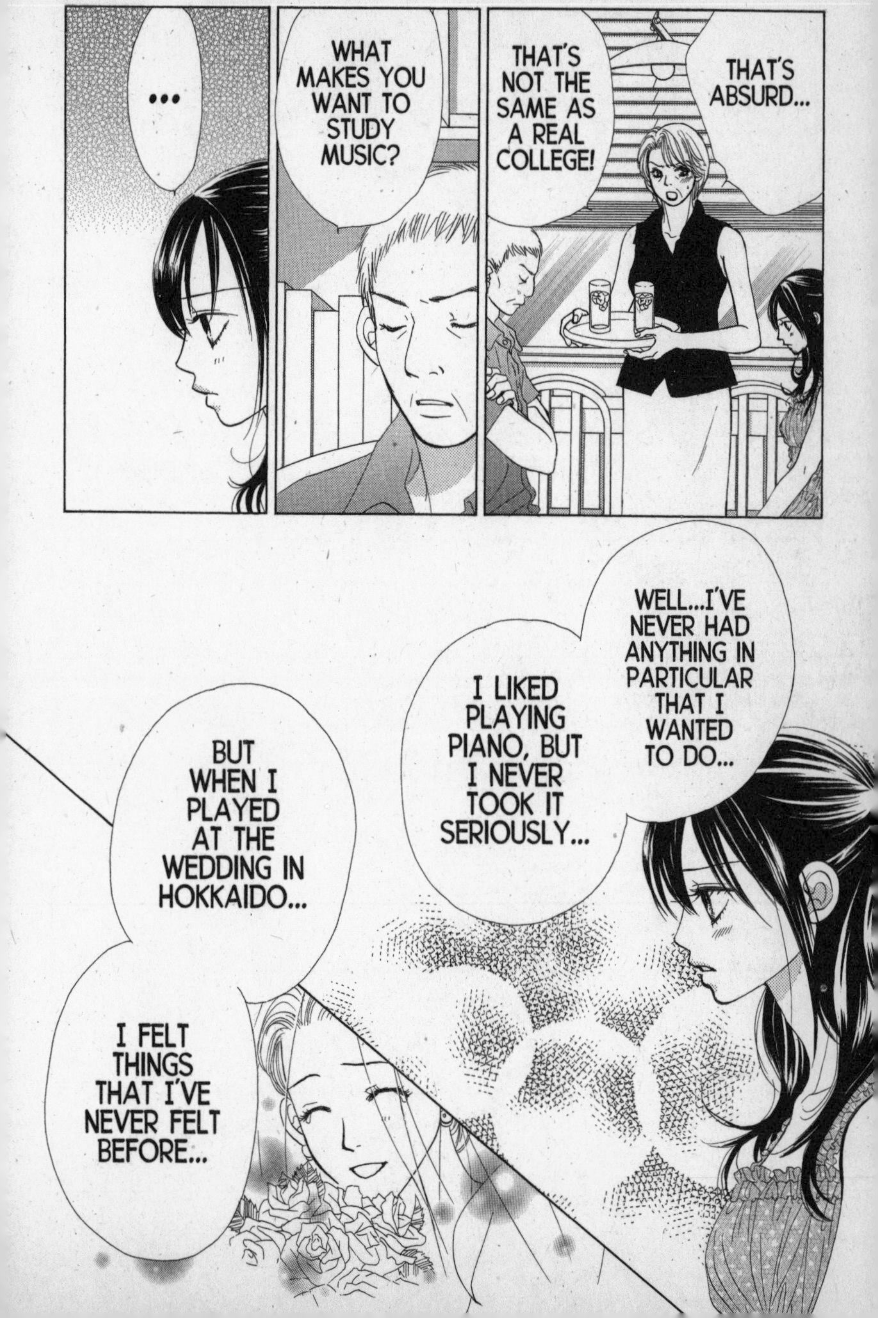
THAT'S ABSURD...
THAT'S NOT THE SAME AS A REAL COLLEGE!
WHAT MAKES YOU WANT TO STUDY MUSIC?
...
WELL...I'VE NEVER HAD ANYTHING IN PARTICULAR THAT I WANTED TO DO...
I LIKED PLAYING PIANO, BUT I NEVER TOOK IT SERIOUSLY...
BUT WHEN I PLAYED AT THE WEDDING IN HOKKAIDO...
I FELT THINGS THAT I'VE NEVER FELT BEFORE...

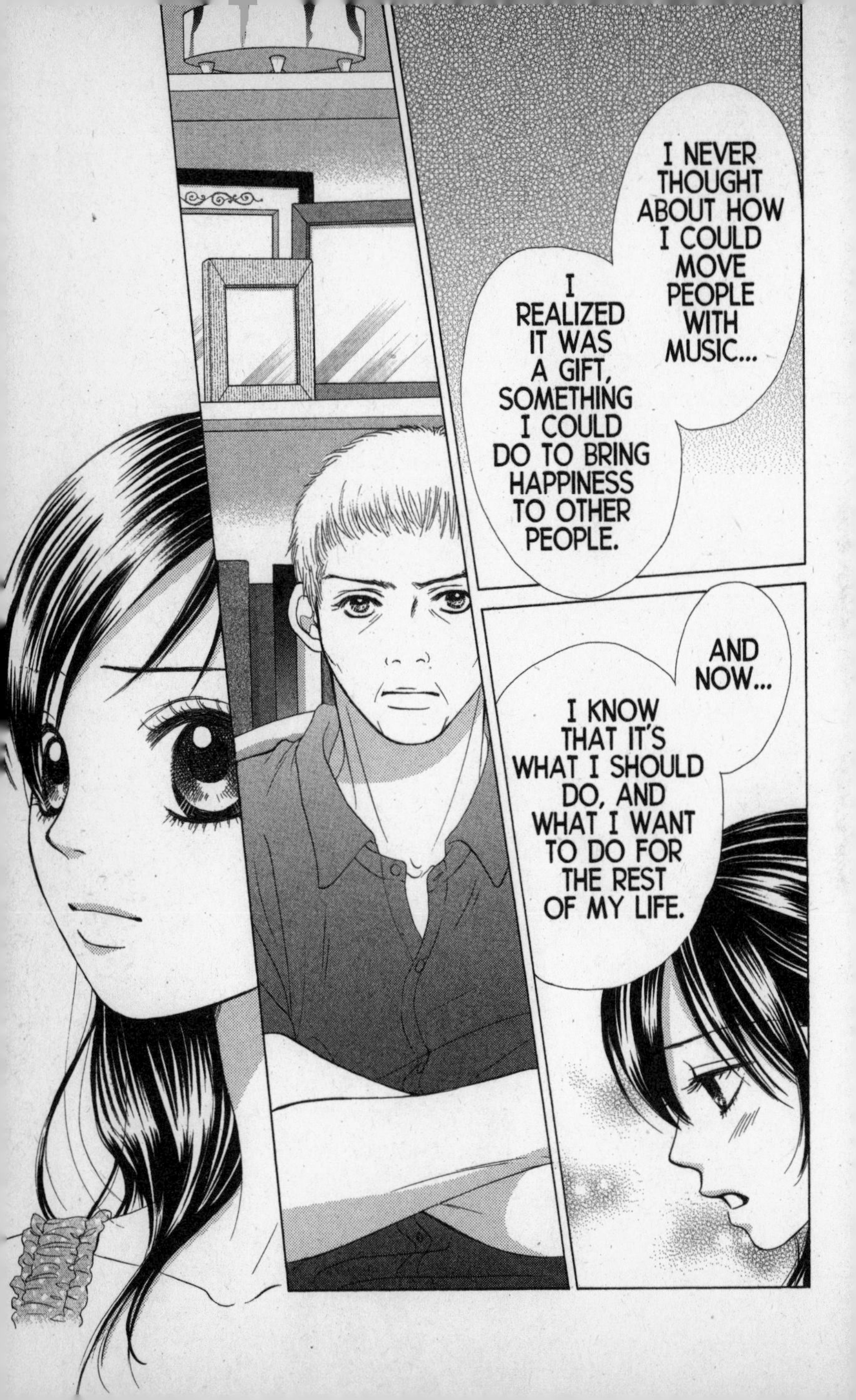
I NEVER THOUGHT ABOUT HOW I COULD MOVE PEOPLE WITH MUSIC...
I REALIZED IT WAS A GIFT, SOMETHING I COULD DO TO BRING HAPPINESS TO OTHER PEOPLE.
AND NOW...
I KNOW THAT IT'S WHAT I SHOULD DO, AND WHAT I WANT TO DO FOR THE REST OF MY LIFE.

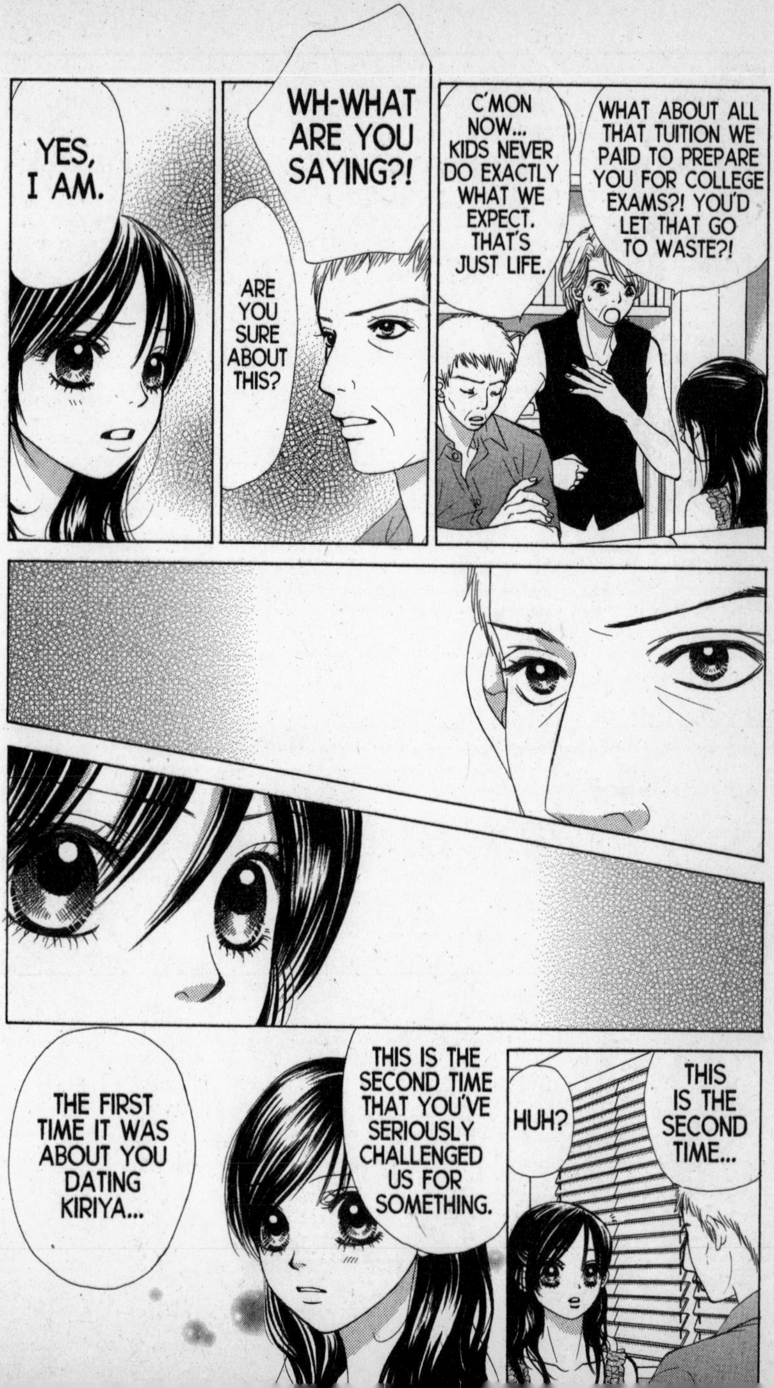
WHAT ABOUT ALL THAT TUITION WE PAID TO PREPARE YOU FOR COLLEGE EXAMS?! YOU'D LET THAT GO TO WASTE?!
C'MON NOW... KIDS NEVER DO EXACTLY WHAT WE EXPECT. THAT'S JUST LIFE.
WH-WHAT ARE YOU SAYING?!
ARE YOU SURE ABOUT THIS?
YES, I AM.
THIS IS THE SECOND TIME...
HUH?
THIS IS THE SECOND TIME THAT YOU'VE SERIOUSLY CHALLENGED US FOR SOMETHING.
THE FIRST TIME IT WAS ABOUT YOU DATING KIRIYA...

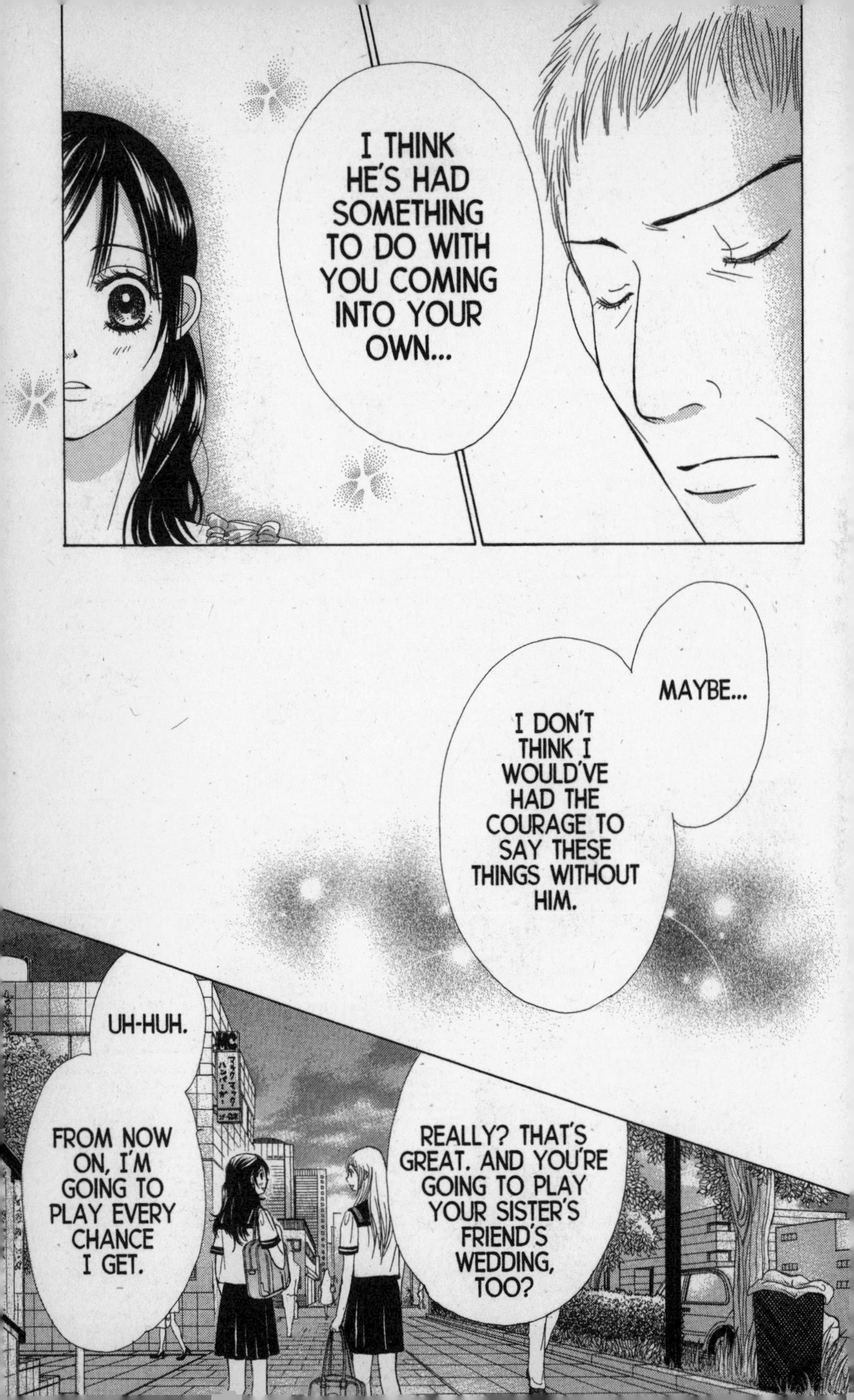
I THINK HE'S HAD SOMETHING TO DO WITH YOU COMING INTO YOUR OWN...
MAYBE...
I DON'T THINK I WOULD'VE HAD THE COURAGE TO SAY THESE THINGS WITHOUT HIM.
REALLY? THAT'S GREAT. AND YOU'RE GOING TO PLAY YOUR SISTER'S FRIEND'S WEDDING, TOO?
UH-HUH.
FROM NOW ON, I'M GOING TO PLAY EVERY CHANCE I GET.

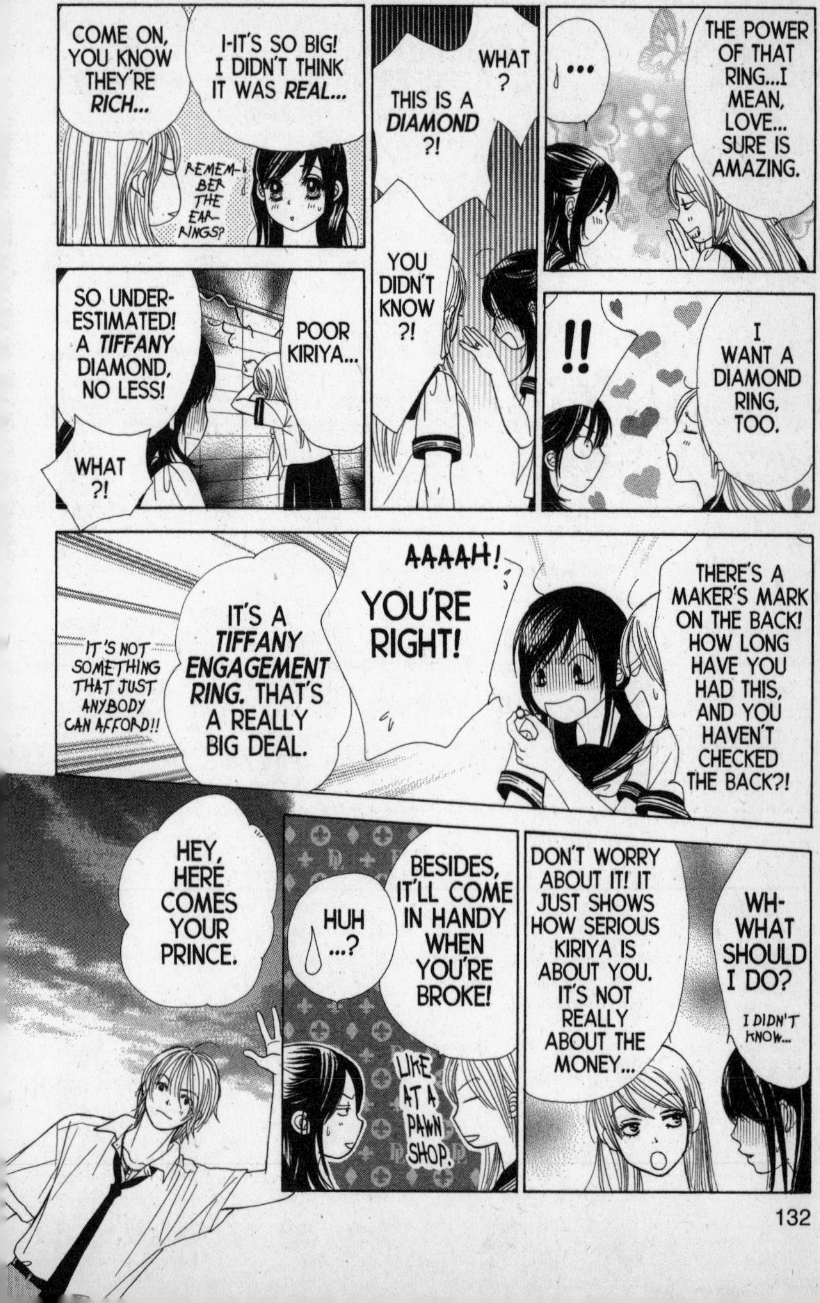
THE POWER OF THAT RING...I MEAN, LOVE... SURE IS AMAZING.
...
I WANT A DIAMOND RING, TOO.
!!
WHAT ?
THIS IS A DIAMOND ?!
YOU DIDN'T KNOW ?!
I-IT'S SO BIG! I DIDN'T THINK IT WAS REAL...
COME ON, YOU KNOW THEY'RE RICH...
REMEMBER THE EARRINGS?
POOR KIRIYA...
SO UNDERESTIMATED! A TIFFANY DIAMOND, NO LESS!
WHAT ?!
THERE'S A MAKER'S MARK ON THE BACK! HOW LONG HAVE YOU HAD THIS, AND YOU HAVEN'T CHECKED THE BACK?!
AAAAH!
YOU'RE RIGHT!
IT'S A TIFFANY ENGAGEMENT RING. THAT'S A REALLY BIG DEAL.
IT'S NOT SOMETHING THAT JUST ANYBODY CAN AFFORD!!
WH-WHAT SHOULD I DO?
I DIDN'T KNOW...
DON'T WORRY ABOUT IT! IT JUST SHOWS HOW SERIOUS KIRIYA IS ABOUT YOU. IT'S NOT REALLY ABOUT THE MONEY...
BESIDES, IT'LL COME IN HANDY WHEN YOU'RE BROKE!
HUH ...?
LIKE AT A PAWN SHOP.
HEY, HERE COMES YOUR PRINCE.

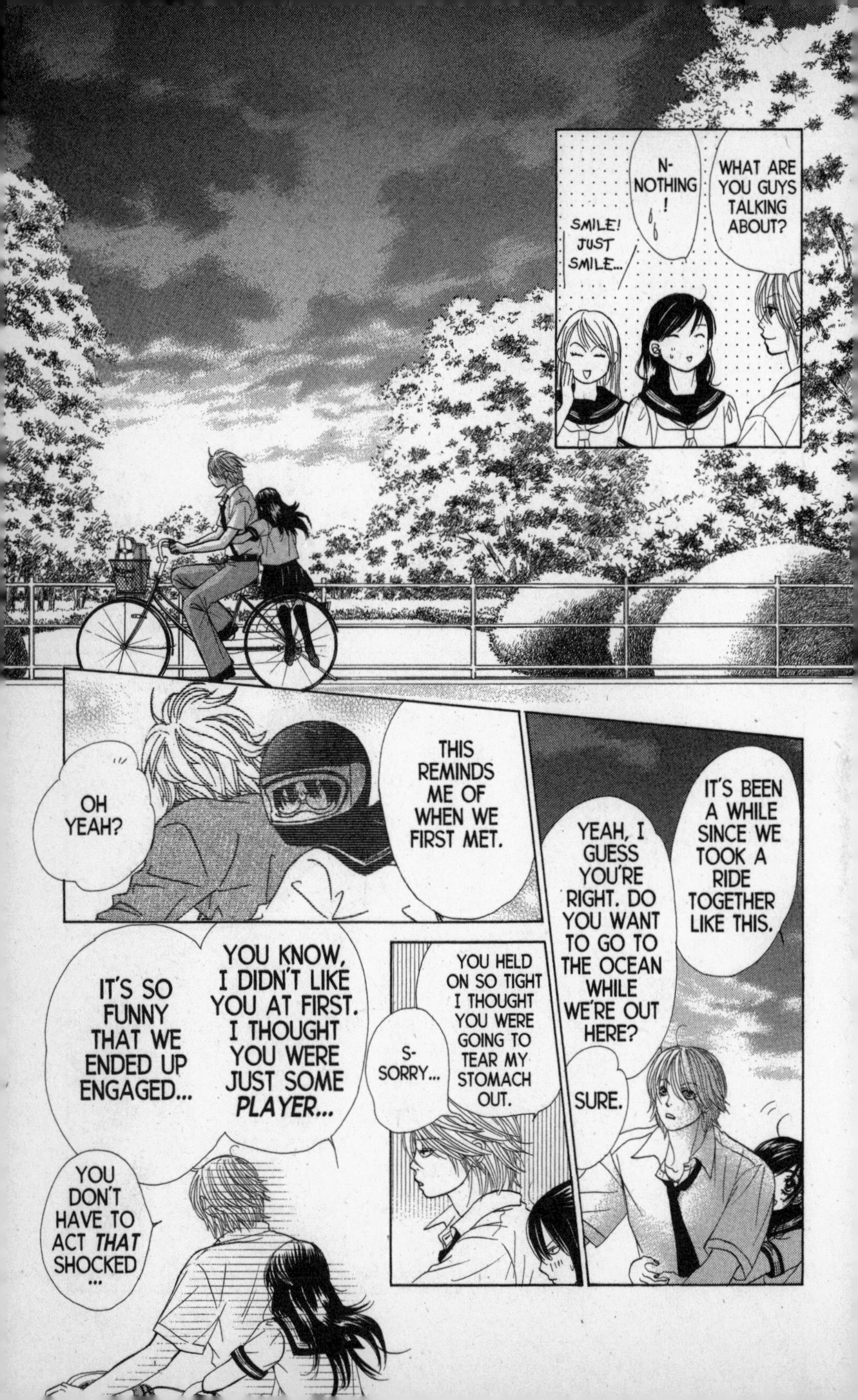
WHAT ARE YOU GUYS TALKING ABOUT?
N-NOTHING!
SMILE! JUST SMILE...
IT'S BEEN A WHILE SINCE WE TOOK A RIDE TOGETHER LIKE THIS.
YEAH, I GUESS YOU'RE RIGHT. DO YOU WANT TO GO TO THE OCEAN WHILE WE'RE OUT HERE?
SURE.
THIS REMINDS ME OF WHEN WE FIRST MET.
OH YEAH?
YOU HELD ON SO TIGHT I THOUGHT YOU WERE GOING TO TEAR MY STOMACH OUT.
S-SORRY...
YOU KNOW, I DIDN'T LIKE YOU AT FIRST. I THOUGHT YOU WERE JUST SOME *PLAYER*...
IT'S SO FUNNY THAT WE ENDED UP ENGAGED...
YOU DON'T HAVE TO ACT *THAT* SHOCKED...

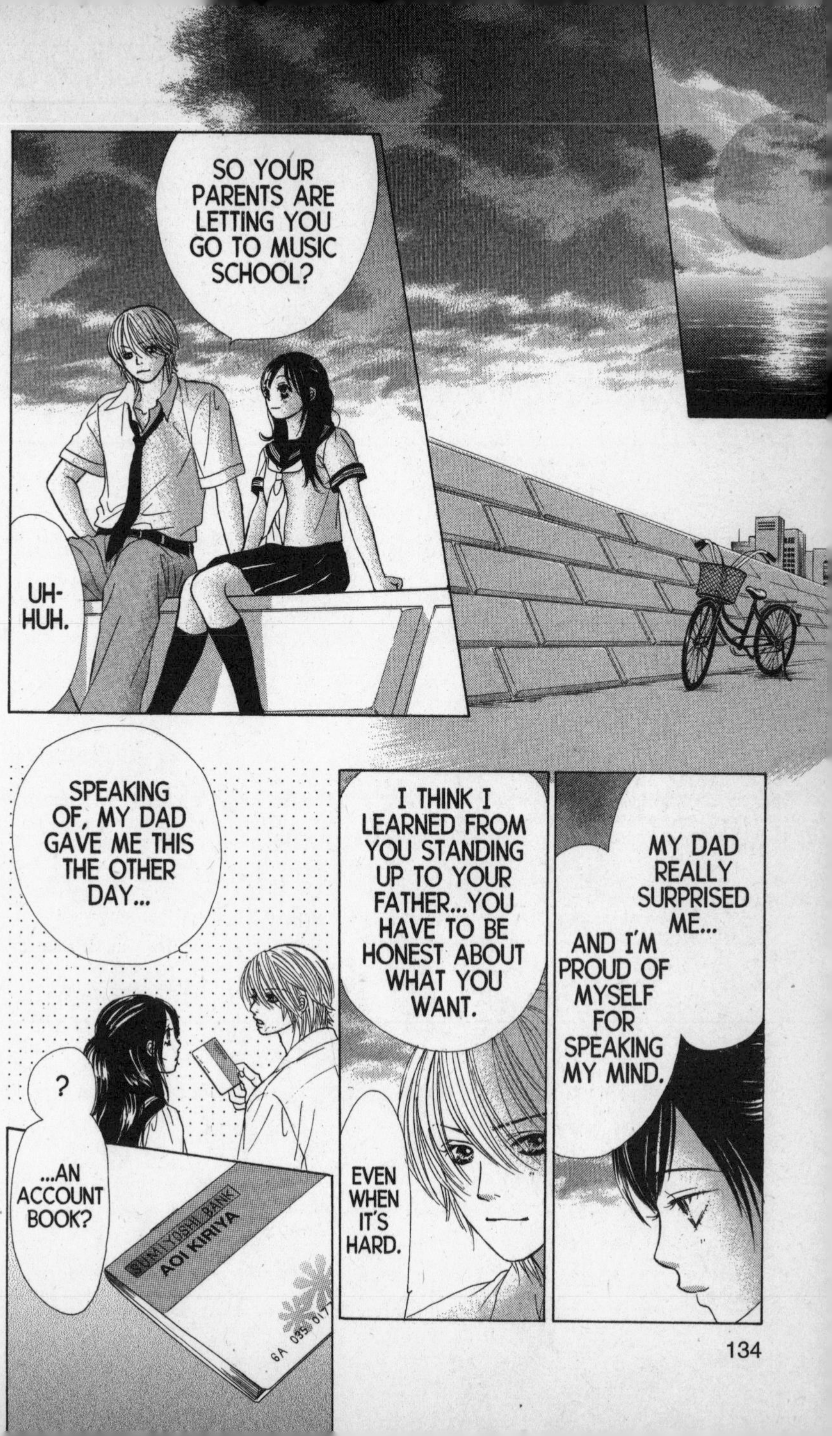
SO YOUR PARENTS ARE LETTING YOU GO TO MUSIC SCHOOL?
UH-HUH.
MY DAD REALLY SURPRISED ME...
AND I'M PROUD OF MYSELF FOR SPEAKING MY MIND.
I THINK I LEARNED FROM YOU STANDING UP TO YOUR FATHER...YOU HAVE TO BE HONEST ABOUT WHAT YOU WANT.
EVEN WHEN IT'S HARD.
SPEAKING OF, MY DAD GAVE ME THIS THE OTHER DAY...
?
...AN ACCOUNT BOOK?
AOI KIRIYA

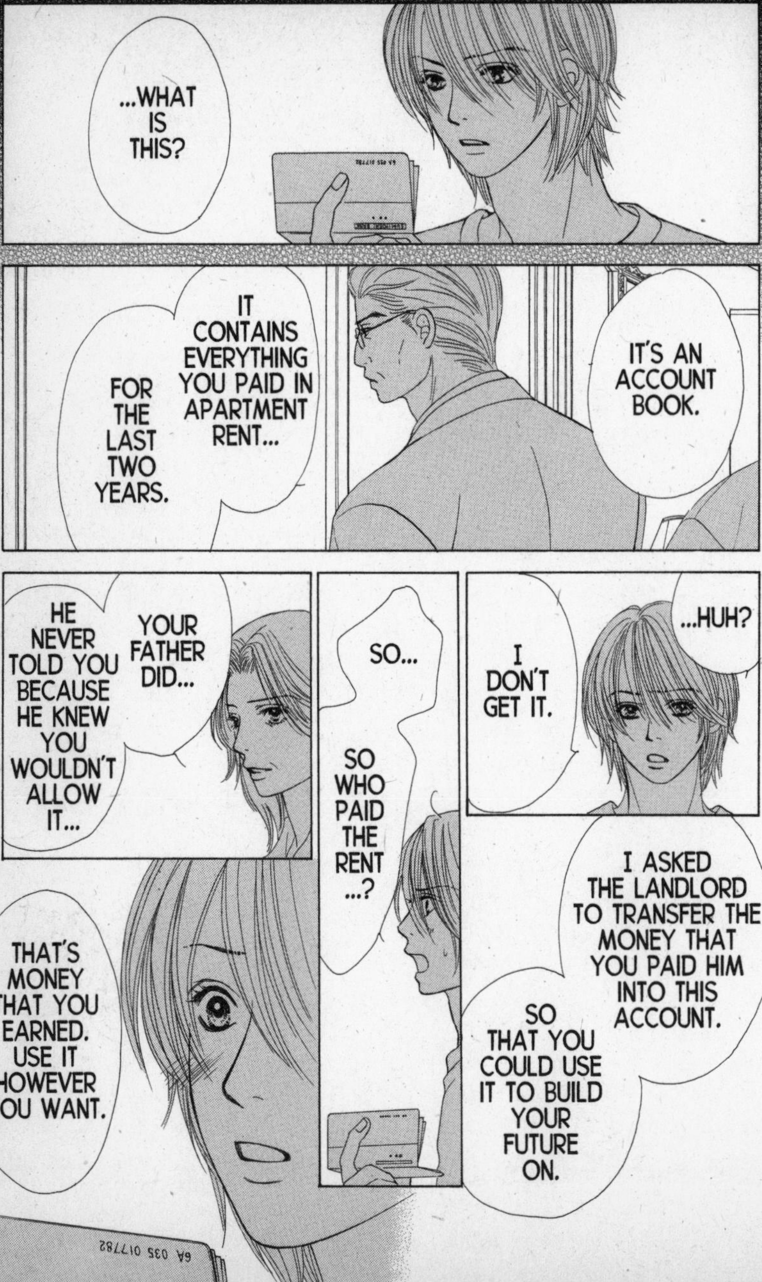
...WHAT IS THIS?
IT'S AN ACCOUNT BOOK.
IT CONTAINS EVERYTHING YOU PAID IN APARTMENT RENT...
FOR THE LAST TWO YEARS.
...HUH?
I DON'T GET IT.
SO...
SO WHO PAID THE RENT ...?
YOUR FATHER DID...
HE NEVER TOLD YOU BECAUSE HE KNEW YOU WOULDN'T ALLOW IT...
I ASKED THE LANDLORD TO TRANSFER THE MONEY THAT YOU PAID HIM INTO THIS ACCOUNT.
SO THAT YOU COULD USE IT TO BUILD YOUR FUTURE ON.
THAT'S MONEY THAT YOU EARNED. USE IT HOWEVER YOU WANT.

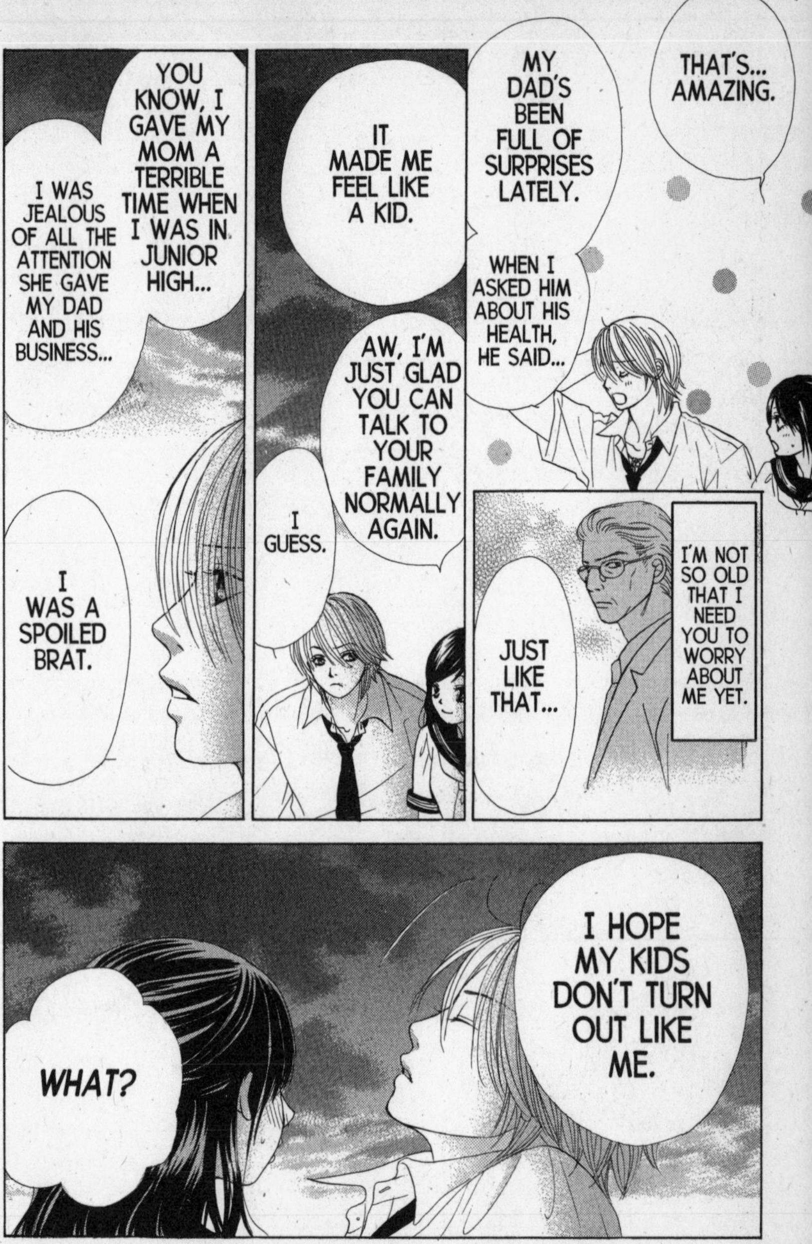
THAT'S... AMAZING.
MY DAD'S BEEN FULL OF SURPRISES LATELY.
WHEN I ASKED HIM ABOUT HIS HEALTH, HE SAID...
I'M NOT SO OLD THAT I NEED YOU TO WORRY ABOUT ME YET.
JUST LIKE THAT...
IT MADE ME FEEL LIKE A KID.
AW, I'M JUST GLAD YOU CAN TALK TO YOUR FAMILY NORMALLY AGAIN.
I GUESS.
YOU KNOW, I GAVE MY MOM A TERRIBLE TIME WHEN I WAS IN JUNIOR HIGH...
I WAS JEALOUS OF ALL THE ATTENTION SHE GAVE MY DAD AND HIS BUSINESS...
I WAS A SPOILED BRAT.
I HOPE MY KIDS DON'T TURN OUT LIKE ME.
WHAT?

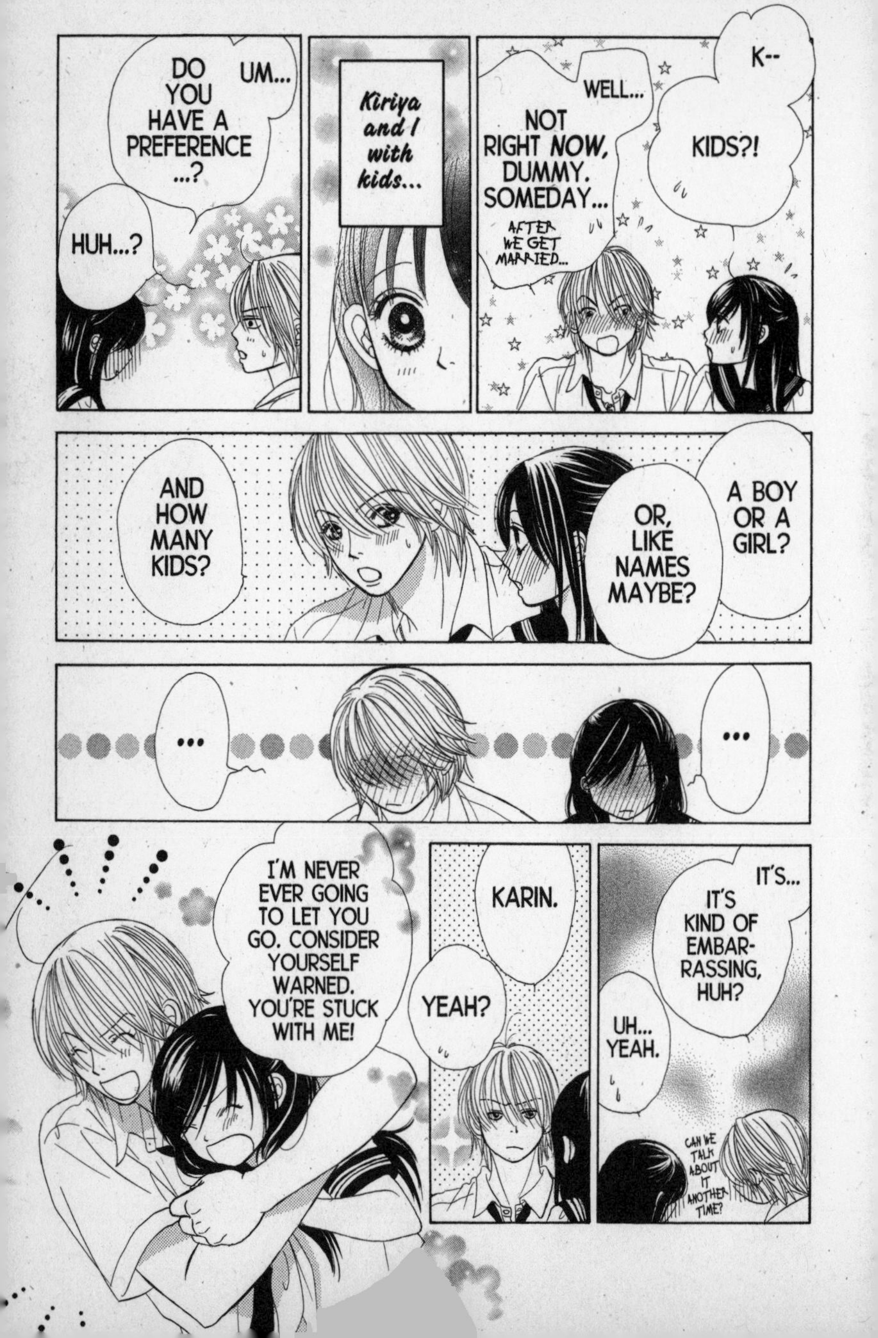
K--
KIDS?!
WELL... NOT RIGHT NOW, DUMMY. SOMEDAY...
AFTER WE GET MARRIED...
Kiriya and I with kids...
UM... DO YOU HAVE A PREFERENCE ...?
HUH...?
A BOY OR A GIRL?
OR, LIKE NAMES MAYBE?
AND HOW MANY KIDS?
...
...
IT'S... IT'S KIND OF EMBARRASSING, HUH?
UH... YEAH.
CAN WE TALK ABOUT IT ANOTHER TIME?
KARIN.
YEAH?
I'M NEVER EVER GOING TO LET YOU GO. CONSIDER YOURSELF WARNED. YOU'RE STUCK WITH ME!

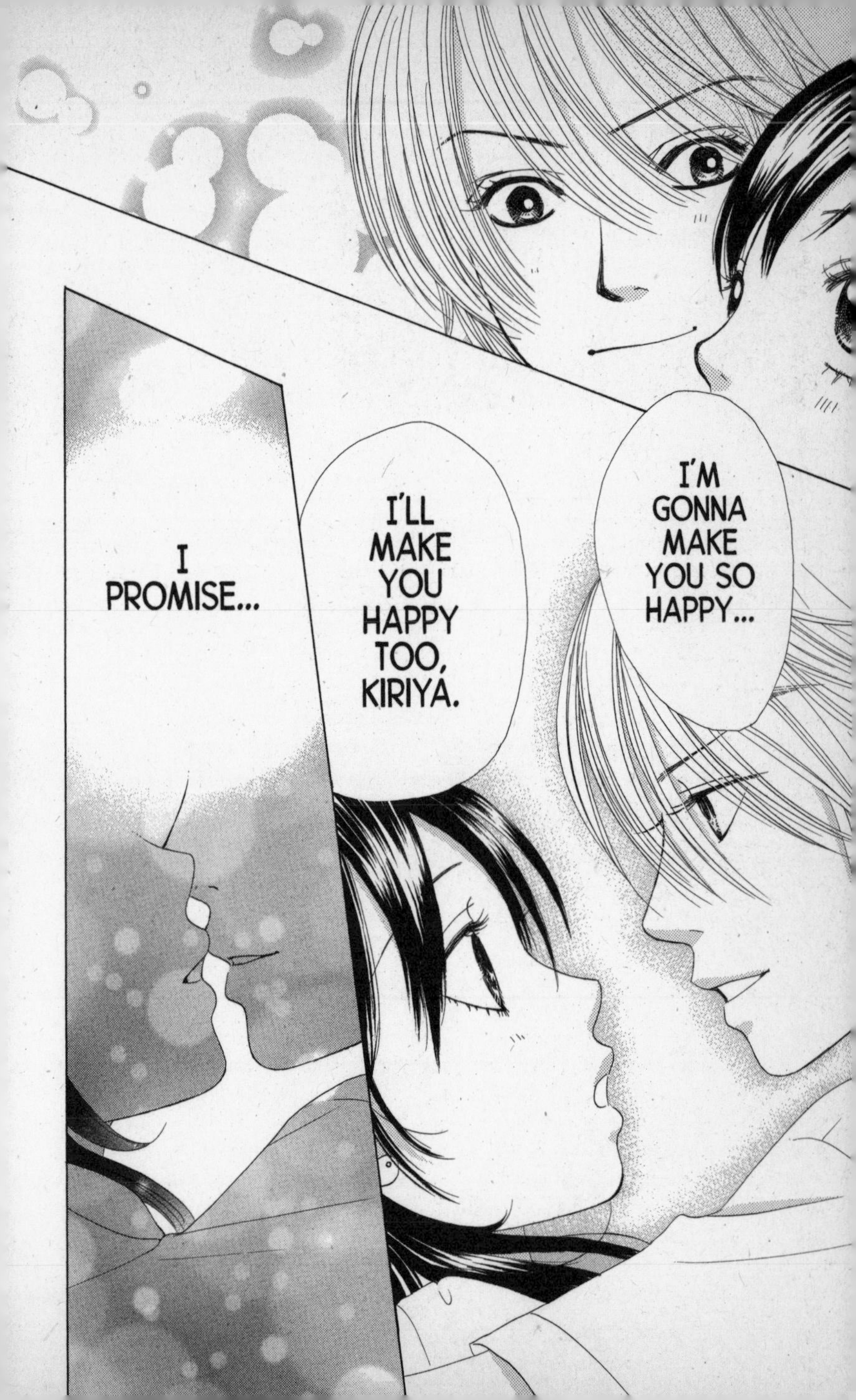
I'M GONNA MAKE YOU SO HAPPY...
I'LL MAKE YOU HAPPY TOO, KIRIYA.
I PROMISE...

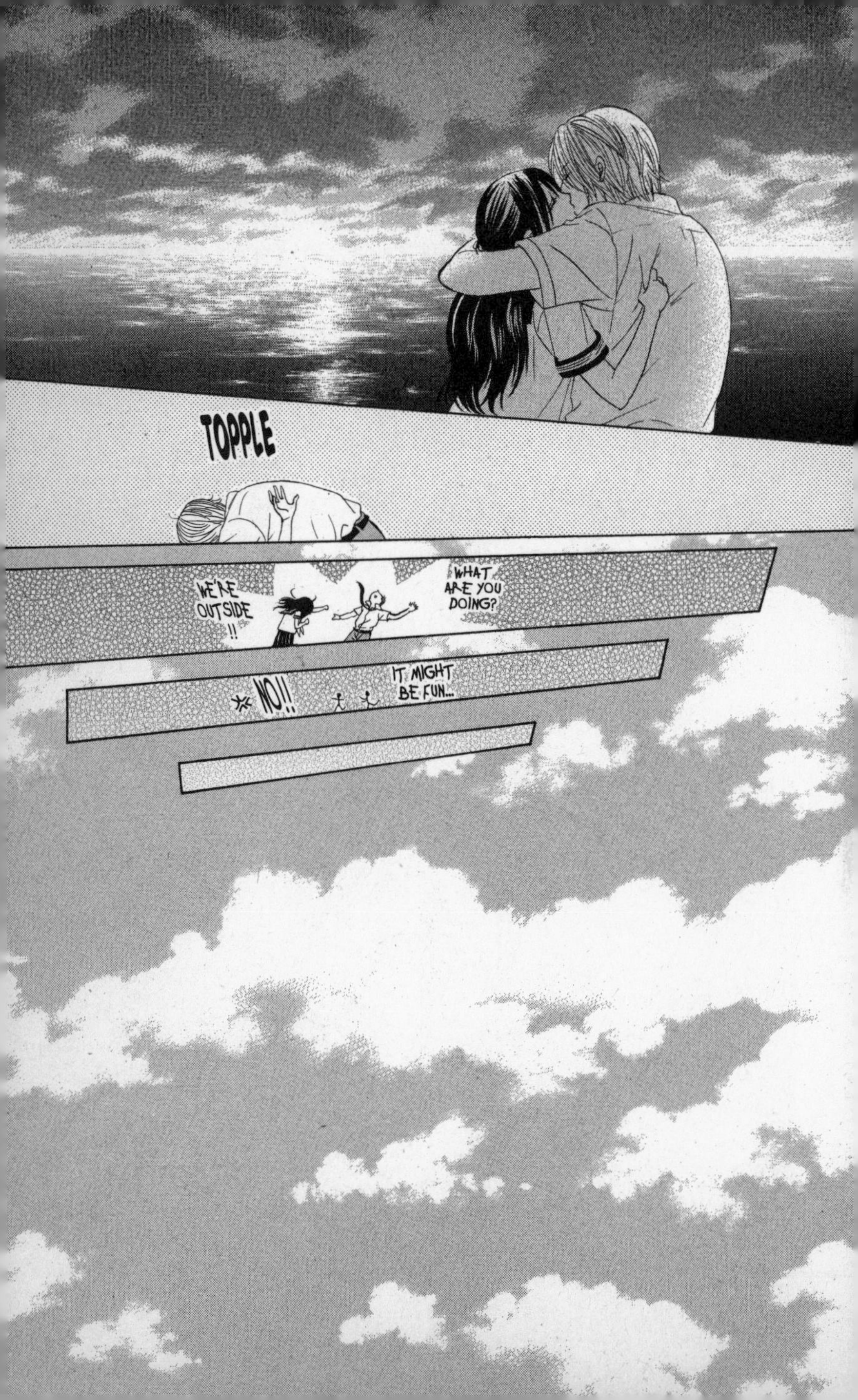
TOPPLE
WHAT ARE YOU DOING?
WE'RE OUTSIDE!!
IT MIGHT BE FUN...
NO!!

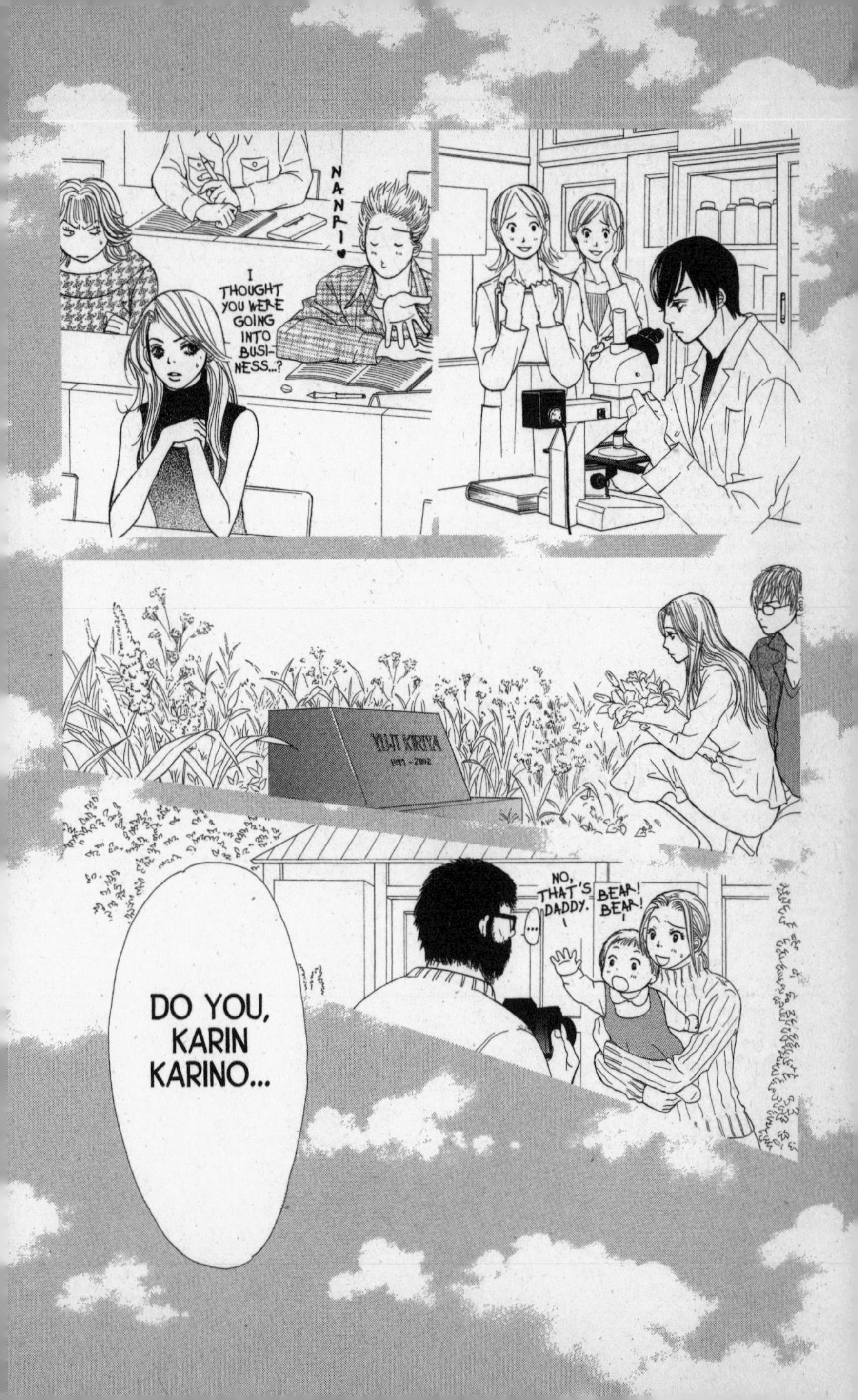
NANPI ♥
I THOUGHT YOU WERE GOING INTO BUSINESS...?
YUJI KIRIYA
BEAR! BEAR!
NO, THAT'S DADDY.
...
DO YOU, KARIN KARINO...

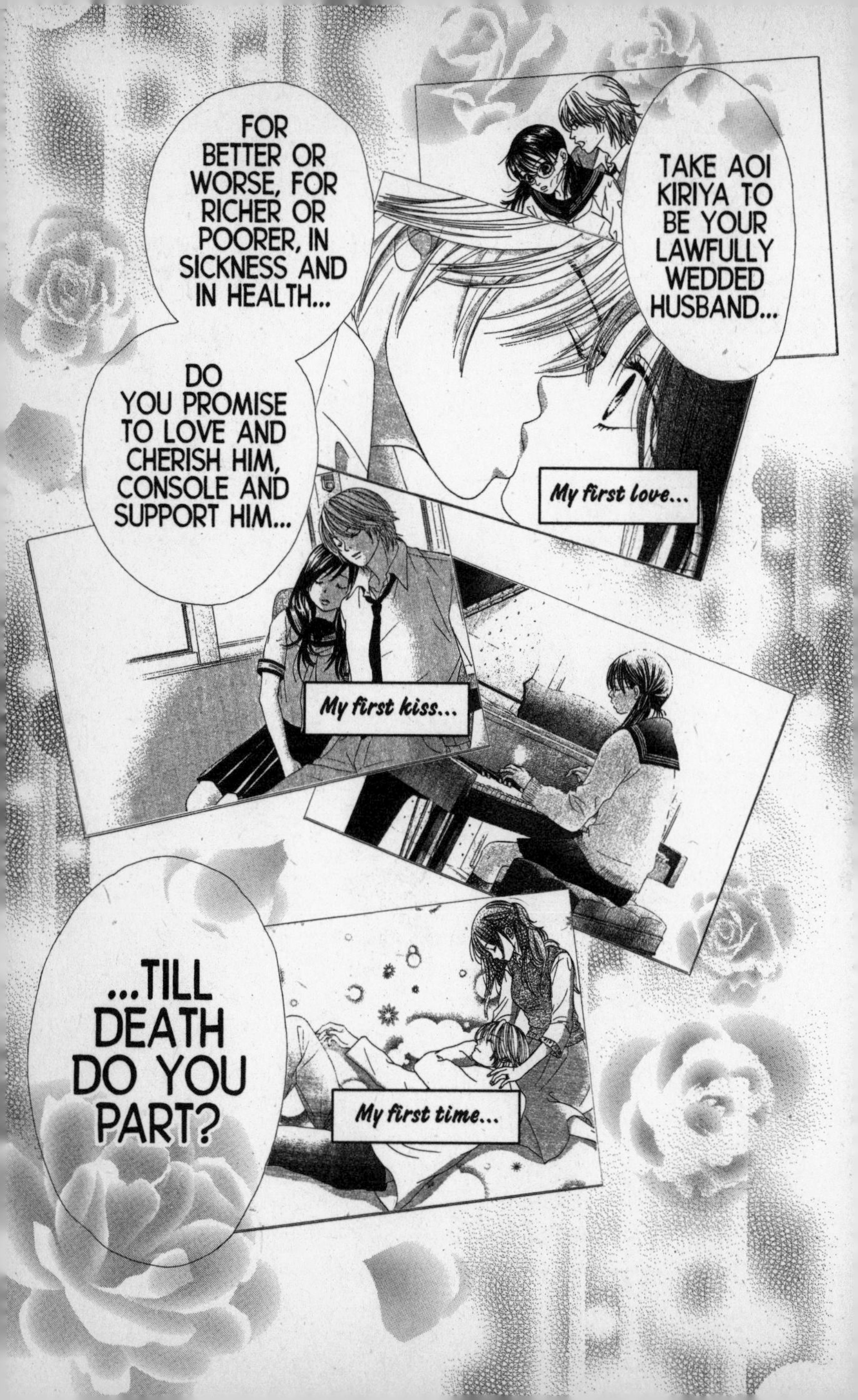
TAKE AOI KIRIYA TO BE YOUR LAWFULLY WEDDED HUSBAND...
FOR BETTER OR WORSE, FOR RICHER OR POORER, IN SICKNESS AND IN HEALTH...
My first love...
DO YOU PROMISE TO LOVE AND CHERISH HIM, CONSOLE AND SUPPORT HIM...
My first kiss...
...TILL DEATH DO YOU PART?
My first time...

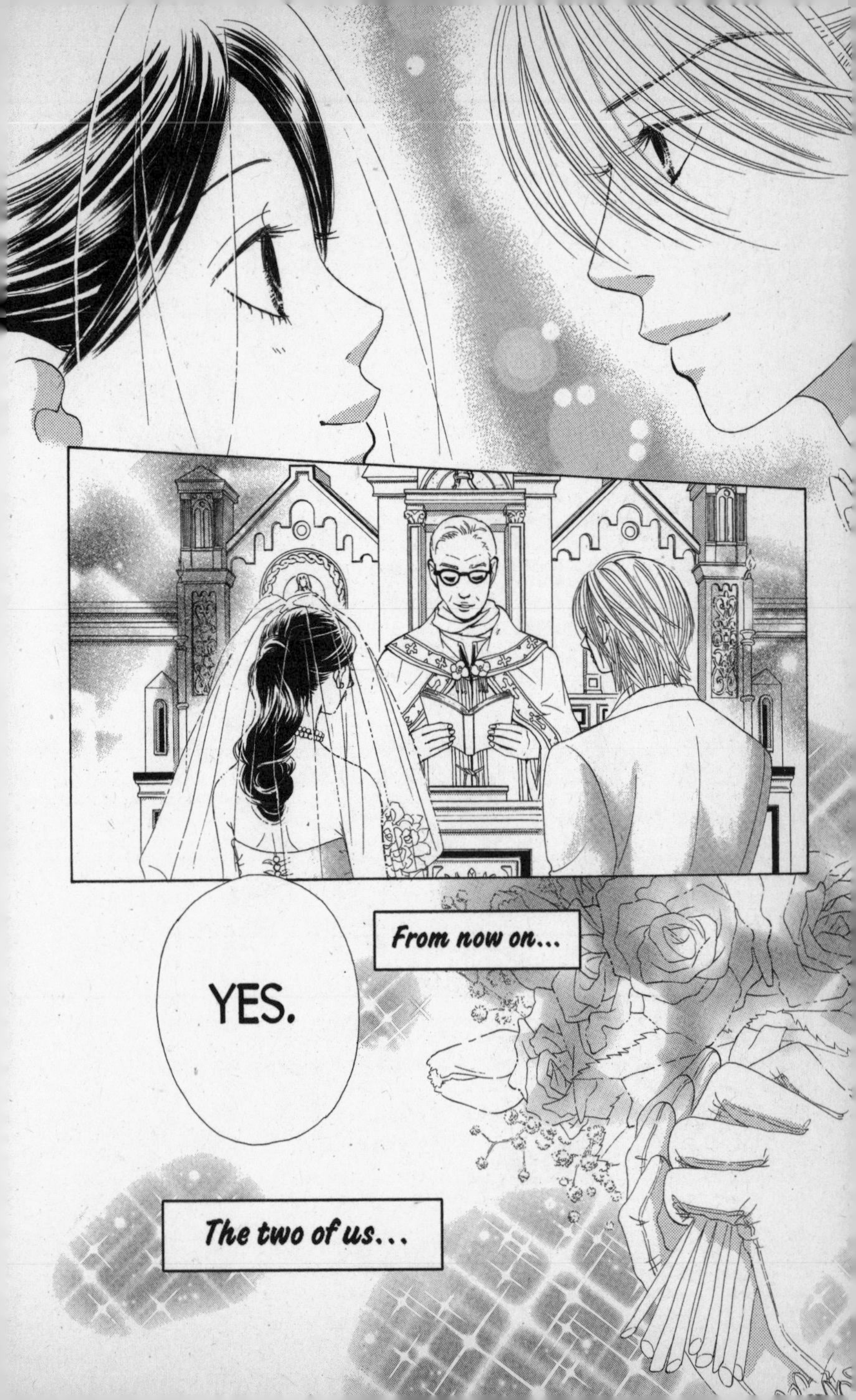
From now on...
YES.
The two of us...

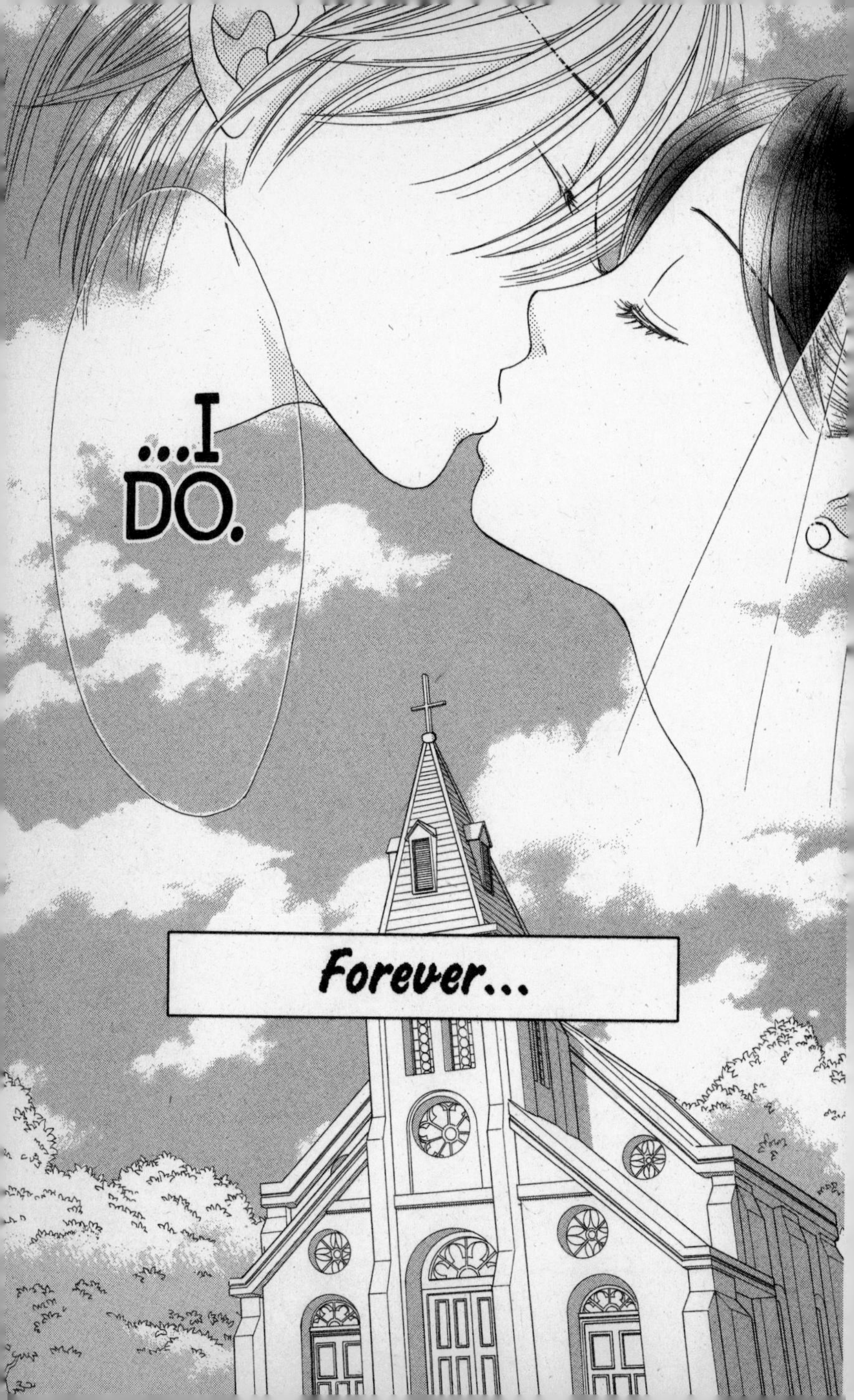
...I DO.
Forever...

[彼] KARE
First Love

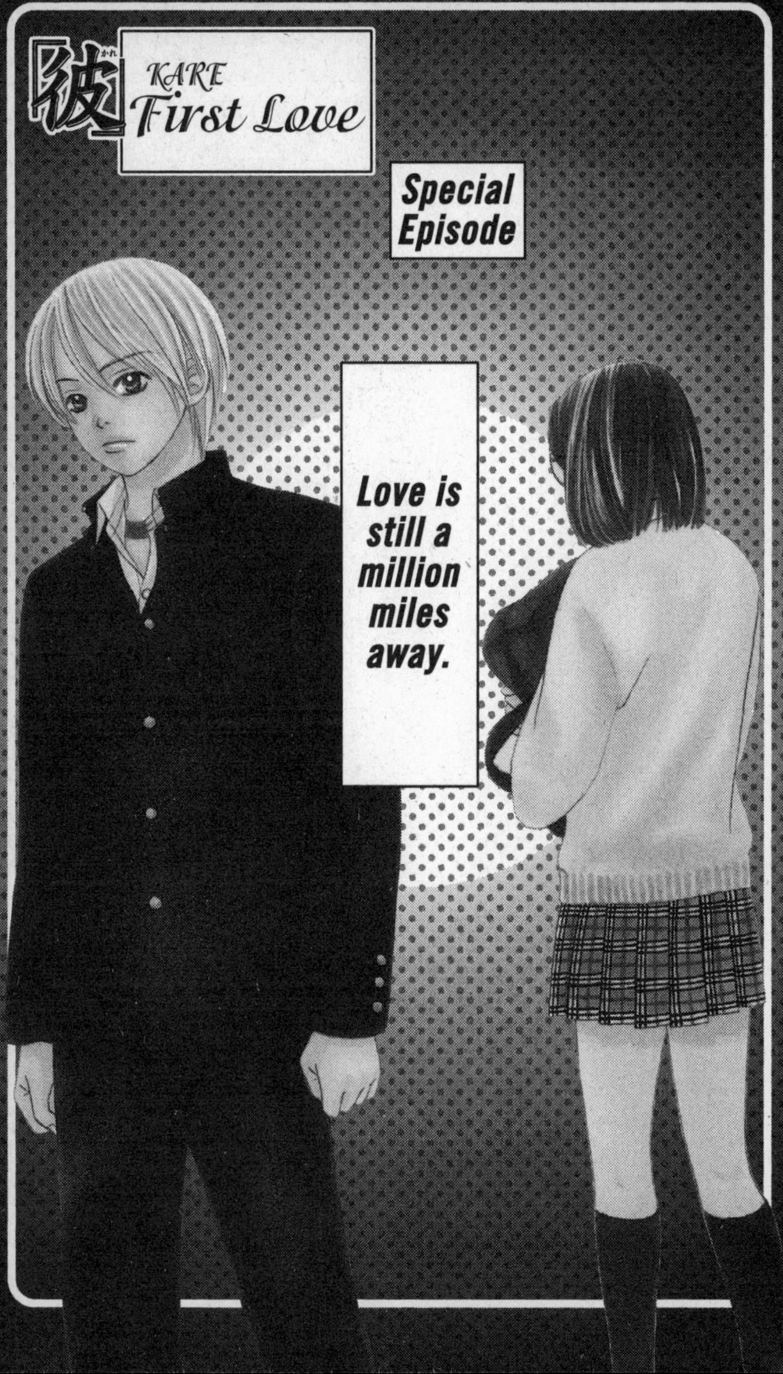

「彼」かれ KARE First Love
Special Episode
Love is still a million miles away.

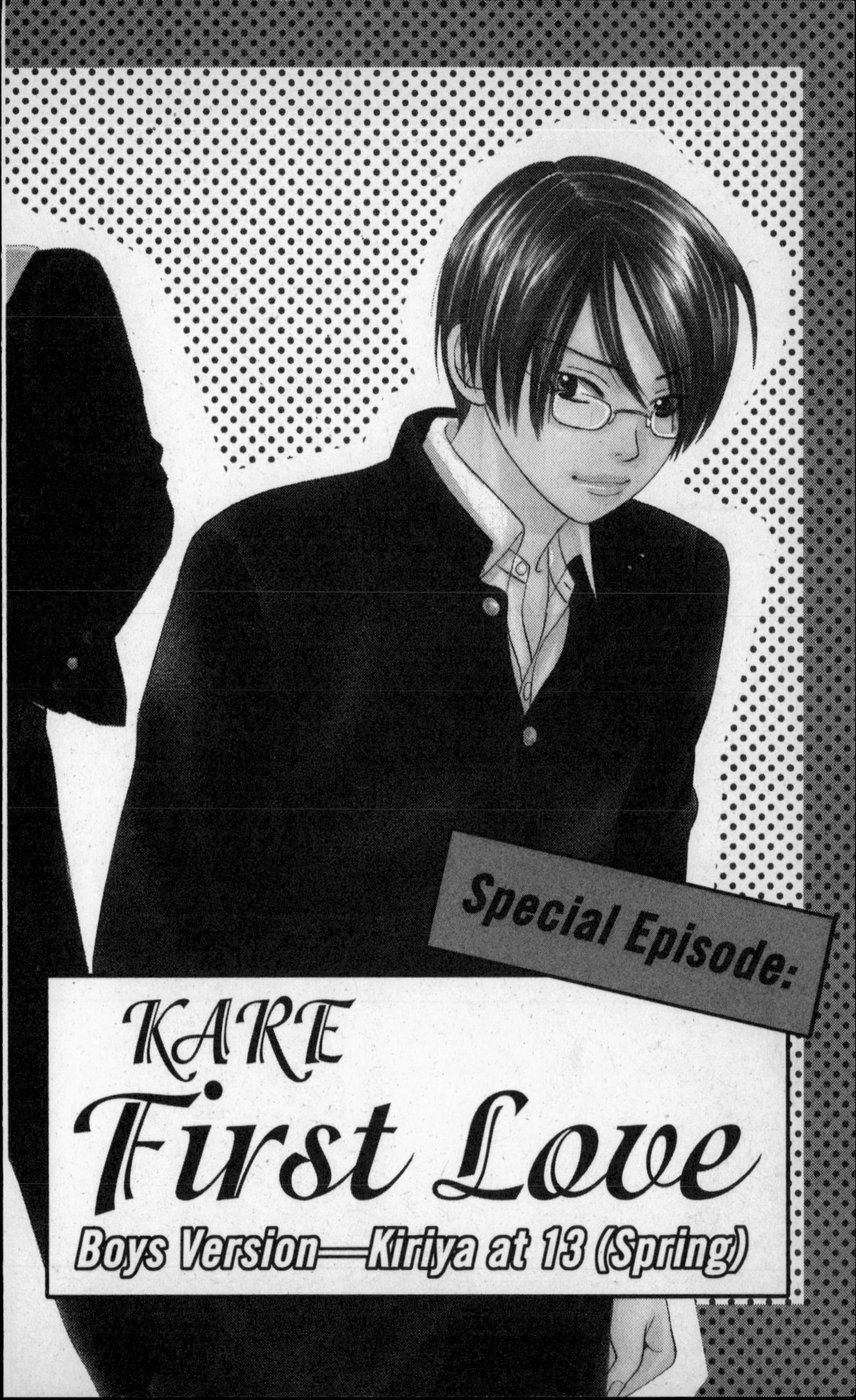
Special Episode:
KARE
First Love
Boys Version—Kiriya at 13 (Spring)

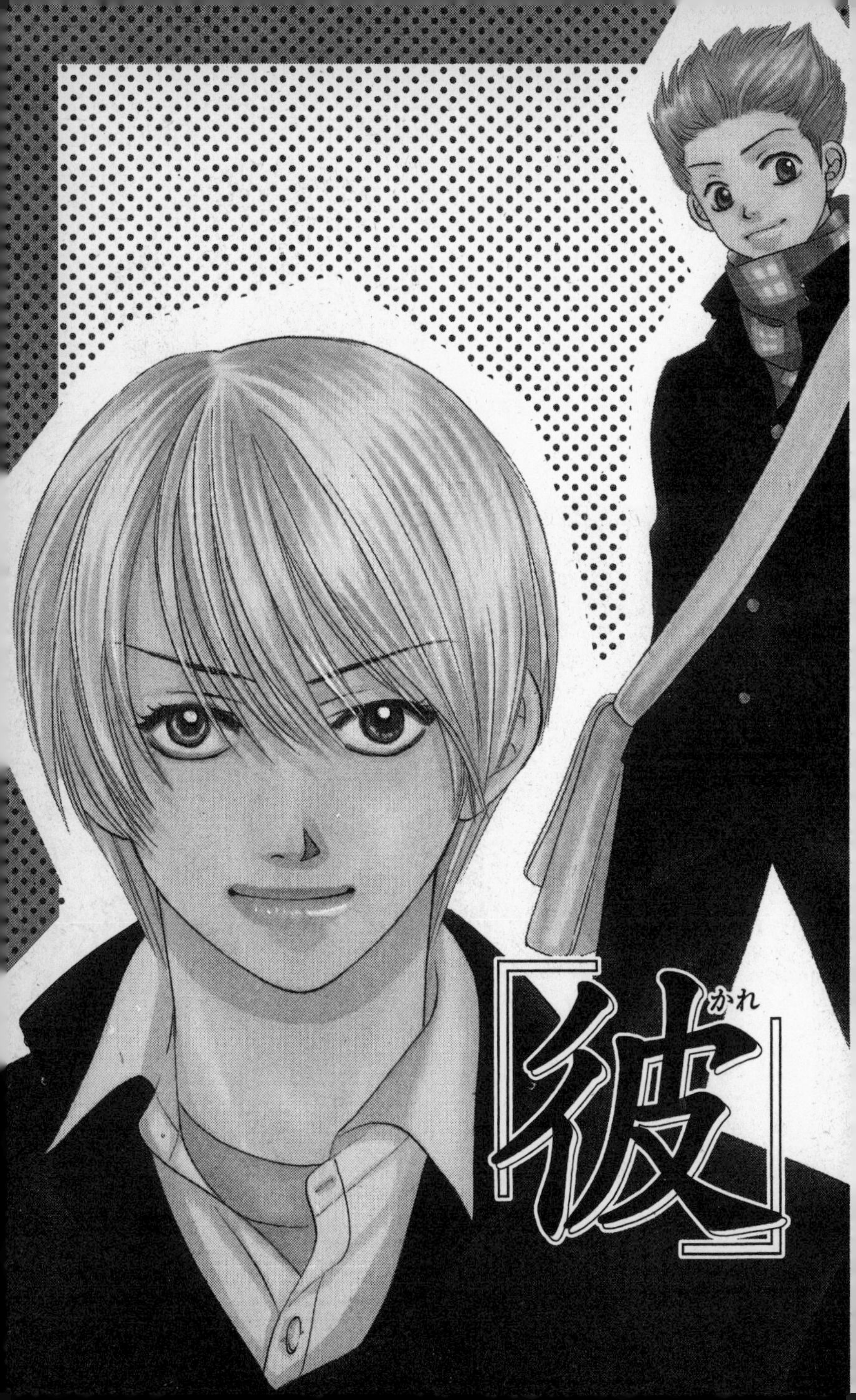
「彼」
かれ

KARE
彼 First Love

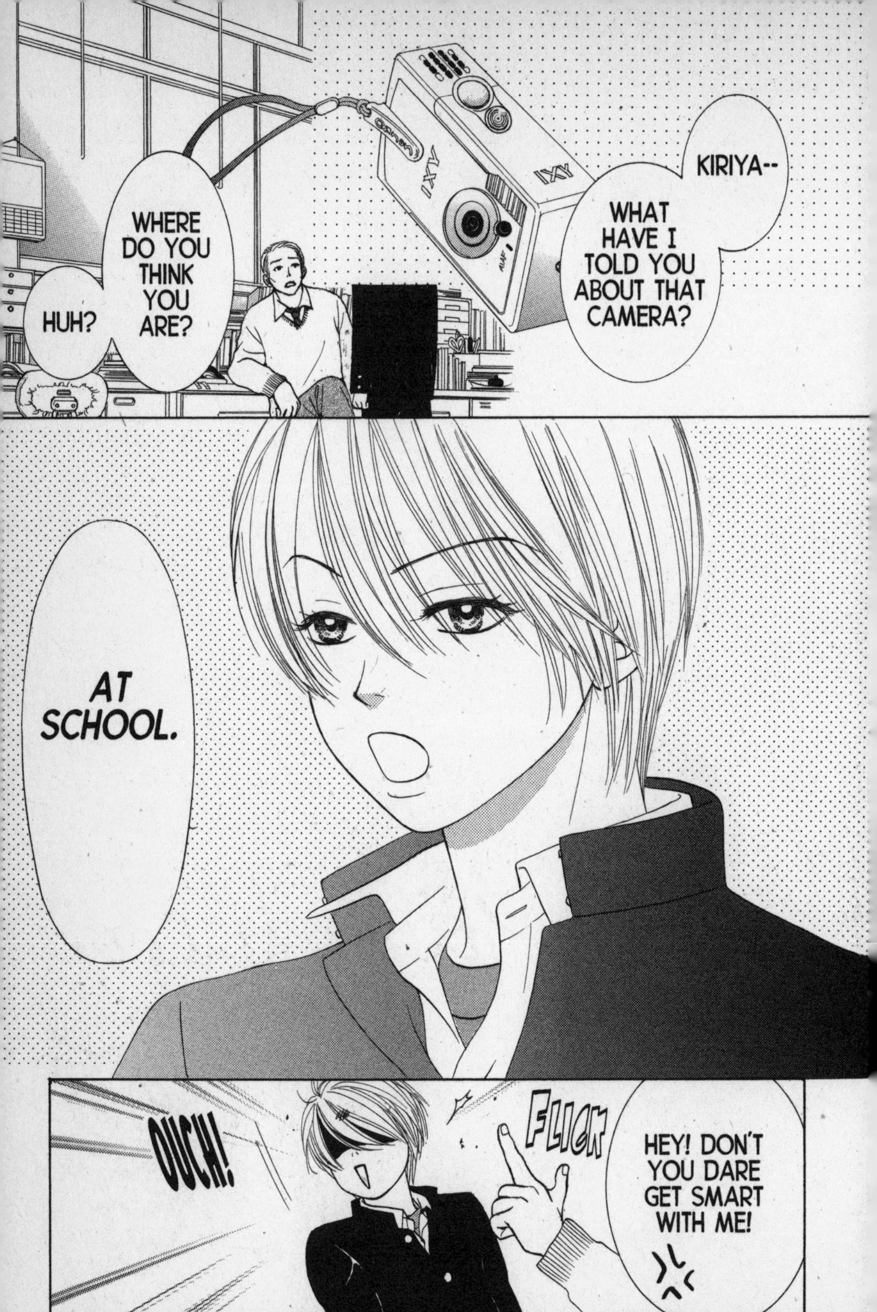
KIRIYA--
WHAT HAVE I TOLD YOU ABOUT THAT CAMERA?
WHERE DO YOU THINK YOU ARE?
HUH?
AT SCHOOL.
HEY! DON'T YOU DARE GET SMART WITH ME!
FLICK
OUCH!

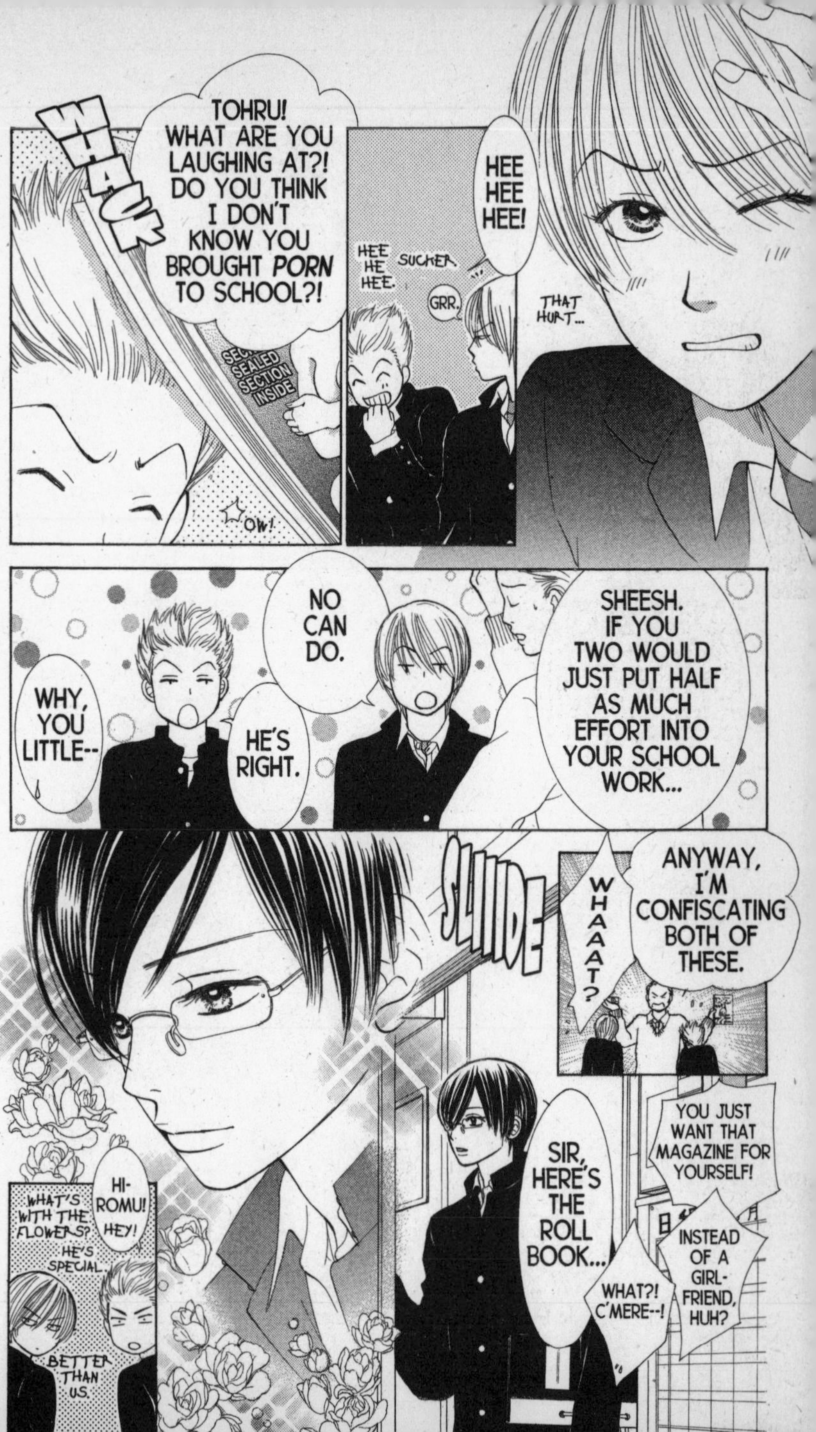
THAT HURT...
HEE HEE HEE!
HEE HE HEE.
SUCKER.
GRR.
WHACK
TOHRU! WHAT ARE YOU LAUGHING AT?! DO YOU THINK I DON'T KNOW YOU BROUGHT *PORN* TO SCHOOL?!
SEALED SECTION INSIDE
OW!
SHEESH. IF YOU TWO WOULD JUST PUT HALF AS MUCH EFFORT INTO YOUR SCHOOL WORK...
NO CAN DO.
HE'S RIGHT.
WHY, YOU LITTLE--
ANYWAY, I'M CONFISCATING BOTH OF THESE.
WHAAAAT?
SLIIIDE
YOU JUST WANT THAT MAGAZINE FOR YOURSELF!
INSTEAD OF A GIRL-FRIEND, HUH?
WHAT?! C'MERE--!
SIR, HERE'S THE ROLL BOOK...
HI-ROMU! HEY!
WHAT'S WITH THE FLOWERS?
HE'S SPECIAL.
BETTER THAN US.

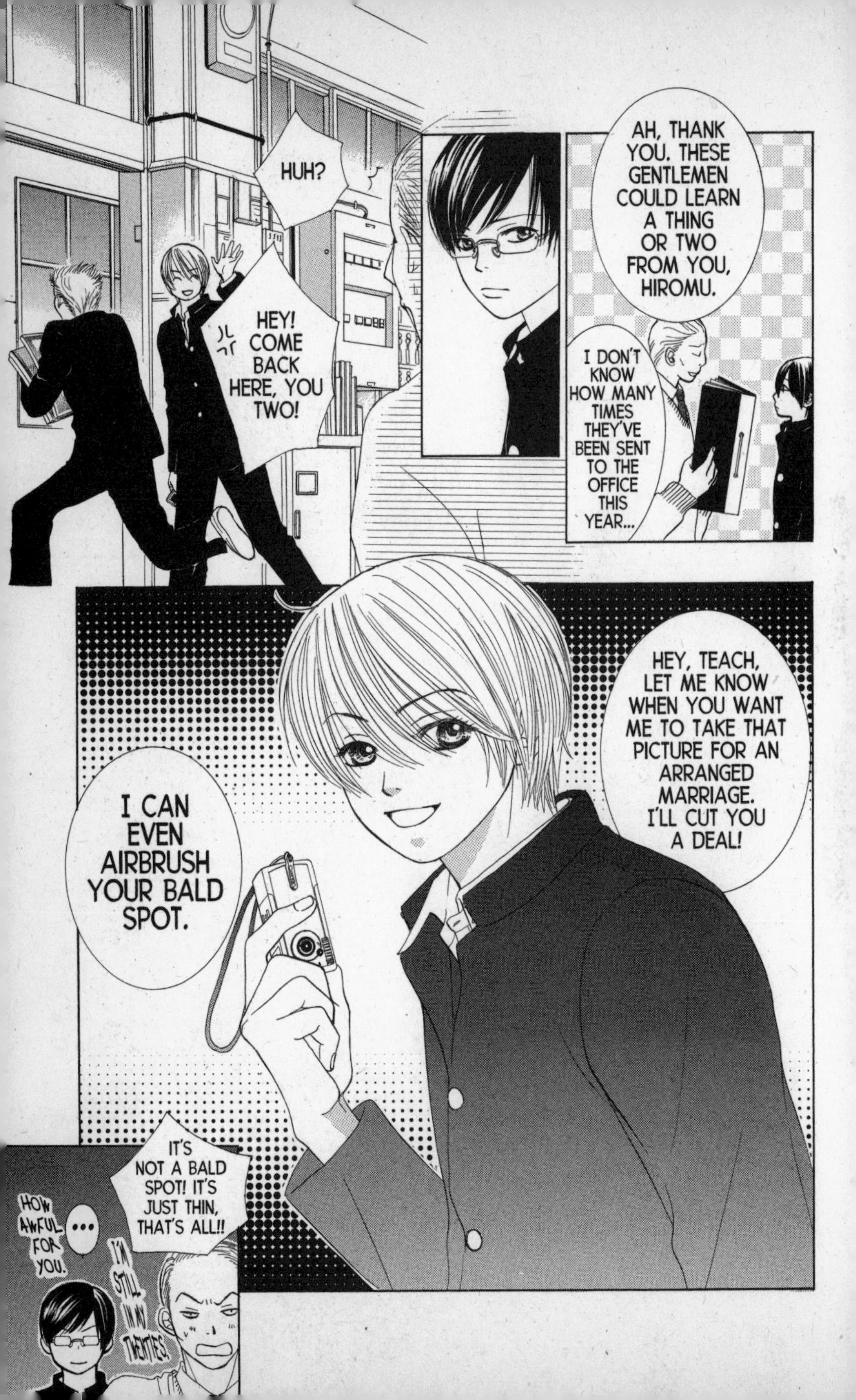
AH, THANK YOU. THESE GENTLEMEN COULD LEARN A THING OR TWO FROM YOU, HIROMU.
I DON'T KNOW HOW MANY TIMES THEY'VE BEEN SENT TO THE OFFICE THIS YEAR...
HUH?
HEY! COME BACK HERE, YOU TWO!
HEY, TEACH, LET ME KNOW WHEN YOU WANT ME TO TAKE THAT PICTURE FOR AN ARRANGED MARRIAGE. I'LL CUT YOU A DEAL!
I CAN EVEN AIRBRUSH YOUR BALD SPOT.
IT'S NOT A BALD SPOT! IT'S JUST THIN, THAT'S ALL!!
...
I'M STILL IN MY TWENTIES.
HOW AWFUL FOR YOU.

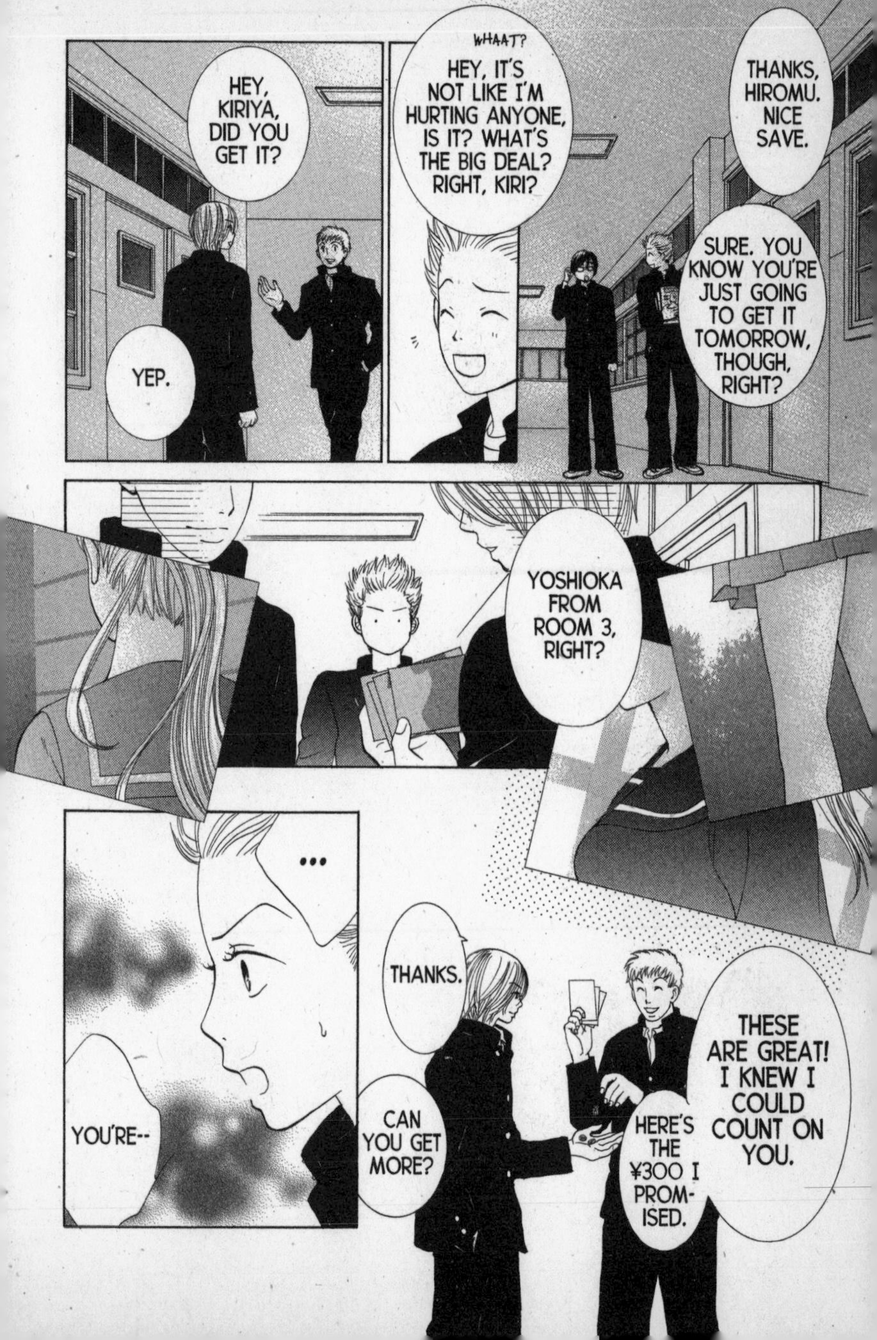
THANKS, HIROMU. NICE SAVE.
SURE. YOU KNOW YOU'RE JUST GOING TO GET IT TOMORROW, THOUGH, RIGHT?
WHAAT?
HEY, IT'S NOT LIKE I'M HURTING ANYONE, IS IT? WHAT'S THE BIG DEAL? RIGHT, KIRI?
HEY, KIRIYA, DID YOU GET IT?
YEP.
YOSHIOKA FROM ROOM 3, RIGHT?
THESE ARE GREAT! I KNEW I COULD COUNT ON YOU.
HERE'S THE ¥300 I PROMISED.
THANKS.
CAN YOU GET MORE?
...
YOU'RE--

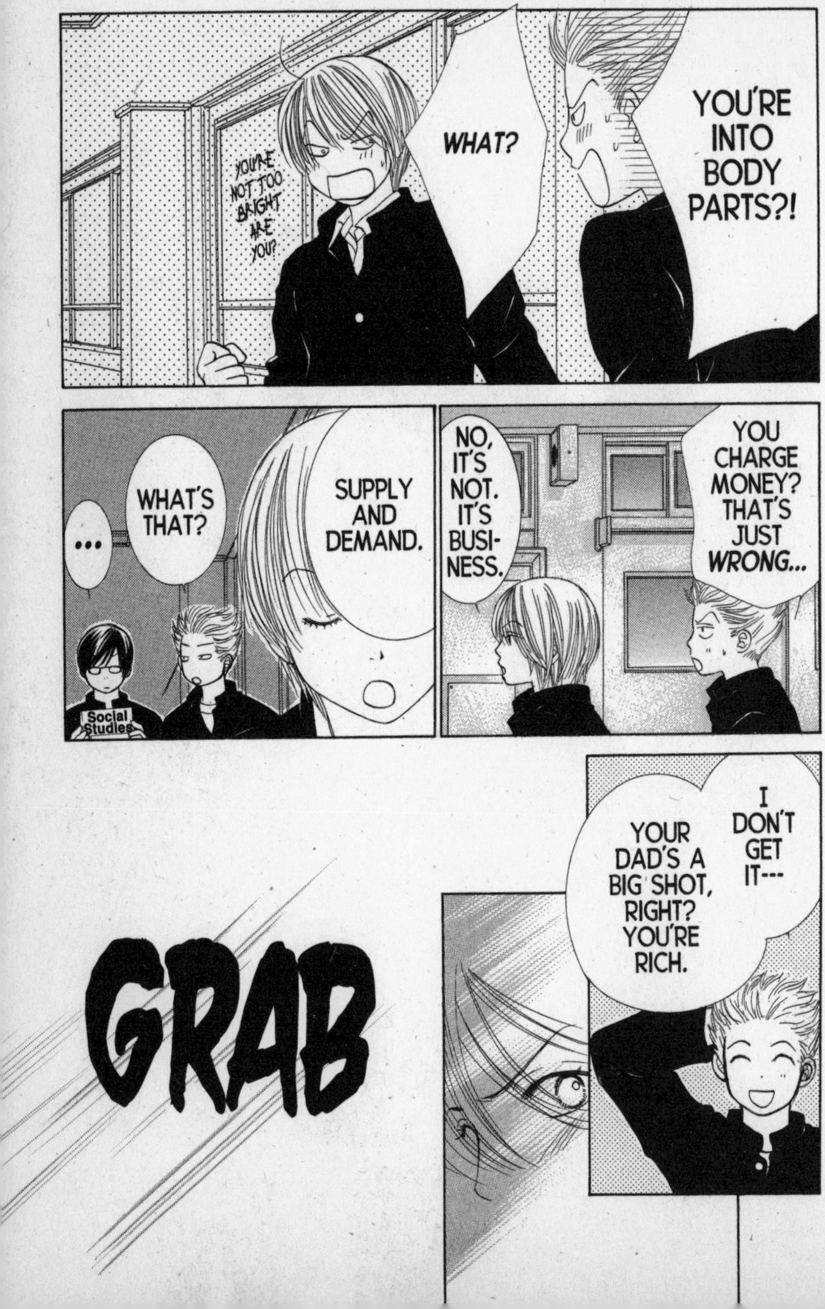
YOU'RE INTO BODY PARTS?!
WHAT?
YOU'RE NOT TOO BRIGHT ARE YOU?
YOU CHARGE MONEY? THAT'S JUST WRONG...
NO, IT'S NOT. IT'S BUSINESS.
SUPPLY AND DEMAND.
WHAT'S THAT?
...
Social Studies
I DON'T GET IT---
YOUR DAD'S A BIG SHOT, RIGHT? YOU'RE RICH.
GRAB

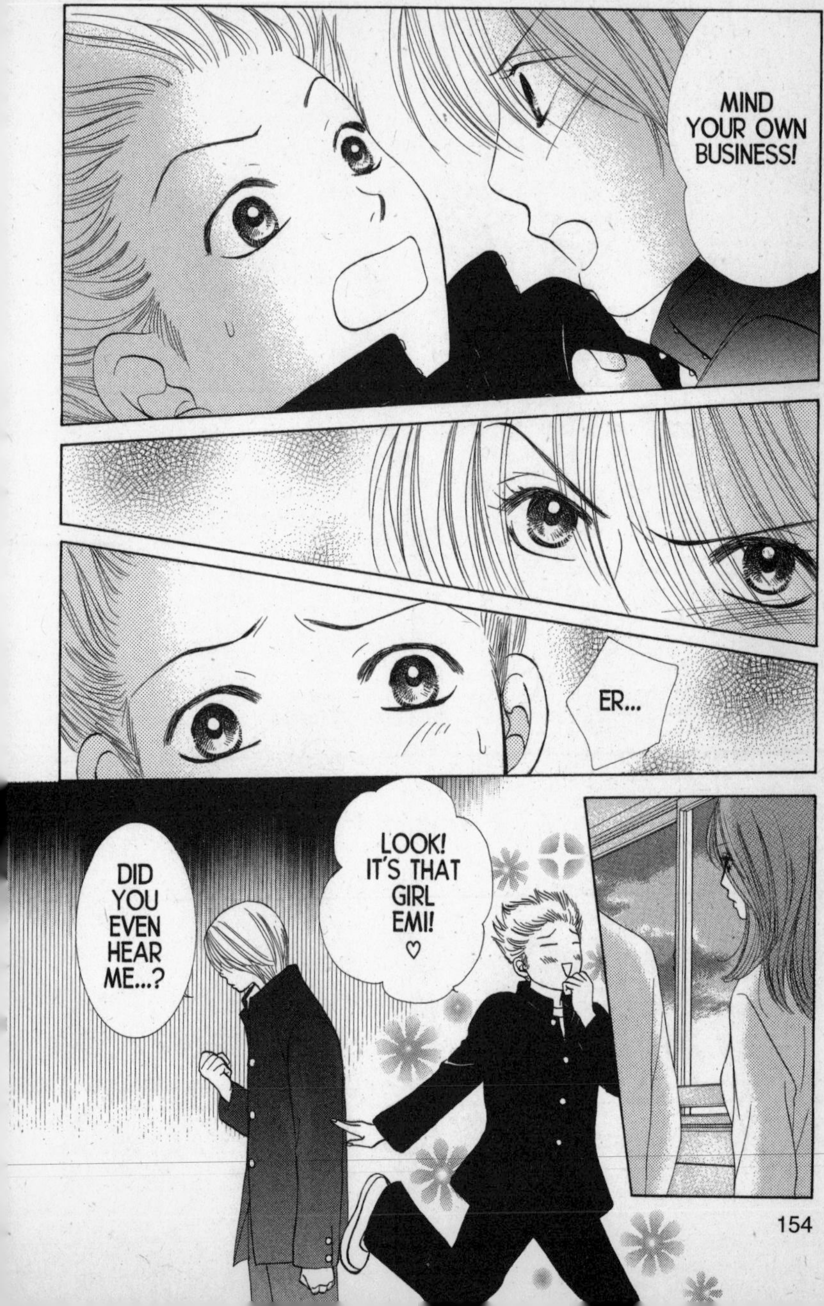
MIND YOUR OWN BUSINESS!
ER...
LOOK! IT'S THAT GIRL EMI! ♡
DID YOU EVEN HEAR ME...?

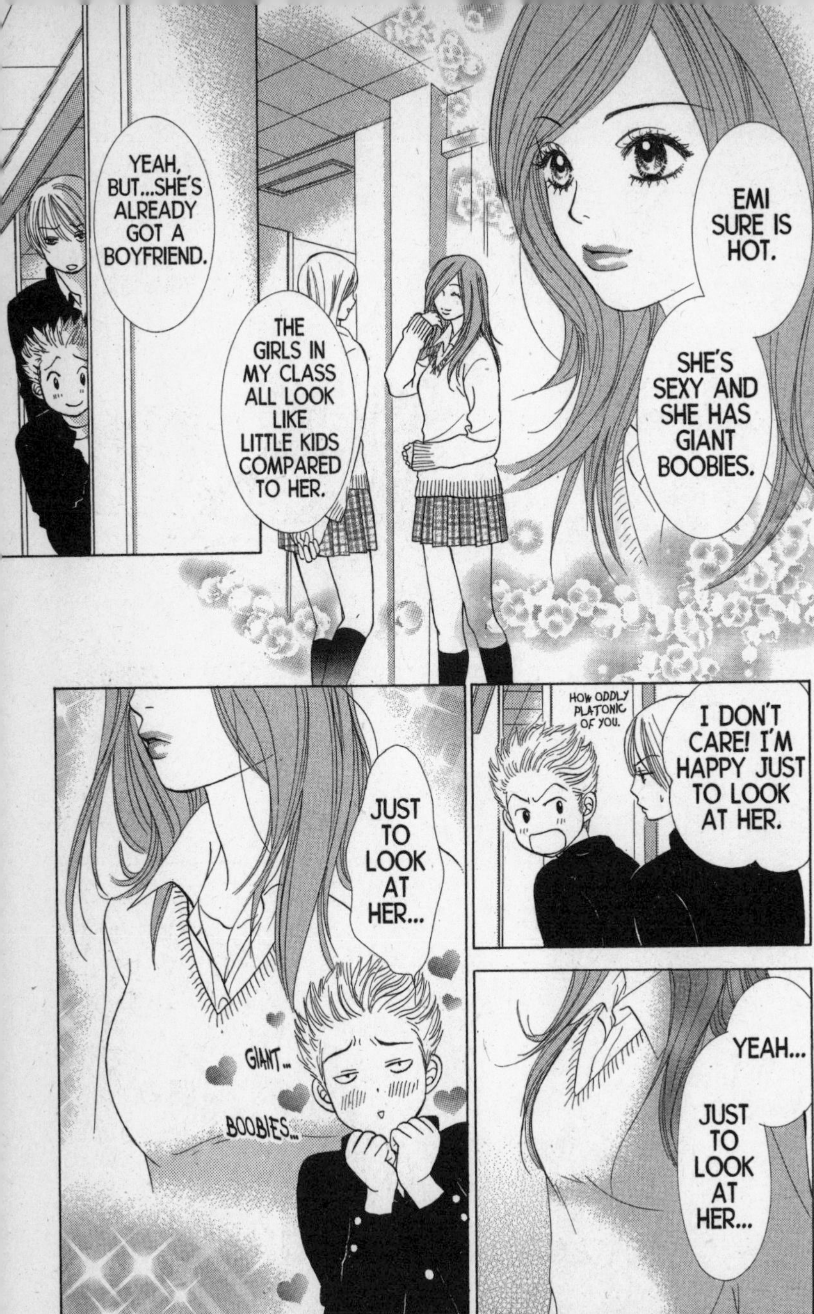
EMI SURE IS HOT.
SHE'S SEXY AND SHE HAS GIANT BOOBIES.
THE GIRLS IN MY CLASS ALL LOOK LIKE LITTLE KIDS COMPARED TO HER.
YEAH, BUT...SHE'S ALREADY GOT A BOYFRIEND.
I DON'T CARE! I'M HAPPY JUST TO LOOK AT HER.
HOW ODDLY PLATONIC OF YOU.
YEAH...
JUST TO LOOK AT HER...
JUST TO LOOK AT HER...
GIANT...
BOOBIES...

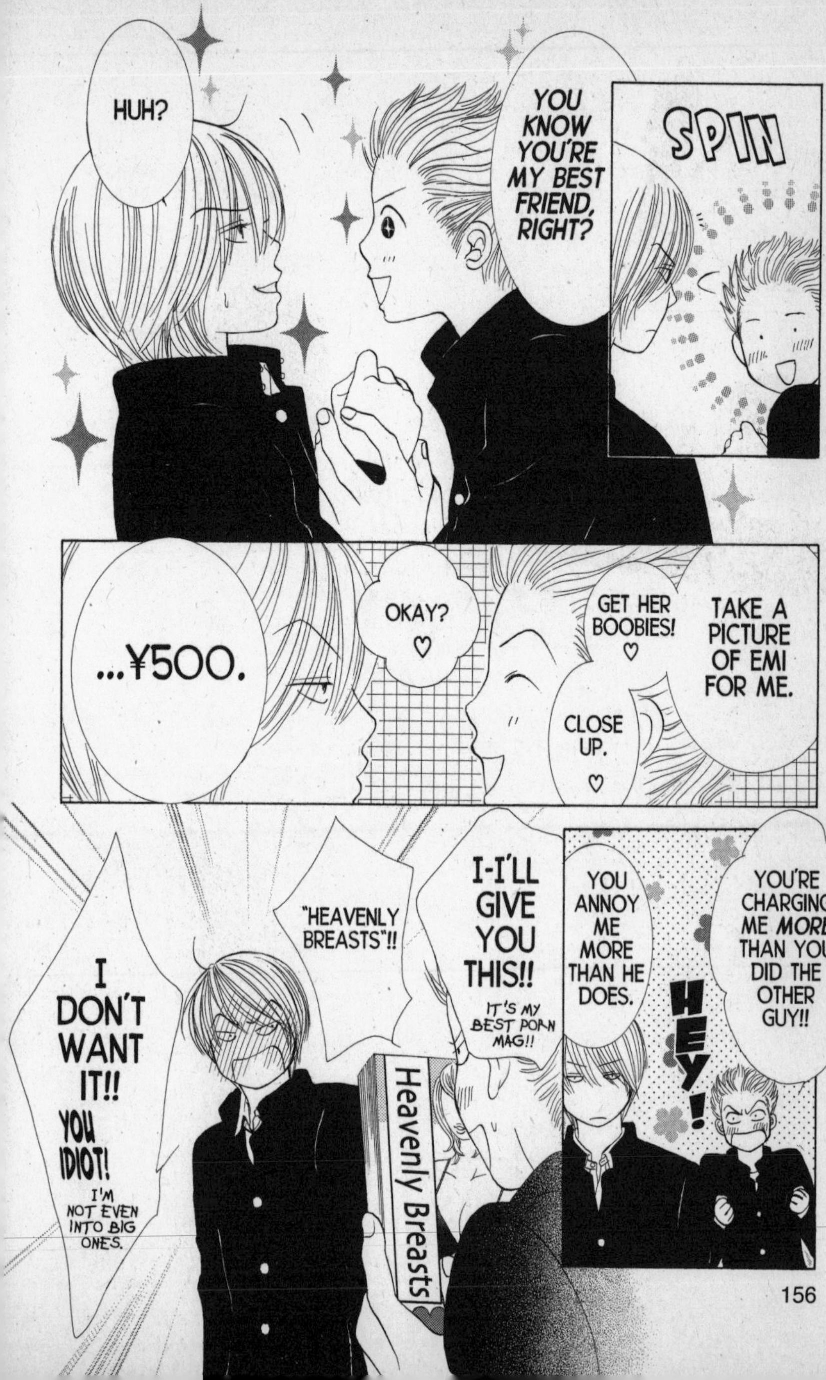
SPIN
YOU KNOW YOU'RE MY BEST FRIEND, RIGHT?
HUH?
TAKE A PICTURE OF EMI FOR ME.
GET HER BOOBIES! ♡
CLOSE UP. ♡
OKAY? ♡
...¥500.
YOU'RE CHARGING ME *MORE* THAN YOU DID THE OTHER GUY!!
HEY!
YOU ANNOY ME MORE THAN HE DOES.
I-I'LL GIVE YOU THIS!!
IT'S MY BEST PORN MAG!!
"HEAVENLY BREASTS"!!
Heavenly Breasts
I DON'T WANT IT!! YOU IDIOT!
I'M NOT EVEN INTO BIG ONES.

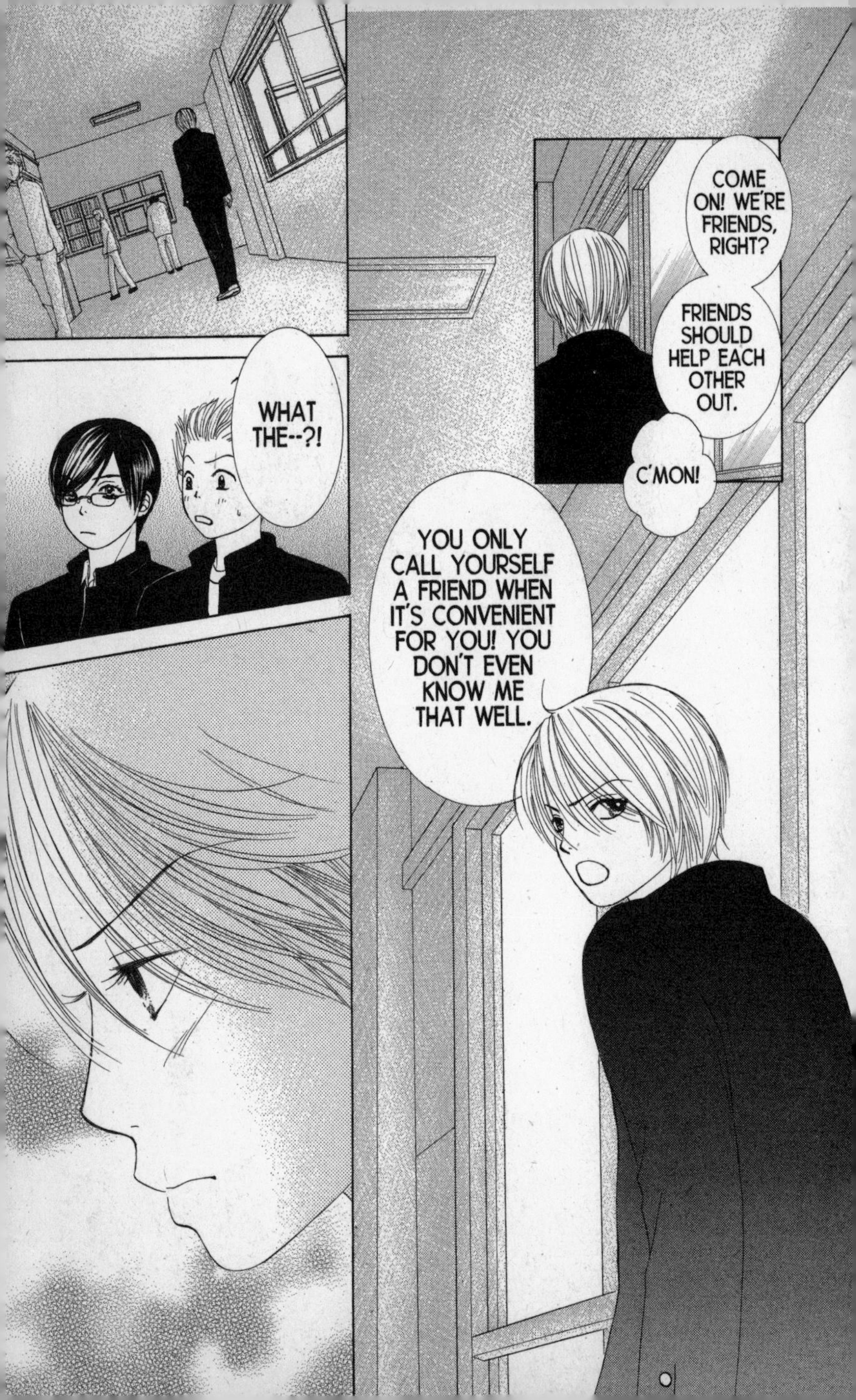
COME ON! WE'RE FRIENDS, RIGHT?
FRIENDS SHOULD HELP EACH OTHER OUT.
C'MON!
YOU ONLY CALL YOURSELF A FRIEND WHEN IT'S CONVENIENT FOR YOU! YOU DON'T EVEN KNOW ME THAT WELL.
WHAT THE--?!

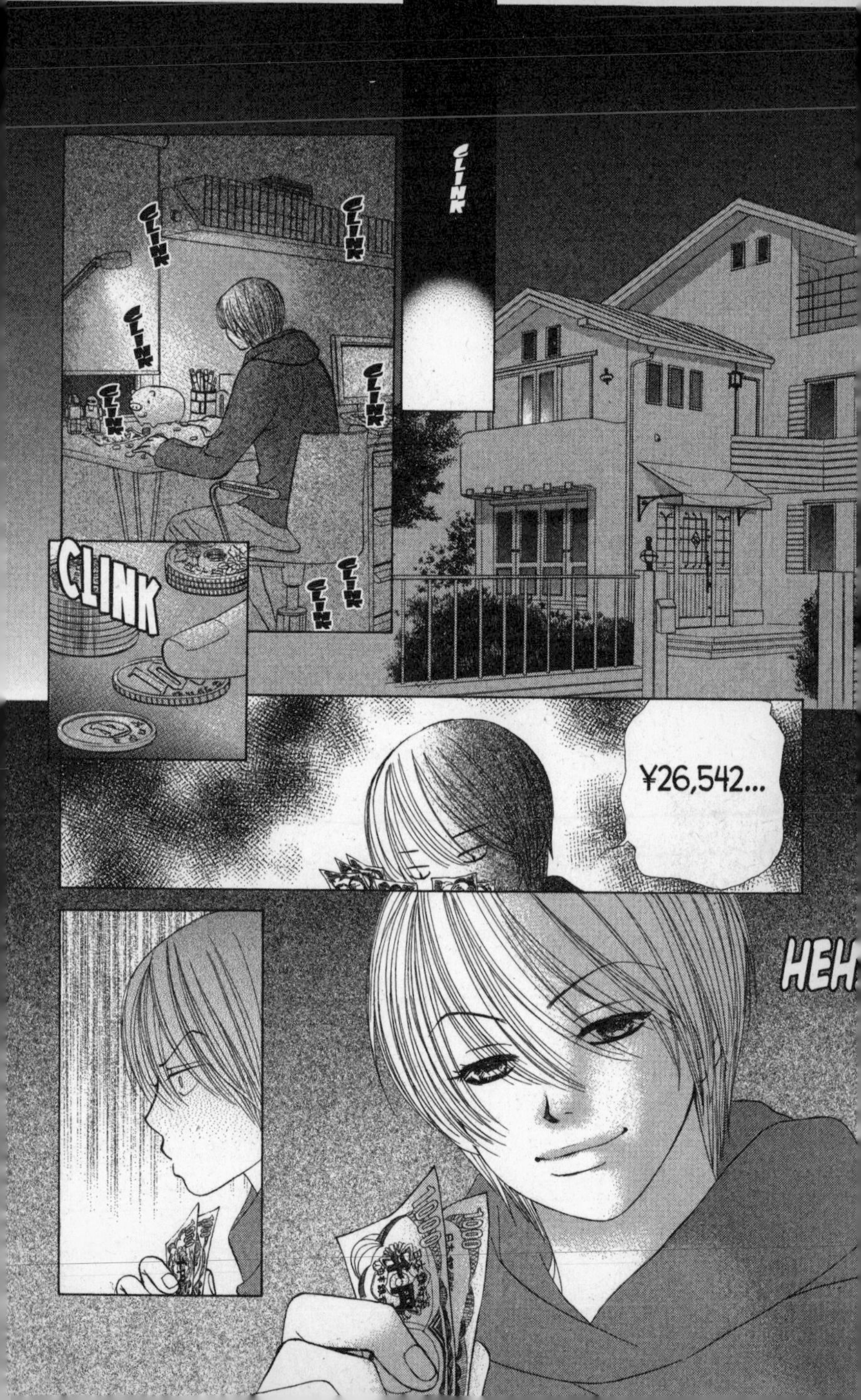
CLINK
CLINK
CLINK
CLINK
CLINK
CLINK
CLINK
CLINK
CLINK
¥26,542...
HEH

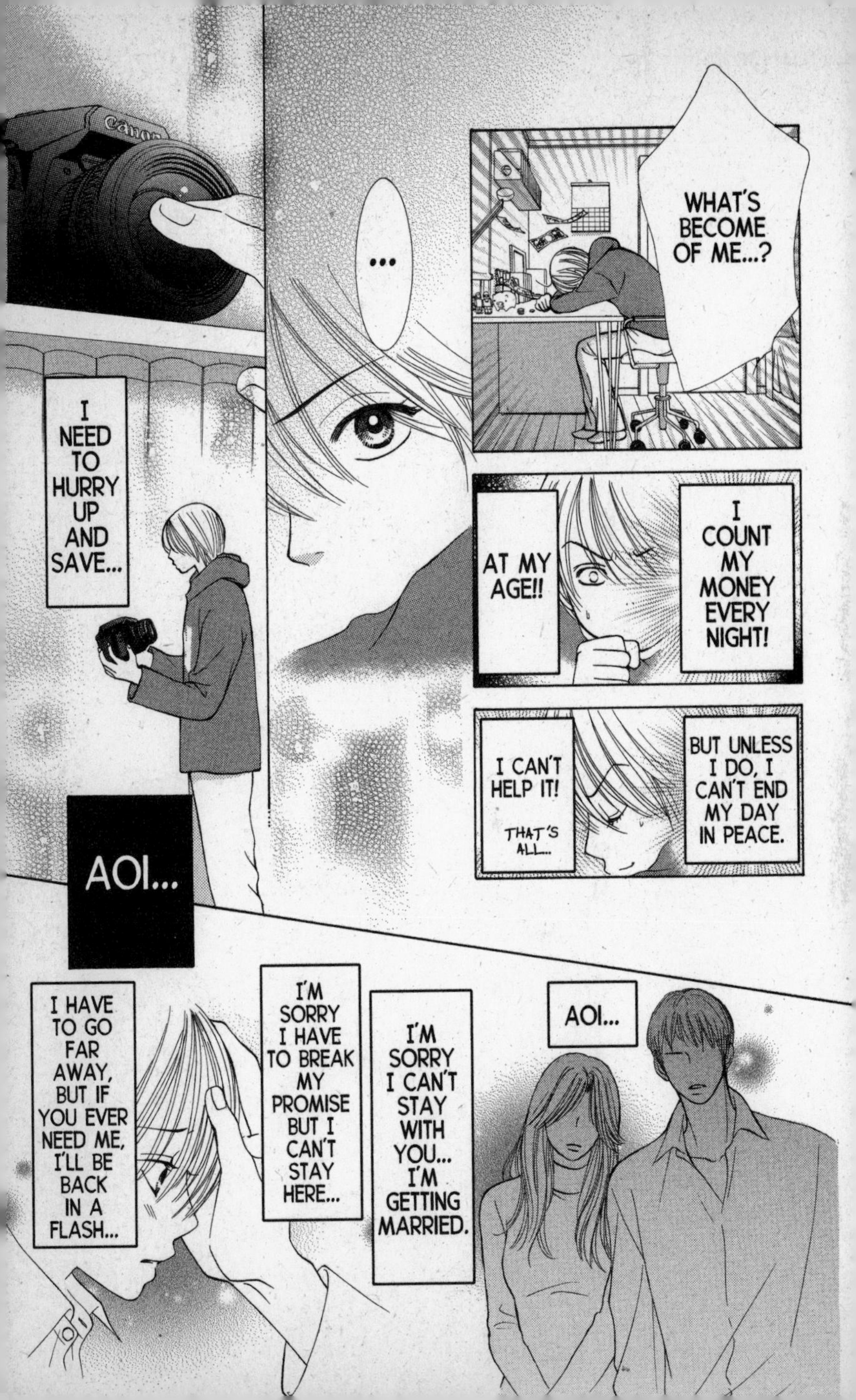
WHAT'S BECOME OF ME...?
I COUNT MY MONEY EVERY NIGHT!
AT MY AGE!!
BUT UNLESS I DO, I CAN'T END MY DAY IN PEACE.
I CAN'T HELP IT!
THAT'S ALL...
...
I NEED TO HURRY UP AND SAVE...
AOI...
AOI...
I'M SORRY I CAN'T STAY WITH YOU... I'M GETTING MARRIED.
I'M SORRY I HAVE TO BREAK MY PROMISE BUT I CAN'T STAY HERE...
I HAVE TO GO FAR AWAY, BUT IF YOU EVER NEED ME, I'LL BE BACK IN A FLASH...

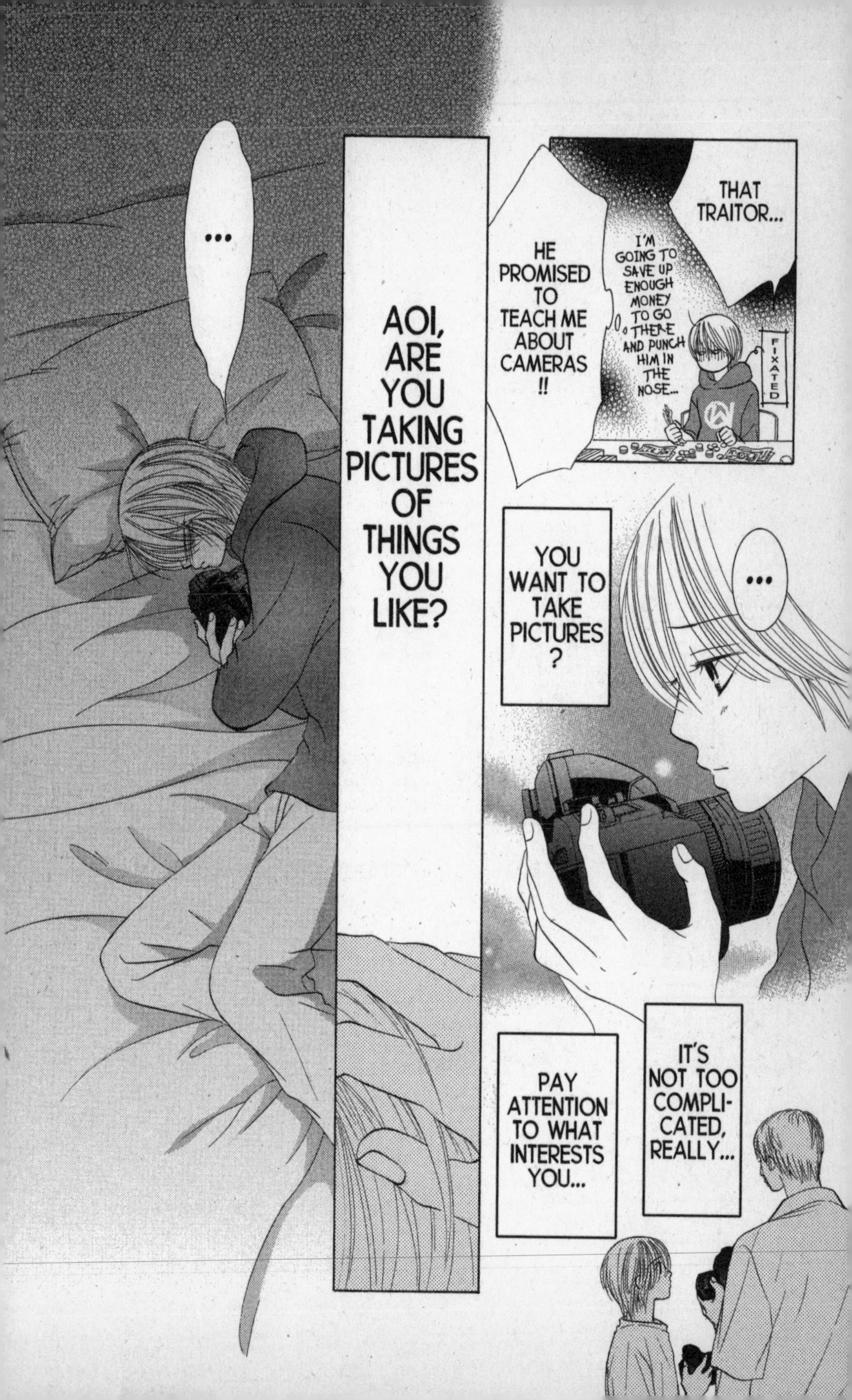
THAT TRAITOR...
I'M GOING TO SAVE UP ENOUGH MONEY TO GO THERE AND PUNCH HIM IN THE NOSE...
FIXATED
HE PROMISED TO TEACH ME ABOUT CAMERAS!!
...
YOU WANT TO TAKE PICTURES?
IT'S NOT TOO COMPLICATED, REALLY...
PAY ATTENTION TO WHAT INTERESTS YOU...
AOI, ARE YOU TAKING PICTURES OF THINGS YOU LIKE?
...

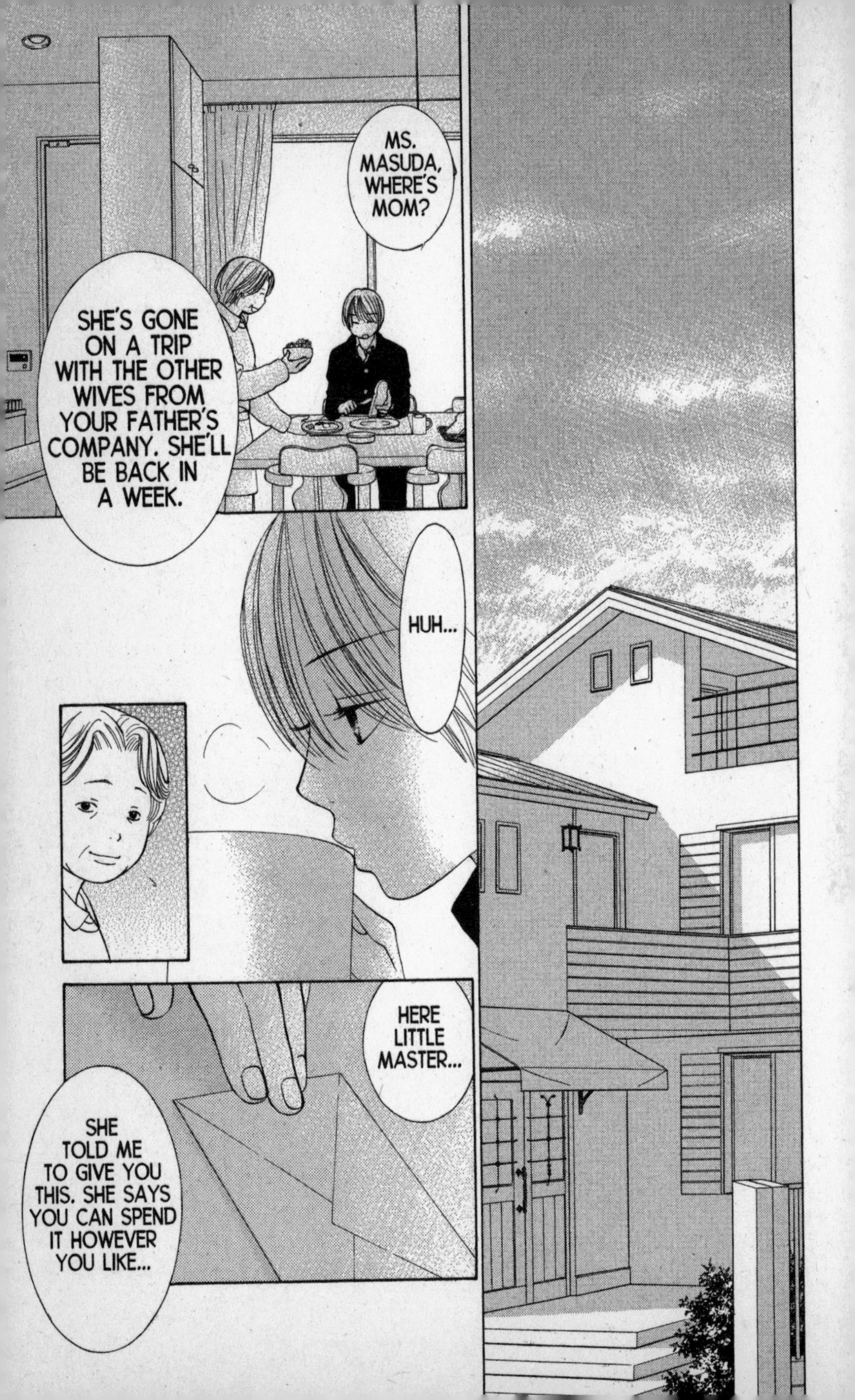
MS. MASUDA, WHERE'S MOM?
SHE'S GONE ON A TRIP WITH THE OTHER WIVES FROM YOUR FATHER'S COMPANY. SHE'LL BE BACK IN A WEEK.
HUH...
HERE LITTLE MASTER...
SHE TOLD ME TO GIVE YOU THIS. SHE SAYS YOU CAN SPEND IT HOWEVER YOU LIKE...

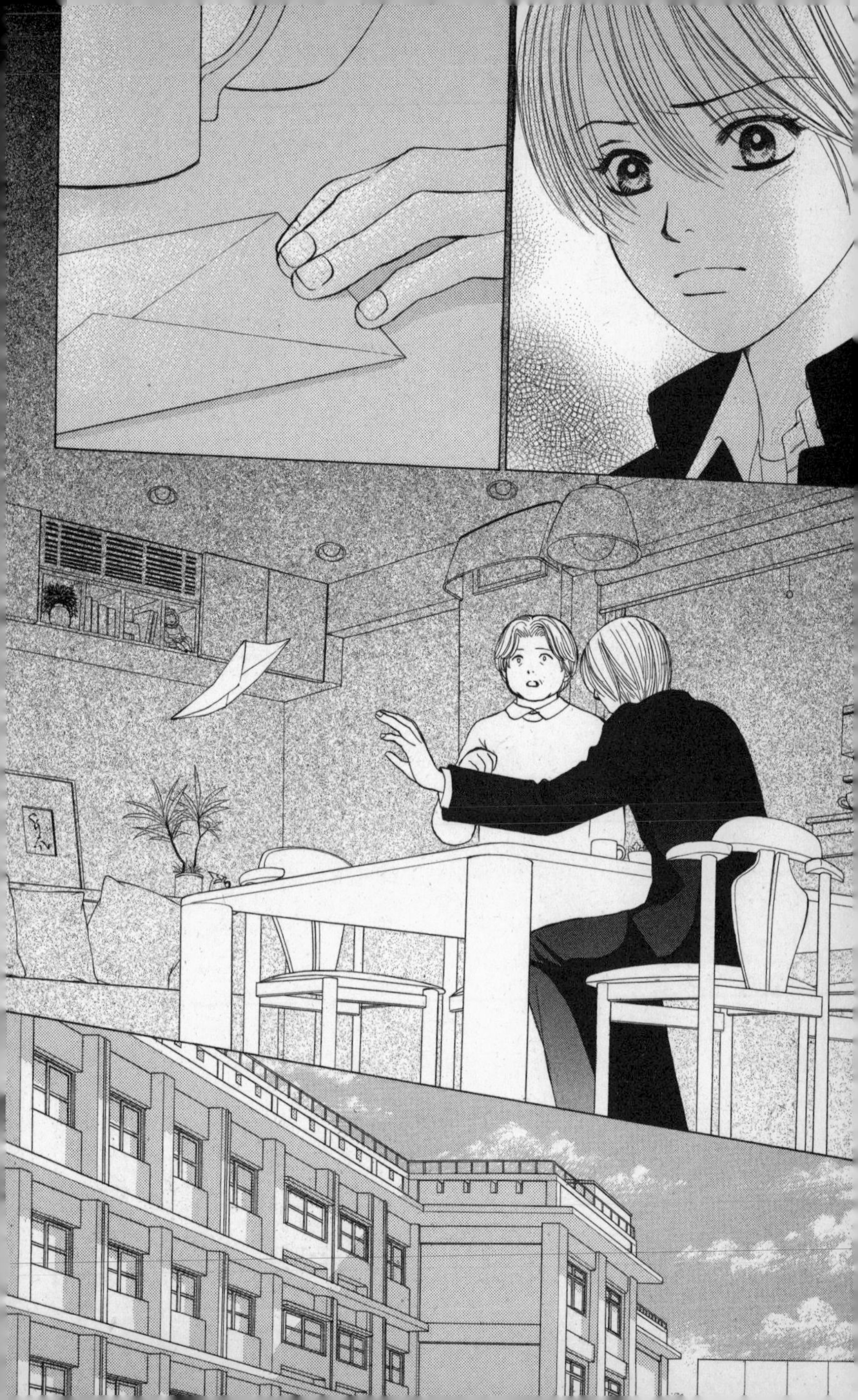

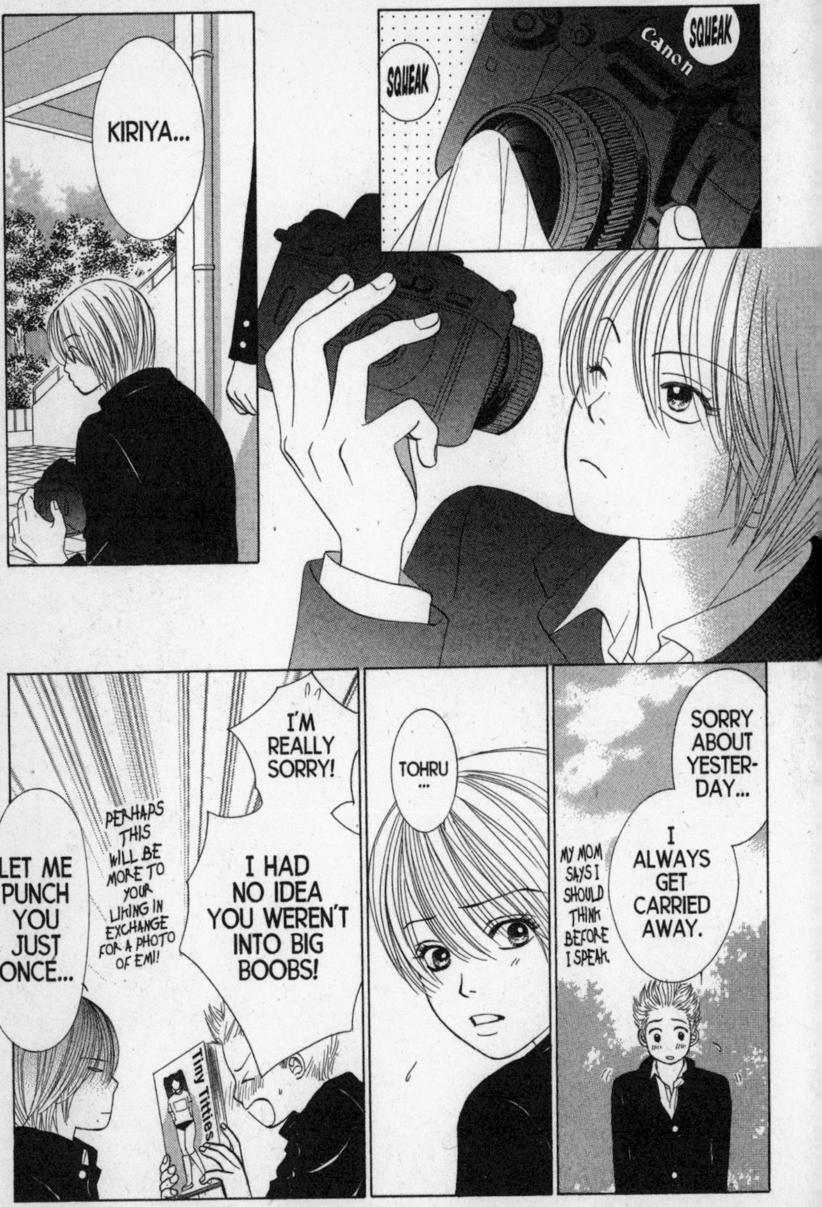
SQUEAK
Canon
SQUEAK
KIRIYA...
SORRY ABOUT YESTER-DAY...
I ALWAYS GET CARRIED AWAY.
MY MOM SAYS I SHOULD THINK BEFORE I SPEAK.
TOHRU...
I'M REALLY SORRY!
I HAD NO IDEA YOU WEREN'T INTO BIG BOOBS!
PERHAPS THIS WILL BE MORE TO YOUR LIKING IN EXCHANGE FOR A PHOTO OF EMI!
Tiny Titties
LET ME PUNCH YOU JUST ONCE...

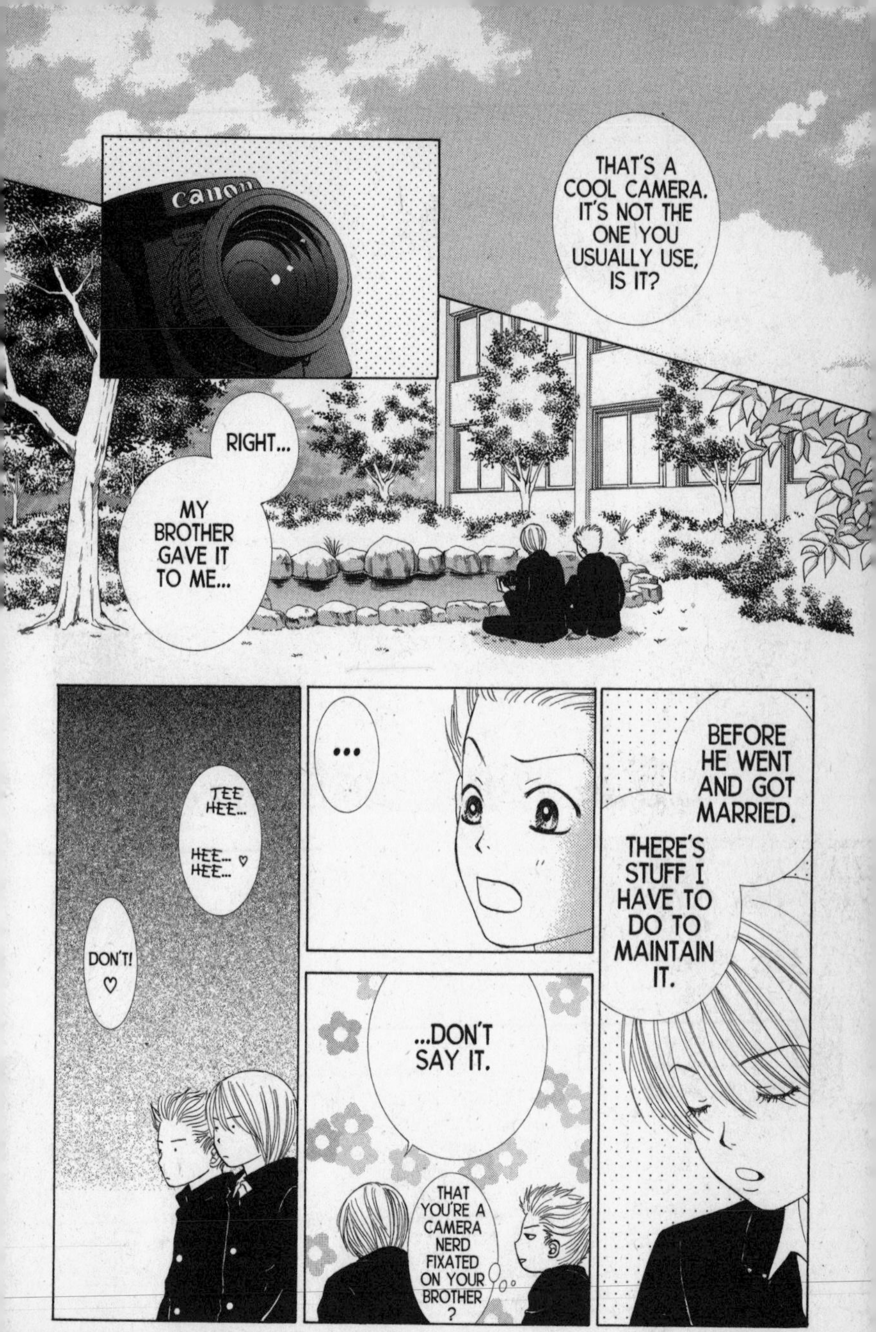
THAT'S A COOL CAMERA. IT'S NOT THE ONE YOU USUALLY USE, IS IT?
RIGHT...
MY BROTHER GAVE IT TO ME...
BEFORE HE WENT AND GOT MARRIED.
THERE'S STUFF I HAVE TO DO TO MAINTAIN IT.
...
...DON'T SAY IT.
THAT YOU'RE A CAMERA NERD FIXATED ON YOUR BROTHER?
TEE HEE... HEE... HEE... ♡
DON'T! ♡

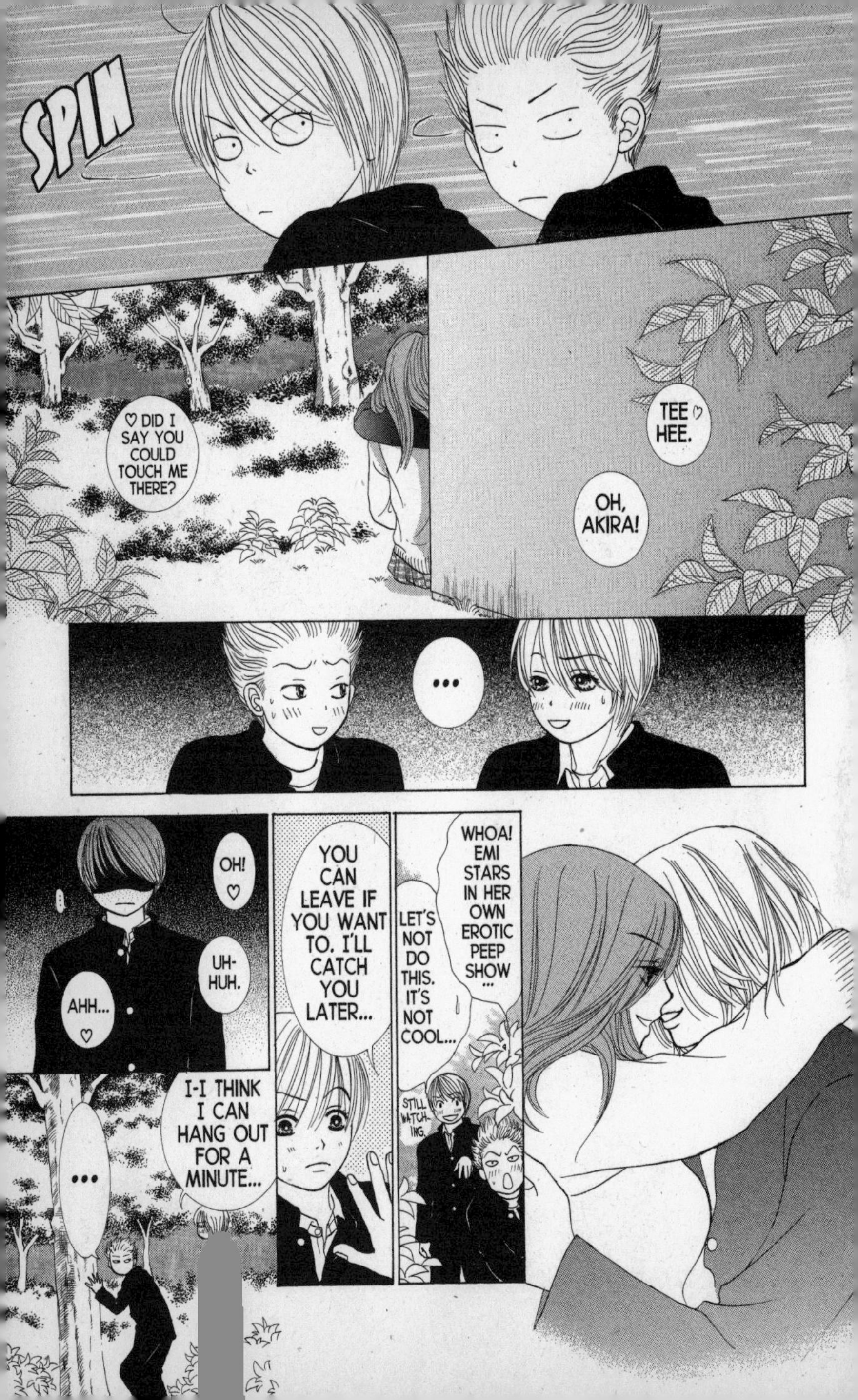
SPIN
TEE ♡ HEE.
OH, AKIRA!
♡ DID I SAY YOU COULD TOUCH ME THERE?
...
WHOA! EMI STARS IN HER OWN EROTIC PEEP SHOW...
LET'S NOT DO THIS. IT'S NOT COOL...
STILL WATCHING.
YOU CAN LEAVE IF YOU WANT TO. I'LL CATCH YOU LATER...
OH! ♡
!
UH-HUH.
AHH... ♡
I-I THINK I CAN HANG OUT FOR A MINUTE...
...

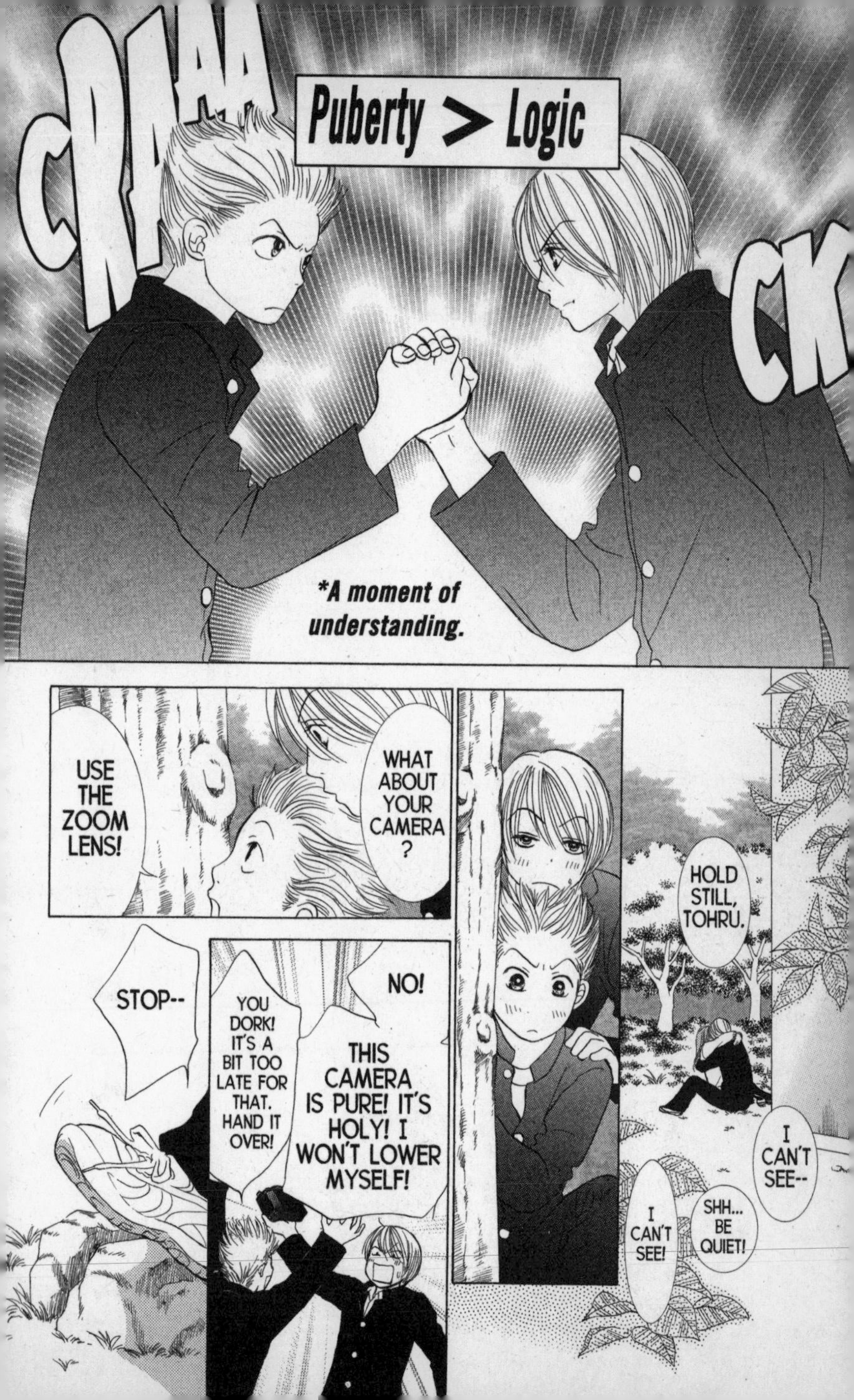
CRAAACK
Puberty > Logic
*A moment of understanding.
HOLD STILL, TOHRU.
I CAN'T SEE--
SHH... BE QUIET!
I CAN'T SEE!
WHAT ABOUT YOUR CAMERA?
USE THE ZOOM LENS!
NO!
THIS CAMERA IS PURE! IT'S HOLY! I WON'T LOWER MYSELF!
YOU DORK! IT'S A BIT TOO LATE FOR THAT. HAND IT OVER!
STOP--

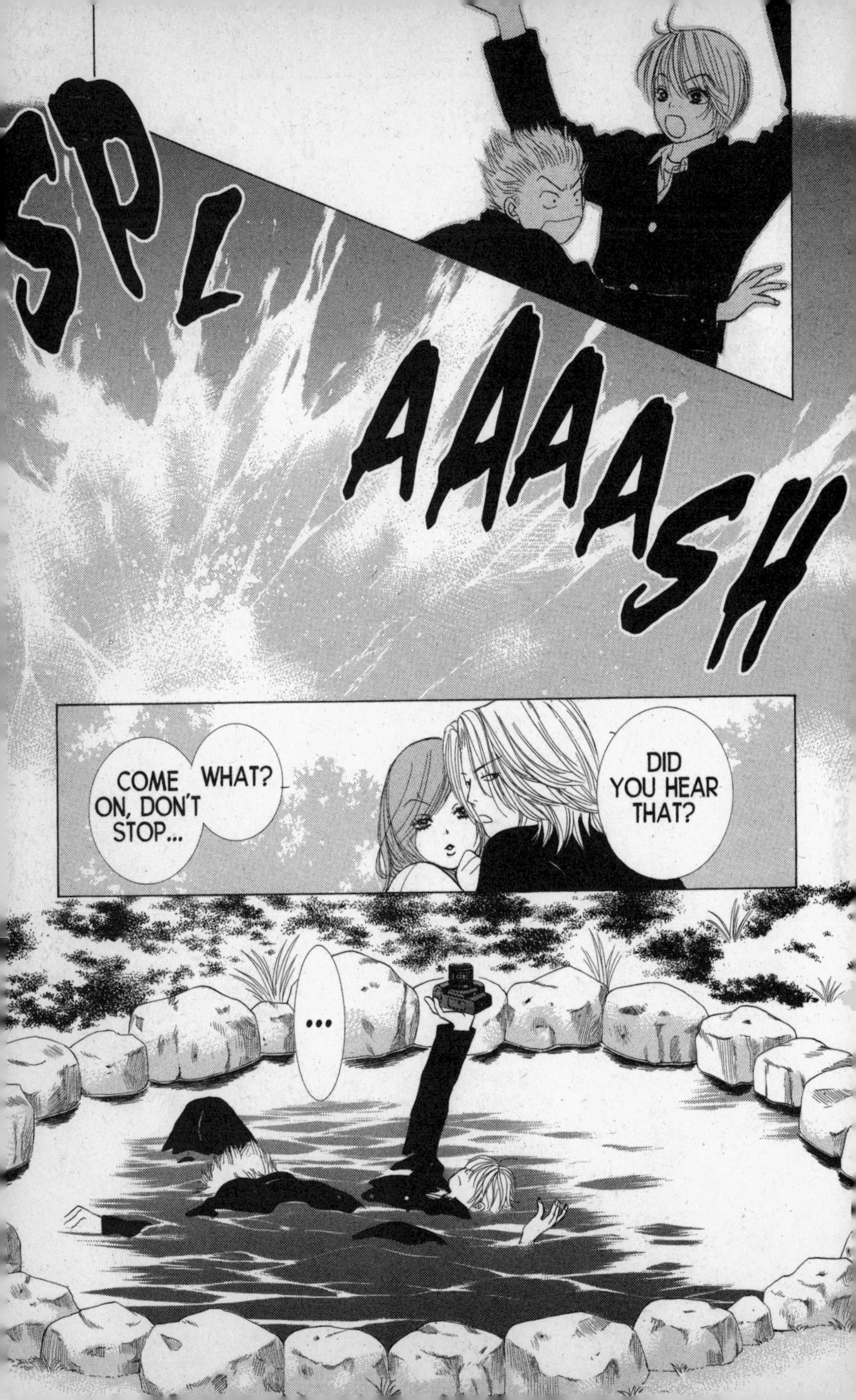
SPLAAAAASH
DID YOU HEAR THAT?
WHAT?
COME ON, DON'T STOP...
...

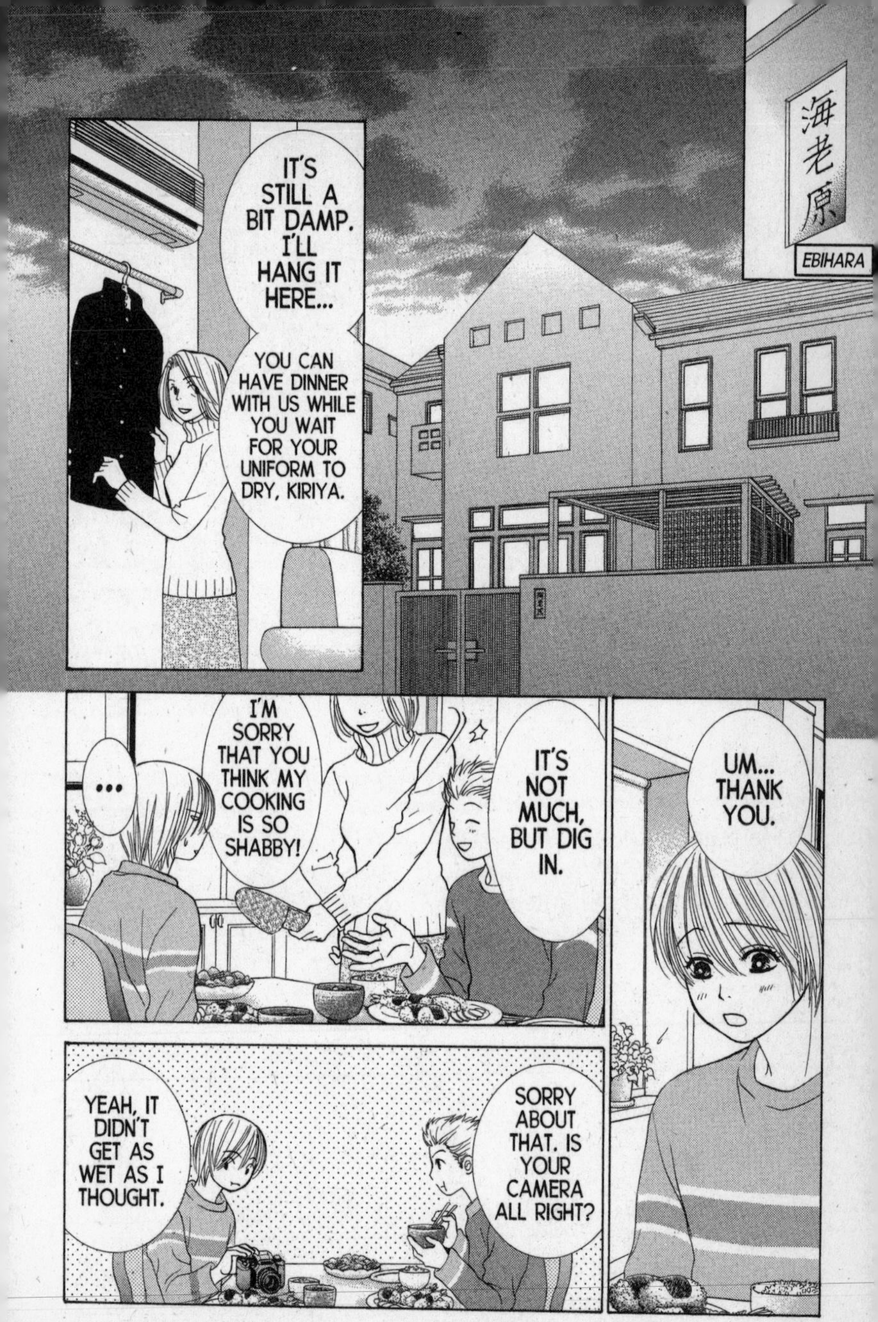
海老原
EBIHARA
IT'S STILL A BIT DAMP. I'LL HANG IT HERE...
YOU CAN HAVE DINNER WITH US WHILE YOU WAIT FOR YOUR UNIFORM TO DRY, KIRIYA.
UM... THANK YOU.
IT'S NOT MUCH, BUT DIG IN.
I'M SORRY THAT YOU THINK MY COOKING IS SO SHABBY!
...
SORRY ABOUT THAT. IS YOUR CAMERA ALL RIGHT?
YEAH, IT DIDN'T GET AS WET AS I THOUGHT.

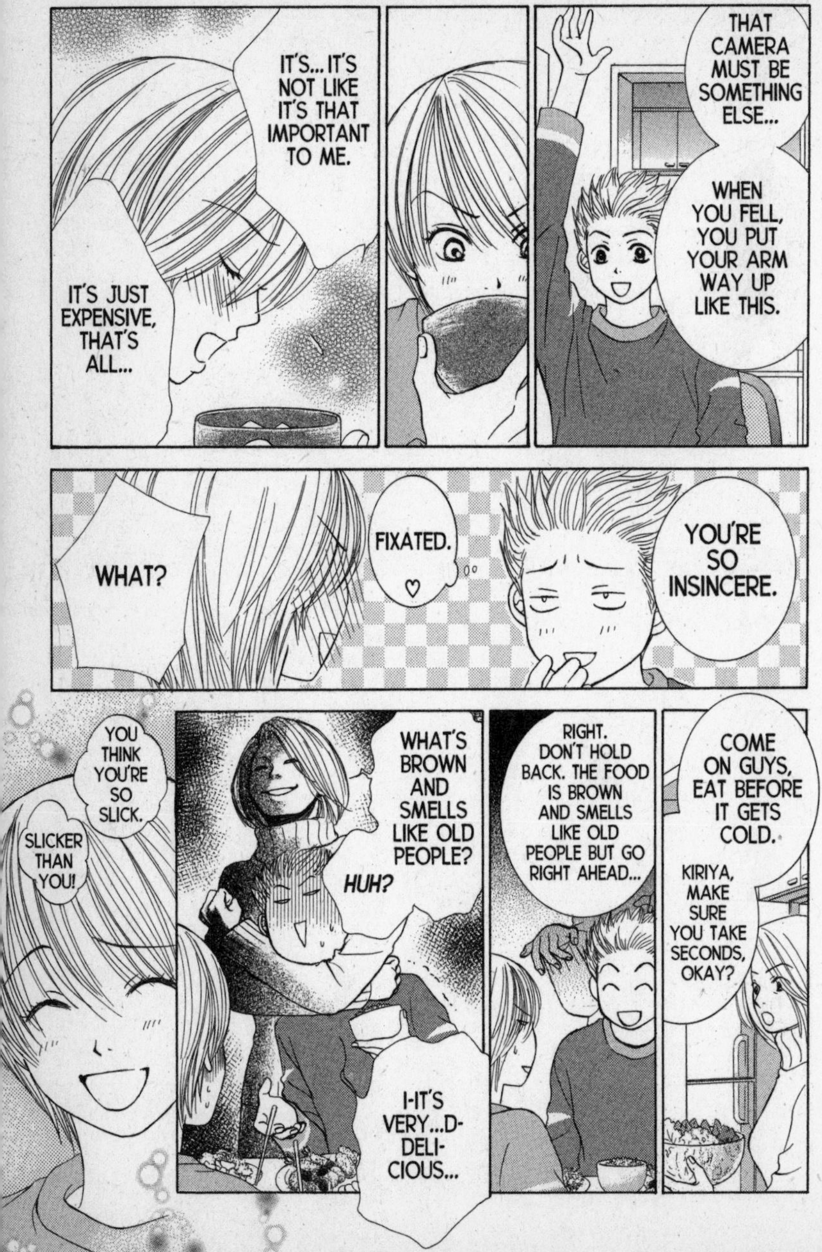
THAT CAMERA MUST BE SOMETHING ELSE...
WHEN YOU FELL, YOU PUT YOUR ARM WAY UP LIKE THIS.
IT'S... IT'S NOT LIKE IT'S THAT IMPORTANT TO ME.
IT'S JUST EXPENSIVE, THAT'S ALL...
YOU'RE SO INSINCERE.
FIXATED. ♡
WHAT?
COME ON GUYS, EAT BEFORE IT GETS COLD.
KIRIYA, MAKE SURE YOU TAKE SECONDS, OKAY?
RIGHT. DON'T HOLD BACK. THE FOOD IS BROWN AND SMELLS LIKE OLD PEOPLE BUT GO RIGHT AHEAD...
WHAT'S BROWN AND SMELLS LIKE OLD PEOPLE?
HUH?
I-IT'S VERY...D-DELICIOUS...
YOU THINK YOU'RE SO SLICK.
SLICKER THAN YOU!

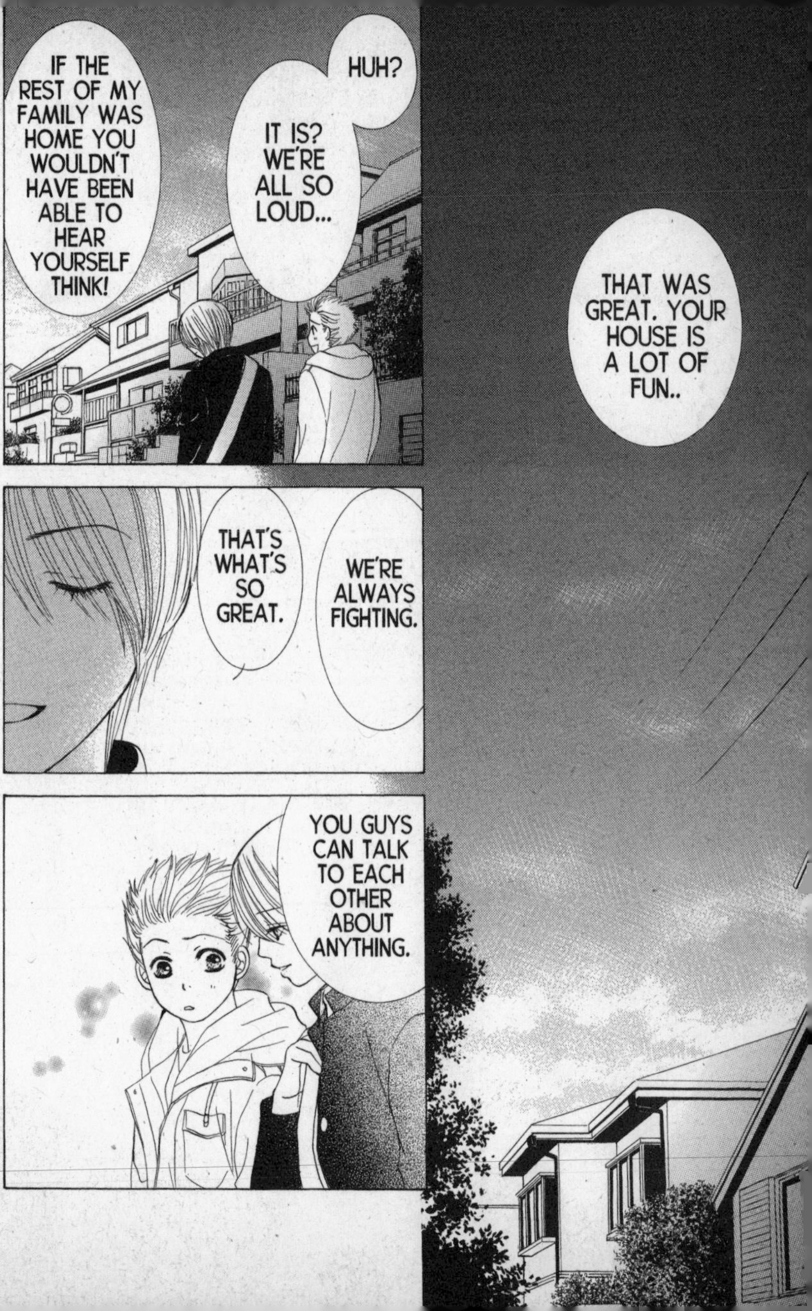
THAT WAS GREAT. YOUR HOUSE IS A LOT OF FUN..
HUH?
IT IS? WE'RE ALL SO LOUD...
IF THE REST OF MY FAMILY WAS HOME YOU WOULDN'T HAVE BEEN ABLE TO HEAR YOURSELF THINK!
WE'RE ALWAYS FIGHTING.
THAT'S WHAT'S SO GREAT.
YOU GUYS CAN TALK TO EACH OTHER ABOUT ANYTHING.

KIRIYA...
IF YOU START PITYING ME, I'LL KILL YOU.
...
I'LL PAY YOU BACK FOR DINNER...
BY TAKING YOUR PICTURE WITH EMI.
HUH?
FOR FREE?!
...

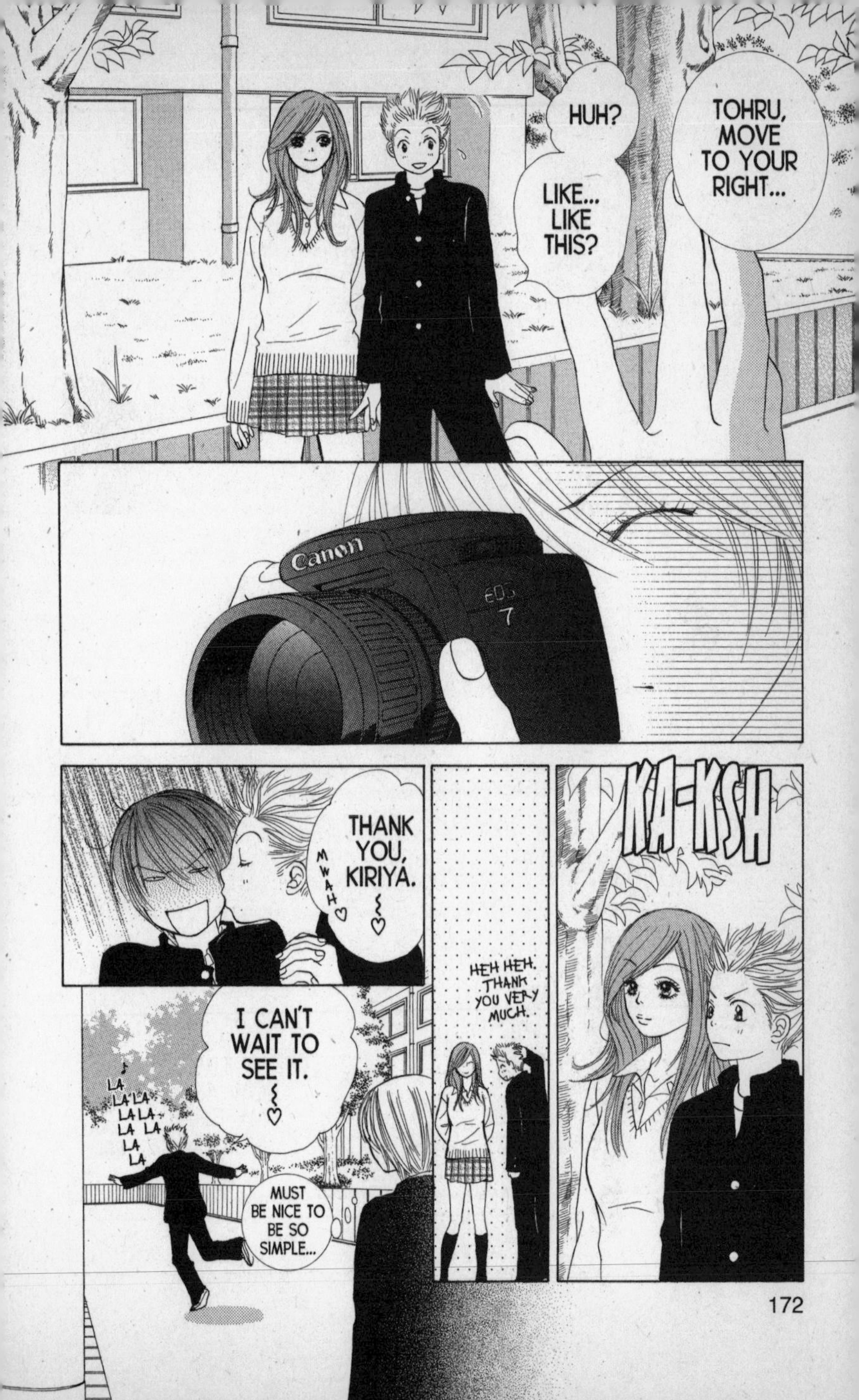
TOHRU, MOVE TO YOUR RIGHT...
HUH?
LIKE... LIKE THIS?
Canon
EOS 7
KA-KSH
HEH HEH. THANK YOU VERY MUCH.
THANK YOU, KIRIYA.
MWAH
I CAN'T WAIT TO SEE IT.
LA LA LA LA LA LA LA LA LA
MUST BE NICE TO BE SO SIMPLE...

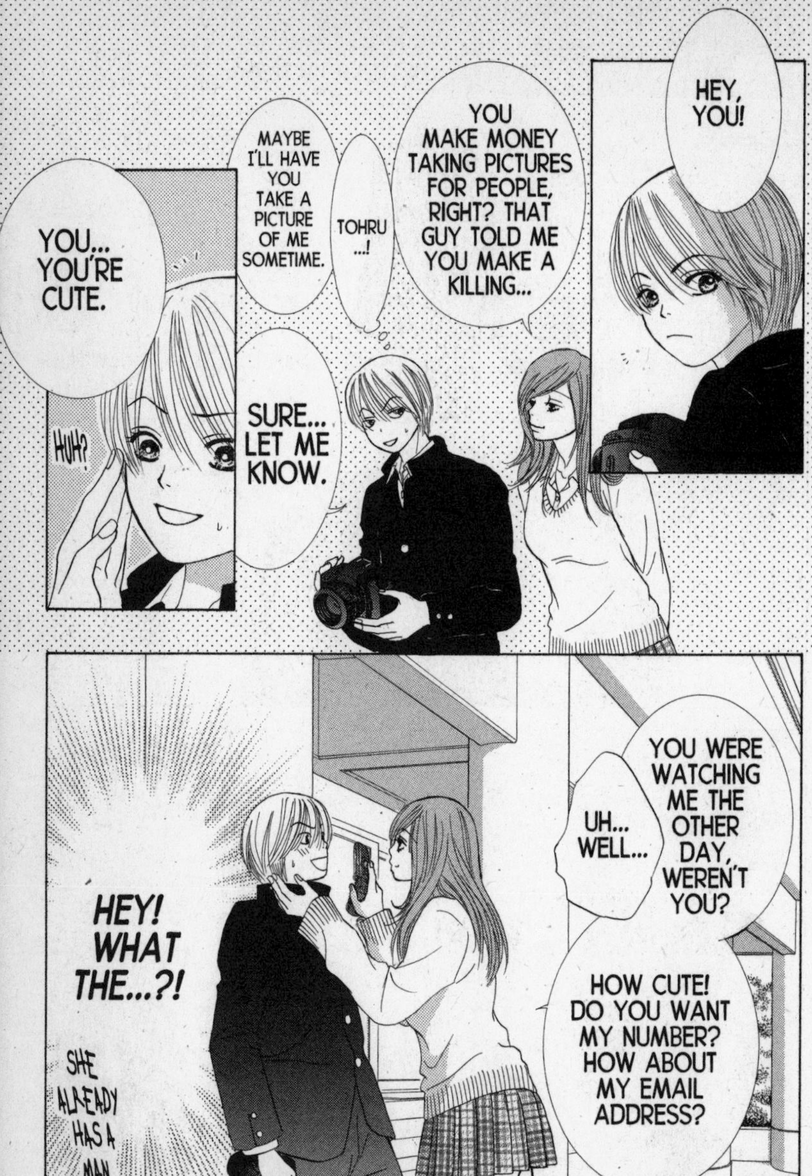
HEY, YOU!
YOU MAKE MONEY TAKING PICTURES FOR PEOPLE, RIGHT? THAT GUY TOLD ME YOU MAKE A KILLING...
TOHRU ...!
MAYBE I'LL HAVE YOU TAKE A PICTURE OF ME SOMETIME.
SURE... LET ME KNOW.
YOU... YOU'RE CUTE.
HUH?
YOU WERE WATCHING ME THE OTHER DAY, WEREN'T YOU?
UH... WELL...
HOW CUTE! DO YOU WANT MY NUMBER? HOW ABOUT MY EMAIL ADDRESS?
HEY! WHAT THE...?!
SHE ALREADY HAS A MAN...

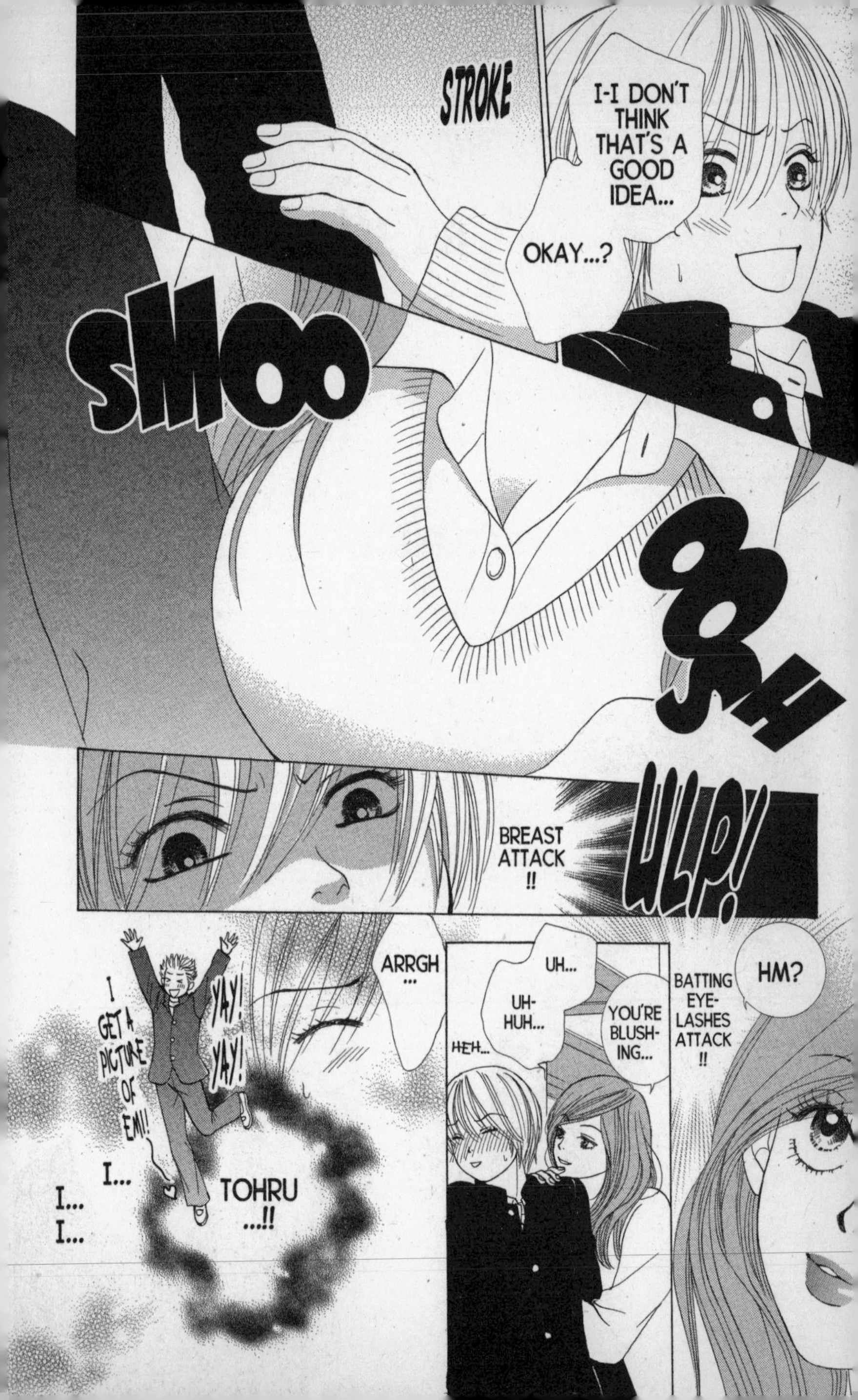
I-I DON'T THINK THAT'S A GOOD IDEA...
OKAY...?
STROKE
SMOO
OOSH
ULP!
BREAST ATTACK !!
HM?
BATTING EYE-LASHES ATTACK !!
YOU'RE BLUSH-ING...
UH...
UH-HUH...
HEH...
ARRGH ...
YAY! YAY!
I GET A PICTURE OF EMI!
TOHRU ...!!
I...
I... I...

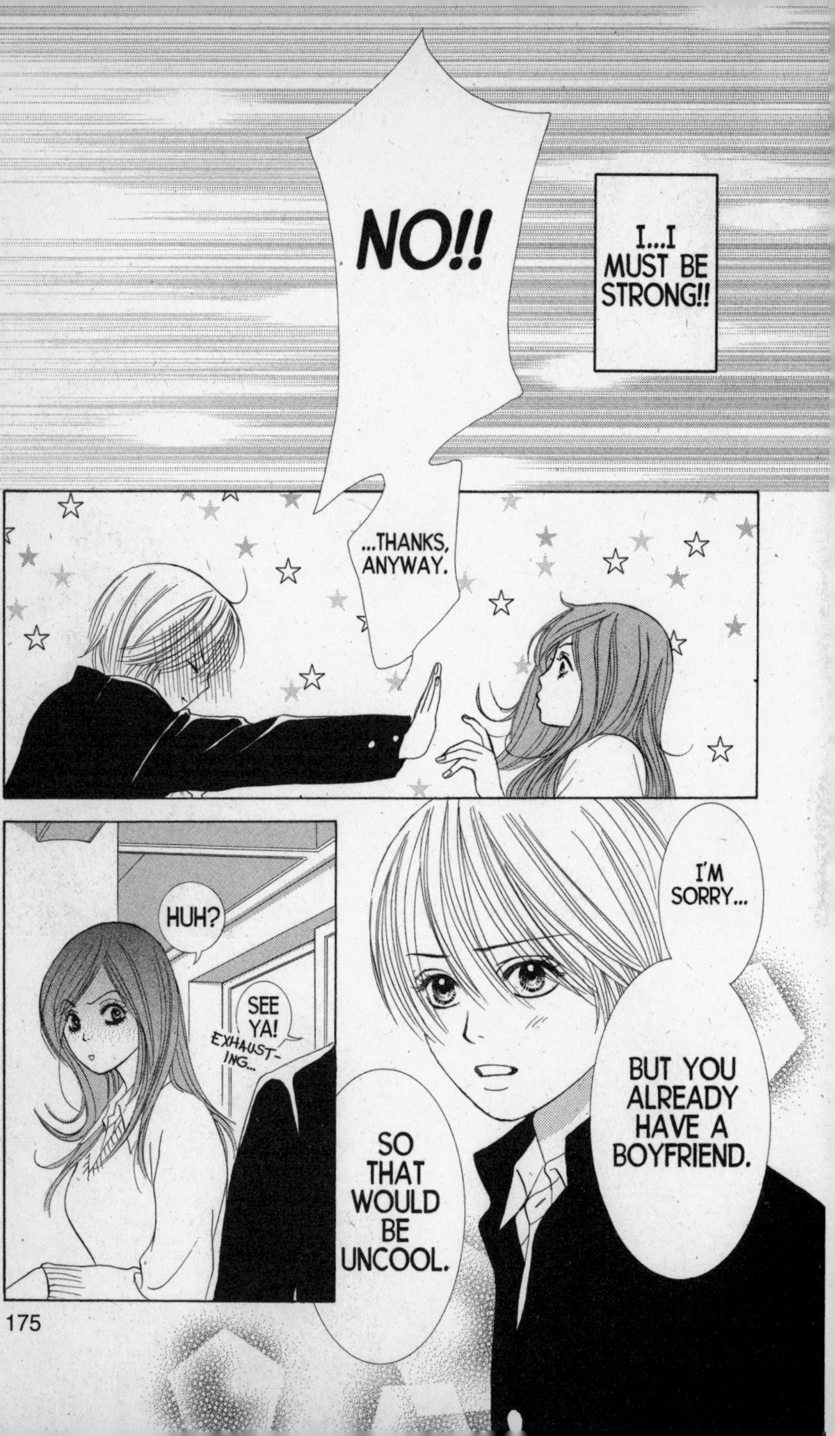
I...I MUST BE STRONG!!
NO!!
...THANKS, ANYWAY.
I'M SORRY...
BUT YOU ALREADY HAVE A BOYFRIEND.
SO THAT WOULD BE UNCOOL.
SEE YA!
EXHAUST-ING...
HUH?

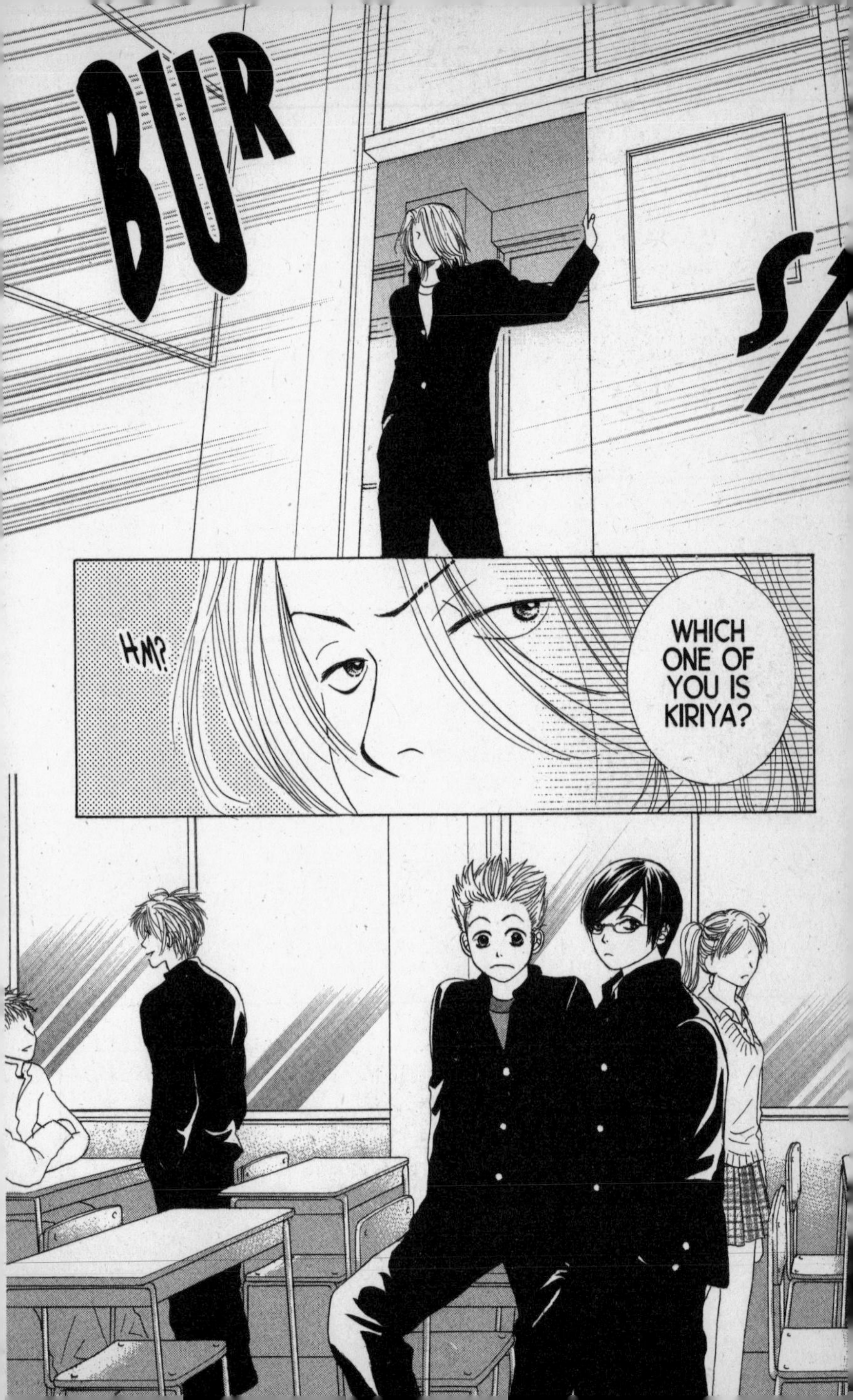
BUR
WHICH ONE OF YOU IS KIRIYA?
HM?

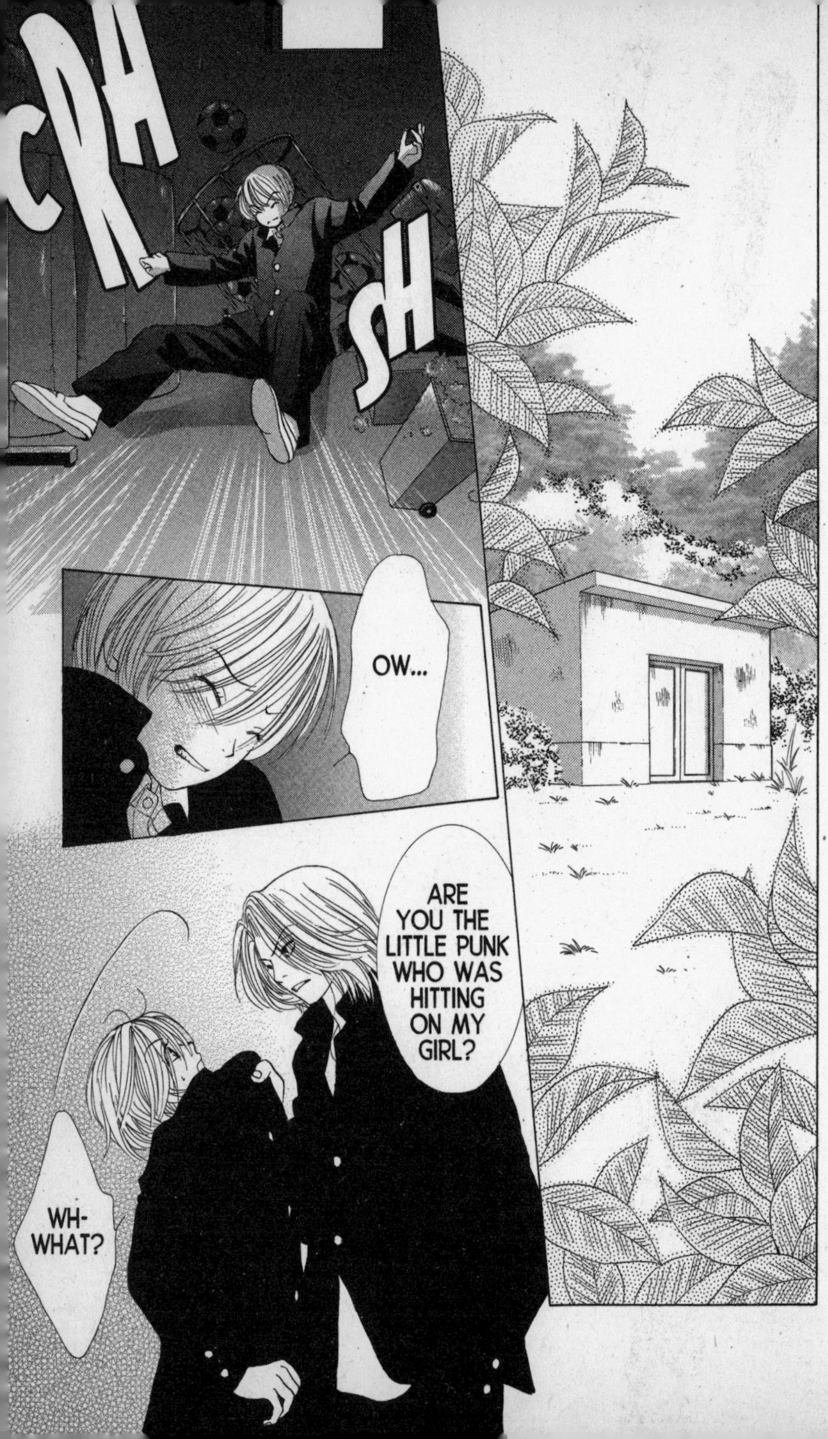
CRA
SH
OW...
ARE YOU THE LITTLE PUNK WHO WAS HITTING ON MY GIRL?
WH- WHAT?

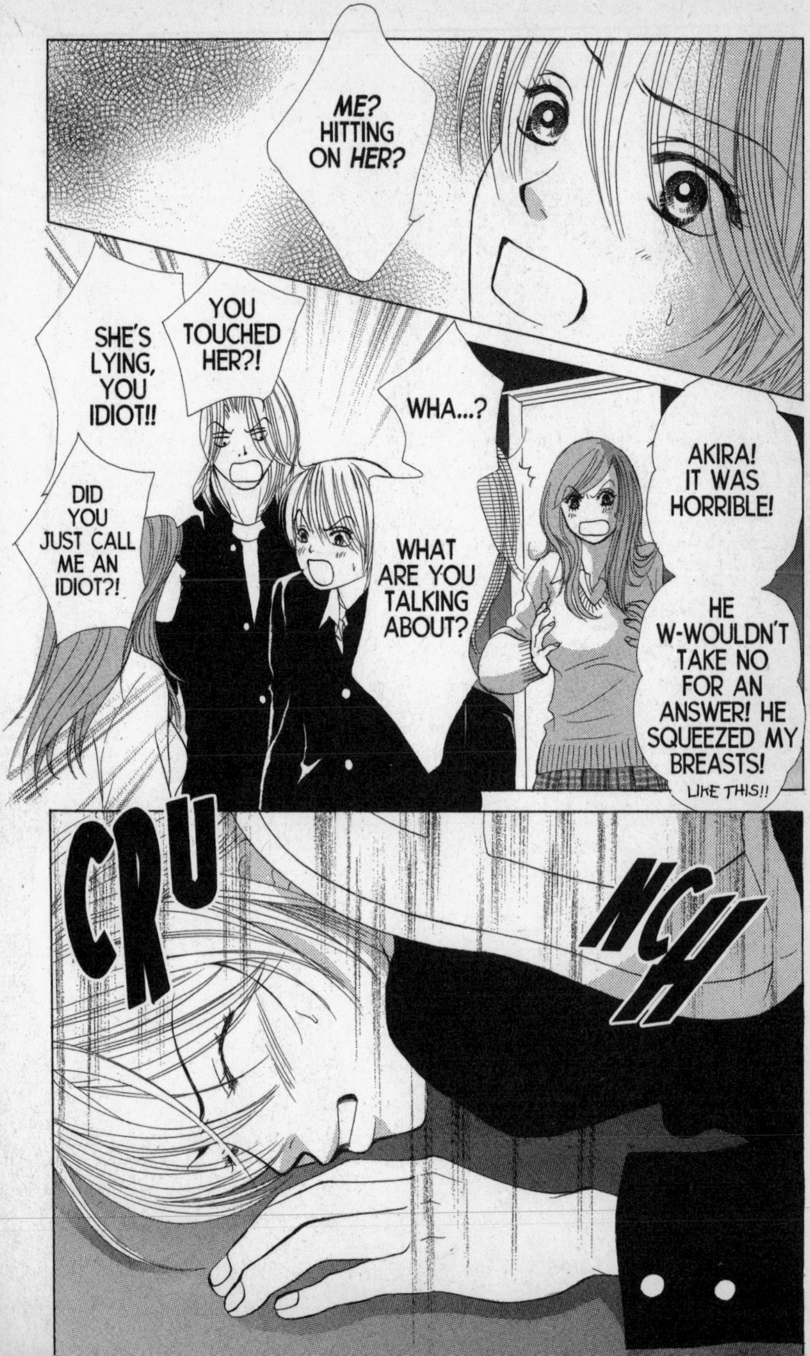
ME? HITTING ON HER?
AKIRA! IT WAS HORRIBLE!
HE W-WOULDN'T TAKE NO FOR AN ANSWER! HE SQUEEZED MY BREASTS!
LIKE THIS!!
WHA...?
WHAT ARE YOU TALKING ABOUT?
YOU TOUCHED HER?!
SHE'S LYING, YOU IDIOT!!
DID YOU JUST CALL ME AN IDIOT?!
CRUNCH

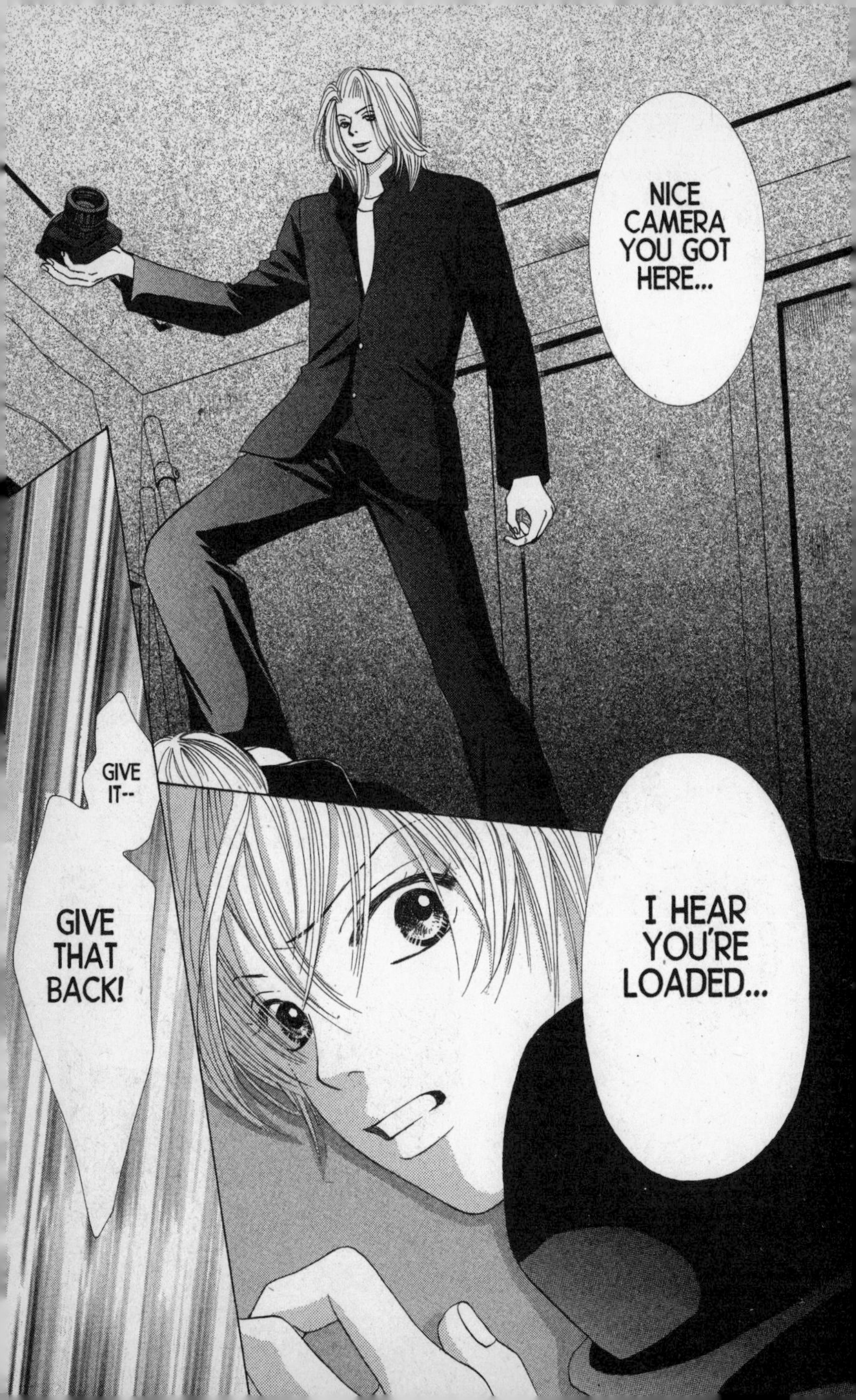
NICE CAMERA YOU GOT HERE...
I HEAR YOU'RE LOADED...
GIVE IT--
GIVE THAT BACK!

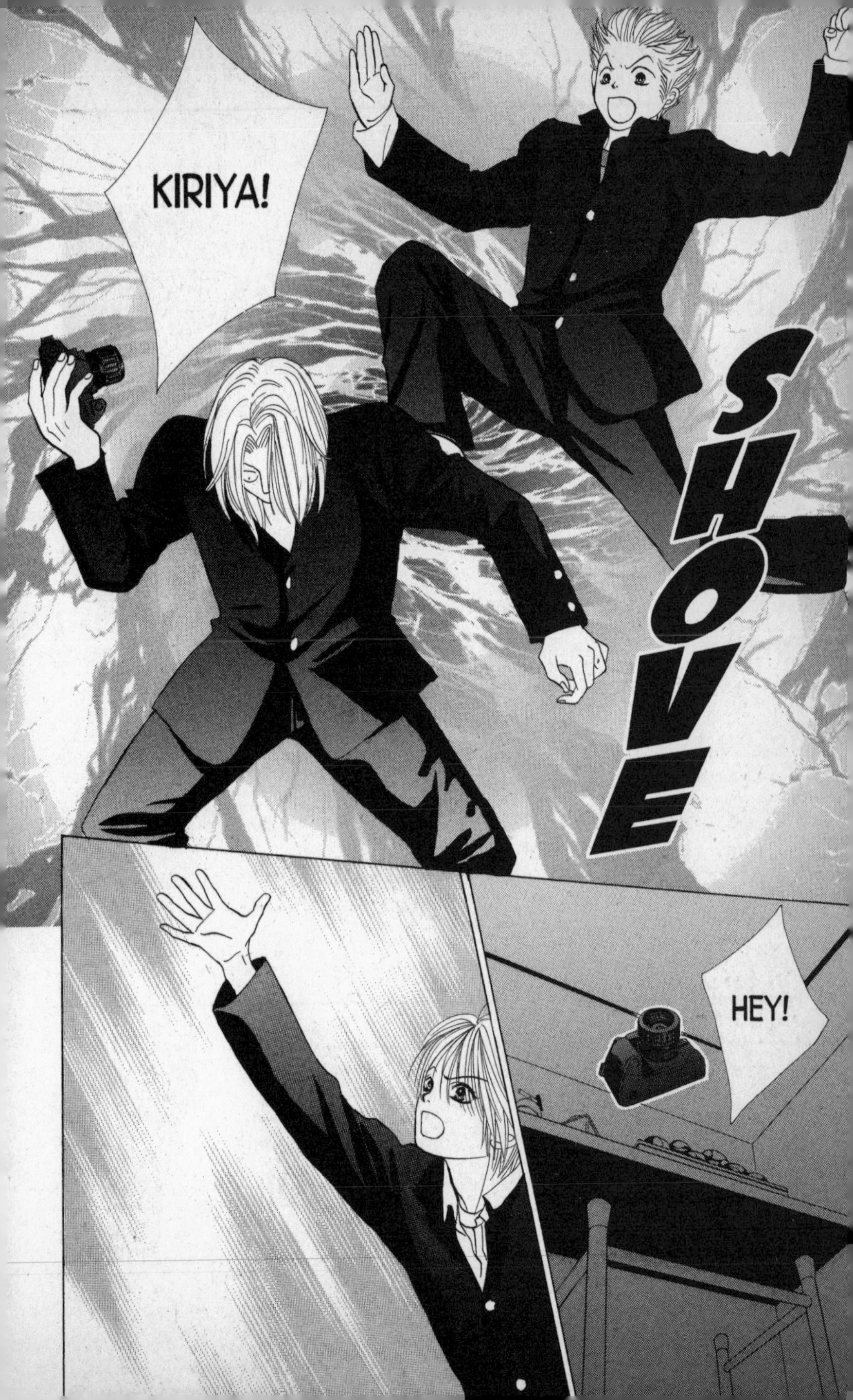
KIRIYA!
SHOVE
HEY!

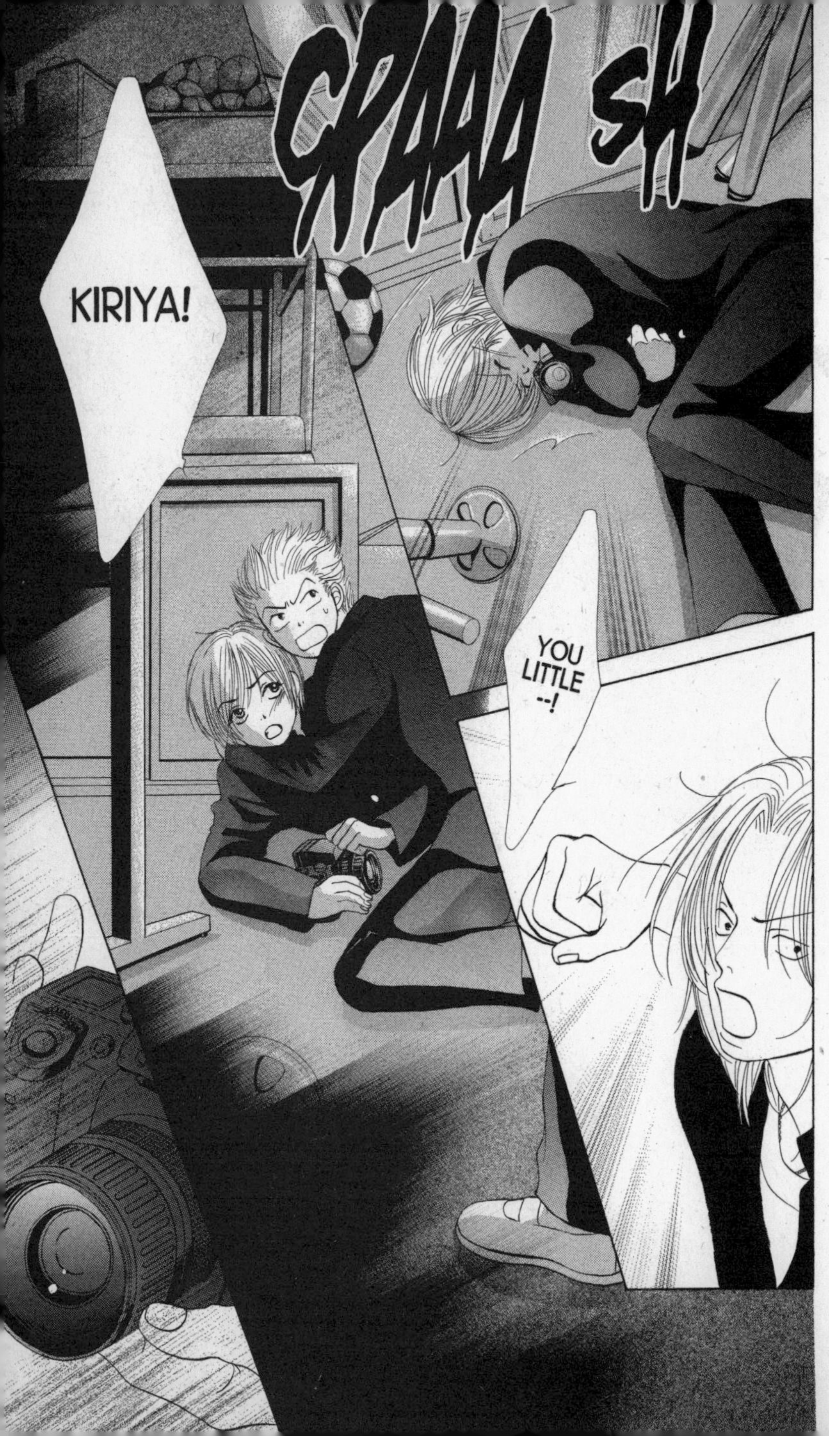
CRAAASH
KIRIYA!
YOU LITTLE --!

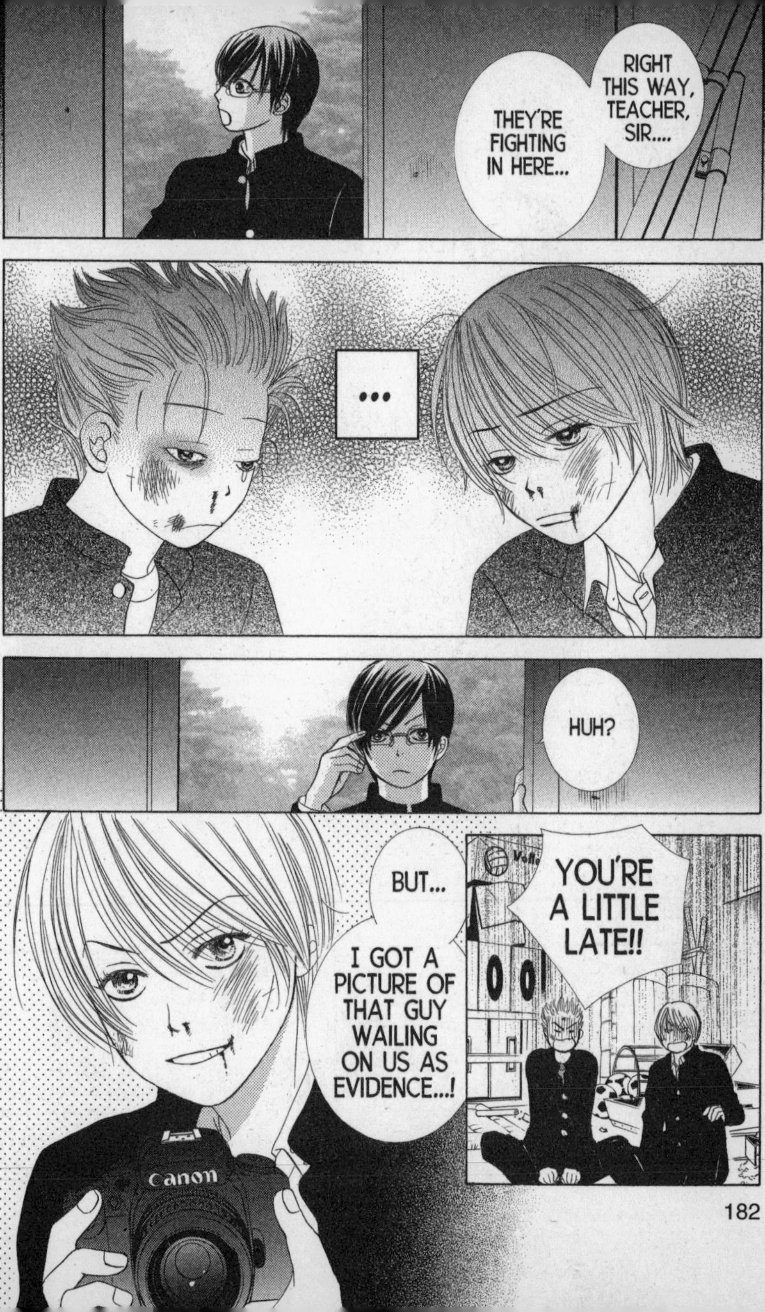
RIGHT THIS WAY, TEACHER, SIR....
THEY'RE FIGHTING IN HERE...
...
HUH?
YOU'RE A LITTLE LATE!!
BUT...
I GOT A PICTURE OF THAT GUY WAILING ON US AS EVIDENCE...!
Canon

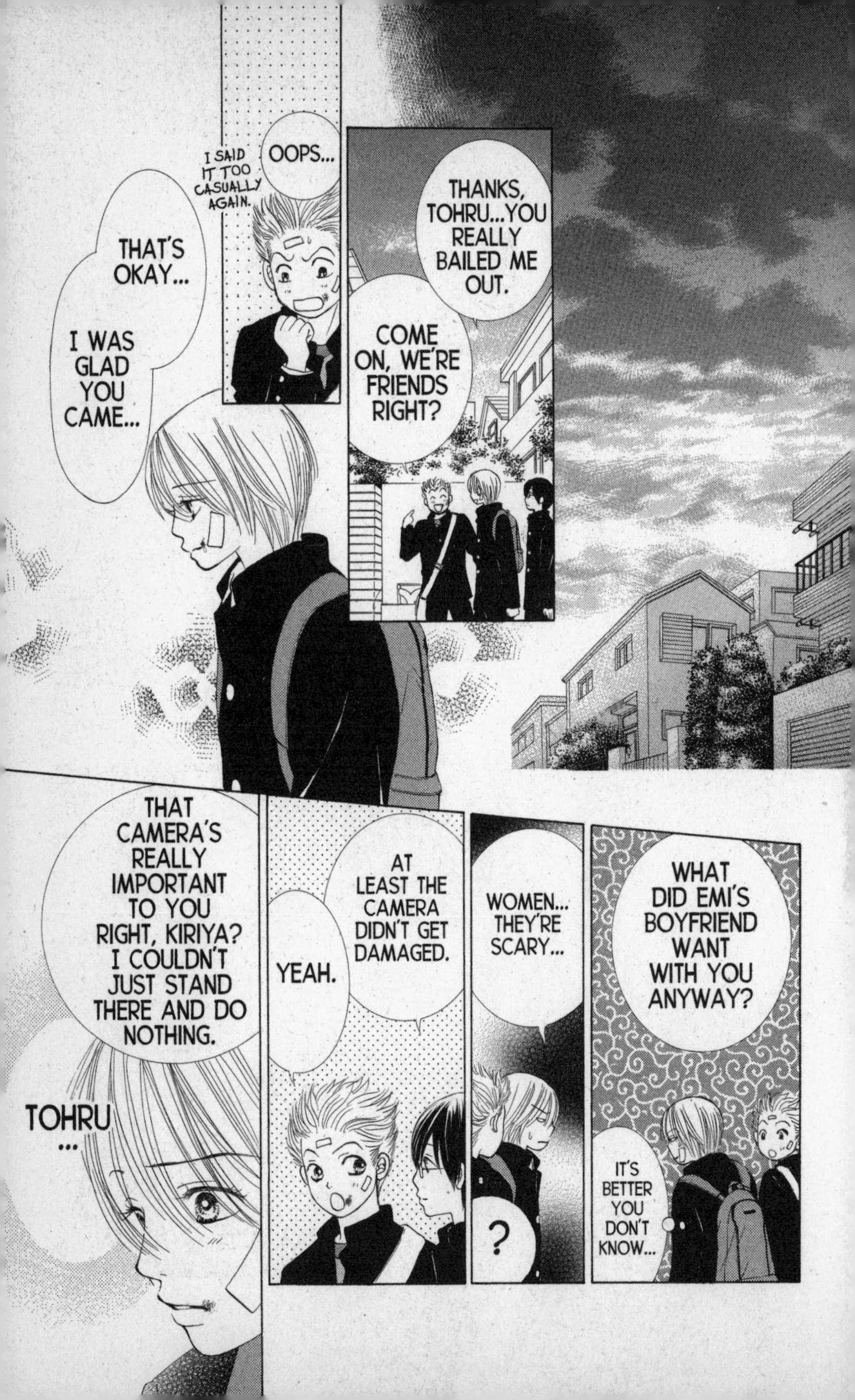
THANKS, TOHRU...YOU REALLY BAILED ME OUT.
COME ON, WE'RE FRIENDS RIGHT?
OOPS...
I SAID IT TOO CASUALLY AGAIN.
THAT'S OKAY...
I WAS GLAD YOU CAME...
WHAT DID EMI'S BOYFRIEND WANT WITH YOU ANYWAY?
IT'S BETTER YOU DON'T KNOW...
WOMEN... THEY'RE SCARY...
?
AT LEAST THE CAMERA DIDN'T GET DAMAGED.
YEAH.
THAT CAMERA'S REALLY IMPORTANT TO YOU RIGHT, KIRIYA? I COULDN'T JUST STAND THERE AND DO NOTHING.
TOHRU...

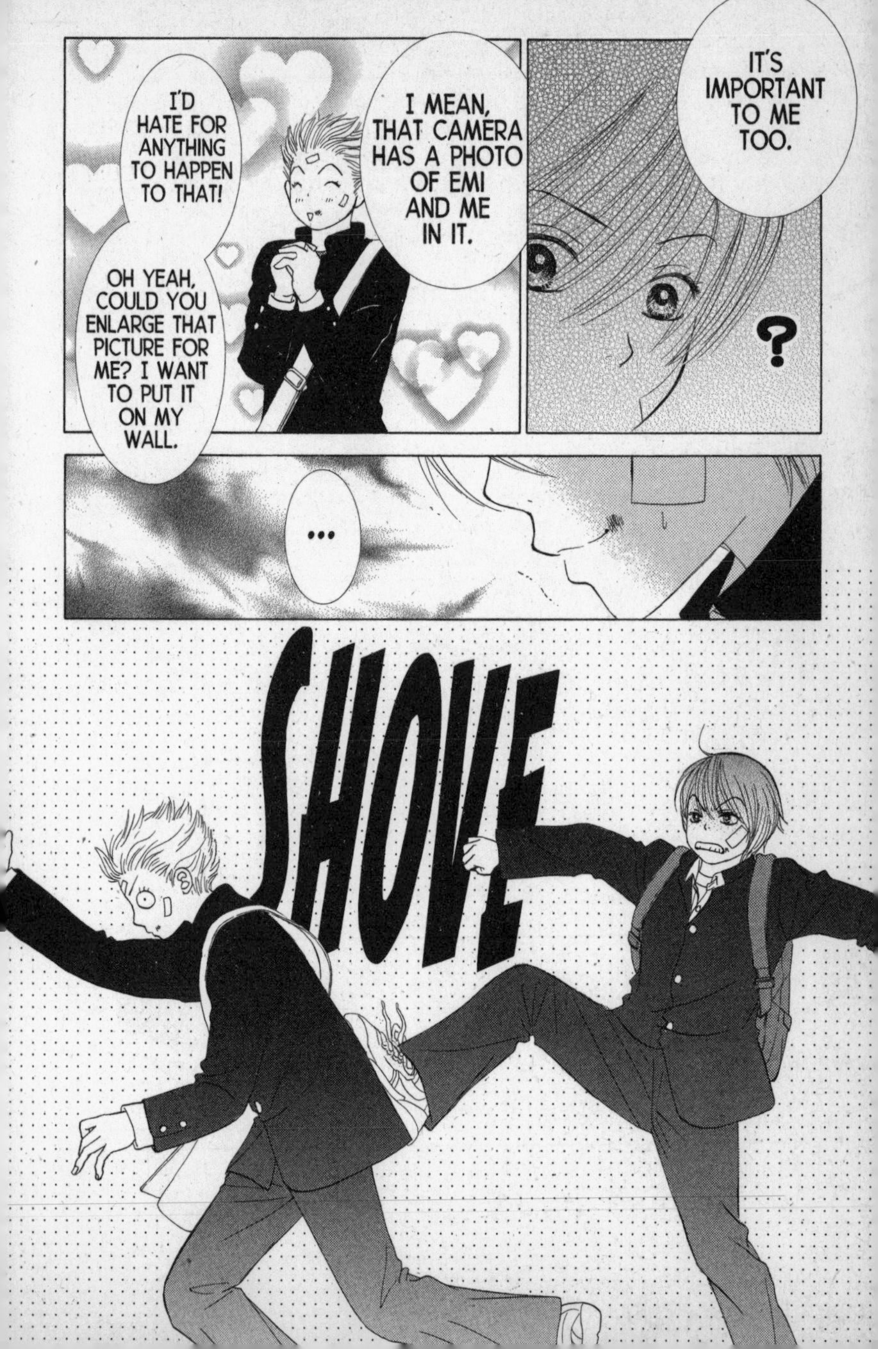
IT'S IMPORTANT TO ME TOO.
?
I MEAN, THAT CAMERA HAS A PHOTO OF EMI AND ME IN IT.
I'D HATE FOR ANYTHING TO HAPPEN TO THAT!
OH YEAH, COULD YOU ENLARGE THAT PICTURE FOR ME? I WANT TO PUT IT ON MY WALL.
...
SHOVE

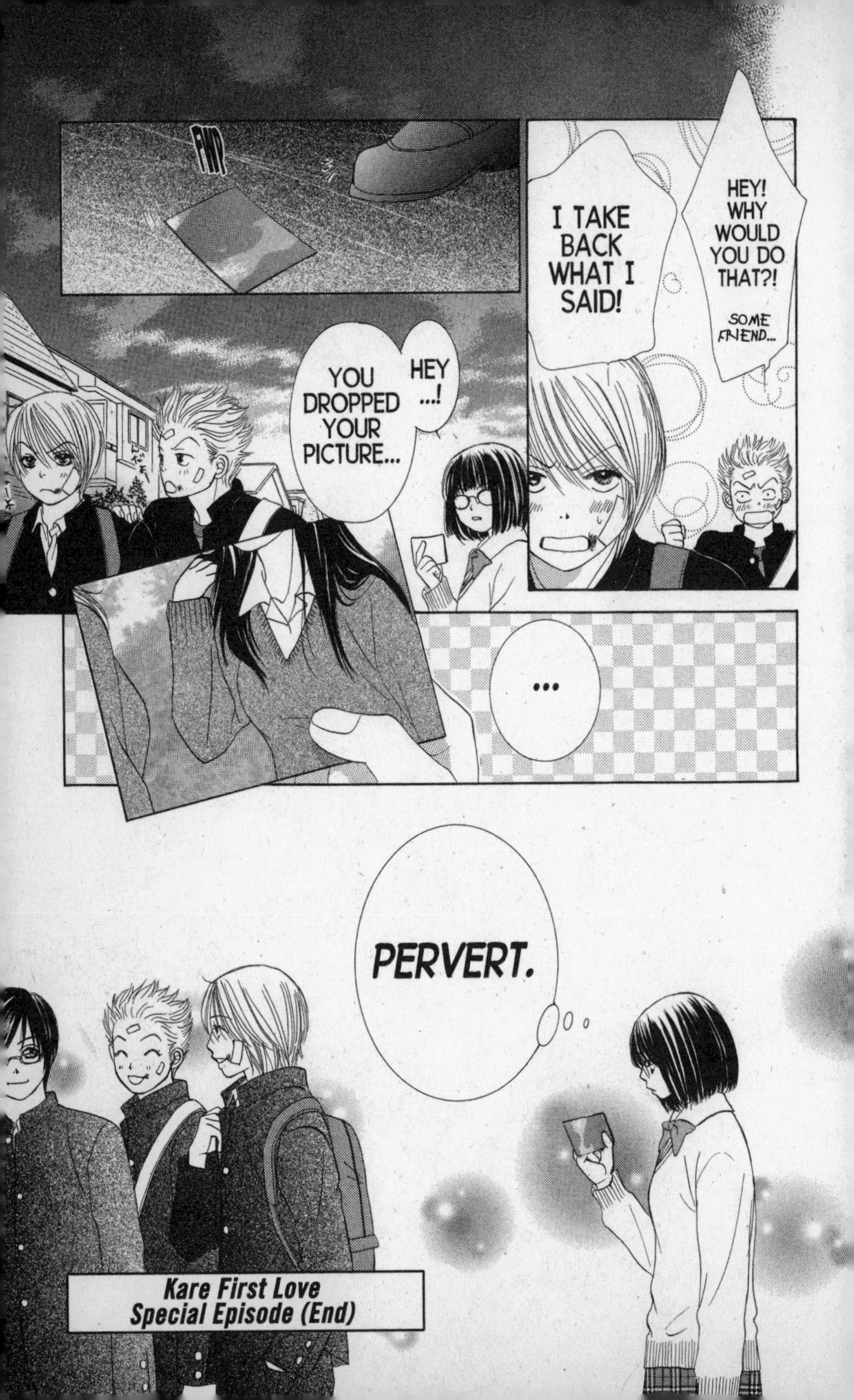
HEY! WHY WOULD YOU DO THAT?!
SOME FRIEND...
I TAKE BACK WHAT I SAID!
HEY ...!
YOU DROPPED YOUR PICTURE...
...
PERVERT.
Kare First Love Special Episode (End)

Kaho Miyasaka's
Official Site

# Love Factory

http://www.k-miyasaka.com/

## Special Thanks To:

**My Assistants**
Madoka Mizuno
Asami Tanimoto
Tomoko Komukai
Makiko Ogawa
Chikako Suzuki
Kayoko Ito
Rie Oishi
Yoko Okamoto

**My Editors**

2001-2002 Makiko Hikichi
2002-2004 Tomomi Sakaguchi
2004-...Tomoko Hikosaka

**And...**
My mother
My sister
My friends
My fans

## Message From the Author

We've finally arrived at the last volume of the series and I'd like to take this opportunity to say a few thanks to all the readers who supported this series from the very beginning; to my assistants, who stuck by me even through the hectic wrap-up phase; to my mother and my big sister, who helped nurse me back to health after my illness; to my friends, who encouraged me and gave me advice; to my editor, who put up with quite a bit from me; and to everyone else without whose help I wouldn't have been able to complete "Kare First Love." Thank you all so much.

# *Kare First Love*

## Vol. 10
### Shôjo Edition
### Story and Art by KAHO MIYASAKA

English Adaptation/Kelly Sue DeConnick
Translation/Akira Watanabe
Touch-Up Art & Lettering/Steve Dutro
Cover and Interior Design/Hidemi Sahara
Editor/Andy Nakatani

Managing Editor/Megan Bates
Editorial Director/Elizabeth Kawasaki
Editor in Chief/Alvin Lu
Sr. Director of Acquisitions/Rika Inouye
Sr. VP of Marketing/Liza Coppola
Exec. VP of Sales & Marketing/John Easum
Publisher/Hyoe Narita

© 2002 Kaho MIYASAKA/Shogakukan Inc. First published by Shogakukan Inc. in Japan as "Kare First Love."
New and adapted artwork and text © 2006 VIZ Media, LLC.
The KARE FIRST LOVE logo is a trademark of VIZ Media, LLC. All rights reserved.
The stories, characters and incidents mentioned in this publication are entirely fictional.

Printed in the U.S.A.

Published by VIZ Media, LLC
P.O. Box 77010
San Francisco, CA 94107

Shôjo Edition
10 9 8 7 6 5 4 3 2 1
First printing, December 2006

**www.viz.com**
**store.viz.com**

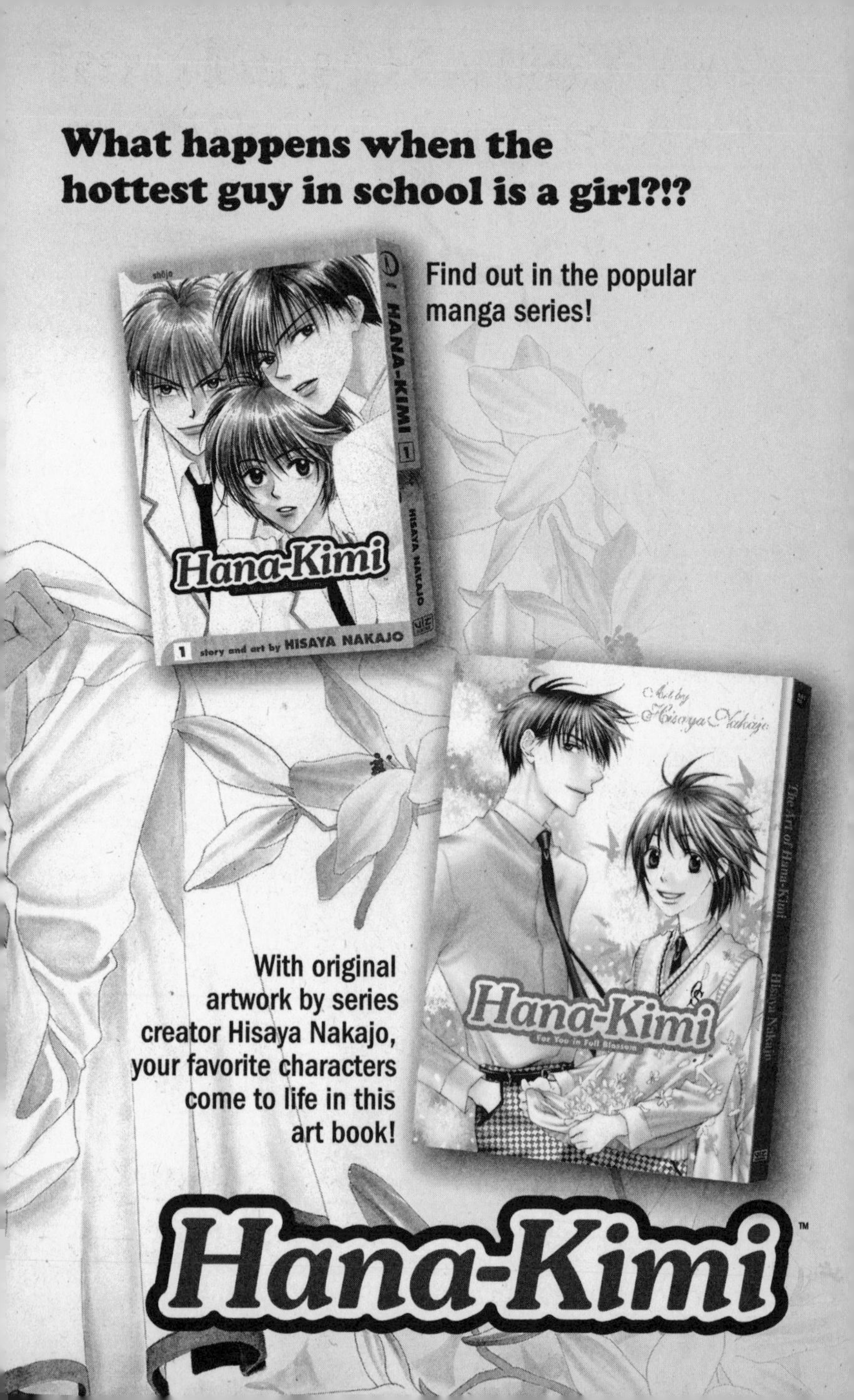
What happens when the hottest guy in school is a girl?!?
Find out in the popular manga series!
HANA-KIMI 1
HISAYA NAKAJO
Hana-Kimi
1 story and art by HISAYA NAKAJO
Art by Hisaya Nakajo
The Art of Hana-Kimi
Hisaya Nakajo
Hana-Kimi
For You in Full Blossom
With original artwork by series creator Hisaya Nakajo, your favorite characters come to life in this art book!
Hana-Kimi™

# Get Your Hana-Kimi Collection in Full Bloom

**Buy yours today at store.viz.com!**

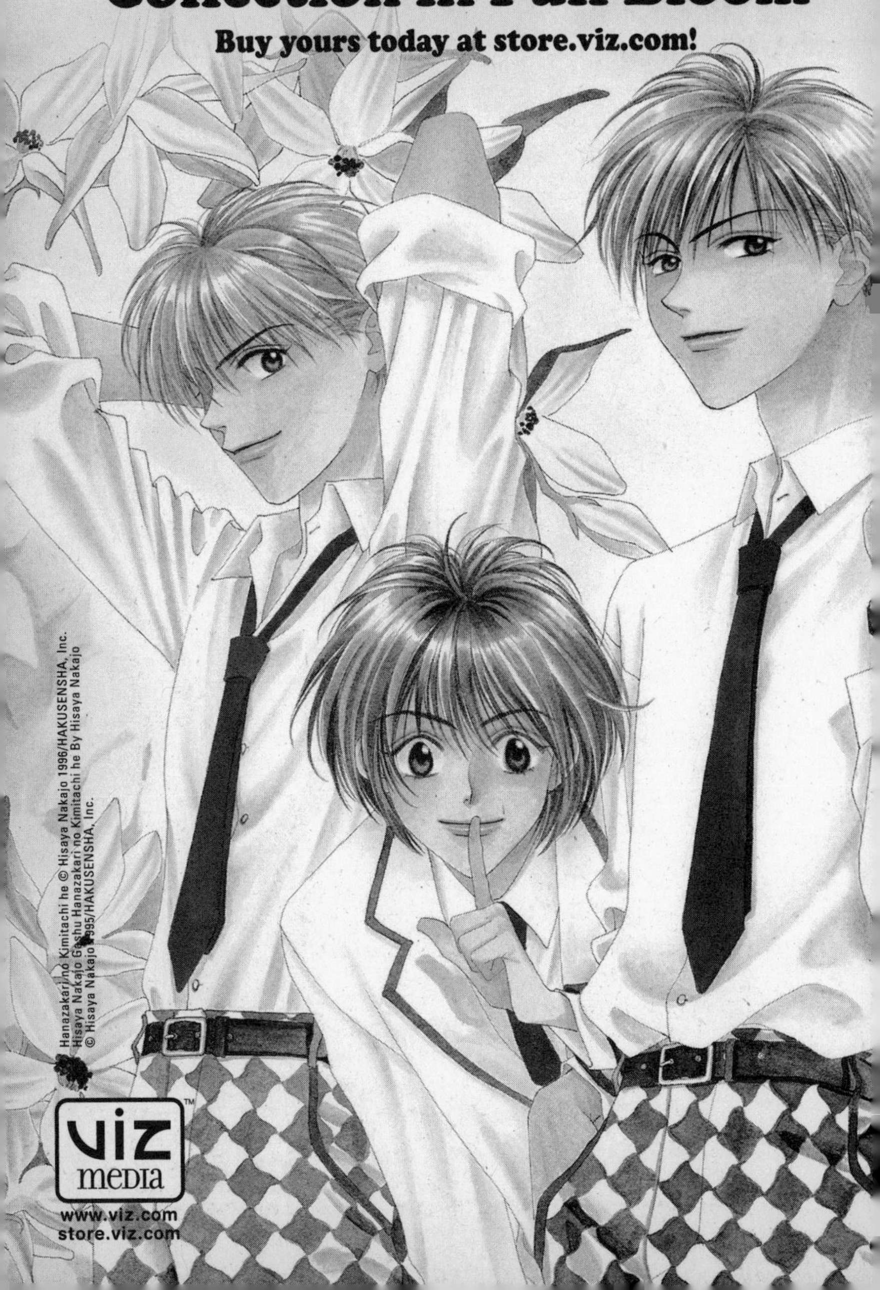

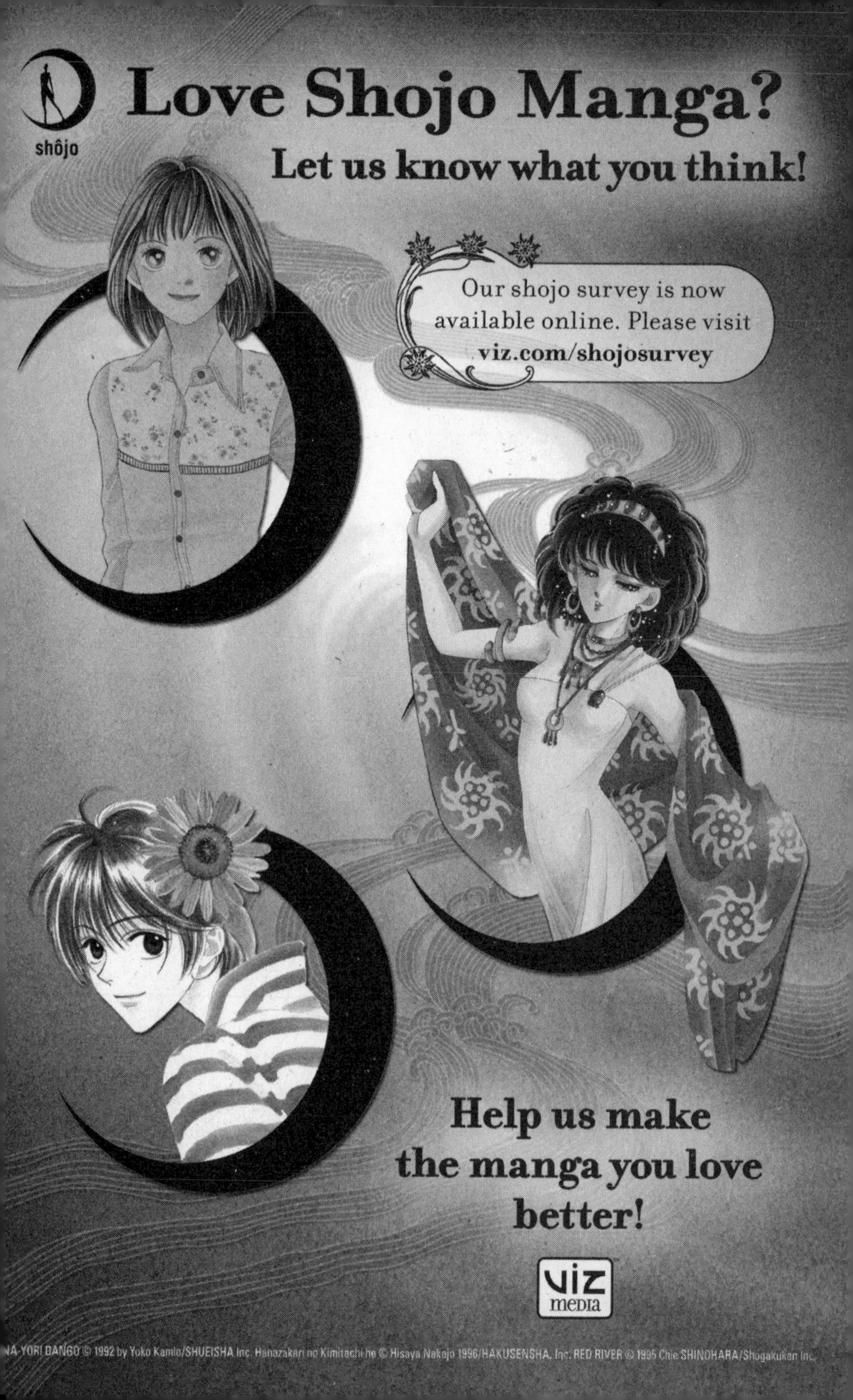
shôjo
Love Shojo Manga?
Let us know what you think!
Our shojo survey is now available online. Please visit viz.com/shojosurvey
Help us make the manga you love better!
VIZ media
NA-YORI DANGO © 1992 by Yoko Kamio/SHUEISHA Inc. Hanazakari no Kimitachi he © Hisaya Nakajo 1996/HAKUSENSHA, Inc. RED RIVER © 1995 Chie SHINOHARA/Shogakukan Inc.